Murder
in
Our
Midst

Murder in Our Midst

The Holocaust, Industrial Killing, and Representation

OMER BARTOV

New York   Oxford
Oxford University Press
1996

Oxford University Press

Oxford New York
Athens   Auckland   Bangkok   Bombay
Calcutta   Cape Town   Dar es Salaam   Delhi
Florence   Hong Kong   Istanbul   Karachi
Kuala Lampur   Madras   Madrid   Melbourne
Mexico City   Nairobi   Paris   Singapore
Taipei   Tokyo   Toronto

and associated companies in
Berlin Ibadan

Published by Oxford University Press, Inc.
198 Madison Avenue, New York, New York 10016

Oxford is a registered trademark of Oxford University Press

Library of Congress Cataloging-in-Publication Data
Bartov, Omer.
Murder in our midst : the Holocaust, industrial killing,
and representation / Omer Bartov.
p. cm. Includes index.
ISBN 0-19-509847-1.—ISBN 0-19-509848-X (pbk.)
1. Holocaust, Jewish (1939–1945)—Historiography.
2. Holocaust, Jewish (1939–1945), in motion pictures.
3. Holocaust, Jewish (1939–1945)—Museums.
4. Genocide.   I. Title.
D804.3.B363   1995
940.53'18'072—dc20   95–11406

9 8 7 6 5 4 3 2 1

Printed in the United States of America
on acid-free paper

For Wai-yee Li

Acknowledgments

I wish to thank a number of friends and colleagues for reading and commenting on drafts of various chapters in this book, and for discussions on the issues with which it is concerned. In Israel: Gulie Arad, Dan Diner, Saul Friedlander, Yosefa Loshitzky, Frank Stern, and Shulamit Volkov; in Germany: Jürgen Förster, Ulrich Herbert, Hannes Heer, Klaus-Jürgen Müller, Reinhard Rürup, Bernd Wegner, and Hans-Ulrich Wehler; in France: Annette Becker and Ashraf Noor; in the United Kingdom: Michael Howard, Ian Kershaw, Tony Nicholls, Jonathan Steinberg, Jill Stephenson, and Jay Winter; in the United States: David Abraham, Elazar Barkan, Diana Barkan, Volker Berghahn, Rogers Brubaker, James Buzard, Geoff Eley, Carole Fink, Michael Geyer, Atina Grossmann, Gordon Horwitz, Anton Kaes, Claudia Koonz, Moshe Lewin, Charles Maier, Andrei Markowitz, Arno Mayer, Peter Novick, Allan Silver, and Liliane Weissberg. I am also grateful to my anonymous readers for numerous constructive comments and suggestions. Special thanks are due to my colleagues at Rutgers University, especially Seymour Becker and Alla Zeide, Rudolph Bell, John Chambers, Ziva Galili, and John Gillis. My dear friends Ilona and Hans Zucker, Paul Holdengräber and María del Mar Sánchez Vivancos, and my parents, Yehudit and Hanoch Bartov, encouraged, supported, and criticized me and my texts to the benefit of both. I could not, and would not, have written this book without my wife, Wai-yee Li: she alone knows how much of her is in it, and it is to her that I dedicate it. I would like to express my appreciation to several institutions that supported me while writing this book: the Alexander von Humboldt Foundation, the Harvard Society of Fellows, the Raoul Wallenberg Visiting Professorship at Rutgers University, and the Rutgers Center for Historical Analysis. I also thank the following journals and publications for allowing me to reprint revised versions of published articles: *Historical Reflections/Réflexions Historiques*, *History and Memory* and its publisher, Indiana University Press, *History Today*, *Tel Aviver Jahrbuch für deutsche Geschichte*, and *The Journal of Modern History* and its publisher, the University of Chicago Press.

Contents

Murder
in
Our
Midst

Man is only a reed, the weakest in nature, but he is a thinking reed. There is no need for the whole universe to take up arms to crush him: a vapour, a drop of water is enough to kill him. But even if the universe were to crush him, man would still be nobler than his slayer, because he knows that he is dying and the advantage the universe has over him. The universe knows none of this.

Thus all our dignity consists in thought. It is on thought that we must depend for our recovery, not on space and time, which we could never fill. Let us then strive to think well; that is the basic principle of morality.

Pascal, Pensées, p. 95

Introduction:
The Past and Present
of Militarized Genocide

We run heedlessly into the abyss after putting
something in front of us to stop us seeing it.[1]

As our century draws to a close, many observers are overcome with a sense of
déjà vu. The intensification of ethnic, religious, and nationalist conflicts, the
inability of the great (and not so great) powers either to settle international
disputes or put their own houses in order, economic dislocation and loss of
optimism, widespread anxieties in the face of a looming "invasion" from the
poorer parts of the world, growing xenophobia and extremism, popular pressure for clear and simple answers to perplexing and ambiguous circumstances,
a general atmosphere of disillusionment, fear, and gloom—it all seems so
familiar. After all, the end of the nineteenth century was also accompanied by
growing chaos in international relations, the disintegration of great empires,
increasing domestic tensions and frustrations, fears of foreign, non-Western
perils along with laments about the decline of the West, racial and cultural
degeneration, and a growing desire for quick, violent, uplifting actions to resolve depressing realities. The current project of "genetic mapping" of humanity, to take just one but to my mind crucially important example, is once more
allied with attempts by both real and pseudo-natural and social scientists to
apply their "findings" to a reorganization of human society and its priorities,
and as such is much closer to the eugenic fantasies of pre-1914 Europe (and
pre-1945 Germany) than many of us would like to admit, reflecting the same
urge to enforce a "scientific" order on a bewildering, unresponsive humanity
that defies all "rational" analyses, categorizations, and forecasts by those charged
with studying and controlling it.[2]

And yet the previous fin de siècle is separated from our own by an era
that has contributed to human civilization a momentous idea, one that, in
accordance with this century's characteristic impatience and pragmatism, was
implemented while it was still being formulated: the concept and practice of
industrial killing. The mechanized, rational, impersonal, and sustained mass
destruction of human beings, organized and administered by states, legitimized
and set into motion by scientists and jurists, sanctioned and popularized by

3

academics and intellectuals, has become a staple of our civilization, the last, perilous, and often repressed heritage of the millennium.

War, slaughter, and genocide, are of course as old as human civilization itself. Industrial killing, however, is a much newer phenomenon, not only in that its main precondition was the industrialization of human society, but also in the sense that this process of industrialization came to be associated with progress and improvement, hope and optimism, liberty and democracy, science and the rule of law. Industrial killing was not the dark side of modernity, some aberration of a generally salutary process; rather, it was and is inherent to it, a perpetual potential of precisely the same energies and ideas, technologies and ideologies, that have brought about the "great transformation" of humanity. But precisely because modernity means to many of us progress and improvement, we cannot easily come to terms with the idea that it also means mass annihilation. We see genocide as a throwback to another, premodern, barbarous past, a perversion, an error, an accident. All evidence to the contrary, we repeatedly believe that *this* time, in *this* war, it will finally be stamped out and eradicated, never to reappear again. Yet even this well-meant urge reveals our complicity in modernity's destructive, unrelenting, intolerant nature. We wish to annihilate destruction, to kill war, to eradicate genocide, by the most effective and deadly means at our disposal. And we want to marginalize the evil, repress it, push it out of our own time and context, attribute it to everything that we are not, to anything that is foreign to our civilization. We thus elect to exist in an illusory reality, occasionally jarred by disturbing incidents of déjà vu, which in turn unleash in us precisely that sense of fear and confusion, that desire for drastic solutions, that anger at a world that refuses to conform to our expectations, that is at the root of modern society's destructive impulse.

The most spectacular and terrifying instance of industrial killing in this century was the Nazi attempted genocide of the Jews. Neither the idea, nor its implementation, however, can be understood without reference to the Great War, the first truly industrial military confrontation in history. This war differed from its predecessors by the magnitude, intensity, and mechanized nature of the killing. To be sure, there were precedents, such as the Russo-Japanese War and the American Civil War; but not only was the Great War a much improved version of those earlier attempts at industrial military confrontations, it was also distinguished by its direct and profound impact on a whole generation of Europeans, both combatants and civilians, as well as their offspring. And it was these European men and women who became the immediate perpetrators, victims, and bystanders of the Holocaust, acting out one of modernity's extreme, yet inherent potentials, whose traumatic effect on subsequent generations is only matched by their desperate attempts to deny its relevance to their post-Auschwitz realities.

It has rightly been pointed out that the Holocaust was not only directly related to the Nazi euthanasia program of killing the mentally handicapped, both conceptually and administratively, but also to a whole complex of scientific thinking on the need and legitimacy of treating human society as an organism to be manipulated by means of a vast surgical operation.[3] Yet it must be stressed that in another respect the genocide of the Jews both differed from the T-4 campaign and was directly related to the Great War, since the very concept of mass killing of human beings by states, as well as the technological and administrative means for actually organizing such vast operations, were lifted directly from the realities of 1914–18. Unlike the killing facilities of the euthanasia campaign, the death camps did not resemble medical installations, but were architecturally and organizationally modeled on the experience of the Great War, incorporating all the attributes of a military environment, such as uniforms and barbed wire, watch towers and roll calls, hierarchy and order, drill and commands. The Holocaust was therefore a militarized genocide, made all the more effective both by killing *all* those targeted for murder and in being safe for *all* those who carried it out. In another sense, however, the experience of the Great War was also linked to the concept of racial hygiene. Prewar fears of the degeneration of humanity were greatly enhanced by the carnage in the trenches, which threatened to bring about the total extinction of the combatants' "healthy" genes and the consequent predominance of the "unhealthy" genes of the shirkers and handicapped. Hence the post-1918 conceptualization of industrial extermination was also meant to redress the balance upset by that first major bout of mechanical killing by means of a massive cleansing operation that would eliminate the threat of genetic degeneration. It is this that we must bear in mind today when we read new/old theories about the potential pollution of the genetic pool in the United States by a genetically (and therefore both socially and intellectually) inferior, but numerically ever-expanding underclass.

This book did not begin as a clearly articulated argument. Rather, it originated in my realization that over the last few years I had become increasingly concerned with the emergence of industrial killing in the First World War, its most drastic implementation in the Holocaust, and its literary and visual representation. It was at this point that I began thinking of putting together some previously published articles as a collection that would present different aspects of my thinking on these issues.[4] But as I went back to these essays, it became clear that I would need to revise them substantially in view of my own clearer conceptualization of the book's thesis. Moreover, I realized that several major chapters would have to be written specifically for this book in order to bring everything together and to discuss at greater length some issues that had meanwhile become important to my thinking. The result is therefore no longer a collection of articles, but a series of discrete yet closely related essays on the emergence, implementation, and representation of industrial killing.

I begin by investigating one crucial factor in the history of war, namely, the persistent tension between the image of personal heroism on the battlefield and the reality of mass, anonymous slaughter. This is anything but a new phenomenon; in the West it can be traced back to the Homeric myth of single combat, to which feudal Europe added the notion of chivalry. In spite of ample evidence to the contrary, the ideal of the heroic individual survived in various

forms well into our own century, reflecting the need of both the warriors themselves and their societies to provide war with an elevating, meaningful, albeit
imaginary content. The Great War, I argue, seemed to shatter this long-
enduring myth once and for all, replacing the heroic individual with factories
of death, the duel with industrial killing.[5] However, as I try to show in Chapter 2,
reactions to the trauma of industrial killing were not limited to abhorrence of
war. While a minority chose to eschew violence altogether, most Europeans
confronted violence with violence, whether by declaring war on war, or by
waging war on its perceived originators, or by vowing to eliminate all potential
enemies, that is, all who were different. With industrial killing having been
introduced to the European (and later of course also to the non-European)
reality and imagery, it was not likely to go away. Ultimately, the traumatic effects of industrial killing were translated by some into a desire to wage it again,
but this time in a more controlled, rational manner, which would ensure the
destruction of the enemy while making certain of one's own survival. In this
sense, then, the Holocaust was a perfection of industrial killing: the victims
would be all on one side, the perpetrators all on the other; the victims would
be totally destroyed, the perpetrators totally safe from destruction, both because of the carefully calculated and controlled manner in which they would
undertake the enterprise of killing, and because by killing those seen as the
cause of war they would remain as the only possible wielders of this instrument of control and domination.

The second part of the book examines more closely several pertinent issues
concerning the Nazi attempted genocide of the Jews. Chapter 3 raises some
general questions on the relationship between antisemitism, the Holocaust, and
National Socialism, arguing that the close links between their interpretations
clearly reveals their historiographical interdependence. This initial discussion
introduces the debates taken up in the following chapters. Thus, Chapter 4
analyzes some problems of German history writing on the Nazi period, especially on the Second World War; Chapter 5 examines the merits and limitations of recent research and polemics on the history and memory of the Holocaust; Chapter 6 looks at the intellectual debate on the nationalization and
institutionalization of the Holocaust and its commemoration, and gauges the
implications of historical relativism for the historiography, representation, and
denial of the Nazi genocide.

It should be noted here that although Chapter 4 was originally written
before the reunification of Germany, and as part of the German historians'
controversy of the mid-1980s, some of the issues it raises seem to me at least
as pertinent today as they were at the time. Rumors about the demise of what
was called in Germany the *Historikerstreit* at the end of the last decade appear
today to have been greatly exaggerated. Indeed, the debate had arguably merely
heralded a new trend in German historiography, quite apart from uncannily
anticipating (as well as providing arguments for) eventual political unification.
One is reminded in this context of the strange history of the Dreyfus Affair: in
the short run, the dreyfusards won; but in the long run, the anti-dreyfusards
had their (albeit relatively ephemeral) day of revenge in Vichy. The difference

is, of course, that in the case of the *Historikerstreit* the long run was much shorter, while the eventual political transformation of Germany has already become a permanent feature of European politics. The untimely death of Andreas Hillgruber, the influential German historian whose last book is discussed in Chapter 4, deprived him of the opportunity to experience the realization of his dream, the final return of Germany to that gaping "hole at the center" caused by the Third Reich's "tragic" collapse and the ensuing control of Europe by the flanking American and Soviet empires. Now that the Soviet Union has vanished, and the United States gives increasing indications of being a declining, isolationist superpower, Germany has regained its traditional role of the power of the center, the arbiter of *Mitteleuropa*, the crucial link between East and West, and the major economic focus of Eastern, but also to a growing extent of Western Europe. Thus, whereas the controversial ideas of Ernst Nolte, that *enfant terrible* of German scholarship, were by and large rejected (even if their impact has been greater than some historians would like to admit), many of Hillgruber's arguments and aspirations have meanwhile become part and parcel of the conventional political and historical discourse, taking place as it does in a radically transformed environment; they no longer seem in any way extraordinary or unique.[6]

Just as historians should beware of declaring any historical event unique (if only because there is no assurance that it will not be repeated in some form in the future—and not necessarily as a farce), so too they would do well not to assert the disappearance of ideas and ideologies simply because they had become temporarily discredited. Antisemitism had lost its effectiveness as a single issue for political parties by the end of the nineteenth century, but its insidious dissemination among mainstream parties made for its reappearance as a respectable "opinion" in much of Europe during the interwar period. Similarly, while scientific racism was rejected after 1945, not least as a result of the Holocaust,[7] it now seems to be experiencing a major revival, along with the rise of neo-fascism, xenophobia, and extremism.

The reappearance of such specters of the past, often camouflaged as scientific "discoveries" or as new and "liberating" forms of discourse and critique, is in turn related to the growing preoccupation of the public with history, memory, and visual representations of the past (and especially of past horrors). The third and last part of the book examines some of these issues. In Chapter 7 I look at the manner in which German filmmakers have tried to recreate their history as a cinematic experience. Concentrating mainly on one specific work, I investigate what it tells us about German intellectual perceptions of (German) history through what I term the representation of absence, that is, the themes with which such cinematic works are (quite consciously and assertively) *not* preoccupied. Here we are presented not merely with a competition of *memories*, but even more crucially with a competition of *victimhood*, precisely because in the context of the German past memory so often recalls horror and its victims. By the same token, history itself is being fought over, and the question of whose history it is, or at least to whom do specific events in the past "belong," finds ample and often fascinating (if also disturbing) expression in such visual representations of evil. While claiming back their history, German filmmakers prefer to represent it as a narrative of their own victimhood. In this, of course, they are also part of a general trend, not least in the United States, whereby the status of victim has become a major attribute of individual and group identity.

Somewhat different aspects of visual representations of evil are also examined in the last chapter of the book. Here I begin with a discussion of war museums and films, arguing that even when they carry an explicit antiwar message, they often implicate the viewer in a fascination with (their inevitably aestheticized representations of) violence. This may partly be avoided, I suggest, by concentrating on the effects, rather than the events, of war. Even in this case, however, we are often confronted with the pathos of the soldier as the victim, rather than the direct perpetrator of violence. Hence, while war museums and films can probably never deliver an unambiguous antiwar message, the most powerful antiwar cinematic representations seem to be those concerned either with war's *truly* innocent victims, especially children caught in the war games of the adults, or with the polluting *memory* of war and its long-term psychological as well as social and political effects.

The difficulties of visual and plastic representation are compounded in the case of the Holocaust. By way of discussing Steven Spielberg's *Schindler's List*, I therefore attempt to evaluate the various options of cinematic representation of the Holocaust, such as other "authentic" fiction films, documentaries using contemporary film material, and oral testimonies. I make a case for Spielberg's accomplishment in reaching a large public both in the United States and in Germany while making a film that largely eschews sentimentality and emphasizes the option of action and resistance among the bystanders. Yet I see *Schindler's List* as reflecting some of the fundamental problems of this genre, in that the extraordinary story it tells may well be viewed by the public as the norm rather than the exception in that universe of industrial killing, while its use of cinematic techniques of representing violence may lead (especially young) viewers to associate the film (and the event it purports to represent) both with the violence of conventional movie "entertainment" and with real-life violence on the streets.

The relationship between the form, content, and context of representation is also the main focus of the last section of the book. In examining Yad Vashem in Jerusalem, the United States Holocaust Memorial Museum in Washington, D.C., and the Simon Wiesenthal Center's Beit Hashoah Museum of Tolerance in Los Angeles, I point out that there seem to be two main narrative options in plastic representations of the Nazi genocide, one oriented toward a Zionist closure, another making the case for tolerance. Moreover, conventional displays depend to a large degree both on the "authenticity" of their artifacts and on their location. The geographical context and its historical implications infuse Yad Vashem with a meaning that goes well beyond the relative poverty of its exhibit, connecting it to the origin of a civilization that culminated in Auschwitz. Conversely, the Holocaust Memorial Museum in Washington, precisely because it is located in the capital of a country that neither experienced the Holocaust directly nor can claim any historical connection to its prehistory, implies the possibility of integrating the genocide of the Jews into an optimistic historical narrative that asserts humanity's march toward a better future, all accidents and misfortunes notwithstanding. Alternatively, the Simon Wiesenthal Center attempts to employ the Holocaust as an argument for tolerance in America's multicultural and increasingly fragmented society, and seeks to appeal to a young generation of Americans perceived as incapable of receiving complicated, ambiguous messages. Its manipulative, electronically sophisticated and intellectually simplistic message is a disturbing example of the manner in which the Holocaust can be recruited for a "good" cause and misinterpreted as a vehicle for a false understanding of the present. Instead of representing the phenomenon of industrial killing as a dangerous potential of modernity, the museum exploits the tools of modernity to provide a conformist, passive perception of contemporary conditions, where emotion replaces action and image obscures reality.

In a recent academic conference, the historian George Mosse noted that the only model for plastic representations of the Holocaust is war museums. This pertinent remark brings us, so to speak, to the beginning, since the great *differences* between war and the Holocaust mean that an unprecedented (rather than unique) event such as the Nazi genocide of the Jews also lacks any precedents of plastic representations. This is most evident in the difficulty of finding an appropriate "end" for such museums, or, as I would put it, in deciding on their narrative. Museum narratives are closely related to their social and ideological context. Thus, for instance, American Holocaust museums in particular shy away from presenting racism as a crucial component of the Holocaust, as well as of the civilization that produced it. The tendency to refer to Nazi racism as a mere reflection of Hitler's personal mania, as Mosse has remarked, is a direct result of the fact that the United States itself is still largely a race-based, rather than class-based society.[8] I would argue further, however, that Western representations of the Holocaust fail to recognize that this extreme instance of industrial killing was generated by a society, economic system, and civilization of which our contemporary society is a direct continuation. In other words, we can note a powerful reluctance to admit that industrial killing is very much a product of modernity.[9] Racism, in this sense, pernicious though it surely is, becomes a crucial factor only thanks to its legitimation by the most representative establishments of the modern state, the scientific and legal communities. Industrial murder is therefore not the product of racism, which merely determines the identity of the victims. Under different circumstances, the victims could be determined according to other categories, similarly legitimized by those institutions whose accumulation of knowledge inaccessible to the lay citizen puts them above our control and provides them with almost unlimited power in our own industrial, bureaucratic, complex societies. As Mosse has rightly argued, while museums may succeed in keeping the memory of the event alive, their real challenge is not to merely ask how, but rather why the Holocaust happened. Yet I fear that this challenge cannot be fully met, since the answer is politically, ideologically, and structurally so subversive of the modern state that it would never be given expression in such state-funded and supported institutions as museums.

Nor can we expect the popular media, which in recent years have shown a growing interest in the Holocaust, to provide the public with anything more than the most superficial and banal interpretation of the event and its implications for our own civilization. It has been argued, however, that the utility of popular media preoccupation with the Nazi genocide might be the prevention of such events in the future.[10] Yet it is difficult to find any evidence for such effects in post-1945 society. Indeed, the question is: What does the public reaction to the genocides and massacres in Bosnia and Rwanda, Cambodia and Burundi, Algeria and Vietnam tell us about the actual effect of the popular media on people's perceptions of, and interactions with, reality and its images? Is it perhaps possible to argue that precisely this massive exposure to images of past violence (in which by definition we can no longer intervene) has accustomed us to view images of present violence *as if* they too were happening in the past, or on a different planet altogether, well beyond our control, though very much subject to our impotent sympathy and empathy? Moreover, could it be that we have grown used to confusing not only between past and present, far and near, but also between real and fictitious, authentic and false, so that staged violence appears to us just as horrifying, or leaves us just as indifferent, as electronic records of real violence? Or, even worse, can this all have been integrated by now into a vast entertainment industry more concerned with ratings and box-office returns than with the moral and political implications of the images it showers on the viewers in such abundant quantities? Have we been made thereby both complicit and numb, curious but distracted?

Thus, we may have reason to fear that the current mechanical reproduction of images of violence is progressively transforming reality into fiction and memory: as we watch an actual genocide taking place right in front of our eyes (on the screen), we are no longer sure whether it is real or staged, past or present, memory or anticipation. We no longer remember the past so as to act against its repetition in the future, but transform the present into a past that precludes all action. The "lessons" we draw from past genocide—namely, that we can no longer act to undo it—are applied simultaneously to the present, which we similarly accept as beyond all control and intervention. The dreadful notion of the Holocaust as a comforting memory (since it is over and done with, and being the very worst of which humanity is capable can by definition not be surpassed), and the no less horrifying exploitation of the Holocaust as a means to legitimize inaction and indifference, conformity and complacency, appear to have become a very real possibility in our present civilization.

This book makes several uncommon connections, between war and the Holocaust, past and present, image and reality. It argues that while the Holocaust belongs both to its past and to its future—our present—and can therefore not be marginalized as an aberration representative only of itself, at the same time it must not be contextualized to the extent that it becomes part of a general history of progress or degeneration, heroism or atrocity. The centrality of the Holocaust for the human experience of modernity has been recognized even by those who seek to deny that it had ever happened. Ultimately, this book is a plea for understanding and compassion. There may perhaps not be any lessons to be learned from the genocide of the Jews; but, all the same, we must know that the killing goes on, and even if we are safe from it today, we may become its victims tomorrow. This is not a memory, not even a history, for the murder is in our midst, and our passivity will be our nemesis.

Images of War
and the Emergence
of Industrial Killing

Man and the Mass: Reality and the Heroic Image in War

They strode out between the two forces, looking so
terrible that the spectators were spellbound. . . .
Paris was first to hurl his long-shadowed spear. . . .
But the bronze did not break through. . . . Then
Menelaus . . . brought his spear into play. . . . But
Paris swerved, and so avoided death. Menelaus then
drew his silver-mounted sword. . . . But the sword
broke . . . he hurled himself at Paris. . . . But
Aphrodite used her powers . . . [and] whisked
him off.[1]

I

War is essentially a military confrontation between two armed groups or organizations of men; yet, at the same time, war seems to present an image of heroic
individuals on whose supreme qualities its outcome depends. Whereas the first
image denotes an impersonal mass, the second implies the centrality of personal valor. Since this fundamental contradiction between the heroic image of
war and its reality can be traced far back in history, and is clearly just as prevalent—or, indeed, much exacerbated—in modern armed conflicts, it appears
to constitute an inherent component of the phenomenon of war as such. Thus,
one question to be posed in this chapter is: Why is this tension between the
abstract ideals and brutal facts of war so persistent, what purpose does it serve,
at what price, and what does it tell us about the nature of human warfare? More
specifically, I will attempt to gauge the impact of industrial killing in the Great
War on traditional Western perceptions of individual heroism. Finally, and by
way of introducing the next chapter, I will suggest some links between the
effects of modern warfare on the individual's relationship with the mass, and
the emergence of genocide as a characteristic phenomenon of the twentieth
century.

For centuries men have gone to war expecting to discover and demonstrate
their heroic qualities on the battlefield; for the most part, confrontation with
reality resulted in disillusionment. Whether physically or psychologically, the
individual was almost invariably annihilated by the mass. And yet, although
preconceived images of war have often had a detrimental impact on its con-

crete conduct, they have simultaneously proved to be an immensely powerful motivating value for soldiers in that they molded their self-perception, provided them with models of behavior, and helped them bear the horrors of reality, enabling them thereby not only to see the actual manifestations of war, but also to envision its ideal, if less obvious essence.

Nowhere has the impact of these contradictory images of war been greater, and the interaction between them more potent, than in the first half of the twentieth century. Consequently, after briefly tracing the roots of the heroic image, the major part of this chapter will be devoted to examining its fascinating transformation in the age of total war. As I claim below, whenever one image of war began to disintegrate, another was already evolving. Modern industrial warfare both greatly accelerated this process and significantly intensified the tensions it produced. Nevertheless, the clash between present conditions and previous images produced a distinctly unmodern new ideal, thereby ensuring similar confrontation in any future conflict. Indeed, one might almost say that modern war's depersonalizing effect, because of both its deployment of huge armies and massive use of sophisticated technology, has only enhanced the need for an heroic image of war. For whatever other aspects it may have stressed, the focus of every such ideal has always been the individual warrior's potential of heroically rising above the multitude and leaving his personal imprint on human history. The harder it became to accomplish this feat in reality, the more men yearned for it. It is this ambivalent relationship between the two contradictory, yet essentially inseparable faces of war that the following pages will attempt to explore. Furthermore, as we will see in later chapters, one consequence of the attempt to preserve the individual in an era of industrial killing has been the attribution of supreme moral qualities to the perpetrators of murder and the denial of humanity to the victims. Hence, by saving the individual, the mass was condemned to death, both figuratively and physically. And, once the verdict was passed, a process was unleashed that by now has become an inherent element of modern civilization.

II

The Greek phalanx dominated the battlefield of the ancient world for some five centuries. Based on a compact formation of heavily armored hoplites, armed with long stabbing spears, the phalanx was virtually invincible as long as it kept its cohesion. However, once discipline faltered and the formation disintegrated, the individual hoplites, weighed down by their heavy equipment, became quite useless.

This crucial need for the men composing the mass to act as a single body was often stressed by Greek sources. The seventh-century poet Tyrtaeus, for instance, appealed to Sparta's warriors to go "shoulder to shoulder . . . into the mêlée . . . setting foot beside foot, resting shield against shield, crest beside crest, helm beside helm."[2] Abiding by these same principles, Xenophon's Ten Thousand frontally charged a much larger Persian host in the battle of Cunaxa in the late fifth century. The enemy "wavered and ran away," but the Greeks nevertheless "shouted to each other not to run, but to follow up the enemy without breaking ranks."[3] Similarly, Alexander the Great won the Battle of Gaugamela when he "promptly made for the gap" created in Darius' front with his massed formations of "Macedonian horse," while "the infantry phalanx in close order and bristling with pikes added its irresistible weight." Hence, the Persian king "was the first to turn tail and ride for safety."[4]

The phalanx was thus both a tactical unit and a state of mind, requiring strict combat discipline whereby no single soldier would either flinch from the enemy or surge forward. Indeed, while absolute uniformity of conduct was essential for maximum effectiveness, individual valor and initiative might have positively catastrophic consequences. This, however, hardly corresponded to the Homeric image of heroic single combat cherished by the Greeks.

Greek soldiers modeled themselves on their heroic ancestors. Tyrtaeus reminded the Spartans that they were "of the lineage of the invincible Heracles,"[5] Xenophon was proud of having reached "Jason's Beach, where the *Argo* is said to have been moored,"[6] and Alexander's first act on landing in Asia was to travel to Troy, where he took "some weapons which were still preserved from the Trojan war," henceforth to be "carried before him. . . . When he went into battle"; indeed, in a striking gesture directly linking him with the epitome of heroism, Alexander "laid a wreath . . . on the tomb of Achilles, calling him a lucky man, in that he had Homer to proclaim his deeds and preserve his memory."[7]

Homer's *Iliad* was all about personal acts of valor, single combat between heroes of noble, if not semi-divine birth, and contempt for the mass. Discipline was anything but common, or praiseworthy, on either side of Troy's walls. Yet the fact that Homer's warriors were fundamentally armed with the same weapons as Alexander's hoplites made identifying with them all the more natural, and coming to terms with the unheroic tactics of phalanx warfare, rooted in the invention of the long pike and the discovery of cheaper metals, all the more difficult.

The contradiction between the obvious efficacy of cohesive tactical formations and the danger that such inglorious warfare might seriously demoralize the individual hoplite, however, was resolved in a number of complementary ways. Tyrtaeus, for one, strongly emphasized the centrality of the individual within the formation, and pointed out the benefits to be gained from outstanding acts of valor. Thus, he considered "warlike strength" to be "the noblest prize . . . for a lad to win in the world," ensuring that "he that falleth in the van" would be "bewailed alike by young and old," and "his grave and his children" would remain "conspicuous among men"; while if he survived the battle, Tyrtaeus promised him the "honor of all," for "he standeth out among his people, and there's none that will do him hurt."[8] Xenophon, on the other hand, described situations wherein the individual could escape the threat of unheroic anonymity by rescuing the mass from a tight corner, as indeed happened when volunteers were sought to save the Ten Thousand from an ambush in a Kurdestan mountain pass. Then, we are told, the "hoplites who came forward were Aristonymus the Methydrian and Agasias the Stymphalian, and Callimachus of Parrhasia."[9]

Alexander, who led even larger hosts into battle than his predecessors, gave his individual hoplites a sense of rising above the mass by personally performing extraordinary feats of heroism. Thus, the king not only demonstrated his own superior qualities, but also acted as a personification of his numerous warriors. Coming himself as close as was possible under the circumstances of his time to the Homeric image of war—indeed, creating his own particular version of the hero-king—he thereby liberated personal heroism from the rigid tactics of faceless formations. By breaking the rules and stepping out of the line, the king enabled his subordinates to share in his anarchic valor while simultaneously conforming to battle regulations. At a crucial moment in the Battle of Granicus, for instance, Alexander characteristically turned the battlefield into a scene of single combat, as he courageously "galloped out in front of his men, struck [the Persian leader] Mithridates in the face with the spear, and hurled him to the ground," with the result that the Persians "began to break just at the point where Alexander in person was bearing the brunt of things."[10]

III

The Roman legion, a more flexible tactical unit, finally ended the long dominance of the Greek phalanx. Yet the Romans also relied on the cohesive, mass infantry formation, fundamentally armed with similar weapons and motivated by the same Homeric image of heroic single combat. Indeed, tracing their history back to the Trojans,[11] the Romans rapidly adopted much of Greek culture and mythology, making Homer a natural starting point for any image of war, and resolving the inherent contradiction between man and the mass in a similar manner by stressing the need for personal courage within the formation, allowing for voluntary acts from without it, and glorifying the feats of heroic leaders.[12]

The simple invention of the stirrup around the sixth century A.D. brought a profound change to the battlefield, and hence also to the image of war. From the moment men could sit securely on a horse, they became real cavalry rather than mounted infantry, and could more accurately and effectively shoot arrows, exchange blows with sword and mace, and, most important, deliver tremendous thrusts with the lance.[13] For the next six centuries, knights wearing increasingly heavier suits of armor came to dominate European wars, sowing the seeds of the new chivalric ethos.

In some respects, during the High Middle Ages the reality of war came as close to its ideal as it may have in the Trojan siege. But here too, the knightly image was widely adopted precisely at a time when it had ceased to reflect contemporary realities, but instead recalled the cleansed heroic memory of an obscure past, making it into a model of behavior for future generations. Thus, in *The Song of Roland*, an epic poem composed in the eleventh century, but based on a real battle between the Franks and the Saracens in A.D. 778, the two leaders finally emerge out of the chaotic slaughter, only to decide the fate of the battle in single combat, thereby personifying the heroic qualities of the individual warrior. Indeed, appropriately assisted by "Saint Gabriel," once Charlemagne "drives his good French blade" into the Emir, we learn that "All's done, all's won; the French have gained the day."[14] Similarly, in *The Nibelungen-lied*, written at about A.D. 1200, we find the "fierce pair," Siegfried and King Liudegast, though at the head of large hosts, fighting each other in heroic iso-lation and providing an example of chivalric excellence increasingly difficult to demonstrate on the real battlefields of the Middle Ages.[15] Even more divorced from the changing realities of war are the heroes of *The Quest of the Holy Grail*, written in the early thirteenth century and set in the Arthurian world of medi-eval romance, where no blood is shed and the chivalric code is strictly observed. There, having stunned an unknown knight in a duel, Lancelot gallantly ties his opponent's horse to a tree, "so that the knight might find it at hand when he revived."[16]

In the course of the following century, however, the face of medieval battle had changed to such a degree that knights, though highly reluctant to recog-nize the fact, became increasingly anachronistic, being repeatedly beaten by Flemish pikesmen and English archers. And yet, precisely because real jousts were gradually relegated to the status of public tournaments, the heroic image could flourish undisturbed—indeed, be greatly enhanced both by its growing distance from the blood and gore of the battlefield and by the consequent, almost inevitable, addition of the most noble virtues to the no longer relevant martial qualities of the knight. Moreover, as the battlefield came to be domi-nated once more by mass, faceless armies of foot soldiers, the need for indi-vidual heroism naturally increased, to be satisfied by an array of legendary knights, giving sense to wars whose reality seemed to have gone astray and, incidentally, also legitimizing an elevated social status no longer justified by real military indispensability. Thus, by putting an end to the knight's actual invincibility, the Hundred Years' War created the need and provided the back-ground for a greatly enhanced chivalric image of warfare, destined to have a major impact on men's expectations from war, and their conduct in it for the next five centuries. In this sense, the wars of the fourteenth and fifteenth cen-turies were in fact image-makers of the highest degree.

This is why Froissart's late fourteenth-century *Chronicles*, though contain-ing a detailed account of chivalry's downfall, nevertheless achieved the author's proclaimed aim of setting on record the "noble adventures and deeds of arms" performed by French and English knighthood "so that brave men should be inspired thereby to follow such examples."[17] And indeed, Crécy and Poitiers turned out to have been not only the graveyards of knightly warfare, but also the fertile breeding ground of the chivalric ideal. For, on the one hand, the "splendidly mounted and armed" French knights kept stubbornly charging the English archers, who proceeded "to shoot into the thickest part of the crowd," "knocking down horses and piercing everything before them with their long barbed arrows"[18] as late as the battle of Agincourt in 1415.[19] But, on the other hand, by the time French siege artillery blasted the English out of Normandy and Guienne in the mid-fifteenth century,[20] both sides had come to realize that if their nobility were to avoid total physical extinction, a way had to be found of adapting the practical implications of the chivalric ethos to the new realities of the battlefield.

The notion of chivalry did not disappear. Instead, European aristocracy found other means of asserting both its social and military superiority, based on the uniqueness of noble character and on its particular brand of heroism in battle. Indeed, in an age bereft of knights, the need for chivalrous conduct, whether in the *salon* or in battle, became all the more urgent. But this entailed a profound metamorphosis in the chivalric image of war. For though its model remained the Arthurian knight, now his moral qualities reigned supreme, while his manner of combat became increasingly symbolic. Instead of being the mainstay of battle, if not battle itself, the knight assumed now the role of its conductor, the chief who sets the rules of the fight, supervises its course, and commands the faceless multitude without himself becoming involved in the bloodshed. In one sense, this was a total reversal of the joust, but replacing martial prowess with moral (and later also intellectual) superiority proved an extraordinarily useful reinterpretation of the chivalric ethos. Personally unsoiled by the grimmer aspects of combat, yet retaining their elevated military and social status, officers of opposing armies found much more in common with each other than with their respective rank and file.

As long as Europe's nobles had refused to give up the martial aspects of knighthood, they were threatened with extinction at the hands of commoners; now the aristocrats could not only continue to dominate their peasants socially, they could also send them to be killed in their stead on the battlefield, in pursuit of the political goals of the ruling elite. Moreover, this newly fashioned chivalric image made it possible to keep asserting the centrality of the heroic and noble individual (seen by and large as synonymous), while simultaneously accepting the incessant growth of ever more impersonal armies.[21] The imagery of war belonged to and was cherished by the officer corps. The rank and file were necessary only to perform the real acts of war on the field; they had no share in the imaginary world that gave it all sense and meaning.

IV

In the next chapter I will trace some aspects of the transformation in Europe's perception of war during the nineteenth and twentieth centuries that followed from the introduction of universal conscription by revolutionary France in 1793. There is little doubt that the national wars of the previous century greatly altered the understanding of the individual's role in battle, and that expansion of nationalist ideologies was both based on, and caused a redefinition of, the physical and psychological mobilization of widespread sectors of society that had previously remained aloof from, though not untouched by, dynastic and religious warfare.[22] In the present context, however, it is necessary to emphasize that it was the Great War, with its lethal combination of the machine gun and barbed wire, backed by heavy artillery capable of firing millions of shells, that completely shattered the European image of war as an exercise in chivalry. Indeed, within a few months of fighting in the summer and fall of 1914, the old European officer corps was virtually wiped out by the new realities of industrial warfare.

Paradoxically, this annihilation of a state of mind, along with the social stratum representing it, showed that the bitter battle waged by Europe's officers against the introduction of the machine gun before 1914 had had more to it than mere thick-headed traditionalism.[23] For what these distant descendants of medieval knighthood sensed was that the new weapons would make them redundant by putting an end to all individual heroism and character, and transforming the battlefield into a factory of death, where victory would be decided by the quality and quantity not of men, but of machines. The total stagnation of the Western Front during most of the war seemed to justify their fears. Personal valor vanished in the labyrinth of trenches, maneuver was blocked by the continuous front, generalship dwarfed by industrial mobilization. For the individual soldier, war became a lengthy wait for certain execution within the confined space of pre-dug graves. It is the links between this reality of the war with its hitherto unimaginable qualities, and its recreation on an even vaster and more horrific scale merely two decades later, that we will discuss in the next chapter. Indeed, one of the most haunting aspects of the post-1918 European imagination is the option of physically experiencing an inconceivable, yet unavoidable and recurring reality.

At the same time, although in a significantly altered sense, the old officer corps ultimately proved wrong. Unlike Japan, which had decided to "give up the gun" in order to preserve the dominance of its feudal aristocracy,[24] Europe managed to maintain its chivalric ethos notwithstanding the rapid development of military technology throughout the early modern era.[25] The European aristocratic officer corps had preserved its position until 1914 by claiming to be endowed with natural leadership qualities, enabling it to constitute the martial and moral backbone of the army, no matter how large and complicated the military organization had become. To be sure, the assertions of a natural noble charisma were under a great deal of pressure even before the First World War, and were indeed largely dismissed once it had taken its first toll. As we will see, however, the aristocracy of the blood was eventually replaced by a new aristocracy of warriors, better adapted to the changing conditions of modern warfare and highly proficient in the exercise of industrial killing. Just as Europe's knights had originated in tough and ruthless mounted soldiers, so too the new nobility of the sword stemmed from among the elite units at the front, as well as from those who hoped to emulate them and further improve their techniques in subsequent wars and undertakings of mass human destruction.

This separation between the new military leaders' social and martial position was certainly enhanced by the fact that the old notions of chivalry were no longer confined to the officer corps. Rather, the chivalric image of war had penetrated far deeper into European society precisely toward the outbreak of the Great War. This was the reason, for instance, for the unprecedented patriotic upsurge experienced by Britain in 1914, whose practical manifestation was a tremendous influx of volunteers that made compulsory conscription initially unnecessary.[26] The "Pals' Battalions" have been described as "a story of a spontaneous and genuinely popular mass movement," the product of "a time of intense, almost mystical patriotism, and of the inarticulate elitism of an imperial power's working class."[27] Indeed, the fact that a growing proportion of society was receiving some kind of education, reading newspapers, and taking a larger part in public life meant that they had become increasingly exposed to the current romantic representations of war as a noble, glorious experience, and wanted to share in it. "Patriotism and national pride were almost part of the Edwardian psyche," we are told, for a generation brought up on boys' adventure stories, tales of exotic colonial wars, and popularized medieval legends. "All imagined that [the war] would be an affair of great marches and great battles, quickly decided."[28]

The French too were influenced by these romantic images of war. Indeed, one historian has written that "one of the keys to French behavior in the summer of 1914 was the widespread conviction that war would turn out to be an adventure, cruel perhaps, but of short duration." This feeling was enhanced by the fact that "most men left home in the firm belief that the French government had had no hand in unleashing the conflict and that unprovoked aggression had to be resisted."[29] Robert Graves also described his decision to enlist as having been motivated by the fact that "the papers predicted only a very short war, over by Christmas at the outside," as well as by his being "outraged to read of the Germans' cynical violation of Belgian neutrality."[30] During the first months of the war, the French press was mainly concerned with such subjects as "French qualities compounded of panache and a Spartan spirit," "the excellence of French soldiers," and "the superiority of French arms," as opposed to "German baseness" and "German cruelty."[31] In this atmosphere *Le Matin* could report on August 7, 1914, that "a sergeant, uncertain how to react to the ovations, raised his rifle and kissed it passionately,"[32] while two days later the *Times* announced the suicide of a retired captain "caused by the feeling that he was not going to be accepted for service."[33]

Across the Rhine, Thomas Mann's intensely romantic portrayal of war in the closing pages of *The Magic Mountain* well reflects its image as cherished by countless German youths before 1914. "Whither has the dream snatched us?" asks the author, looking down to the real world from his imaginary Alpine sanatorium: "It is the flat-land, it is the war." There he observes "a volunteer regiment, fresh young blood and mostly students" who now "fix their bayonets" and charge forward, while "the horns enforce them, the drums roll deepest bass." Though some are hit, "the wood emits new swarms" for, we are told, "They are glad to be here—albeit with boundless anguish," and this, to Mann's mind, "of itself, is a noble and a shaming thing." This joy of battle envelops even the main protagonist, the hitherto unheroic Hans Castorp, who now appears "running, his feet heavy with mold, the bayonet swinging in his hand," and yet, "unaware . . . half soundlessly," is singing a sweet romantic tune. The next moment Castorp is assaulted by a howling "hell-hound . . . a huge explosive shell, a disgusting sugar loaf from the infernal regions. . . . The product of a perverted science." But soon Castorp is up again, "all unconsciously singing," until he finally "vanishes out of our sight."

Mann's ardent youths charge like medieval knights with fixed bayonets to the sound of trumpet and drum; they swarm out of the forest like Rome's Germanic nemesis, yet they are cruelly confronted by anonymous, deadly projectiles, true representatives of an unromantic, hostile, foreign, un-Germanic world. Nevertheless, as the author bids farewell from his now much more heroic Castorp, he concludes that the experience may well be worthwhile, for although the young man's chances of survival are poor, "Adventures of the flesh and in the spirit . . . granted thee to know in the spirit what in the flesh thou scarcely could have done." Indeed, asks Mann, "Out of this universal feast of death, out of this extremity of fever . . . may it be that Love one day shall mount?"[34]

But for many real participants, the horrors of the war actually produced the kind of fascination with extremity so powerfully celebrated in Ernst Jünger's *In Stahlgewittern (Storm of Steel)*. Here we find the author expressing from the very first page that "unbelievable awe" with which his unit, newly arrived at the front, "strained to hear the slow beat of the rolling-mill of the front, a melody to which we would become accustomed for long years." The "feast of death" created an addiction to the "breath of the battle" among the soldiers, just because they sensed "that almost all of us would be devoured." Certainly this was a product of the images and expectations of war prevalent among youths "raised in a period of security" and filled with a "longing for the extraordinary, for the great danger." Thus, when war broke out, it "gripped us like an intoxication." Leaving for the front "in a shower of flowers, in a drunken mood of roses and blood," these enthusiastic recruits were convinced that this "war must surely deliver us to the Grand, the Powerful, the Festive," expecting it to be "a manly act, a joyful infantry battle over blooming, blood-bedewed meadows." Indeed, they could think of "no more beautiful death in the world" than in such a war, and their greatest fear was that they might not "be allowed to join in."[35]

This fascination with death, this obsession with annihilating both one's enemies and oneself in a horrific, awesome festival of destruction, this mixture of archaic, mythological memories with the endless resources of modern industry and technology, had a profound effect on the European psyche and imagination. This was indeed the birth place of industrial killing: Auschwitz could neither have been imagined, nor constructed and set to work, without the experience and memory of the Great War, where many of the architects and executioners of the "Final Solution" underwent their "baptism of fire."

And yet, in spite of this fateful legacy, the First World War might have been expected to erase forever all romantic notions of battle, since that vast factory of death seemed to have "destroyed the very elements of human individuality: courage, hope, enterprise, and a sense of the heroic possibilities in moral and physical conflict."[36] The old images no longer corresponded to reality. Instead of charging over a green meadow, soldiers preparing to go over the top were shocked "looking up and seeing the coarse green grass growing along the parapet flying into the air as the bullets' stream hit it. It was just like the effect produced by a lawn mower being used without a grass box."[37] Dignified conduct on the battlefield was outright suicidal. A German machine gunner in the Somme saw an English officer "walking calmly, carrying a walking stick" as he led his men forward. "When we started firing we just had to load and reload.

They went down in their hundreds. You didn't have to aim, we just fired into them."[38] A French soldier in Verdun recalled that a German "officer came out of the ground two hundred yards away, followed by a column-of-four—their rifles were at the slope, and it looked like a parade." As they opened fire, "The officer dropped dead fifty yards off . . . his men piling up and dropping next to him. It was not to be believed."[39] Another German in the Somme remembered that the English "lay in piles," and when they resumed the attack, "they weren't walking this time, they were running as fast as they could but when they reached the piles of bodies they got no farther."[40] Determination, discipline, and cohesion similarly turned out to be lethally counterproductive. A single burst of machine-gun fire could not destroy a battalion, but "if the line of men perseveres with a determined gallantry, over a long open approach, the end is certain."[41] In precisely this manner the 1st Newfoundland Battalion lost 658 men out of a total of 752, along with all 26 officers, within forty minutes of the attack on the German line,[42] and a Highland battalion, which retreated "as though they were on a barrack square," was traversed by a German machine gun "until the last man fell."[43]

Thus indeed the heroic image was shattered by a horrific reality, inexplicable because unprecedented, and unbearable because it contrasted so totally with expectations.[44] To be sure, different generations reacted differently. The youths of 1914 rushed to one war and found themselves in another; the men of 1917 knew already full well what to expect, and while some of them rebelled against it, others hardened themselves with a combination of cynicism, mysticism, and nihilism; the youngsters of 1919 had spent four years preparing to go into the inferno only to find that the war was over just as they believed themselves to be ready for it.[45] But, as Henry James had remarked, "The plunge of civilization into this abyss of blood and darkness" revealed "what the treacherous years were all the while really making for and *meaning*." This was "too tragic for any words"[46] because it had retrospectively given the lie to all previous notions of honor and decency, glory and dignity. Europe was preparing itself for new concepts of decency and honor, more akin to those propagated by Himmler's SS than to Walter Scott's *Ivanhoe*. The chivalrous, it seemed, had shared the fate of the battalion from the soldiers' song, which had been left "hanging on the old barbed wire."[47] Coming under a barrage, even the greatest heroes began "shaking and twitching, their mouths contracted in a hideous spasm, their teeth chattering." The longing "to be there" had gone up in smoke, and as one corporal muttered, "If this is what it's like, I hope I'll be killed off now."[48]

V

The confrontation between the chivalrous image and the industrial horrors of modern warfare, however, did not merely produce bitter disillusionment. For one thing, reality took a long time to undermine the image even among those presumably best suited to adapt to new conditions on the battlefield. Thus, it has been pointed out that throughout the Great War the generals had refused to recognize "the relationship . . . between the art of war and the state of technical knowledge," clearly demonstrating that "In 1914–18, chivalry was still virtually the rule, which was regression even from Greek antiquity, when Hephaestus, god of armor, was at least the equal of Ares, god of war."[49] Moreover, while physically learning how to exist in the new reality, combat soldiers sheltered from its mental implications by retreating into what has been aptly described as a world of "reinvigorated myth . . . a throwback way across the nineteenth and eighteenth centuries to Renaissance and medieval modes of thought and feeling." This paradox of "a myth-ridden world . . . in the midst of a war representing a triumph of modern industrialism, materialism, and mechanism" was at the very core of the Great War; for without the former it would have been impossible to bear the latter. A typical example of this "plethora of very un-modern superstitions, talismans, wonders, miracles, relics, legends, and rumours"[50] was the story of the English bowmen of Agincourt who had come to the rescue of their countrymen, soon transformed in men's imagination into "real" angels firing unseen arrows at the Germans.[51]

Coming face to face with the realities of modern warfare did not resolve the tensions and frustrations that sparked that extraordinary outpouring of joy and excitement the war was initially greeted with, though it did profoundly transform people's perceptions of war, to the extent that today we find the sentiments of the men of 1914 almost inconceivable. Artists and intellectuals, especially but by no means exclusively in Germany, "reacted to the outbreak of war in July 1914 with a sort of relief," with a sense that "the war was to bring redemption from a long period of intellectual and artistic dearth," and "put an end to the extreme diversification of cultural life which had set in during the last decades," all thanks to that "enormous wave of national enthusiasm, engulfing all sections of the population."[52] But in 1918, along with the disillusionment caused by defeat after four years of unprecedented bloodshed, it turned out that the "initial hope that the war might lead to the emergence of a genuine German culture, free from all alien influences, had not come true at all." Indeed, the gulf between various sectors of the German intellectual community only deepened even more, as was also the case in France, although, as we will see in the next chapter, with very different consequences. Hence, while during the postwar years German avant-gardist literature and art chose "war and its inhuman nature . . . as an even more important theme than had been the case during the First World War itself," "the reservations among the more traditional sections of the German cultural community vis-à-vis Western 'civilization' had lost none of their vigor." These "sharp divisions within the German cultural community" no doubt played a major role in the rise of Nazism and the collapse of the Weimar Republic.[53] They also paved the way for the appearance of a new chivalric ethos, better suited to industrial killing, bureaucratic efficiency, and state-controlled nihilism.[54]

The soldiers' "baptism by fire," said to have produced "an initiate generation" possessing "a secret that can never be communicated,"[55] constituted the background for the emergence of a refashioned image of war, one that has by and large molded people's perception of war ever since, the numerous instances of mass killing and genocide in the intervening years notwithstanding. This image was derived from both the technological and psychological struggle to salvage the individual from the mechanical slaughterhouse of the trenches, and to re-discover valor and nobility, meaningful self-sacrifice and devotion. For a time it had seemed that the notion of personal heroism would finally be destroyed by industrial warfare; in fact, however, merely a few more technological and tactical innovations were needed to break the military stalemate on the West-ern Front and thereby also breathe a fresh spirit into the image, reshaping and adapting it to the new conditions. By 1918, the new heroic individual emerging from the trenches was already eager for a new test of arms—and indeed made sure that it would not be long delayed. Thus, the Great War, rather than being the "war to end all wars," became only the originator of the phenomenon of industrial killing that has come to characterize the twentieth century.

European knighthood had originated in a successful combination of man and horse. The new elitist ethos of 1918 was the combination of man and machine. This had two important consequences. First, while chivalry was an-nihilated in 1914 in a mechanical war, by 1918, man had learned to control machines and ride them over entrenched masses deep into the enemy's rear. Henceforth the new knights of war were the tankmen and pilots, the subma-rine crews and the highly trained, well-equipped troops of the assault battal-ions. Thus, that seemingly insurmountable obstacle of barbed wire and ma-chine gun, heavy artillery and foxhole, was overcome, and the impersonality of war consequently appeared to have been done away with; or, at least, men could once more be persuaded that war would give them the opportunity to demonstrate personal heroism. Just as their ancestors had learned to maintain their chivalrous posture without charging into clouds of arrows, so the new heroes no longer had to march calmly into machine-gun fire; now they could drop bombs from the sky, race in armored vehicles, and wreak destruction from the depths of the ocean—no longer faceless, or at least no longer an insignifi-cant element in a vast multitude of similar individuals, and yet a hundred times more deadly than that anonymous mass once buried in the trenches.

Second, however, the increasingly sophisticated and numerous death ma-chines, and the constantly improved systems of control and organization that the effective deployment of such machines made imperative, not only greatly enhanced the ability to implement industrial killing, but also considerably al-leviated the psychological burden of participating in killing operations and provided a convenient mechanism for overcoming (or at least avoiding) the moral questions that had still plagued the generation of 1914. Indeed, the perverse logic of this new ethos of war and killing dictated that those involved most directly in the planning, organization, control, and implementation of industrial killing became the elite, the inheritors of chivalry and the forgers of a new moral and ethical code of behavior. This also meant that the distinction between soldiers and civilians, whether they belonged to the enemy's camp, or constituted one's own human reservoir, became increasingly blurred, and that various categories of human beings could more easily be defined as ex-pendable or harmful and therefore eliminated in large numbers without any major technical difficulties or moral qualms. In this sense we can say that the

Great War not only created the preconditions for indiscriminate bombing of civilian targets, slave labor, state-controlled famine and depopulation, deployment of nuclear weapons, and death camps; it also made for the emergence of an elitist ethos that viewed the perpetration of industrial killing as a noble duty dictated by a new and more profound as well as more relevant interpretation of morality.

Some of the following chapters will elaborate on various aspects of this second, most significant outcome of the redefinition of the relationship between man and the mass, and man and the machine, that emerged from the Great War. In the present context, however, it is useful to note that while the armies of the Second World War were even larger than those of 1914–18, the individuals who manned these huge hosts seem, by and large, to have been less permeated with that sense of total insignificance and helplessness that characterized their Great War predecessors. It was, of course, the far more numerous civilian non-combatants who found themselves in physical and psychological circumstances that, though often much more extreme (depending largely on who and where they were), were nevertheless related in more than one sense to those of the men of the trenches. As for the soldiers, to a large extent it was the new ethos of the elite that liberated the individual from the impersonality of the mass, reawakening the notion of personal, and therefore meaningful, heroism. This had much to do with the greater emphasis on ideology prevalent among all sides in the Second World War, whether one was fighting for *Volk*, *Führer*, and *Reich* (and against "Judeo-Bolshevism" and "plutocracy"), for the Cradle of Communism and Mother Russia (and against "fascism"), or for Democracy and the Free World (and against "Totalitarianism" and "Tyranny"). Thus, the soldiers of 1939–45 give one the impression of having been much more convinced of fighting for a "good cause," and against more or less absolute Evil, than the men of the Great War.[56]

Moreover, along with the sense of fulfilling a mission in the name of humanity (or those parts of it deemed worthy of consideration by whichever ideology one preferred or was compelled to adopt), and not entirely divorced from it, the interwar period saw a general expansion of military elites in all European armies, as well as some non-European ones. Consequently, the mass, large as it had grown, came to be subdivided into an array of arms, formations, and units, each with its own particular identity and speciality. The elites, small by definition, took up the role of the hero-king in that they gave an example of heroism and provided the rest of the mass with a sense of its own potential individuality. But, in this case, the widespread penetration of technology into the armed forces also made for the emergence of soldier/technicians, men of specialized knowledge filled with professional pride and a sense of their indispensability as experts and individuals alike.[57] Thus, alongside the inevitable infantryman, who still made up the largest portion of the fighting element, appeared the combat elites, ranging from armored and motorized formations to airborne divisions, shock battalions and commando companies, on the one hand, and, on the other, the growing army of non-combatant soldiers, mechanics and electricians, radar operators and photography experts, intelligence officers and code-breakers, without whom no bomber could take off or find its target, no tank could drive or fire, no submarine could be sent into the ocean or be reached once there. Both categories of soldiers also tended to develop their own particular states of mind: whereas combat elites might become politically identified and ideologically motivated, non-combatant professionals often assumed a politically indifferent, technocratic attitude, or preferred to focus on their task and ignore its political and/or moral implications.[58]

The ordinary soldier in between these two extremes, the conscripted civilian who still did most of the fighting and dying in the Second World War, has become less common since 1945, as many Western countries tend to rely on smaller, more specialized armies, occasionally narrowing down the gap between the elitist image of war and its reality. This was most evident in postwar colonial conflicts, where a variety of elite units were employed, ranging from the French Foreign Legion and paratroopers, to the British SAS, to the American Marines, Green Berets, and airborne forces, the latter neatly combining the cavalry tradition with the most updated (and often just as gruesome) helicopter tactics. Indeed, whenever an attempt was made to use conscripts in these wars, as happened during the French Algerian war and in the United States' involvement in Vietnam, public resentment ultimately forced governments to pull out of the conflict.[59] Yet while the trend in post-1945 Western nations is to do away with general conscription (with all the implications this may have for their reconceptualization of national identity[60]), we should keep in mind that the combat elements of military elites have on occasion wielded a great deal of influence on both the army and the civilian sector. An interesting example of how the character of a whole army (and to some extent of civilian society as well) was molded by a minute military elite was provided by the Israeli Defense Forces, first formed around the nucleus of the pre-state *Palmach* units, and later reorganized on the model of the 101 commando unit, which in turn led to the creation of the paratroopers. These and many other such elite units were often very fertile breeding grounds for political involvement, either left-wing (like the *Palmach*) or right-wing (like the French paratroopers), Nazi (like the *Waffen-SS*) or communist (like the GPU or NKVD detachments). Indeed, this predilection for politics was closely connected to the elitist sense of a mission, which in turn formed the core of the combat motivation of these units.

All this notwithstanding, it must be said that much of the post-1945 combat elite ethos has always been nothing but a highly potent myth (reminiscent of post-Agincourt knighthood). Since Hiroshima and Nagasaki, nuclear weapons have for the first time in military history introduced the possibility of war without soldiers, without battlefield experience, and most certainly devoid of all memory, being instead the technician's ideal, total destruction at the tip of one's finger. The politically indifferent technocrat will by definition strive to perfect this kind of warless war and make unleashing it all the easier for anyone willing to try, no matter what their ideological stance may be. Nor, of course, are all scientists politically indifferent, though they may find themselves occasionally serving regimes that end up being too nihilistic even for their taste, as happened, for instance, in the case of the far from indifferent biologists, physicians, physicists, rocket makers, nuclear scientists, and a wide array of scholars from related fields in Nazi Germany.[61] Moreover, in conventional wars too, massive use of technology has continued to threaten soldiers with the loss of individual identity. Not only was the Second World War, even more than its predecessor, actually won by the nations with the greatest industrial and demographic resources, but the most concrete manifestation of technological and industrial capacities of that war, the one-thousand bomber raids, could have been no less destructive of individual heroism than the Greek phalanx, similarly deriving their effect from sheer concentration of numbers and determined adherence to formation. Yet here too, the crew of the bomber could feel itself simultaneously waging its own, private, intensely personal and heroic war—riding one machine against another, isolated in the air, in the airplane, in the cockpit and the gun turret, just like Tyrtaeus' hoplite who, though in line with all his comrades, ultimately had to fight a single enemy warrior opposite him, and in doing so it was he, and he alone, who decided the outcome. Thus, when the alienation of man from machine in the mechanical warfare of the Great War had been resolved by man mastering the machine for his own use, and in spite of the fact that mechanized warfare in the Second World War was materially even more destructive, the image of war as an expression of individual heroism could be revived, at least as long as one ignored the threat of atomic war, that most impersonal of all conflicts.

The machine had forced the individual back into the mass, and it was the machine that enabled him to rise again from the multitude. Paradoxically, precisely by achieving that apparent liberation from mechanization, men rapidly learned how to turn other multitudes, to which they themselves did not belong, into anonymous masses that could this time be physically destroyed without presenting any threat to the perpetrators' sense of individual humanity. No wonder that machines take up so much of this century's artistic, literary, and cinematic imagination. Fascination with the machine, and terror from it, the joy of riding it and the fear of being trampled by it, the power it puts in one's hands and the insignificance into which it reduces the individual—all these are recurring themes in the paintings, novels, and films of our time, more often than not in the context of war, or war-like situations of passion and violence, and accompanied by powerful political, ideological messages.[62] And as it was the new elites springing out of the trenches who had mastered the machine and had risen above the multitude, it was also their perceived right to lead the whole of society into the new age. Indeed, seen from the perspective of civilian society, the ethos of the elite was no longer confined to the members of elite units, but to the community of warriors as a whole, to the men who had come to possess that "secret that can never be communicated," and had thereby become the very best and noblest part of humanity. This too was an important heritage of the Great War, an ideal of existence whose recreation came to obsess both those who had experienced it and, even more so, those who had been denied it by reasons of age—that is, the potential soldiers of its second run.

Thus, alongside the trauma of a depersonalizing, dehumanizing war, there flourished an ideal view of the front, as remolded in men's memories and hopes, firmly founded on the cult of togetherness, of living the (imaginary) real, dangerous, fast, and deadly lives of heroes bound to each other by their shared experience and yet remaining individuals separated from the wretched mass. It was this mixture of disillusionment and nostalgia, image and reality, dream and nightmare, that permeated the literature of the Great War, including works described as anti-militaristic. Henri Barbusse's *Under Fire* and Erich Maria Remarque's *All Quiet on the Western Front*, Robert Grave's *Goodbye to All That* and Ernst Jünger's *Storm of Steel*, as well as books concerned with later wars such as Norman Mailer's *The Naked and the Dead* and Michael Herr's *Dispatches*, all reflect a fascination with war not cleansed, but actually enhanced by its horrors.[63] As they inevitably experience the realities of war through the interpretative filter of its image, men remain perpetually attracted to its deadly essence, for it is only by exposing themselves to its dangers, they believe, that they might be allowed to achieve individual heroism, uniting thereby image and reality. Indeed, as one Great War veteran wrote, "in that fascination lies War's power," for "Even those who hate her most are prisoners to her spell. They rise from her embraces, pillaged, soiled, it may be ashamed: but they are still hers."[64]

The new elitist ethos of war, combining ancient notions of heroism and chivalry with modern technology, methodical planning with irrational aspirations, outright nihilism with sensual passion, may be said to have found its most typical expression in European fascism. The *Sturmbataillone* of the *Kaiserheer* were in more than one sense the precursors of the SA and SS (often by way of the *Freikorps*), just as the *arditi* paved the way for the *fasci*.[65] Here was a fascination with technology bound together with an attempt to rediscover the heroic virtues of the past, an obsession with surpassing the limits of human endurance combined with a longing for death, an assertion of individualism along with a passionate desire to merge with the mass. To a considerable extent, the ideal *Kämpfer* of the *Waffen-SS* constituted the epitome of this century's struggle between man and the mass (as expressed by perpetrators, *not* as experienced by victims): belonging to the elite of the Aryan race, noble in blood and by conviction, he expressed the rebellion against the faceless multitude, the mundane and the cynical, the dull and the hopeless; but, paradoxically, he also represented the longing to become part of the whole, to act in unison, to follow orders and to avoid all decision and responsibility, to erase one's particular features and cease being alone. In many ways, this was but a modern version (but also perversion) of the Homeric and knightly ideal of individuality best expressed within a community of warriors, life as a constant war, battle as the essence of existence, (glorious, meaningful) death as the ultimate goal of being. The twentieth century greatly enhanced the destructiveness of war, as well as the soldiers' desperation in view of the vast impersonal forces at play. But fundamentally the heroic image of war has remained unchanged in content and purpose. Indeed, the claim often made by military elites that their political and social philosophy should be adopted by the state employing them has much to do with the soldiers' ethos, according to which they constitute not merely an instrument of power, but also offer an alternative way of life, and state of mind, for humanity as a whole (and here we can consider also non-

European cultures such as Japan). The Homeric hero, the medieval knight, the SS officer, the French paratrooper (as well as the Samurai), all represent a view of human existence, reflecting and molding a social and political reality by practicing their image of war on the battlefield, and striving to adapt the reality of their civilian environment to their martial ethos.

VI

These examples seem to indicate the existence of a dialectical relationship between the image of war and its reality; as the two contradictory components of the soldier's perception of events clash on the battlefield, they invariably produce a synthesis, adapting the previous imagery to present experiences. This new image of war will then be carried into the next military confrontation, only to clash once more with a newly changed reality.

The Homeric image of heroic single combat dominated the minds of men for centuries in a Greece whose mode of fighting was the rigid, disciplined, impersonal phalanx. This contradiction was overcome by finding other means of expressing individual valor: stressing the qualities of each man within the phalanx, praising those operating out of the line in situations that necessitated such actions, and allowing ample room for the heroic leader, whose license to break the rules of combat and commit extraordinary feats of courage enabled the rest to stay in formation and yet share in his glory.

The chivalric image of war emerged from a mode of fighting adopted by European knights. Technically, the duel between two heavily armed horsemen was for a while the reality of war, just as Homeric single combat may have been in the distant past. However, only when this reality of war vanished due to the changing conditions on the battlefield did the joust achieve the status of an ideal image, by now associated with virtues hardly connected with its actual military origins. Gradually a strange transformation took place, whereby the noble knight, the very essence of the warrior, became the European officer, whose role was to direct and supervise the battle, not fight it. Applying violence was sublimated into giving orders, and individualism, tied with social and moral superiority, could be retained, the appearance of large infantry formations notwithstanding.

The Great War, with its massive use of technology and seemingly unlimited reserves of manpower, shattered the chivalric ethos of the officer corps. An industrial confrontation that gave birth to such terms as "*Menschenmaterial*" and "*Materialschlacht*," that is, which considered human beings as mere pieces of material, and battle as a clash between inanimate objects, did not seem to leave any room for individual heroism. But the gradual growth of the new specialists, who both broke the stalemate at the front by channeling technology to their own purposes and did away with the depersonalization of war by creating the mystique of the elite, provided powerful evidence for the phoenix-like quality of the heroic image. Interestingly, the struggle for individuality manifested itself once more in the attitudes of the European officer corps. The new officers to emerge from the Great War returned, one might say, to their tradi-

In the closing pages of Thomas Mann's *The Magic Mountain*, as we recall, the author asks whether "Out of this universal feast of death, out of this extremity of fever . . . may it be that Love one day shall mount?"[26] Published in 1924, Mann's novel was begun before 1914, and expressed the romantic view of war prevalent at the time. Just as pre-1914 war plans combined the extensive use of railroads for the execution of complicated tactical maneuvers with what has been called the "myth of the offensive," so too the literary imagination yearned for "Love" to spring out of what soon became a no-man's land scarred with millions of shell craters and machine-gun bullets. And just as the *offensive à outrance* ended up in decimating a whole generation of enthusiastic youngsters, and had to be replaced by new tactics more suitable for the changed reality of warfare, so too the old romantic image of war was eventually transformed, even though this transformation did not necessarily lead to the abandonment of the search for a "higher" or "deeper" meaning of battle.[27]

Even before the Great War ended, many Europeans were already preoccupied with studying its "lessons," gauging its implications, and preparing both materially, politically, ideologically, and psychologically for the possibility of a second round. Since the war was begun with a series of offensives, which within a few months turned into a lengthy and costly stalemate, finally broken by another series of offensives, two contradictory consequences to be drawn from this experience seemed equally valid. It was possible to argue, as the French did, that the best strategy in modern war was defense, at least until one marshalled enough material resources, and sufficiently depleted those of the enemy, to make the offensive once more cost-effective. But it was just as rational to assert, as the Germans did, that the only way to avoid the bloody stagnation of the last war was to launch a rapid and powerful offensive right at the opening of hostilities. Hence, both the French Maginot Line, and the eventual German concept of *Blitzkrieg*, were derived from the experience of 1914–18. Although there were numerous other political, demographic, strategic, and ideological reasons for the war plans finally implemented by these two nations (as well as by many others, most notably Britain and the Soviet Union), there is little doubt that they were both based on differing images of the same event, namely, the Great War. Clearly, fear of destruction led one side to plan a war whereby the enemy would be kept outside the country's territory by means of a defensive "wall," while convincing the other side to rescue itself from potential defeat by rapid destruction of it rivals. For the military and political mind, Mann's "feast of death" had relatively simple and unambiguous implications: either keep it away from yourself or do it to others. The only "Love" we can detect here is obviously love of oneself (or by extension one's nation), as is indeed inevitable where politics and the military are involved.[28]

Literary minds, however, and especially those of writers who (unlike Mann) had been directly exposed to the realities of the fighting, revealed a much more ambivalent attitude toward the phenomenon of mass, industrial killing, while at the same time no longer espousing that vague and sentimental pre-1914 romanticization of war that still informed Mann's generation.[29] In these texts we can clearly note the realization that something quite new had taken place, something whose consequences still continue to haunt our civilization today. Moreover, we can also perceive that while the preoccupation with the enormity of the war produced in some a powerful urge to prevent such an event from ever happening again, it also contained the perilous potential of actually stimulating its reenactment, on an even vaster and more horrific scale. This is the crux of the matter: that the occurrence of industrial killing, inevitably accompanied by its representation, made its recurrence all the more likely.

As early as 1916, the French author Henri Barbusse published *Le feu*, the first realistic Great War novel in any European language. For the very first time readers who had not been to the front and had depended on the censored and propagandistic reports of the newspapers could learn what the fighting really looked and felt like. But Barbusse was not aiming merely at exposing the reality of war, the blood and gore of the trenches, the horrific deaths and mutilation of the soldiers, and the seething anger of the front-line troops on realizing the comfort and complacency of those who had remained safely in the rear. Rather, Barbusse's intention was to make some sense of the slaughter—indeed, to provide the war with a higher purpose, even if that purpose differed substantially from that ascribed to it by the government, the generals, or the media.[30] In this he was not wholly different from Mann; but his was a revolutionary romanticism, while Mann's was still traditional and patriotic, linked to the liberal-conservative cultural elitism that characterized his wartime, liberal-nationalist perception of the war expounded in his *Betrachtungen eines Unpolitischen*.[31]

While Mann appeals for love, Barbusse demands justice. Justice would mean the end of War, not merely the end of this specific massacre; and that greater goal may call for yet more bloodshed. Only this time, the fighting may be not against a foreign enemy, but against the perpetrators of War and injustice, the enemies of the soldiers, the enemies of the people. If this was pacifism (and Barbusse was a major figure in the interwar pacifist movement until his death), then it was active, militant, revolutionary pacifism.[32] Barbusse's protagonists, their "eyes full of slaughter," proclaim the solidarity of soldiers: "Two armies at death-grips—that is one great army committing suicide." They know that "It should not have been." But theirs is not a passive, certainly not a hopeless attitude. Some reflect the hopes of millions: "Perhaps it is the last war of all." To be sure, there are those who no longer believe that there will ever be an end to the killing; for them the world is rotten to the core: "Stop war? Stop war? Impossible! There is no cure for the world's disease." But this is not the author's position, although he clearly agrees with another protagonist that the end will not come of its own accord: "It is the French Revolution beginning again." "Let thrones beware!" Indeed, his vision is of universal awakening and liberation, for otherwise how could one ever justify mass killing? Those soldiers of Europe, those "thirty million slaves, hurled upon one another in the mud of war by guilt and error," finally "uplift their human faces and reveal at last a burgeoning Will." Barbusse offers a vision of hope and redemption: "The future is in the hands of these slaves, and it is clearly certain that the alliance to be cemented one day by those whose number and whose misery alike are infinite will transform the old world."[33]

Here were two options, one of pacifism and another of revolutionary action. And while the former was potentially passive, the latter had, at least initially, mainly domestic implications: The task was to transform one's own state and society, hoping that the same would happen beyond the country's borders. It was, in a sense, an optimistic view, but one born of despair, anger, disgust. And it was a view that extolled the simple, fighting soldiers, those who were the victims of the war, and who would, one hoped, make certain that another war would never happen again, or, if it did, that it would be a revolutionary war to end injustice, subjugation, "slavery."[34]

Interwar imagery presents a highly favorable view of the simple soldier; it contains little acknowledgment of the fact that it was, after all, those very same soldiers who had actually carried out the killing; just as it fails to grapple with the fact that it was the People who had produced the shells, the bullets, the guns and the bombs, the newspapers and propaganda leaflets, without all of which the war, and especially *that*, total war, would have been impossible. In this imagery, War is the enemy, its human instruments the victims. This view of victimhood without perpetrators was not without its dangers. The misery of the trenches seemed to have ennobled their inhabitants, and though many of those who glorified the soldiers expressed explicitly antiwar, antimilitarist views, their rhetoric was anything but unambiguous, and its implications were consequently not necessarily at all what their propagators had had in mind. For at least one possible elaboration of this image was the view that if the actual killers were not to be blamed for the killing, and if one nevertheless needed to blame some human agency, then it was precisely those who were allegedly *not* involved in the killing (and the dying), or, better still, those who had opposed it, who deserved punishment: it was they who had betrayed the nation and stabbed it in the back. Not surprisingly, this role was often ascribed to the Jews.[35]

Barbusse represents the advent of industrial killing as the shock that would awaken humanity to the realities of its condition of enslavement and induce it to wage a war of liberation against a corrupt ruling class, thereby eliminating the preconditions for war; other writers sought a more personal meaning in mass slaughter. Erich Maria Remarque, whose *All Quiet on the Western Front* (1929) sold more copies than any other Great War novel, was and still is considered to have been a major antiwar, even pacifist figure. Yet his novel too contains that ambiguity of which I have spoken, generally ignored by his critics. Remarque's lost generation, whose representatives reappear in his later works (such as his 1931 *Der Weg Zurück* and 1937 *Drei Kameraden*), consists of disillusioned, cynical, once-patriotic and naive men, whose only contact with the postwar world is through their comrades and the memory of the fallen. Though they do not long to be back "there," they feel at home nowhere else. Remarque, unlike Jünger, did not find any aesthetic beauty in the war; nor did he join the *Freikorps* and continue the war by other, terrorist means, as did von Salomon—who just missed the war—along with many other veterans.[36] And yet, reading his account of life and death on the Western Front, we find that for him it was there, and there alone, that man could discover his true qualities and potential. In war, he says, man learns how to face death, how to confront destruction, how to transform himself into an animal determined to survive at all cost. In war, man is redeemed only by killing: "We have become beasts. We do not fight, we defend ourselves against annihilation," for, "when Death is hunting us down . . . we can see his face . . . we can oppose him; we feel a mad anger. No longer do we lie helpless, waiting on the scaffold, we can destroy and kill, to save ourselves, to save and to be revenged." And in that battle for survival, in that killing, there is an exhilaration, a new self-knowledge, perhaps not wholly recognized by the author and yet present in his text, and much more readily acknowledged by other members of his generation who chose a wholly different path after the fighting had ended. As they charge, writes Remarque, something happens to the soldiers: "we run on, overwhelmed by this wave that bears us along, that fills us with ferocity, turns us into thugs, into murderers, into God only knows what devils; this wave that multiplies our strength with fear and madness and greed of life, seeking and fighting for nothing but for our deliverance." Indeed, he admits, this energy of the fight, this mad desire to survive, is stronger than even the most powerful moral sanction and emotional tie: "If your own father came over with them you would not hesitate to fling a bomb at him."[37]

Remarque, to an even greater extent than Barbusse, seems frightened by his discovery of what the insanity of the war had released in him. But just as Barbusse believed that the destructive energies of human beings could be channeled to serve the cause of justice, so Remarque appears to imply that knowledge of the brutality and irrationality of war would finally convince men never to fight again. And yet neither of them, precisely *because* of their commitment to render the experience of war as realistically as possible, could avoid revealing its fascination, its power to transport men to physical and mental states previously unknown to them. This was the intoxication of murder on a vast, unprecedented scale. Many feared the killing, others feared the intoxication; some could not have enough of both.

Barbusse and Remarque found some universal meaning or at least purpose in the war. It would be, they fervently hoped, a war to end all wars, even if, paradoxically, it was precisely in that war that they discovered the endless capacity of men to destroy. They admired the soldiers, and, in that, they also admired themselves, for in spite of its harsh realism, there was in their writing, as in many other war accounts, a measure of narcissism of the kind perfected, perhaps, by Hemingway.[38] That this antiwar, pro-soldier literature had a tremendous effect on a whole generation of young readers (indeed, on many subsequent generations) is undeniable, but what this effect actually boiled down to is more difficult to determine. Some, no doubt, came to fear and hate war; but others read these accounts quite differently, regretted having missed the horror, and hoped to emulate those most directly involved in it, those who had physically perpetrated it and yet had achieved the status of heroic victims, the main element in the newly forged romantic image of war in which growing numbers of interwar youths yearned to partake.[39]

In this respect, there is little doubt that Ernst Jünger was more sincere than many other contemporary writers. Jünger did not seek a universal purpose in the war; he only wished to satisfy his own fascination with death and extremity. His was quite literally a personal pleasure at observing and participating in this "universal feast of death." From this perspective we can say that Jünger was indeed endowed with highly (post)modern sensibilities, which may explain to some extent his current popularity. His attraction to war and violence was akin to our own fascination with horror, cinematic, journalistic, televised, and fictionalized, in our own cities and in faraway places.[40] But in other respects he was closer to his *Freikorps* contemporaries, since he not only observed, he simultaneously killed himself—and with some pleasure too, it would seem.

Now this phenomenon, this celebration of limitless, round-the-clock destruction, brings us to the other alternative reaction to this first great instance of industrial killing. Jünger's aim is neither to condemn, nor to prevent, nor even to justify total war. His goal is to master an unavoidable, unstoppable condition that, fortunately, also has some positive aspects to it, both aesthetic and, in his later writings, also social and political.[41] Thus, in his 1930 essay *Total Mobilization*, he recognizes that the whole world is once more preparing for war, and suggests that in such a world it is better to be armed oneself; in his 1980 postscript to this essay he acknowledges that this universal condition has still not fundamentally changed.[42] Hence war, for Jünger, much as he may personally enjoy it, exists beyond personal actions and desires and can be viewed almost as a natural phenomenon. What matters is to retain control over this perpetual condition of potential mass killing; do it to others, lest it be done to you (and while you are at it, make the most of it). This attitude, incidentally, also goes some way to explain Jünger's eventual distance from the Nazis. Content with his own aesthetic pleasure and attraction to war, Jünger's world-view contains no overt fatalism or pessimism, nor the expectation of an approaching apocalypse; instead, it is wholly narcissistic and nihilistic; *Volk*, Führer, and *Vaterland* have a distinctly second priority for him. Even his own son's death in battle in 1944 elicits from him (in the privacy of his diary, which, however, he later published) the following startling comment: "Since he was a child he had always striven to emulate his father. Now he has done much better right from the start, surpassing him [his father] so completely."[43] Thus, his son had accomplished (for him) the death he had always yearned for (but had so well avoided with that unsurpassed instinct of a survivor who is still alive as I write now, precisely fifty years later); the son had made it possible for the father to keep on writing about his fascination with death, an amazing ability to pour forth a stream of words of which death would have surely deprived him (and his readers). We find no remorse in Jünger's diary for having provided his son with this example; here too he is wholly sincere, for he truly believes that such a death, in battle, by a bullet through the head, is fascinating (even, presumably, for the mind that must endure its own annihilation). The intervening years between the two world wars did nothing to lessen his voyeuristic interest in other men's destruction. Indeed, as a Wehrmacht officer in occupied Paris, Jünger was engaged in executing German deserters and is reported to have been "interested in observing how a person reacts to death under such circumstances," a predilection he characterized as "a higher form of curiosity."[44] It is this mentality that cannot but make us think of the SS officer looking through the peephole in the door of the gas chamber to see how people "react to death under such circumstances."[45]

The other aspect of this same activist reaction to the experience of industrial killing in 1914–18 is best represented by Louis-Ferdinand Céline. Jünger's narcissistic nihilism contained no particular hatred, not even disgust of others. His is a detached, cool (and cruel) eye, unblinking, apparently fearless, with a hint of derision. In this he is still not wholly fascist, though quite capable of perpetrating "banal evil" (a description of his potential he will surely disagree with).[46] We may, of course, doubt the sincerity of his "pure" aesthetic vision, which, after all, provided a retrospective justification for the more bestial instincts aroused in him (as in any other soldier) during the actual act of killing. Aesthetic contemplation after the fact makes for distance, and distance enables the viewer to impose a "higher" meaning on what was ultimately an expression of that which is most base and brutal in human nature. Céline, in this sense, is more honest, for he reacted to industrial killing with greater terror and disgust than any of the writers mentioned here. Céline's nihilism is of a wholly different quality, for while Jünger will (at least claim to) watch or perpetrate murder simply out of curiosity, Céline wants to destroy the world (and especially the Jews in the world) because it is so utterly ugly and depraved. Having experienced the concerted attempt of a whole industrial complex to kill him, he is now quite ready to destroy everything that complex represents (to his mind). Céline, like so many (much less articulate) fascists of his time, is filled to the brim with visions of torture, suffering, pain, and perversion. He yearns to wipe the slate clean, once and for all, though he fears that too, lest he be destroyed in the process.

For Céline, as for Jünger, there is no comradeship, "love," compassion. In this both lack one aspect of fascism present in Remarque who cherishes that very comradeship that came to be extolled by fascism. It was Remarque who wrote of that "great brotherhood, which adds something of the good-fellowship of the folksong, of the feeling of solidarity of convicts, and of the desperate loyalty to one another of men condemned to death, to a condition of life arising out of the midst of danger, out of the tension and forlornness of death—seeking in a wholly unpathetic way a fleeting enjoyment of the hours as they come." To be sure, he acknowledged (as no true fascist would have done) that this was "at once heroic and banal,"[47] but he remained nostalgic nevertheless, even in his later (and lesser) writings. Nevertheless, it is the combination of Jünger's fascination with killing and Céline's utter and complete disgust with humanity (and himself) that leads us directly to Auschwitz. It is this fear of perversion and boundless attraction to it, this longing for purity and obsession with filth, this indifference to the fate of others and immeasurable hatred of anything human, which we must keep in mind when we turn to discuss the Holocaust:

This war, in fact, made no sense at all. It couldn't go on.

Had something weird got into these people? Something I didn't feel at all? I suppose I hadn't noticed it . . . .

"In a mess like this," I said to myself, "there's nothing to be done, all you can do is clear out . . . ."

I never felt so useless as I did amid all those bullets in the sunlight. A vast and universal mockery . . . .

Could I, I thought, be the last coward on earth? How terrifying! . . . . All alone with two million stark raving heroic madmen, armed to the eyeballs? With and without helmets, without horses, on motorcycles, bellowing, in cars, screeching, shooting, plotting, flying, kneeling, digging, taking cover, bounding over trails, root-toot-tooting, shut up on earth as if it were a loony bin, ready to demolish everything on it, Germany, France, whole continents, everything that breathes, destroy destroy, madder than mad dogs, worshipping their madness (which dogs don't), a hundred, a thousand times madder than a thousand dogs, and a lot more vicious! A pretty mess we were in! No doubt about it, this crusade I'd let myself in for was the apocalypse!

You can be a virgin in horror the same as in sex. How, when I left the Place Clichy, could I have imagined such horror? Who could have suspected, before getting into the war, all the ingredients that go to make up the rotten, heroic, good-for-nothing soul of man? And there was I, caught up in a mass flight into collective murder, into the fiery furnace . . . . Something had come up from the depths, and this is what happened.[48]

IV

In March 1936 one of the leaders of French pacifism, Félicien Challaye, in a response to Romain Rolland, pointed out that the ultimate evil was war, not Nazism. Hence he concluded that the destruction of war had to be avoided at all cost. Furthermore, Challaye insisted on the distinction between the "struggle against internal Fascism . . . which we accept" and "the struggle against external Fascism," which "takes on necessarily the aspect of war." And on this point he saw no compromise: "We want nothing to do with war, even that which is baptized antifascist and revolutionary. We are convinced, moreover, that one does not bring freedom on the tip of a sword, nor democracy in foreign troops carriers."[49]

This was an admirably steadfast position to take, and one that eventually led Challaye to claim that Pétain had "saved the country in imposing the armistice," and to insist on the "duty to collaborate with Germany."[50] Céline too had become convinced that France could not survive another war. Moreover, by 1937 he was certain that it was the Jews who were about to bring a second round of mass slaughter to the world, and concluded that the only way to prevent industrial killing was to commit it oneself: "War, for us as we are, means the end of the show, the final tilt into the Jewish charnel house." The seeds of Céline's rabidly antisemitic essays *Bagatelles pour un massacre* and *L'École des cadavres* were sown in 1914. Evasion of murder could come only through its perpetration, through the total elimination of all Jews, and, by extension it seems, of the rest of humanity along with them.[51] Céline, of course, was not alone in expressing such views, though his use of words was quite incomparable.[52] For on the other extreme of the political map, opposing pacifists like Challaye but about to join him in the collaborationist camp, were organizations such as the fascist league *La solidarité française*, whose leaflets warned the French of the "Red Fascism" of "social-communist Judeo-freemasons" conspiring "against the freedom of thought, against the family, against the nation," threatening to bring "fire and bloodshed to France just as it had brought it to central Europe, Russia, and now Spain," and about to incite "sabotage against the national defense and a bloody revolution."[53]

By this time the Nazi regime had already consolidated its power in Germany, had passed the Nuremberg laws, and was frantically preparing for another war. Less than five years after Céline had called for a general annihilation of the Jews, Hitler, who shared the French writer's general disgust with humanity, obsession with filth, and maniacal antisemitism, unleashed the "Final Solution of the Jewish Question," a program of industrial, bureaucratically organized genocide he believed would save the world from a repetition of the industrial killing of the Great War. As early as 1939, only two years after the publication of Céline's *Bagatelles*, Hitler proclaimed in a major speech to the Reichstag: "Europe cannot find peace until the Jewish question has been solved. . . . [I]f the international Jewish financiers in and outside Europe should succeed in plunging the nations once more into a world war, then the result will not be the Bolshevizing of the earth, and thus the victory of Jewry, but the annihilation of the Jewish race in Europe!"[54]

With the outbreak of the Second World War, escape from industrial killing by evasion became increasingly difficult; only a few people in Europe could safely remain pacifist, at least as long as they did not join the fascists. Nazi Germany had chosen the other path, escape by perpetration. This did not save Germany from being ultimately devastated, although not before it had destroyed large parts of Europe and brought about the death of even greater numbers of people than in 1914–18. But it did make for the creation in the most concrete form possible of the nightmare of industrial killing that had haunted the European imagination since the Great War. The killing was more efficient, the victims more varied in age and gender, and the cost for the killers miniscule in comparison. Had it not been for the war raging around this "concentrationary universe," it would have indeed been the ideal answer to the Western Front of 1914–18. It even resembled images of Hell more closely. George Steiner has suggested that "The camp embodies . . . the images and chronicles of Hell in European art and thought from the twelfth to the eighteenth centuries," and that "these representations . . . gave the deranged horrors of Belsen a kind of 'expected logic.'" Indeed, to his mind the death camps "are *Hell made immanent*. They are the transference of Hell from below the earth to its surface. They are the deliberate enactment of a long, precise imagining."[55] To be sure, images of Hell force themselves on us whenever we read descriptions of the Holocaust, and such images often also haunted the inmates and cheered the perpetrators. But this was a hell whose immediate origins were geographically and chronologically much closer, one which had already been seen on earth. For the Holocaust was far more directly the almost perfect reenactment of the Great War (and its own imagery of hell), with the important correction that all the perpetrators were on one side and all the victims on the other. Everything else was there: the barbed wire, the machine guns, the charred bodies, the gas, the uniforms, the military discipline, the barracks. But this reenactment had the great advantage that it was *totally* lethal for the inmates and *totally* safe for the guards. And the killing too, needless to say, was *total*.

Arriving at the camp, inmates were beset by a sense of unreality, disbelief, shock.[56] This did evoke in many a memory of hell, but their descriptions often resemble those of soldiers arriving at the front, who were similarly struck by its "hellish," nightmarish appearance: "All around us were screams, death, smoking chimneys making the air black and heavy with soot and the smell of burning bodies. . . . It was just like a nightmare and it took weeks and weeks before I could believe it was really happening."[57] If we recall the accounts of Great War soldiers quoted in the previous chapter, we will realize where this universe of industrial killing, both its reality and the imagination that brought it into being, comes from. But it is, of course, immeasurably worse; the war is by now believable, since it happened, and is happening again (the Great War provides the image; the Second World War provides the context). *This* instance of industrial killing can still not be believed even by its victims; it is only after the fact that we accept it, and thereby also accept the possibility of its reenactment: "Not far from us, flames were leaping up from a ditch, gigantic flames. They were burning something . . . little children. Babies! Yes, I saw it . . . Was I awake? I could not believe it . . . No, none of this could be true. It was a nightmare."[58] This "dream of Hell,"[59] now actualized, was so total, so close to images internalized over many centuries, that the victims had to force themselves to accept its reality: "Many times I felt I must be dreaming, and I would call to myself: 'Wake up! Wake up! You are having a nightmare!' I would look around me, trying to wake up, but alas, my eyes kept on seeing the same dismal picture."[60] And what is the picture? It is hell, it is war, it is a death camp: "Every chimney was disgorging flames. Smoke burst from the holes and ditches. . . . Sparks and cinders blinded us. Through the screened fence of the second crematory we could see figures with pitch forks moving against the background of flames. They were . . . turning the corpses in the pits . . . so that they would burn better."[61]

It has been rightly noted that "the drift of modern history domesticates the fantastic and normalizes the unspeakable. And the catastrophe that begins it is the Great War."[62] Fiction has no business where such testimonies are heard: "I stood in front of the pit quaking. For a fleeting moment I saw my companions in the pit. Some of them were still moving convulsively. I heard a loud rifle volley, then silence and darkness. . . . Is this death? . . . . I try to raise myself. . . . I cry out . . . "Are any of you alive?" . . . But in the pit . . . no one moves."[63] Viewing this world of industrial killing from the inside, as seen by those on whom is was perpetrated—that is, those who made evasion, who made escape possible—is terrifying, numbing, shattering. And yet it evokes memories, memories of the Great War (novels, films, photographs, oral testimonies), and memories of hell, whose imagined reality, which informed the creators of these human worlds, fades in comparison to their achievement.

This is not a world of sacrifice, but of victimhood, and perhaps its most terrifying aspect is that it is based on the assumption that the victim is necessary. This victim is not a sinner; he does not go to hell for his actions, but in order to make it possible for others not to end up in the eternal flame. Therefore he is a modern figure, in a modern, man-made hell, where industrial murder is perpetrated by those who want to be saved from it. In this world, God is just as superfluous as fiction; but human imagination is omnipotent, for it both makes for this world's creation and its perpetuation. And from this perspective, this is anything but an unimaginable reality.

Yet there is much reluctance to associate the imagery of the Great War with the Holocaust. This has to do both with the discomfort of perceiving national wars as instances of industrial killing and with the general tendency to insist on the uniqueness of the Holocaust, or at least on the differences between genocide and war. But while there is clearly a distinction to be made between the mutual killing of soldiers and the wholesale massacre of defenseless populations, it is crucial to realize that total war and genocide are closely related. For modern war provides the occasion and the tools, the manpower and the organization, the mentality and the imagery necessary for the perpetration of genocide. With the introduction of industrial killing to the battlefield, the systematic murder of whole peoples became both practical and thinkable: those who had experienced the former could imagine and plan, organize, and perpetrate the latter. All that was needed was the will to act, and by the end of the Great War there were not a few men who believed that their only escape from the hell of modern war was to subject others to the industrial killing they had barely survived.

II

The Holocaust:
Histories, Memories, Stories

Antisemitism, the Holocaust, and Reinterpretations of National Socialism

The truth is, Auschwitz refutes
creator, creation, and the creature.
Life as an idea is dead.
This may well be the beginning
of a great new era,
a redemption from suffering.
From this point of view only one crime
remains: cursed be he who creates life.
I cremate life. That is modern
humanitarianism—the sole salvation from the future.[1]

There is a common tendency to view the Holocaust as a well-ordered plot, in which antisemitism led to Nazism, Nazism practiced genocide, and both were destroyed in a spectacular, "happy" end. This is a tale most people would like to believe, university students and filmgoers, book readers and television viewers. It breeds complacency about our own world. It refuses to acknowledge that this is a story without a clear beginning and with no resolution. For this reason one finds it such a difficult period to teach; we strive to provide our students with a more comforting, rational, logical, palatable explanation for an event that would otherwise threaten to undermine our civilization's fundamental values and beliefs. And yet we know that would be false; the story has not been resolved, its plot has not been revealed. Ultimately, the world we live in is the same world that produced (and keeps producing) genocide.[2]

This chapter will examine several aspects of the postwar discourse on antisemitism, genocide, and Nazism. I will begin by discussing some characteristic features of the scholarly interpretations and popular images of each of these three phenomena, noting the extent to which these debates were molded over time by chronology, geography, ideology, and changing sociopolitical as well as cultural circumstances. I will then attempt to assess the implications of these differing views on the relationship between the causes, essence, and consequences of the Holocaust for the study and deeper understanding not only of the Event itself, but also of the nature of modernity. This will then lead me to a final discussion of some aspects of Nazism that the above causal model tends to underestimate, though they were both crucial to the theory and practice of genocide and are still very much present in our own society. By touching briefly on the role of the medical and legal professions in the formulation and realization of National Socialist policies, I will thus argue that the world in which we live is still anything but free from the profound contradictions of modernity that made Auschwitz possible.

I. Antisemitism

Roughly speaking, we contrast two basic views about antisemitism: one that sees it as a permanent aspect of Jewish life in the Diaspora ever since the Exile (or even before), another that perceives it as a political/ideological/social phenomenon firmly rooted in late nineteenth-century European society and by and large discredited, apart from some more remote corners of "Western civilization," following 1945. Each interpretation defines the phenomenon itself differently so as to be able to fit it into its own understanding of antisemitism's historical context. Hence, while the former views anti-Jewish sentiments as a cluster of religious, social, economic, and political prejudices, the latter stresses the differences between traditional anti-Jewish feelings and actions among the Christian population of Europe, seen as primarily related to religious biases and social exclusion (as well as economic activity), and modern, political, demagogic, "scientific" antisemitism, rooted in a combination of new racial theories, modernization and its effects on society, and nationalism, sometimes invoked along with imperialism and colonialism.[3]

The interesting point to be made at this juncture is that in spite of the fact that the representatives of these two interpretations of antisemitism have often clashed bitterly with each other, and have indeed come from wholly different ideological backgrounds, they have by and large agreed on the role played by their conflicting versions of antisemitism in both the rise of Nazism (or totalitarianism) and in the genocide of the Jews (or also in some cases of other categories of human beings by this and other totalitarian regimes). The proponents of perpetual antisemitism are thus content within the framework of an historical interpretation that explains everything, even the seemingly inexplicable, and which, while professing a grim, perhaps permanent pessimism, at least provides one with a sense of stability associated with any historical "law." Similarly, the supporters of contextualized antisemitism, who view it as part and parcel of modernity, the nation-state, industrialization, and mass society, can also employ their (more complex) interpretation as a tool for understanding what would otherwise seem to defy reason. Since modern society does not appear to be on the way out, postmodern fears or aspirations notwithstanding, this latter view also offers a measure of comforting (albeit explosive) stability in a highly fluid and bewildering environment.[4]

Supporters of the traditional view of anti-Judaism seem to come from two very different camps: the orthodox and the Zionist. For the orthodox it is a given that the gentiles are constantly threatening the Jews, as has been the case, from their perspective, ever since biblical times. For the Zionists, who had rebelled against the orthodox world, it is just as obvious that the gentiles would always be against the Jews, with the important qualification that the best defense and remedy for this situation is not prayer and trust in God, but statehood.[5] For both these groups the Holocaust, however catastrophic it surely was in personal human terms, serves the ideological (or theological) purpose of fortifying their understanding of Jewish fate and history. The Zionists obviously could say that had the Jews lived in a state of their own, none of this would have happened (or, at least, things would have happened differently). The orthodox have argued that the Holocaust not only proved the biblical truth that all the gentiles are against the Jews, but also that the only way to continue Jewish existence after the catastrophe is to go back to the old ways, since that would be the real victory of the Jews over all their foes.[6]

Some of the most brilliant (Jewish) minds who have written on antisemitism as generated by its socioeconomic and ideological context (including the role played by the Jews themselves within gentile society) have been accused of suffering from that modern disease of "Jewish self-hatred."[7] Yet Hannah Arendt, the main target of such attacks by (both Diaspora and Zionist Israeli) Jews holding the traditional view, in fact argued that antisemitism was a major factor in the appearance and spread of totalitarianism and its accompanying facet of mass murder and genocide. Some interpretations of antisemitism, however, do indeed minimize its role in either the genocide of the Jews or generally the emergence of totalitarian regimes of one kind or another. The difference between these interpretations has to do, among other factors, with their chronological distance from the event, as well as with personal and national perspectives. Thus, for instance, during the Second World War German antisemitism was not often invoked as a major motivating element in the fight against Nazism, not least due to actual or suspected antisemitic sentiments among the populations of the Allies (and in Soviet Russia also due to Marxist interpretations of fascism that excluded antisemitism a priori as a substantial factor). After the end of the war and the discovery of the death camps antisemitism seemed for a while to be the key for explaining the barbarization of German society. But the rhetoric of the Cold War and its insistence on the similarity between Stalinism and Hitlerism replaced antisemitism with totalitarianism, followed in the 1960s by refashioned leftist theories of fascism, which again saw class tensions, late capitalism and imperialism as much more central than antisemitism.[8]

Personal factors were often also crucial in discussing antisemitism. Jews who had been persecuted as Jews by the Germans and their collaborators had no time for interpretations that relegated anti-Jewish sentiments to a secondary place. Conversely, Germans who had lived through the period performing their various duties without much contact with actual Jews beyond perhaps some faint memories of prewar neighbors, or encountered the term Jew as an administrative abstraction, could not accept arguments that made Nazi Germany appear to have been mainly populated by rabid antisemites. Hence also the often exaggerated differentiation made between Jewish and gentile historians writing on Nazism, which for some reason assumes that the latter can achieve greater detachment and objectivity than the former.[9]

Detachment and empathy seem to be also related to chronological distance, with the result that in recent years it has become much easier for some historians to view antisemitism as relatively unimportant in explaining politics and ideology in the twentieth century, while calling for greater empathy with those whose own fate had allegedly been obscured by the overemphasis on Jews in previous scholarly work.[10] It is of course a manifestation of the cunning of history that just as the distance from 1945 allows one to speak about *that* past with more detachment (or to call for new subjects of empathy), the present seems to provide one with an ever growing array of instances where racial and religious prejudice and hatred are gaining political importance.

In the political arena, antisemitism has been abused by all and sundry. Israeli governments have sought to legitimize their policies by accusing their critics and enemies of antisemitic sentiments;[11] German governments have sought renewed international respectability by well-orchestrated public proclamations of Philosemitic feelings.[12] Both the Left and the Right in Europe have accused each other (not without reason) of harboring antisemitic ideas. Indeed, since 1945 antisemitism, like fascism, has become a term of abuse hurled at one's enemies, while not altogether disappearing both as a private sentiment and as a loosely concealed public platform. Given the growing chronological distance from the Holocaust, it is not unreasonable to expect that at some point in the future antisemitism will regain some of its lost influence, not least by seeping in from those parts of Europe where the collapse of communism left the public open to the rejuvenation of old prejudices.[13]

II. The Holocaust

In speaking about the Holocaust we may also begin by a basic distinction between the eschatological and the scholarly interpretation. At the same time, however, we should note that in spite of the clear differences, there exists in fact a measure of overlap between these two points of view. Just as what might appear to be a purely academic explanation may reveal at a closer look some deeply ingrained, often irrational and inexplicable beliefs and sentiments, so too the eschatological interpretation of the second half of the twentieth century will tend to employ arguments and evidence taken from scholarship and science in order to fortify its own interpretative universe. Hence we must bear in mind that when applied to such an event as the Holocaust—that is, to a disaster carried out by human beings that nevertheless threatens constantly to escape reason or to wholly undermine the very concept of humanity—even this fundamental distinction remains highly tenuous, since the rules of logic or systems of belief on which it is based are constantly threatened by the nature of the abyss they seek to explain.[14]

Leaving the eschatological view aside (since it is, at least by definition, self-contained and foolproof), the constant flux in the secular interpretation of the Holocaust, its many shifts between detachment and sentimentality, harshness and doubt, and ultimately extreme openendedness, demonstrates not only that by and large the secular universe is a less secure one than the theological, but, more specifically, that the Holocaust as an event, by its very extremity, indeed its apparent alienation from its modern, progressive, optimistic, scientific, and rational context, has become a threat to our own post-Holocaust secular world, both because of what it was and because of our helpless inability to grasp it as a whole. It is the protean nature of the Event, its refusal to be tied down to any single meaning and definition, that makes it appear so horrifying even at a distance of two generations.

The secular interpretation of the Holocaust is thus in some respects more difficult than the eschatological. The religious strive to justify God, but since God's justice is inherent to their existence, their struggle is one of belief, not of reason; and once God has been justified, so has Man, who is after all only a tool in God's hands. The secular strive to justify Man, or Man's Civilization, but they remain men even if they cannot justify humanity. Yet survival as men in a world devoid of humanity, while possible (as opposed to religious existence in a world devoid of God, which is ultimately a contradiction in terms), is the secular equivalent of hell. The difficulty of coping with this predicament can be seen not merely on the abstract level, but also more specifically in the various attempts to come to terms with the Event.

The Event: In much of the English-speaking world it is called the Holocaust.[15] This is a highly evocative term, of course, since it carries with it the connotation of sacrifice, without specifying who sacrificed whom for what. If the Jews were the victims, the Nazis the slaughterers, what then was the purpose of the sacrifice? Interestingly, the term is used indiscriminately by secular scholars (as well as intellectuals, the media, politicians, laymen, even survivors), signifying once more the overlap between history and myth, the rational and the metaphysical, empiricism and belief. Some use the surprisingly more neutral Hebrew term, Shoah, meaning great disaster, and applied also to such natural catastrophes as floods and earthquakes. The French prefer the more precise term génocide, which is exactly, though not completely, what the Event was about. The Germans use the no less precise, but more troubling term Judenvernichtung, more disturbing both because it was employed by the Nazis themselves and because "destruction of the Jews" evokes a scientific, methodical, detached, clinical operation, whereas an alternative term such as, for instance, "murder of the Jews," would have provided it with a sorely lacking moral dimension.[16]

The various terms used by different groups and nationalities are not the result of mere linguistic coincidence, though at the same time they are also not to be taken as signifying clear and obvious divergences in interpretation and understanding. The fact is, after all, that these terms are used also by Jews who speak the languages mentioned here, and though they may not be unaware of their significance, they usually, though not always, tend to accept them. Nevertheless, I would argue that the names given to the Event (itself a term employed by one scholar loath to use any other[17]) are of some importance. A multiplicity of names for an event, an object, a phenomenon, may signify a confusion as to its essence, an unease with its presence, fear and anxiety at calling it *what it really is*. The Jews had a name for their God, but were allowed neither to write nor pronounce it. They therefore gave their God many other names, which were, however, never *ha'shem ha'meforash*, the name of God pronounced in full. God was unthinkable, therefore His name was unpronounceable, to the extent that He was called simply "The Name" (*ha'shem*). Hence the divine entity, whose name was unpronounceable, became a name denoting an entity whose features were inconceivable.

The multiplicity of names for the mass murder of the Jews is to some extent the obverse side of God's multiplicity of names. In both cases the thing itself cannot be given a name or, rather, its name cannot be pronounced, for pronouncing it would bring an end to all things. Instead, many other names are given, yet with the knowledge that none of them precisely describes the phenomenon it tries to evoke. Only that in the one case we are speaking about heaven; in the other, about hell.

Because we are speaking about an inconceivable, yet multi-named hell, the choice of ersatz names is indicative of the conscious and unconscious motivations of those who employ them. "Holocaust" is a name that provides the Event with meaning, and that meaning carries deep religious, Judeo-Christian connotations. Though this may have been the reason for its wide acceptance rather than for the initial choice of the term among English speakers, there can be little doubt that "Holocaust" is a highly appropriate concept to nations that, while having experienced the Event from afar, are culturally susceptible to providing meanings (whether concrete and empirical or mythic and metaphysical) to phenomena and intolerant of things inexplicable. If the Holocaust cannot be given a good historical explanation (and many would argue that it can), then at least it must be endowed with a meaning; if it was mass murder, then it must yield some sacrificial value; if it was genocide, then it must have had some purpose for humanity. Indeed, the very use of the term "Holocaust" already provides us with a meaning even before we begin to articulate it. Especially in a society such as the United States, where the secular and the religious are so closely intertwined, Holocaust means sacrifice, God, purpose. The Jews (were) sacrificed for the good of humanity. Having accepted this fundamental precondition, one can turn to the details with less trepidation.

The term Holocaust arrived in Germany in the wake of the screening of the American television series of the same name.[18] It was a strange path to take, as bizarre as the effect of this Hollywood soap opera rendering of genocide on German society's perception of its Nazi past. The ambivalent attitude of Germans toward both the Event and the film is neatly reflected in the confusion between the two whenever the word "Holocaust" is employed. *Judenvernichtung* thus remains the definitive term, even though not all the Jews were actually "destroyed." For German speakers the term seems natural, since it describes the Event with unadorned clarity, not to say brutality. Nevertheless, it has the effect of creating detachment, both personal and moral; it has a bureaucratic ring, an administrative dimension, a military neatness; hence it also appears neutral. When one's neighbor is murdered next door, one does not say that he was destroyed, not even in German. When the population of Hamburg or Berlin or Dresden burned to death in the hundreds of thousands, one did not say they were destroyed, neither then nor now. The cities were destroyed, the houses were destroyed, even the artworks were destroyed, but the people died, or were killed, or were murdered. The Jews, however, were destroyed, even in the most recent German scholarship on the Event.[19] *Holocaust* is a sentimental American movie; *Judenvernichtung* is a detached, objective, reliable, scholarly term. Coming to "terms" with, or "overcoming" the past, that great German problem, calls for an appropriate word to denote its darkest chapter, a term perhaps not consciously chosen (rather adopted directly from the SS) but somehow wonderfully malleable to the uses to which it is put.

The term *génocide* has the same clinical and precise connotations as *Judenvernichtung*. But while the latter refers to a specific group, the former inevitably tends to generalize (although one American historian with French connections has proposed the term Judeocide[20]). The Germans are concerned with the destruction of the Jews, both because it is what is best remembered by others, and because focusing on that enables them to set aside the larger numbers of people "destroyed" who were not Jews, such as Russians, Poles, Gypsies, the mentally and physically handicapped, and so forth. The French have no qualms about calling the thing by its name—genocide—yet prefer to maintain their distance from it not merely by employing a legalistic terminology but by associating it with all other genocides. While the English and Americans were on the other side, and the Germans at the center, the French hovered on the periphery. According to the French perception of the war, all kinds of terrible things happened in it, such as occupation, collaboration, resistance, destruction, and genocide. It was a terrible (but also heroic) time, and everyone suffered terribly (though some behaved more heroically than others).[21] Thus, while the Germans, even when they present themselves as victims, can nevertheless not escape "their" *Judenvernichtung*, the French see the genocide of the Jews as the counterpart of their lot under the occupation, and even then, or perhaps precisely because of this perception, the Resistance tends to assume a somewhat higher moral ground, since it actually fought against the Nazis, while the Jews were merely "passively" killed.[22] Genocide therefore becomes detached both because it provides a commonly accepted definition of any instance of mass killing and because this specific instance is not seen as a specifically French affair. Precisely because unlike the American and English case, mass murder took place at a greater geographical proximity and with wide-ranging French collaboration, it becomes necessary to define it accurately and unsentimentally, and to associate it with one's own sacrifices, rather than one's complicity.[23] In English one can speak of "Holocaust," since one had nothing directly to do with it and ostensibly fought against it; in French that would not do, for it would diminish the sacrifice of the Resistance and increase the guilt of the nation as a whole.[24]

In Israel, as well as among some scholars and artists, the Hebrew word *shoah* is used to describe the Holocaust. Modern Hebrew uses the word *shoah*, that is, disaster, in many other contexts as well, such as "nuclear disaster" (*shoah gar'init*), "air disaster" (*shoah avirit*), "natural disaster" (*shoat teva*), and so forth. The term "Shoah" is an accurate description of the genocide of the Jews from a Jewish perspective, since it evokes the fact that this was indeed a disaster for the Jewish people. It is free from any religious connotations, yet is not as detached as the French and German terms. At a second look, however, the very fact that it is often associated with natural disasters, or with spectacular man-made catastrophes, makes it particularly useful within the Israeli/Zionist context. Associating the Holocaust with a natural phenomenon such as the eruption of a volcano would mean that just as it is impossible to prevent the volcano from erupting but possible to move house to a safer location, so too it was impossible to prevent the Nazis (or gentiles) from trying to kill the Jews but *was* possible to recreate a Jewish national existence that would have both hampered fulfilment of such aims, and made death more honorable, since it would have come only after organized military resistance (and here we hear echoes of the *Résistance*). Hence while not a "holocaust" in the sacrificial sense, "Shoah" has an didactic aspect, in that it serves as a constant reminder that the Jews in the Diaspora, who lived on the edge of a volcano, had refused to heed the warnings of the Zionists and consequently perished. The Event itself is taken therefore almost as a given, as a natural law, as being anything but surprising. If not ordered by God, it was at least an historical inevitability. If it did not justify God, it legitimized the Jewish state. After the Holocaust, Zionism needed none of the pre-Holocaust justifications; it seemed *natural* (to Zionists) that Jews must live in their own land, just as it seemed *natural* that the gentiles would try to murder them, especially as long as they did not achieve statehood.[25]

Ironically, Israel as a state behaves like any other state, and expects to be treated in this manner by the international community. That means that although the Shoah was seen as a manifestation of the old Jewish sentiment that "the whole world is against us" (another irony since this ancient belief was mobilized to change the conditions that prompted it), the state of Israel, which seemed the obvious, *natural*, and most positive conclusion to be drawn from the Shoah largely set this sentiment aside. Nevertheless, Zionism has always retained remnants of this anxiety, to the extent that one might say that the peace process now unfolding in the Middle East was made possible also (though certainly not only) by the disintegration of traditional Zionism in Israeli society. At the same time, one must point out that for Israelis the Disaster (*Ha'shoah*) is distinct from any other catastrophe, and still predominates much of the political, intellectual, and cultural discourse in the country. As we will see in Chapter 6, the role played by the Shoah in the formation of Israeli identity cannot be overestimated, and can only be compared to, or be seen in an uneasy partnership with, the Arab-Israeli conflict.[26] A people that chose to call one of the central events in its recent history the Disaster is naturally prone to paranoia, anxiety, hysteria, and manifestations of brutality. It also either consciously or unconsciously chose thereby to ignore or repress some of the most glaring aspects of the Disaster from which it sprang into national existence.

III. National Socialism

Despite appearances of uniformity both during its existence as party and regime, and in the decades following its demise, Nazism has always meant different things to different people. For some it was an ideology, a political movement, a creed, an aspiration, an explosion of hopes and frustrations; for others it was an abomination, a manifestation of humanity's darkest side, the embodiment of Evil, hell on earth. There were (and are) those who viewed it as a hodgepodge of inarticulate nonsense manipulated by a crafty, ambitious, and ruthless clique, or as an insignificant, if unpleasant blip on a thousand years of German culture, most likely a foreign import from Asiatic barbarism, combined perhaps with the depraved ideas of decadent *fin de siècle* French intellectuals; others have described it as the culmination of German history since Luther, or as merely an extreme example of what the German character is capable of. Just as during its political existence Nazism managed to attract people from very different social and educational origins, not least because of the ambiguity of its message and its refusal, or inability, to put down any written dogma, so too after its demise it has been open to the most contradictory interpretations (and uses).[27]

Such interpretations of National Socialism are, to be sure, not innocent of national, ideological, and personal biases. They also reflect the changing perspectives of different generations, as well as the political circumstances under which they were formulated. Indeed, as we will see in Chapters 5 and 6, Nazism and the Holocaust still constitute the focus of several crucial discourses concerned with the relationship between history and fact, truth and denial, memory and authenticity. Arguably the most extreme interpretations of Nazism were put forth by those most remote from its actual manifestations, and those closest to its very center. Thus, immediately after the war deterministic historical essays were written by English and American scholars who sought to prove that German history had taken the "wrong turn" some four hundred years before Hitler appeared on the scene, making the final emergence of Nazism only a matter of time.[28] In the Federal Republic of Germany attempts were made at the time to understand "how it could have happened" (to the nation of Goethe and Schiller), and theories were promulgated according to which Nazism was the equivalent of foreign conquest by a group of gangsters, or at least the forceful imposition on the nation of culture of a combination of narrow militaristic interests, fanatical political extremists, deluded conservatives, and mob leaders.[29] Curiously, this latter version of Nazism had more than a little in common with that which emerged in the German Democratic Republic, where Nazis (or rather fascists) and Germans were kept strictly apart, to the extent that a "real German," a "man of the people," could not have been by definition a fascist, and a fascist could not have possibly been a "real German." Being fascist (or Nazi) was thus almost the same as being a foreign implant or a member of a dying class (just as in the 1960s anyone who disagreed with one's politics was by definition a fascist or a communist).[30]

A more profound trend in the analysis of the origins of National Socialism developed in the 1960s, initiated perhaps first and foremost by exiles from the Third Reich, men and women raised in the fold of "German culture" who, following the Nazi "seizure of power," had been forced to flee the nation to which many of them were deeply attached. Here a more serious attempt was made to link Nazism to earlier periods in German history, and especially to the pre-1914 Reich, or, in some cases, to the birth and development of German nationalism over the preceding century.[31] This brand of analysis, which was taken up by German scholars as well, was seen by many of their colleagues as an unwarranted attack on some of the more glorious chapters of German national history.[32] Besmirching the *Kaiserreich* with Nazi roots was not popular in a nation that found it hard enough to accept that its more recent past was a very dark one indeed. The French had their *Belle Epoque* and the Germans wanted to retain theirs as well, driven by an even more urgent need to mythologize the pre-1914 era than that of the French, whose own inglorious period of occupation and collaboration was hard enough to swallow.

With the debate over the origins of Nazism having exhausted itself during 1970s, attention turned back to the regime itself. Here one might note two major clusters of interpretations: first, intentionalism versus functionalism (or structuralism), and, second, comparability versus uniqueness.[33] However, both controversies were arguably driven by the same need to "come to terms" with, or "overcome," the past in a period of renewed German self-assertion that already anticipated reunification (without anyone expecting it to come quite so soon). Because many of the most interesting and stimulating works of research in this period came from Germany, and because some of the major non-German scholars writing on National Socialism were obviously influenced by their German colleagues, if not indeed coached by them, it is difficult to distinguish here between national biases, although the psychological motivation of individuals often differed substantially. Moreover, this trend was not evident only in scholarship, but also in film, literature, theatre, and, of course, political discourse and media preoccupations.[34]

Both clusters of debates were, as such, not new at all. Questions regarding the function and importance of Hitler's position in the Third Reich, as opposed to the bureaucratic and administrative structure and inner logic of the modern (totalitarian) state, were raised even before the end of the war.[35] Nevertheless, there was a new twist to the debate, for while the functionalist interpretation began as an attempt to discredit the previous conspiratorial theories about Nazism and to show that much larger sectors of society had actually been involved in running the "Hitler state," it ended up by drawing a highly depoliticized picture of the Third Reich where nobody was actually responsible for, let alone guilty of, anything, since everyone was involved as a smaller or bigger cog in a monstrous, faceless, and ultimately uncontrollable machine. The structure, rather than being the creation of human agents, was thus presented as having molded and dehumanized the men who worked for it, a representation of past realities somewhat akin to the terrifying visions of the future constructed by such filmmakers and writers of the interwar period as Fritz Lang and Franz Kafka.[36]

Similarly, the issue of the uniqueness of (the evil nature of) the Third Reich was anything but new. In fact, this question was raised already during the regime itself, if not indeed even before the Nazi "seizure of power." The favorite contender for the position of originator of evil, violence, brutality, inhumanity, and so forth, was naturally enough always the Soviet Union, which served this useful purpose from its very inception to its somewhat pathetic demise.[37] Other (similarly long-standing) competitors for this title were colonialism and imperialism (with the British concentration camps during the Boer War an understandably popular choice), the North American annihilation of the Indians, and the Turkish genocide of the Armenians.[38] Interestingly, in the search for comparable genocides during the mid-1980s, the Turkish massacre of the Armenians was invoked once more, while millions of Turkish *Gastarbeiter* and their families who had lived for many years in the Federal Republic were being denied German citizenship.[39] Other, more recent cases of mass slaughter were also mentioned, with the Right's most frequent choice being naturally enough the mass murder committed by the Khmer Rouge in Kampuchea.[40] Nevertheless, Soviet Russia was always seen as the most pertinent example both because it shared a so-called totalitarian character with the Third Reich and because of the direct relationship between the two, whereby both indeed learned a great deal from each other in techniques of control and manipulation, brutality and massacre, expansion and domination. The mutual fear (tinged at least in the case of some individuals such as Hitler and several of his generals with awe) between the two regimes, and the nightmarish visions of their expected fate under the other's domination, span a history that begins as early as the *Freikorps* of the immediate post-1918 period and reaches beyond the recent revisionist tirades of Ernst Nolte and his supporters.[41]

Intention and structure, similarity and uniqueness—these are issues of crucial importance to all parties involved in the debate over the nature and implications of Nazism. Yet they are slippery concepts, whose clarification often leads one in precisely the opposite direction than that originally intended. If, for instance, we can show that structure played a major role in the formulation and implementation of policies in the Third Reich, and draw the (not necessarily self-evident) conclusion that we have thereby diminished the importance of both ideology and individuals, we may find ourselves inadvertently also raising questions as to the nature of postwar German society and the extent to which the (bureaucratic, legal, administrative, educational) structures on which it is founded differ markedly from their predecessors.[42] After all, would this not be one of the implications of emphasizing long-term, slow-changing socioeconomic structures? Similarly, if we show to our own satisfaction that the Third Reich was just as evil, murderous, and totalitarian as other nations at other times, or that at least it had strong competitors for the title of "Evil Empire," what are the consequences to be drawn from this finding? Does it reflect on human nature, or the nature of modernity, on capitalism or imperialism, on totalitarian ideologies, or on Western civilization? Does it in any way alleviate the burden of guilt from those who perpetrated evil? Paradoxically, uniqueness becomes relative in this context. Nazism was unique for the Germans; no one else came up with quite the same idea, or carried it out in quite the same manner. By the same token, the Holocaust was unique to Nazism, as it was to the Jews, which is why many Jews insist so strongly on maintaining its uniqueness. Although the Jews had experienced many horrific massacres in the past, the Holocaust was unprecedented in their experience. But then the massacre of the Armenians was unprecedented for them, and has remained unique in *their* experience. And if the Nazi genocide of the Jews had certain unique characteristics (as it certainly did), those are not diminished by comparison with other cases of genocide or mass killing.

Reinterpretations of National Socialism and the Holocaust are often bound together. In recent years, however, new work has appeared in Germany that focuses on the relationship between Nazism and modernity.[43] Here we find arguments according to which not only was Nazism produced to a large extent by a crisis of modernity,[44] but, at the same time, actually ushered in the modernization of German society.[45] According to such arguments, this was achieved not merely by a ruthless attack on the traditional order so as to create the basis for authoritarian rule, nor by the destruction Hitler had brought on his people (as has been argued before),[46] but also by positive policies and actions carried out during the Nazi regime, which created the infrastructure later used by the Federal Republic to transform postwar German society. In this literature the Holocaust is rarely discussed, even though it featured at least one quite unique aspect of modernity, namely, the invention of death factories.[47] Calls for a search after more positive aspects of even this darkest period of German history have intensified during the 1980s, accompanied by the demand for a greater degree of empathy with the historical protagonists of the period and a lesser emphasis on moralizing rhetoric.[48] One instance of a conscious attempt to rewrite the history of the war from a new, national perspective will be examined in much greater detail in the next chapter. Meanwhile, a younger generation of German scholars has begun heeding the advice of its elders (often in unexpected ways) by proclaiming detachment (from the horror) and empathy (with the perpetrators and the bystanders, as well as with the fate of the nation as a whole). This may be much less than a Rankean revolution, but it can no longer be viewed as a mere fad.

Some bizarre and disturbing echoes of this new view of the past can be heard in present-day Germany, whether among certain more respectable political circles, or among extremist groups of one variety or another. That German historians have not only been influenced by the changing climate of public opinion, but have actually anticipated it, is an interesting finding especially in the case of a nation whose scholars normally prefer to isolate themselves from current affairs. The extent to which this reemergence of the German Mandarins from their ivory tower has led some scholars to call for a "historicization" and "contextualization" and of the past, and the relationship between this trend and the more blatant kind of revisionism à la Ernst Nolte, is still an open question.[49] One may only wonder whether the growing sensitivity of German scholars to the effects of their findings and interpretations on the public's sense of national identity and historical heritage is such a happy event after all.

IV.   Interpretations

By and large, when discussing the relationship between antisemitism, the Holocaust, and National Socialism, we can speak of two models of interpretation. The intentionalist model assumes a direct and causal link between these three elements. According to this view, antisemitism, and especially its modern, political, pseudo-scientific version, was the core and essence of the Nazi movement, and hence the Nazi state was inevitably bound to end up carrying out the threats and intentions of its propagandists, namely, the physical annihilation of the Jews.[50] A personalized version of this interpretation will perceive Hitler as the focus of both the long-term impact of antisemitism and its direct link with the "Final Solution."[51] The functionalist model hypothesizes a weaker, more indirect relationship between these three phenomena. Hence, the study of antisemitism is seen as an independent field of inquiry, while its impact on the rise of Nazism is not thought to have been of crucial importance. In other words, while National Socialism is regarded as a much more complex phenomenon than merely the political manifestation of antisemitism, the argument is made that antisemitism functioned neither as its main engine and motivation, nor constituted the most attractive feature of the Nazi movement for its activists and followers.[52] Finally, the Holocaust is understood not as the inevitable consequence of the Nazi regime, and certainly not as the premeditated goal of Nazi policy makers, but rather as the result of a specific juncture of circumstances and conditions during the war, combined with the structure of the state and the regime as they evolved throughout the prewar years.[53]

Now although the old debate between intentionalists and structuralists has lost much of its ardor, and proponents of both have been moving toward a middle position, some elements of the debate were lost sight of in the fray and have not been recuperated since. Indeed, instead of leading to a more comprehensive analysis of the complex relationship between widely differing elements resulting in a general crisis in Western civilization (whether *inherent* to it, or its *aberration*), we have witnessed a growing fragmentation, specialization, preoccupation with detail and reluctance to draw more general conclusions. Hence the issue of antisemitism was first separated from that of Nazism and the Holocaust; then specialists of National Socialism concentrated on detailed studies of such aspects of the Nazi period as daily life (to the exclusion of the victims of the regime); and finally Holocaust experts have begun increasingly to concentrate on the mechanics of the "Final Solution," the decision-making process, the role of bureaucrats on different levels, and so forth.

From this perspective we can therefore speak now of another, perhaps more subtle division between two discourses on what has been called the "*Zivilisationsbruch*" of Auschwitz, its causes, context, and implications.[54] While on the one hand we find detailed studies of minor episodes in the history of the Holocaust, the Third Reich, or antisemitism, on the other hand we find more or less acute generalization on the meaning of the Event. What seems to be lacking is an attempt to tie together the different strands that lead to and from Auschwitz, to trace both the origins and the consequences, to employ the knowledge collected so meticulously by scholars yet not to get lost in the details and lose sight of what one is actually confronting.

That a close relationship exists between the elements mentioned above not only in the historical past, but also regarding its reconstruction, is evidenced by the fact that reinterpretations of any one of the factors I have noted seems to have a direct effect on the whole interpretative edifice. This was demonstrated as early as 1950 by Hannah Arendt, whose reinterpretation of anti-semitism formed the basis of a new explanatory model of totalitarianism, whatever its faults and merits. Conversely, the more extreme functionalist arguments have not only postulated a weak and ineffective Führer,[55] but have also relegated antisemitism to a relatively irrelevant role in the implementation of genocide against the Jews (a view which *is*, of course, directly related to Arendt's analysis of Eichmann, his function, and personality).[56] The recent interest in the *Alltagsgeschichte* of the Third Reich has, on the other hand, had contradictory consequences, either demonstrating the extent to which German society was Nazified, thanks not least to pre-existing racist and political prejudices, or, on the other hand, by presenting a picture of normality and resistance to extremity through a stubborn adherence to old routines, beliefs, and loyalties.[57] By the same token, a comparison between the films *Heimat* and *Nasty Girl*, for instance, reveals how differently the daily life of a small community can be portrayed in recent German representations of the past.

It would be foolish to deny that vested interests are involved in the different presentations of the relationship between the constituting elements of the Holocaust, as well as their continuing impact. Germany is now in the process of both detaching itself from the Nazi past and accepting a certain version of it with less discomfort than ever before. Jews in many countries, including Israel, find this process painful, yet they too are showing signs of being ready to accept that the past is gradually receding. Scholars everywhere are sharing this sense of growing detachment, and welcome it, while searching for new and different ways of approaching a heavily researched area. As I will argue in the last part of this book, intellectuals and writers, filmmakers and media people, are still powerfully drawn to (while often being also strongly repelled by) this seemingly unprecedented example of man-made extremity, but are simultaneously showing signs of impatience with old representations and are searching for new, ever more disturbing ways of dealing (or avoiding to deal) with the Holocaust.

It is more than sheer irony that while the debate over the study and representation of unprecedented inhumanity continues, we are constantly exposed to new examples of human cruelty and depravity, to scenes of rape and massacre, torture and mutilation. What is the relationship between *this* and the past? What does the endless slaughter in the former Yugoslavia, for instance, with all its links to the Nazi occupation and the indigenous fascists, tell us about the roots of the Holocaust? What does our understanding of the relationship between racial prejudice, brutal political systems, international indifference, and industrial killing teach us about the future?

All this notwithstanding, and despite the similarity between the Holocaust and other mass murders in history, the case before us is unfortunately not only more complex, but also more disturbing and threatening. For while we may believe that given the humanizing effects of education and democratization, both prejudice and abuse of power might be curbed, few of us would contest the need for, or in any case the inevitability of, continued advance in the fields of science and technology. Yet it was in conjunction with the development of modern science and technology that the mass killing of the Jews (along with many other categories of human beings targeted by the Nazis) took place. This aspect of the relationship between antisemitism, the Holocaust, and National Socialism still needs to be explored.

V.   Modernity

It would seem that our main difficulty in confronting the Holocaust is due not only to the immense scale of the killing, nor even to the manner in which it was carried out, but also to the way in which it combined the most primitive human brutality, hatred, and prejudice, with the most modern achievements in science, technology, organization, and administration. It is not the brutal SS man with his truncheon whom we cannot comprehend; we have seen his likes throughout history. It is the commander of a killing squad with a Ph.D. in law from a distinguished university in charge of organizing mass shootings of naked women and children whose figure frightens us. It is not the disease and famine in the ghettos, reminiscent perhaps of ancient sieges, but the systematic transportation, selection, dispossession, killing, and distribution of requisitioned personal effects that leaves us uncomprehending, not of the facts but their implications for our own society and for human psychology. Not only the "scientific" killing and its bureaucratic administration; not only the sadism; but rather that incredible mixture of detachment and brutality, distance and cruelty, pleasure and indifference.[58]

Hence the genocide of the Jews, its causes, and its context, must be seen as part and parcel of a phase in European civilization that blended modernity and premodernity into an often dangerously explosive mixture (though, of course, also a highly creative one, not only in the science of murder). This potent, stimulating but frequently lethal potion, made of ancient prejudices, hatreds, and violent instincts, on the one hand, and of organizational techniques, methods of production, and resource exploitation, on the other, opened the way for the mobilization of individuals whose natural inclinations, talents, and abilities would have been rendered quite harmless in a premodern era, yet within the context of a barbarous modernity cast them in the role of great executioners.[59]

The Holocaust can therefore be seen as the culmination (but neither the beginning nor the end) of a process begun in the late eighteenth century and still continuing, whose first paroxysm of violence was the Great War, and whose subsequent repercussions can be seen among the millions of victims of the post-1945 era.[60] It is characterized by the missile-wielding religious fanatic, or the cool-headed scientist directing a slave colony of rocket builders, the brutal guard with a given quota of bodies to be disposed of on a daily basis, and the official busy with his schedules of trains bringing anonymous masses of passengers to destinations from which they never return. It is also characterized by two types of professionals essential to the fabric of modernity—the physician and the lawyer.

Modern society cannot be imagined without these two figures. They represent the greatest achievements of human and political science. Humanity's

physical well-being is at the hands of the doctors, and its sociopolitical organization at the hands of the lawyers. Even if we manage to conduct most of our
lives out of hospital and away from the courtroom, it is our awareness of their
existence that makes us into modern people. Take the doctors away from us
and society will be struck by epidemics returning it to bygone periods of fear
and ignorance, mysterious death and rampant disease. Take away the legal
system that binds together the modern nation-state and the international system
and our lives would slip back into a chaos reminiscent of Hobbes's nightmare.

It is precisely because of our complete dependence on these two professions, our awareness that they represent the essence of our modern existence,
that their participation in the construction and implementation of an evil (mistakenly) perceived by us as primeval, as a reversion to a premodern, if not
antimodern world, is so disturbing. For by observing this fact we come to understand that the seeds of modernity also contain the potential of moral perversion, then as now.

The point is not, of course, that doctors and lawyers collaborated with a
dictatorial or murderous regime due to opportunistic reasons or human weakness. Individually, they were and are as human as the rest of us, and should
not be expected to behave any better than soldiers, politicians, university pro-
fessors, journalists, writers, train drivers, or sewage workers. The point is, rather,
that they were crucial for the *construction* of the system to which they then
yielded, that without them things could not have possibly gone so far, or would
not have taken that path at all.

To legitimize themselves in a modern world, antisemitism, Nazism, and
genocide all needed two crucial elements: a scientific stamp and a legalistic
sanction. Antisemitism could not have achieved the support of both the masses
and the elite, the mob and the school teachers, without being made part of an
elaborate racial theory allegedly tested and proven by the most prominent
authorities in the fields of human sciences. In this sense too, and not only the
organizational one, the so called euthanasia of the mentally ill and physically
handicapped, and the genocide of the Jews, cannot be seen separately from
one another. Eugenics was a science that ruled that some forms of life were
undeserving of life. The regime at hand merely had to draw the practical conclusions and carry out the death sentence. National Socialism, which harped
incessantly on notions of purity of race, would have been the laughingstock of
Germany had its scientists shown the imbecility of this idea. Instead, it was the
scientists who gave an academic garb to racism or, rather, invented scientific
racism as a modern version of pure and simple prejudice and fear of the other.
Finally, the Holocaust, the systematic "extermination" of human beings would
have been unthinkable without the medical profession's "detached" evaluation
of these human beings as not only inferior and therefore unworthy of life, but
as positively dangerous to the national Aryan body and therefore doomed to
quick and efficient, yet of course wholly unemotional, elimination. This is what
makes the Holocaust central to our era, for it was founded on a scientifically
sanctioned, indeed ordered, brutality.[61]

The same can be said about the legal profession. Unlike its predecessors, the modern state must function within a legal system if it does not wish to disintegrate from within under the pressure of contradictory economic, social, and political forces each pulling in its own particular direction. Chaos is inadmissible, hence everything must be done in the name of the law. At the same time, once things *are* done in the name of the law, it no longer matters what they are, for they *are* legal, and any further scrutiny of their nature is unnecessary—indeed, may be construed as subversive. The law, however, is open to interpretations, and these are given to the legal profession. Hence both the formulation (in varying degrees, depending on the political system) and the interpretation of the law is highly dependent on the members of the legal profession. They represent man-made law (that is, state order), just as the physicians represent biological law (that is, natural order). Between the two of them is the span of modern man's existence.

In this respect modern antisemitism would be inconceivable without the collaboration, indeed the active participation, of the legal system. The biologist can say who is a Jew in "scientific" terms. Yet these remain irrelevant to the state until the lawyer defines them legally. A Jew is a person with such and such characteristics that can be determined in such and such a manner. Modern state antisemitism is distinguished from traditional antisemitism precisely by its combination of biological and legal definitions. National Socialism as a political system could not have survived without constant and active support from the legal machinery of the state, as well as new legal theories justifying the rule of the Führer and written by the greatest legal experts of the period. Finally, the Holocaust could not have taken the course it did without constant legal advice, support, legitimation, and participation, which not only smoothed the relations between the various agencies concerned with the implementation of the "Final Solution," but also eased the consciences of the individuals involved. There is nothing more calming to a man involved in actions that seem inherently dubious than being told by an expert that they are quite legal. Thus, while the doctors sanctioned murder, the lawyers legalized crime. It is a legacy with far-reaching consequences.[62]

In conclusion, it would seem that quite apart from the causal ties between antisemitism, National Socialism, and the Holocaust, what distinguishes them and puts them all in the same context is that they were extreme and yet characteristic outgrowths of modernity. Late nineteenth-century notions of progress and improvement were not wholly false. In many ways the life of the individual has improved. But the association between material improvement and moral progress was based on a misunderstanding of the inherent nature of modernity. In the modern world, certain organizations, professions, institutions, have immense power over the life and mind of the individual. Yet the power of knowledge and direction, though associated with moral sanction, does not imply any elevation in the quality of morality, indeed, in many ways may work in the opposite direction, since its legitimation is only its own power, the extent of its own knowledge, not recognizing any other limits or sanctions. The scientist who reaches the "scientific" conclusion that some people deserve life more than others sees this as a truth that no one in the world can refute. "Scientific" laws about humanity will tend to become moral judgments. The individual scientist may decide to keep these "findings" to himself precisely because he perceives their moral implications, but by doing so he will be acting against the essence of his own profession, of scientific "progress," and sooner or later another member of his profession will apply the allegedly value-free rules of science more rigorously, whatever their social, political, and moral implications. The same can be said about the the legal profession, whose business is man-made laws. Laws are not expressions of some metaphysical moral order. If the scientist "finds" certain categories of people to be inferior, and the state rules that they should be eliminated, the role of the lawyer is to make sure that the law pertaining to this case be as well formulated, as clear and all-encompassing as possible. Once the law is there, the interest of the legal profession is that it be followed, just as it is the interest of the scientist that the natural law he has discovered be obeyed.

In the modern state, the discovery of laws in nature, the enactment of laws for society, the construction of bureaucratic and administrative systems that would ensure the teaching, imposition, and enforcement of these laws on the citizenry, can be achieved with greater efficiency than at any other point in the past. In the absence of any binding religious commitment or authority, the makers and formulators of natural and civil laws define the limits of our existence, and it is the administration and technical capacities of the state that impose them on us. We have nowhere else to turn, for there is no other sanction or institution. And because we know now the barbaric essence in modernity, its potential of scientifically and legally sanctioned and state controlled evil, we enjoy our liberty and freedom as citizens of Western civilization with a sense of fear and foreboding.

4

Historians on the Eastern Front: Andreas Hillgruber and Germany's Tragedy

But the red hordes are devastating our country and
therefore we must fight on. . . . This is . . . our plain
duty in view of the terrible fate which threatens us if
we surrender. . . . It is our plain duty also to the
destiny which has placed us geographically in the
heart of Europe and which we have obeyed for
centuries: to be the bulwark of Europe against the
East. Whether or not Europe understands or likes
the rôle which fate has thrust upon us . . . does not
alter by one iota our European duty. We are
determined to be able to hold our heads high when
the history of our continent, and particularly of the
dangerous times ahead, is written.[1]

I

In 1950 Hannah Arendt reported on a six-month visit to postwar Germany,
the homeland she had fled seventeen years earlier. Some of her impressions
recorded in this essay, only recently published in the Federal Republic,[2] ring
a disturbingly familiar note today, in view of the controversy initiated by a
number of Germany's most prominent scholars over the possible need to revise
and reinterpret the history of the Third Reich.

Five years after what Friedrich Meinecke had termed the "German Catastrophe,"[3] the reality of the Nazi crimes, the war, and the defeat, Arendt wrote,
still dominated all aspects of life in Germany, whether it was recognized or
repressed; yet the Germans had already discovered various ways of coping with
their recent past. Thus, in reference to the death factories of the Third Reich,
Arendt often heard the claim being made that the Germans had only done what
others were also capable of doing or might still do in the future. Consequently,
anyone who raised the issue was immediately suspected of trying to justify
himself. Indeed, the policies of the Allied Powers toward Germany were seen
as a successful campaign of revenge: in this view, everything that had happened
to the German people during the final years of the war and in the wake of the
"capitulation" was simply the consequence of a well-executed plan of revenge.

This argument, Arendt added, had a tranquilizing effect on the population, as it proved that all human beings were sinners in equal measure.

Far worse, however, according to Arendt, was the attempt by the Germans to escape reality, manifested in the practice of dealing with facts as though they were mere opinions. Each person had a right to his own opinion; in the context, this meant that each individual had a right not to know. Indeed, a powerful desire *not* to know the facts was the real reason behind this newly discovered freedom of opinion. The average German, wrote Arendt, believed that this general contest of opinions, this *"nihilistic relativism"* regarding the facts, was the true essence of democracy. This she viewed as an important legacy of Nazi propaganda, which, unlike that of non-totalitarian states, was based on the concept that *all* facts should be altered and *all* lies should be made to appear true. Reality was thus no longer the sum of hard, undeniable facts, but a conglomerate of changing circumstances and slogans that might be true one day and false the next. In postwar Germany, she emphasized, this had given rise to a complete inability to distinguish between facts and opinions.[4]

The attempt by the historian Ernst Nolte to "relativize" the horrors of the Third Reich by pointing to other criminal regimes, and particularly by a comparison with Stalin's Soviet Russia,[5] seems far less revolutionary once we have read Arendt's 1950 account. Nolte, however, has already been criticized by many of his German colleagues, although others have come out just as strongly in his defense.[6] What concerns me here, therefore, is Andreas Hillgruber's book, *Zweierlei Untergang: Die Zerschlagung des Deutschen Reiches und das Ende des europäischen Judentums*,[7] attacked by Jürgen Habermas, but viewed much more kindly by most other participants in the debate.[8] It should be pointed out that whereas Nolte has expressed doubts concerning the uniqueness of the Holocaust, Hillgruber has voiced similar doubts concerning the Wehrmacht's war of annihilation in the Soviet Union. Nolte views the Gulags as both more "original" (*ursprünglicher*) than the death camps and as the source of a precedent by allegedly sanctioning the extermination of whole categories of human beings. Hillgruber, in turn, emphasizes the crimes committed by the Red Army, claiming that both their practice and their underlying concept were essentially quite similar to those of Hitler's soldiers. Both historians, therefore, may be said to have the same objective in mind: to demonstrate that the murderous policies of the Third Reich, whether directed against the Jews or the Russians, were comparable to the policies pursued by Stalin and possibly other regimes as well. The implication, clearly stated by both, is that one can, at least to some extent, explain Hitler's policies and the conduct of his soldiers by reference to their knowledge and fear of what they could expect at the hands of the Russians.[9]

The first essay in Hillgruber's slim volume can be criticized, as I will presently argue, for several reasons. More than anything else, however, it is an attempt to explain, and to rationalize, the stubborn resistance put up by the troops of the Wehrmacht against the Red Army during the final, desperate months of the war, when it was clear to anyone in his right mind that the war had been hopelessly lost. The author's central thesis is that Germany's soldiers kept fighting to the bitter end because they believed that in so doing they were making it possible for the population of the Eastern Provinces of the Reich to escape from the Russians and flee to the West. Moreover, he asserts that the valiant efforts of the troops did in fact succeed in limiting the extent of the Soviet advance and thereby saved the Reich, and indeed the whole of Central Europe, from being "flooded" by the Red Army, keen as it was on carrying out an "orgy of revenge" on Germany's defenseless civilian population. This was what Nazi propaganda claimed at the time, this was what motivated the soldiers, and, according to Hillgruber, this was also the reality of the situation.[10]

In this chapter, I will first present Hillgruber's arguments and examine what appear to be his main theses regarding the war waged by the Third Reich in the East. I will then demonstrate that the author, in his acceptance of the notion that Germany's troops were motivated by the propaganda being pumped into them in increasing quantities, tends to confuse between their subjective view of the situation, the opinions of the propagandists in the rear, and the historical truth, or at least a sincere effort to arrive at as close an estimation of it as possible. This approach, I will claim, has had a profound and disturbing impact on both the methodology and the language of Hillgruber's work.

II

One of the author's initial assumptions is that the men on the Eastern Front were fighting for a cause, one with which, incidentally, Hillgruber seems very much to sympathize, at least as regards the final months of the war. Hillgruber's empathy with the troops is not only a consequence of his openly stated objective to scrutinize the events in the Eastern Provinces of the Reich through the soldier's rifle-sight, having rejected all other perspectives as unrepresentative or unhelpful; rather, it is grounded in his belief that what the men were fighting for was indeed worth their sacrifice.

This is not to say that Hillgruber is unaware of the implications of such a perspective. Quite the contrary, he willingly concedes that as long as the frontiers of the Reich held firm, the much-accelerated mass murder of the Jews could continue unhindered. Nonetheless, he prefers to deal separately with these two phenomena, because, as he writes, while the soldiers were indeed "protecting" the gas chambers, they were also doing their best

> to prevent the worst: the threatening orgy of revenge by the Red Army against the German population for all the crimes carried out—by whichever German agencies that may be—in the years 1941 to 1944 in those parts of the Soviet Union occupied by German troops.[11]

Time and again, Hillgruber repeats in rather plastic terms (although not quoting any eyewitness accounts) how terrible the danger threatening the defenseless population of the Reich really was. In an essay of 74 short pages, we repeatedly encounter the "vicious," indeed "barbarous" Red Army, about to "flood" Germany and presumably intent on destroying the whole of Western civilization. Apparently it was only the Wehrmacht's desperate sacrifices that saved us all from this forbidding fate: Hitler's troops protected Europe from Stalin's hordes. For this reason, having eliminated all other possible perspectives, Hillgruber makes the following assertion:

> Looking at the winter-catastrophe of 1944–45, the historian is left with only one position, even if in specific cases it is difficult to sustain [einzulösen]: He must identify with the concrete fate of the German population in the East and with the desperate and costly [opferreichen] efforts of the German Eastern Army and the German Navy in the Baltic Sea, which sought to defend the population of the German East from the orgy of revenge of the Red Army, from the mass rapes, the arbitrary murders and the indiscriminate deportations, and to keep open the flight routes to the West over land or sea for the East Germans in the very last phase [of the war].[12]

As I have already noted, Hillgruber is well aware of the difficulties stemming from this approach, and states them clearly. Yet he often seems to be carried away by his "historicization" of the events. It is of course true, he writes, that the Germans committed crimes in Russia, though it does not seem to be clear to him who were actually responsible for these crimes (implying that they were much more the affair of the SS than of the regular army). However, for the soldiers of late 1944, as well as for the (presumably German) historian writing about them, all that was and is irrelevant. Leaving aside the fact that a number of works based on extensive scholarly research have already demonstrated how deeply involved the Wehrmacht was, on all levels, in the killing of many millions in the occupied parts of the Soviet Union,[13] the question remains as to how narrowly historians can "historicize": how much can they limit the scope and time-span of their investigations, how short can they consider the memories of both their protagonists and their readers to be, how much should they themselves consciously forget? Many of the soldiers fighting on both sides in 1944 had passed through Russia in 1943, some devastating it, others witnessing the destruction and its aftermath. The Wehrmacht had pursued a policy of "scorched earth" and "desert zones" ever since its first retreats in the winter of 1941–42, and it played a major role in the ruthless exploitation of the Russian civilian population to the point of widespread starvation; it was centrally involved in the mass murder of prisoners of war and in the extermination of other political enemies and biological *Untermenschen*.[14] Can the historian refuse to take into account even the memories of those with whom he wishes to empathize? Should he present them as having flat, one-sided personalities with no concern but for the immediate present?

Hillgruber's attempt to deal with this problem raises more questions than it answers. Thus, he writes that by early 1945 the military situation was leading to

> Rapes on a hitherto hardly conceivable scale, thousands upon thousands of murders and mass deportations, which included the systematic implementation of forced displacements of around 500,000 Germans. The cry "the Russians are coming" became the alarm signal throughout the East. Naturally this had to do with revenge, which the soldiers of the Red Army now took for the crimes carried out by the Germans on Soviet land between 1941 and 1944;

but this explains only the vast scale of the excesses, not the phenomenon of rape and murder itself. For such incidents occurred also during the Red Army's march into other countries. The fact that the same outrages occurred not only as early as the entry of the Red Army into Poland, but also in 1944 in Rumania and Hungary, indeed even during the "liberation" of north-eastern Yugoslavia in 1944–45, suggests a wider context: the Soviet conception of war, which had universally adopted such manifest barbarous traits during the Stalinist epoch.[15]

Hence we find that the Red Army was simply barbarous in its behavior, raping and murdering everyone everywhere in an unprecedented manner. No mention is made here of the "Barbarossa Orders," which promulgated the notion that the war on the Eastern Front should not be fought by the Wehrmacht according to any accepted custom or law, since it was a "war of ideologies" directed against a vast horde of Slavic *Untermenschen* led by a criminal "Jewish-Bolshevik clique." Nor are we told here about the many collaborators in the countries of Eastern Europe Hillgruber mentions, individuals who committed countless crimes both against their own people and in occupied Russia. All Hillgruber tells us is that the Red Army was a wholly objectionable, criminal, and barbarous lot.

The soldiers of the Wehrmacht were not alone in this tremendous effort "to save what could still be saved" from the clutches of the Red Army, writes Hillgruber. Rather, men of God were also involved, along with respectable members of the white-collar professions and numerous representatives of both the civilized countries of Western Europe and the less fortunate East:

> Some unknown individuals outdid themselves at that time as the catastrophe broke upon them—leaders of refugee columns, clergymen, doctors, Frenchmen, Belgians, also Polish prisoners of war, who along with the Germans strove toward the West, and not least also the German soldiers, who held the eastern bridgeheads... as long as possible, in order to enable the salvation of the population from the sea.[16]

The extent to which the peoples of the West were indeed making great sacrifices in order to stem the tide of the red "flood" can be seen, in Hillgruber's view, from the fact that even the SS Divisions "Nordland," "Wallonien," and "Nederland," composed of "Scandinavian, Belgian, and Dutch volunteers," and the SS Division "Charlemagne," established by "French volunteers," were all drawn into the attempt to save the Eastern Provinces of the National Socialist Reich, "whereby the European conception of the SS was to be demonstrated once more."[17] One is reminded in this context of Abel Tiffauges in Michel Tournier's *Le roi des aulnes*, that eccentric French prisoner of war who finds himself directing an SS youth training camp in Prussia, and ends up escaping the Russians with Goethe's poem ringing in his ears—except that Hillgruber's heroes do not carry even a single Jewish boy to safety.[18]

The collapse of the Ardennes offensive in the West made it clear even to the most optimistic that the end was drawing near. Yet, writes Hillgruber, the fact that the armies in the East continued to fight saved both the civilian population and the Wehrmacht soldiers from the "even more gruesome consequences" that would have ensued had they surrendered and thereby become exposed to the arbitrary will (*Willkür*) of the Red Army in the depth of winter.[19] Hence the gradual retreat, which cost many lives on both sides, was justified, though not, as the author hastens to assure us, for the reasons Hitler had in mind. Nonetheless, Hillgruber feels constrained to quote the Führer's call to the Eastern Army issued as late as 15 April 1945:

> Berlin remains German, Vienna will become German again, and Europe will never become Russian.[20]

This revealing indication of the whole trend of Nazi propaganda at the time, which did its best to persuade both the Germans and the Western Allies that the Reich was in fact defending Western civilization from the "Asiatic flood," is left, quite significantly, without any comment by the author.

By page 42 of his essay, Hillgruber has brought us to the final capitulation of the Reich and then moves on to a discussion of the broader international context, though up to this point the reader had been under the impression that the author's aim is to describe events only in the Eastern Provinces. This second discussion, however, also aims at "relativizing" the history of the period and demonstrating the culpability of all nations involved in the horrors of the war. Hitler's war (and in this context we are led to believe that Hitler was in fact the only person to be blamed) was indeed waged as directed "according to the radical, racially and ideologically informed conception [*rassenideologisch geprägten Konzeption*]" of the Führer.[21] But although the Germans liquidated sections of the Polish leadership,

> Stalin executed a comparable policy in those parts of East Poland left to him, through deportations and murder operations against the Polish leadership stratum.[22]

As for the war in Russia, the Reich aimed at establishing a so-called "Eastern Empire" by liquidating the Bolshevik leadership, systematically decimating the Slav masses, and exterminating the Jews. A *"Generalplan Ost"* spoke of forcing more than thirty million Slavs to relocate to Siberia, and replacing them with German settlers in vast areas of Western Russia, the Ukraine, and the Caucasus. Yet Hillgruber maintains that the traditional German leadership never took Hitler's ideas, as expressed in *Mein Kampf*, seriously, and goes on to say that opposition circles actually attempted to change his policies. Hillgruber admits that those circles had initially served the Nazi state, and that when they finally decided to move against Hitler, time was running out and they no longer had any real influence on the affairs of the Reich. Yet he does not consider the possibility that the "liberal-conservative opposition" acted only out of fear that Hitler was doing great harm to Germany's national interest and leading the Fatherland down the road to catastrophe, while as long as he had been successful the "opposition" was more than passively pleased with the realization of its own, more traditional expansionist policies.[23]

Moreover, according to Hillgruber, even such notorious characters as the SS officer and "expert on partisans" Bach-Zelewski made efforts to arrive at a certain "understanding," presumably with Lithuania, an act that was "halfheart-edly encouraged" by none other than Himmler, "whose Europe-concept had for long differed from Hitler's in some details."[24] In which "details" Himmler actually deviated from Hitler, the author fails to point out; one might remark, however, that the *Europa-Konzept* of the SS hardly left any room for com-promises with Slavic and Jewish *Untermenschen*. Yet Hillgruber concludes this discussion with the following assertion:

> Nevertheless, the Eastern political concept of the liberal-conservative opposi-tion deserves a just appreciation; it was the only active alternative in Germany to Hitler's radical utopia. Common to both conceptions, that of Hitler and that of the liberal-conservative opposition, was only the conviction that Europe must be organized and led, or in Hitler's view, ruled, from the center, by the Ger-man Reich.[25]

This point should not be overlooked: the "only" idea the opposition had in common with Hitler was that Europe must be ruled or at least "organized and led" by Germany. The disagreements had to do merely with the means by which this could be achieved, and even here it was clearly the "liberal-conservatives" who made the compromises. Indeed, by the end of his essay, the author comes to bewail precisely the fact that owing to the policies of both the Soviet Union and the Western Allies, as well as the defeat of the Third Reich, this did not come about; Hillgruber views the absence of a German-led European center as a general European tragedy.[26]

This fateful consequence was brought about, we are told, by the determi-nation on the part of both Britain and the Soviet Union to put an end to Germany's control over central Europe; a power position that, as Hillgruber readily admits, had served as the basis for the expansionist policies of the Reich ever since Bismarck. Thus, Churchill is quoted as having wished to create a "fat, but impotent" Germany, totally demilitarized but economically healthy.[27] Indeed, the author claims that the idea of expelling entire populations was entertained by all nations involved in the war:

> The widespread idea in Germany during the First World War of ethnic cleans-ing [*völkischen Feld- und Flurbereinigung*], which was carried out by the German and and Soviet sides since the beginning of the Second World War in September 1939, was now—without it being possible to find direct links to the expulsions of portions of the population in the East—also introduced by the British side as an element in their own war plans, as it appeared likely to promise long-term security for their own role of leadership in Europe.[28]

Having thus demonstrated to his own satisfaction that Britain's war plans were as ruthless as Germany's, or at least were directed toward the same ends, Hillgruber goes on to say that once it became clear that the Soviet Union would attempt to push its own territorial control as far west as possible, neither Brit-ain nor the United States showed any interest whatsoever in the fate of Germany's Eastern Provinces. The author attributes this attitude, which he finds both surprising and thoughtless, to the "extremely negative, cliché-ridden image of Prussia," the "fixation on Prussia" of the Western leaders, which had little in

common with the actual state of affairs in Nazi Germany.[29] Hillgruber's peculiar interpretation of the international political context of his main theme—
the fate of eastern Germany—thus links a willingness on the part of the Western Allies to uproot whole populations with a number of outdated biases
regarding a presumably no longer existent Prussian militarism. Only by examining Hillgruber's undocumented speculations and astonishing simplifications
of the international situation before and during World War II can we arrive at
a full appreciation of still another, equally undocumented contention of the
author, one that would apparently seek to turn the entire understanding of the
politics of that period on its head:

> The annulment of the Munich agreement of 1938 *by the British government
> in August 1942* [my emphasis] was already tied together "explicitly with the
> agreement on principle to the transfer of the Germans out of Central Europe."[30]

We are thus asked to believe that it was Britain's foolish decision to reject
in 1942 (!) the agreements made in Munich, tearing Czechoslovakia apart and
yielding to Hitler's threats and the British public's apparent lack of enthusiasm for another war, rather than Germany's annexation of the rest of Czechoslovakia and the invasion of Poland in 1939, which had such grave consequences
for the fate of the Eastern Provinces of the Reich, described with much emotion by the author:

> Every town, every settlement, every region which the German troops were
> forced to give up with the collapse of the Eastern Front in winter 1944–45,
> was in a wholly elementary sense lost forever for Germany and for its German
> inhabitants.[31]

What conclusions does Hillgruber draw from his analysis of the general
political context, and what significance does he attach to his main theme within
that context? Having followed his line of argument up to this point, we should
perhaps not be surprised to read that, by the author's criteria, it is only the
conquest of Prussia that deserves the undisputable title of a "tragic process":

> Whether the concept of tragedy can be employed regarding the events which
> peaked in the Second World War may be left undecided; guilt and fate, legiti-
> mate claims and manifest injustice, arbitrariness and entanglement are indis-
> solubly mixed together here. But in the case of the events in the German East
> in 1944–45 one may well speak of a tragic process, [since] the hopelessness
> of the situation for the soldiers and the inhabitants of the eastern region is
> evident.[32]

The survivors of the Eastern Army, with which Hitler had attempted to destroy
the Soviet Union, were now protecting the ever-shrinking Reich. Close behind
the front, the Nazis were exterminating the Jews at an ever-increasing tempo,
a fact that, according to Hillgruber, "certainly only a part of the soldiers and
the German population knew or guessed at the time." Nevertheless, he refuses
to discuss the interconnection between these two phenomena, and is clearly
more interested in, and moved by, the former, that is, the tragedy of *his own
homeland* and compatriots:

But in precisely this situation the German Eastern Army also struggled—only partly informed of the Allies' war aims by the half-truths of the National Socialist propaganda—in desperate defensive battles for the preservation of the independence of the German Reich's great power position, which according to the will of the Allies was to be smashed.[33]

Finally we arrive at Hillgruber's central and, it must be said, deeply disturbing conclusion:

> And the German Eastern Army defended in an entirely elementary sense the people of precisely these Prusso-German Eastern Provinces, who were threatened by the gruesome fate of having their homeland flooded by the Red Army, as the hate-filled propaganda campaign of the Red Army had demonstrated. . . . The oft-repeated claim of National Socialist propaganda, that the only alternative was between Hitler and Stalin, now became a reality for the Germans in the East.[34]

This tragedy, concludes Hillgruber, was caused by an approach to politics that had been generally accepted ever since the Great War: the Turks had practiced genocide against the Armenians and had uprooted the Greeks; Hitler and Stalin carried out policies of liquidation in their "spheres of interest"; Great Britain and the United States had come ever closer to the notion that there should be a mass resettlement of populations in east-central Europe, "in complete contradiction of their humanitarian traditions."[35] Germany was to undergo "de-Prussianization," and be turned into a "fat, but impotent" country whose population was to be re-educated and democratized.[36] Hillgruber, unwilling perhaps to accept the fact that the Federal Republic, at least, is indeed a fat, although certainly not an impotent country, which reaps the benefits of its rather successful democratic system, comments:

> Thus it has become an open question, whether the history of the Germans as a nation formed by the establishment of the Reich has run out, or whether it nevertheless still has a future.[37]

The ultimate conclusion was that the destruction of Germany's role as a major power in the heart of Europe spelled defeat for the whole continent.[38] Harking back perhaps to both the old *"Europa-Konzept,"* coupled with the more recent anti-Americanism on one side of the political spectrum, and the fear of communism on the other, Hillgruber ends his essay on an appropriately pessimistic note:

> The new flank-powers [*Flügelmächte*], the Soviet Union and the USA, now made Central Europe into their respective area of operations [*Vorfeld*] in the world-political confrontation which began directly following their victory.[39]

III

Hillgruber's essay is intriguing on a number of counts. First, because it clearly accepts the notion that the Wehrmacht troops were motivated by a cause, one that extended beyond their immediate concerns and their group of comrades-in-arms. Second, because it demonstrates that a close correlation existed between those motivating causes and the National Socialist propaganda that was being pumped into the civilians and soldiers of the Third Reich ever since Hitler's "seizure of power." Third, because it describes what took place along the Eastern Front very much in the same terms of, and in apparent agreement with, the principle arguments advanced by National Socialist propaganda (arguments that, incidentally, have also often been repeated by Wehrmacht generals in their postwar memoirs published, to be sure, mostly at the height of the Cold War).[40] Fourth, because of the striking difference between the choice of words used by the author in his first essay (examined above) and in the essay immediately following it, the subject of which is the mass murder of the Jews.

Before discussing these points, a few general remarks on the fundamental historical concept underlying Hillgruber's essay may be in order. It has been pointed out that the author chose to describe the collapse of the German Eastern Front from the perspective of the soldiers. This in itself is a very problematic position, since it fixes events within a very narrow span of time and takes for granted a unanimity of opinion, as well as a striking lapse of memory, among the troops. Moreover, the author does not provide us with any empirical evidence for this assertion. In historical research, few things are as difficult as demonstrating that an entire group of human beings shared a common belief in something, be it what it may. To some extent, this is probably the reason why so many historians have chosen, mistakenly in my view, to neglect the role played by ideology in human action, and have preferred to concentrate on issues that readily yield concrete data and are thus amenable to quantitative analysis. Hillgruber, however, does not even bother to state the fundamental difficulties involved in any attempt to "gauge" belief.[41]

What frees the author from the necessity of coping with this dilemma is that in fact he does not do what he has promised his readers: the essay is *not* an examination of the collapse in the East from the perspective of the soldiers involved, but rather an outline of Hillgruber's personal opinion, supported by some selectively chosen evidence as to what occurred there, its underlying causes, and the reason why the troops fought on so tenaciously until the bitter end. Apart from a few quotes of high-ranking officers, we are not presented with even a single soldier's point of view. However, if in fact it is not the troops' perspective that the author has in mind, if the views presented are his own, then one is justified in expecting that Hillgruber as an historian would strive for as balanced an analysis as possible. This leaves us with the question as to what this essay, in fact, is really all about, and what are its aims? To put it rather bluntly: the text reads like an account by a veteran who had fought on the front and has attempted to place his own personal experience within a historical context that would justify his and his comrades' actions, or, as Hillgruber would probably prefer, sacrifices. Being neither "history from below" nor "history from above," it is rather a "history from within (myself)," from the perspective of one's own experiences, memories, and prejudices. Consequently, it is often confusing, contradictory, and simplistic, shifting from the personal to the impressionistic, and providing no satisfactory answers to the questions it raises.

The first point of interest I indicated has to do with the motivation of the soldiers. Having also grappled with questions regarding the troops' conduct on the Eastern Front, I too believe that Wehrmacht soldiers were not motivated solely by loyalty to their comrades or a particularly effective system of manpower administration, as has been argued by other scholars concerned with this issue.[42] I have already demonstrated elsewhere that because of the tremendous casualties sustained by the Wehrmacht in the East, one cannot accept the "primary group" thesis, according to which men continue fighting mainly out of a sense of comradeship with other members of their combat unit. Formations were so frequently smashed in the Russian campaign that one can hardly speak of any continuity in the manpower composition of such units, or of loyalty to individual soldiers or commanders at the lower echelons. If there was such "primary group" loyalty, it may well have existed more as an idea than as a reality, and this would bring us back to a certain type of ideological motivation.[43] Other studies have already shown the extent of indoctrination among Wehrmacht troops, disseminated by the highest political and military authorities of the Reich and reaching down to the smallest and most isolated units at the front.[44] Moreover, there are numerous indications that this propaganda was welcomed, indeed demanded by the combat formations, and was perceived by junior front-line officers as essential to the enhancement of their men's *esprit de corps* and the stiffening of their morale.[45]

The importance of a "cause," and the danger of its absence, can also be demonstrated in many other military confrontations. The difficulty lies, of course, in showing its positive effect, for soldiers often speak about the "cause" when they begin to doubt its truthfulness. Thus, for example, German soldiers arguably spoke more about the reasons for fighting in 1918 than in 1945, because the end of the Great War was marked by a growing dissatisfaction with the military and political leadership, whereas even in the final months of World War Two, the majority of German prisoners of war expressed belief in the Führer, as has been shown by a number of polls.[46] The same can be said about the Vietnam War, whose justice was much more widely discussed in the United States than that of World War Two. In Israel too, soldiers began to talk about the "cause" for which they were fighting only when doubts appeared regarding its applicability. Thus, the 1973 War was seen by most as "just," indeed as a war for survival, but the failures of the military and political leadership were extensively discussed both in the rear and at the front. The war in Lebanon was criticized by the civilian population and the troops because there were questions as to whether it was necessary, or rather unavoidable, which in Israel is still by and large considered to be the essential precondition and justification for fighting and dying for one's country.

The second point already indicates the inherent contradictions in Hillgruber's argument. Not only does the author accept the notion that the men were in fact moved by the propaganda that rained down on them, he constantly confuses between that propaganda and what he views as the historical reality, or, phrased differently, his own truth. Ultimately, as quoted above, he states quite bluntly that Nazi propaganda regarding the terrible fate that Germans could expect in the event of a Soviet victory was completely true.[47] This is a bold admission, not only because he feels no need to make any reservations, but also because it ties up well with the third point, namely the language the author employs to describe the events. Here one is struck by Hillgruber's personal anxiety in the face of the approaching "Flooding [*Überflutung*] of the homeland by the Red Army,"[48] which wholly matches his ability fully to empathize with the German population's fear of the "Flooding of their homeland by the Red Army,"[49] and by his obvious relish in speaking of the Russians' crimes in such terms as "Orgie of revenge [*Orgie der Rache*],"[50] "Revenge orgies [*Racheorgien*]," "mass rapes [*Massenvergewaltigungen*]," "arbitrary murders [*willkürliches Morden*]," "indiscriminate deportations [*wahllose Deportationen*],"[51] "Rapes on a hitherto hardly conceivable scale, thousands upon thousands of murders and mass deportations,"[52] "the phenomenon of rapes and murder," the "manifest barbarous traits [*barbarischen Züge*]" of Soviet soldiers' conduct,[53] the potentially "even more gruesome consequences [*noch grauenhaftere Folgen*] for the wholly unprotected German population" had it been "delivered to the arbitrary will (*Willkür*) of the Red Army," in which case the "extent of the catastrophe would have been . . . greater,"[54] and finally the good fortune that "the German Eastern Army defended" the population from a "gruesome fate [*grauenvolles Schicksal*]" promised them in "the hate-filled [*hasserfüllte*]" propaganda of the Soviet Union, whose real purpose, of course, was "the extinction of Germandom [*die Auslöschung des Deutschtums*]."[55]

It would be pointless to quote extensively from the innumerable propaganda leaflets, brochures, orders of the day, speeches, and other indoctrination material that was liberally distributed among the Wehrmacht troops and in which precisely this languages was employed.[56] A few examples must therefore suffice. It is interesting to begin with some quotes from senior army officers, since they were considered more immune to Nazi ideology and, precisely for that reason as well as their position in the military hierarchy, may have had a significant influence on the troops' state of mind and conduct. Thus, the commander of the 47th Panzer Corps issued the following order of the day on the eve of the invasion of the Soviet Union:

> The Führer has called us again to battle.
> It is now our task to destroy the Red Army and thereby to eradicate Bolshevism forever, the deadly enemy of National Socialism.
> We have never forgotten that it was Bolshevism which had stabbed our army in the back during the [First] World War and which bears the guilt for all the misfortunes which our people have suffered after the war. We should always remember that![57]

On October 10, 1941, Field Marshal von Reichenau called on the troops of his Sixth Army to understand once and for all the true nature of the war and conduct themselves accordingly:

> The essential goal of the campaign against the Jewish-Bolshevik system is the complete destruction of its power instruments and the eradication of the Asiatic influence on the European cultural sphere. . . .

In the East the soldier is not only a fighter according to the rules of warfare, but also a carrier of an inexorable racial conception [*völkischen Idee*] and the avenger of all bestialities which have been committed against the German and related races.[58]

In December 1941, the commander of the 2nd Army Corps urged his men to exert themselves to the utmost in battle by posing the rhetorical question:

What would have happened had these Asiatic Mongol hordes succeeded to pour into Europe and particularly into Germany, laying the country waste, plundering, murdering, raping?[59]

As for the propaganda leaflets distributed among the troops, such as the newssheet *Mitteilungen für die Truppe*, an even harsher language was employed here, often presenting the Russian enemy as the Devil incarnate:

Anyone who has ever looked at the face of a red commissar knows what the Bolsheviks are like. Here there is no need for theoretical expressions. We would insult the animals if we described these mostly Jewish men as beasts. They are the embodiment of the Satanic and insane hatred against the whole of noble humanity. The shape of these commissars reveals to us the rebellion of the *Untermenschen* against noble blood. The masses, whom they have sent to their deaths by making use of all means at their disposal such as ice-cold terror and insane incitement, would have brought an end to all meaningful life, had this eruption not been dammed at the last moment.[60]

In this manner, the troops of the Wehrmacht were prepared for the invasion of the Soviet Union, exhorted to go about it even more ruthlessly during the campaign, and frightened into a fanatic resistance during the final, bitter months of the war in the East. Much of this vocabulary did not simply disappear with the "capitulation" of the Third Reich, but rather still lingers in divisional chronicles, soldiers' memoirs, certain types of journals, and, unfortunately, in some historical writing as well. It is more than likely that such vivid descriptions of the enemy's inhumanity, coupled with the license given them by the "Barbarossa Orders" and many other commands at various levels of the army, were taken by the troops as a directive to inflict on the Red Army and the Russian civilian population what otherwise would be done to the Germans. Indeed, the Wehrmacht's barbarous activities on the Eastern Front have been amply demonstrated.[61] We are not dealing here with an "opinion," as Hillgruber would have it ("by whichever German agencies that may be"[62]), but with conclusive documentary proof, drawn from the Wehrmacht's own files. Even the heavy emphasis on "rape" and "orgy" was characteristic, as we have seen, of contemporary linguistic usage; depraved sex and Satan went well together in both the practice and the propaganda of the Third Reich. The "male fantasies" of the Freikorps' commanders seem to have travelled a long way.[63] But even while constantly being threatened with Russian males' capacity for raping German women, the Wehrmacht troops were also warned about having any contact with Russian women, because

intercourse with female civilians is not only unworthy of the German soldier, but also carries with it the danger of being exploited or harmed by a spy, of falling into the hands of a female partisan and of being terribly mutilated or infected with venereal diseases or other infectious diseases. Russian physicians have pointed out that from their own experience up to 90 per cent of the female population is infected with gonorrhea and 50 per cent with syphilis.[64]

This does not mean, of course, that there were no rapes, but rather that they were considered as racial, not moral offenses. At the most, German soldiers might be accused of contact with enemy agents, for

the Russian woman is prepared to make unscrupulous use of her physical advantages and of our soldiers' confidence for purposes of espionage in the interest of the war.[65]

Conversely, when the Red Army entered Germany, it was (German) women who were presumably "clean," and the soldiers, Russian this time, who were diseased.

The argument that the Wehrmacht had in fact defended Europe from the "Russian flood" was used quite frequently after the war, and was often seen rather favorably by Americans and West Europeans involved in the Cold War and ignorant of the nature and scope of Germany's crimes in the Soviet Union. The Stuka ace Rudel, described by an RAF colleague in the introduction to the English translation of his memoirs as "a gallant chap,"[66] wrote how certain he was, even after he had heard of Hitler's suicide, that as long as "the Red Hordes are devastating our country . . . we must fight on," not just to save the disintegrating Third Reich, but for the sake of the whole of Western civilization:

It is our plain duty to be the bulwark of Europe against the East. Whether or not Europe understands the role which fate has thrust upon us . . . does not alter by one iota our European duty.[67]

Similarly, the much admired Panzer General Heinz Guderian also noted in his memoirs that German officers had

had to sacrifice many a privileged and many a well-loved tradition . . . in order to prevent their country from being overwhelmed by the Asiatic Bolshevik flood that threatened Germany from the East.[68]

Furthermore, Guderian found it necessary to explain that Hitler

was clearly aware of the threat that the Soviet Union and the communist urge to world hegemony offered both to Europe and to Western civilization. He knew that in this matter he was in agreement with the majority of his fellow-countrymen and, indeed, with many good Europeans in other lands.[69]

Thus, we find Hitler and his soldiers, having destroyed as much as they possibly could of European civilization, posing as its staunchest defenders, not only in the propaganda of the time, but also, so to speak, posthumously, in their memoirs and in the history books written about their "desperate," their "tragic" war against Bolshevism.

All this is not to say that the Red Army did not commit numerous outrages and crimes, although there was indeed a fundamental difference between its conduct and that of the Wehrmacht, conveniently ignored by the apologists for Hitler's soldiers, which we will examine below. Rather, it is the language employed here by a professional historian that is so disturbing. Had Hillgruber displayed a certain flair for emotionally charged terms, notwithstanding their unpleasant connotations, throughout this volume, perhaps one would have had to allow this as an idiosyncrasy of style. However, the fact that immediately following the first essay the author goes on to describe the mass murder of the Jews, and employs a totally different style in which to do so, raises the question anew. It has already been pointed out that the title given to his slim volume is rather peculiar, since it claims to deal with the shattering, or destruction of the German Reich (*Die Zerschlagung des Deutschen Reiches*), signifying an active act of annihilation, as opposed to the end of European Jewry (*Das Ende des europäischen Judentums*), implying a passive withering away of the Jews. Yet, not only were the Jews murdered in a highly organized manner that demanded a major concentration of effort, manpower, and resources for a country simultaneously involved in a vast military confrontation, as indeed Hillgruber himself rightly points out in the second essay of his book, it is also erroneous to speak of the "end of European Jewry," since there are millions of Jews still living in Europe, principally in the Soviet Union, but also in the West. Even if this can be excused as being a rather unfortunate choice of phraseology, the titles of the essays themselves, not commented on previously in my discussion of the Hillgruber volume, give rise to additional questions.

The first essay is entitled *The Collapse in the East 1944/45 as a Problem of German National History and of European History*; the second is entitled *The Historical Place of the Extermination of the Jews*.[70] Thus, we are to understand that while the "collapse in the East" was, indeed still is, a problem both for German national history and for European history as a whole, the historical position of the "extermination of the Jews" has yet to be determined. Presumably, it is not at all an obvious part of Germany's national history, nor of European history. The history of the Jews themselves interests the author only as the history of antisemitism, and one cannot maintain that he discusses the historical or cultural significance of the Holocaust either, apart from enunciating some familiar and well-worn clichés. However, although this appears to me to be a central issue in any debate on the deeper significance of Hillgruber's (and many other so-called revisionists') attempt to take a "new" look at his country's history, I will concentrate here only on one aspect of this problem.

What seems to me most striking is the nature of the language employed by Hillgruber throughout his second, much shorter essay on the Holocaust. As if by a stroke of magic, all emotional, plastic descriptions have vanished, replaced by the "bureaucratese" used by numerous other historians, as well as by the murderers themselves. Here, strangely enough, the author is no longer burdened with the dilemma of which perspective he should chose. This is a clear, balanced, dry, and precise sketch of the events leading up to and including the execution of the program of genocide against the Jewish people. Any empathy with the protagonists is completely lacking. To quote just one representative example from the essay:

At this point the preparations for *"Aktion Reinhard"* of SS-Gruppenführer Globocnik were put into action; as of December 1941 the eradication was translated into action in Chelmno, as of March 1942 in Belzec and a few weeks later in Sobibor and Treblinka, by the personnel of *"Aktion T4"* by means of the "tested" method of gassing by engine exhaust fumes in hermetically closed spaces. *"Aktion Reinhard"* claimed as victims the majority of the Polish Jews crowded into the "large ghettos" since the end of 1939, as well as—about ten per cent of the victims—Jews from the Netherlands, from the territory of the Reich, from Macedonia, from Bulgarian-occupied Thrace, from France and Belorussia [Weissruthenien]. The number of Jewish victims in Chelmno reached more than 150,000 people, in the extermination camp Belzec between 500,000 and 600,000, in Sobibor some 200,000, in Treblinka 900,000 people (the vast majority from the area of Warsaw), in the camp Maidaneck, by Lublin, which served many purposes (and was not included in *"Aktion Reinhard"*) 50,000 to 60,000 Jews out of an overall number of 200,000 people killed there (in Maidaneck Zyklon B already served as the means for murder).[71]

And so on. Now some historians before Hillgruber have chosen to write on the Holocaust in this detached manner, and have argued that this is the only way in which scholars can deal with such an unprecedented, ghastly phenomenon, one that defies human imagination and understanding. This is precisely the reason why "historicization" seems so difficult in the case of the Third Reich. Yet Hillgruber has chosen to "historicize" one aspect of Nazi Germany, while completely rejecting this method in another. And, as he himself admits, both are closely interconnected.[72]

This brings us back full circle. In an article entitled "A Plea for the Historicization of National Socialism," the historian Martin Broszat has argued that forty years after the event, the time has come to place the Nazi period within a broader chronological and geographical perspective, and to do away with the "distance" preserved by scholars dealing with the Third Reich. As things stand now, "The ability to feel one's way empathetically into the web of historical interconnections [*das Einfühlung in historische Zusammenhänge*] evaporates along with the pleasure of narration,"[73] Broszat writes, implying that we must begin once again to empathize with our protagonists. This is, in his opinion, particularly necessary, since "not all the historically significant developments that occurred in Germany during the Nazi period merely served the regime's goals of inhuman and dictatorial domination."[74] Broszat's thought-provoking, if far from unproblematic contribution to the historiographical debate on Nazism has unfortunately led to a number of essays that seem to suffer from precisely that "nihilistic relativism" noticed by Hannah Arendt in 1950. Opinions and historical facts become hopelessly mixed, comparisons are made that cannot stand up to careful scholarly analysis, empathy turns into uncritical identification, truth becomes a matter of one's own, or one's national, point of view. Ranke's dictum regarding the writing of history "as it really happened" has been perverted into the writing of history "as I would like to see it," or "as the group I had chosen had seen it" and, far worse, this is then presented as historical truth. If Hitler's "rat cage" remark can be taken not only as indicative of his fear of the Gulags,[75] but also as proof of their having provided the origin for the Nazi death camps, then, by the same token, an emotional description of the collapse of the German East can serve as proof of the similar or rather identical nature of the criminality of the Third Reich and that of the Soviet Union, with the rest of the world trailing not far behind. Again, one is struck by the acuteness of Arendt's observation that, already five years after the end of the war, many Germans were saying that all human beings were evil and capable of similar crimes and therefore, if we are all sinners, then none of us is to blame.

However, the historian dealing with the Nazi period must be well aware that there was a crucial difference between the policies of the Soviet Union and those of the Third Reich. Nazi Germany was bent on murdering entire peoples, numbering many millions, in a highly organized, industrialized, and systematic manner; moreover, the regime had done its utmost to achieve this aim right to the last moment. Not only were the Jews doomed to extermination, but at least twenty to thirty million Russians as well, along with countless other "biological" and political enemies. Those who survived, particularly in the eastern *Lebensraum* of the Reich, were to be enslaved as complete and total *Untermenschen*, and to lead lives far worse than those of domestic animals. Wherever possible, this policy was carried out with what was called in the language of the time "ruthless determination." Had Nazi Germany won the war, Eastern Europe would have remained a vast death factory for centuries, ruled by a *Herrenvolk* who would refuse to consider its inhabitants as human beings. In no way can this be said about the Soviet Union. Stalin did indeed establish dictatorial, cruel, even criminal regimes in Eastern Europe, which subjugated their peoples to totalitarian systems complete with secret police forces, the elimination of civil rights, prohibitions on political organization, curtailment of the freedom of expression, and so forth. But even Stalin, let alone his followers, never intended to enslave and exterminate the population of Eastern Europe, the German Democratic Republic included. He did kill millions of his own people, and justly earned the title of one of the greatest butchers of all time. However, he never attempted to do to the Germans what they had almost succeeded in doing to the Russians. East Germans are in no immediate danger of being exterminated (not more, at least, than any of us in the event of a nuclear war), and are certainly not considered by their own regime or the Kremlin as *Untermenschen*. Indeed, the GDR is today one of the most prosperous countries in Eastern Europe.[76] If, for some inexplicable reason, Hillgruber had chosen the fate of the Eastern Provinces of Germany as the only incident in the Second World War worthy of being called a "tragedy," then we must remember that the collapse of Soviet Russia and a Nazi victory, although it would have saved Prussia, would have spelled a much greater, indeed quite unimaginable tragedy. No such simple comparisons should be allowed, for some regimes are far more criminal than others. The German people did not rise up against its dictator, and was liberated (without the inverted commas favored by Hillgruber when using this term in his essay) from his curse by a tremendous effort on the part of many nations. The German people paid a heavy price; however, even in defeat, it took a greater toll on its real and imagined enemies than the suffering inflicted on it. If the Federal Republic has taken the path toward the search for national identity, let it not dwell on the evil of mankind, but face up to its own past.

An Idiot's Tale: Memories and Histories of the Holocaust

She should have died hereafter:
There would have been a time for such a word.
To-morrow, and to-morrow, and to-morrow
Creeps in this petty pace from day to day
To the last syllable of recorded time
And all our yesterdays have lighted fools
The way to dusty earth. Out, out, brief candle!
Life's but a walking shadow, a poor player
That struts and frets his hour upon the stage
And then is heard no more. It is a tale
Told by an idiot, full of sound and fury,
Signifying nothing.[1]

Perhaps the one thing that all the books considered here[2] have in common, apart from their preoccupation with the Holocaust, is that they fill the reader with an almost unbearable sense of despair and helplessness regarding not only the past but also the present. It is, in the true sense, a tale that signifies nothing. Indeed, it is precisely the meaninglessness of the event, made all the clearer now with the benefit of hindsight, the utter uselessness of it all, the total and complete emptiness in which this hell on earth unfolded, that leaves us breathless, bereft of the power of thought and imagination. And what is especially frightening is the impossibility of learning anything from the Holocaust, of drawing any lessons, of putting its facts to any use. Seen from this perspective, questions such as "Could it happen again?" or "Was the Holocaust unique?" appear irrelevant. Humanity has brought on itself so much meaningless, useless, utterly idiotic suffering over the intervening five decades, and so much of this suffering appeared for a while, as it still does for some, meaningful and significant, that we, in our double roles as members of the human race and as its historians, must conclude that despair is probably the safest reaction—as human beings, because it seems that our ability to cause each other pain and suffering far exceeds even our imagination; as historians, because what we say about the past never seems to have any positive impact on the future and, moreover, does not appear particularly useful even in understanding the past itself.

All this may seem excessively pessimistic, in line with a general trend of cultural pessimism that appears to be sweeping the Western world in the wake of economic depression and the shattered hopes of yet another, post-Cold War, brave new world. After all, if the Holocaust was the worst that humanity was capable of, and if we can write and read its history, then perhaps we may *hope* that the worst is already over (even if *logically* it may well be repeated).[3] We now can devote ourselves to preventing a recurrence of this horror and ensuring thereby a better world for our children. History may not lead to certain progress, but the near future (which is all that concerns us as mortals and parents) can certainly be better than the present, just as the present is better than the past (some of us have moved up the social ladder as compared with *our* parents, though others have already found even that no longer possible).

To comfort ourselves with such assertions, we try to be selective in our exposure to and interpretation of contemporary events. The "civilized" world's inaction in the face of the continuing massacre in Bosnia, or the recent genocide in Rwanda, has its rational explanation, and for all too many observers, and most crucially all the relevant political and military decision-makers, it must have nothing to do with that same world's inaction during the Holocaust. The resurgence of racism in Germany, and the German government's insistence on a definition of citizenship based on blood, must not evoke any memories. The passivity of peaceful citizens who spent long years of normality next to a brutal concentration camp can have nothing to do with our own pursuit of scholarship only a couple of blocks away from slums teeming with violence and despair.

The relationship between history and memory; the relevance of the past for the present; the interaction between victim, perpetrator, and bystander; truth and relativity, abuse of the historical record and subjective recollection— these are the themes the books discussed here attempt to confront.[4] They are, at least to my mind, also of immense importance for our present day concerns. Although not all of these works are equally satisfying as scholarly, polemical, or philosophical texts, their overall importance is derived not only from the subject that forms the focus of their concern, but also from the highly illuminating and in part unconventional perspectives they have chosen for their analyses.

I. The Facts of the Matter

Those who wish to "get the facts right" and escape from the rhetoric, simplifications, exaggerations, and sheer inaccuracies of lesser scholars and popular writers would be well advised to turn to Christopher Browning's recent collection of essays, *The Path to Genocide*. In a field in which demagogy often serves to cover either ignorance or ideological motivations (and often both), it is a relief to find a historian whose judgments are sound and whose archival work is both extensive and highly relevant.

The Path to Genocide addresses some of the most important issues of the "Final Solution," and is particularly noteworthy for shifting the focus to what Browning recognizes as a crucial yet relatively neglected and misunderstood period, namely the years 1939–41. By analyzing Nazi resettlement and ghettoization policy, Browning is able to demonstrate the limitations of both previous schools of interpretation on the nature of National Socialism, especially concerning its Jewish policies.[5] The "intentionalist" interpretation, which argues that everything the regime had done up to the actual unleashing of the "Final Solution" was merely in preparation for a preconceived plan,[6] is shown to be untenable in view of the fact that while concentrating the Jews in the ghettos of Eastern Europe several alternative plans were seriously considered and only at a relatively late stage was the decision made to carry out mass murder. The "functionalist" school, which has claimed that the "Final Solution" emerged from local initiatives by middle-ranking Nazis faced with an impossible logistical situation and that it was only subsequently adopted by the regime,[7] is also shown to be contradicted by the evidence, since the logistical, administrative, and technical aspects of the genocide of the Jews clearly necessitated coordination from the top, without which the construction of the death camps would have been out of the question.

Browning therefore manages to change the terms of the debate by analyzing the archival evidence and demonstrating that the increasingly polarized positions of the two schools are no longer founded in the documentation. In doing so he shows the importance of empirical work when combined with lucidity of mind. In the course of presenting his own highly modified "functionalist" interpretation, Browning also effectively demolishes the arguments of two contentious German scholars, Götz Aly and Susanne Heim, who in recent years have elaborated a new and in some ways even more extreme and disturbing version of "functionalism" than that originally proposed by Martin Broszat and Hans Mommsen.[8] Aly and Heim argue that the initiative for the "Final Solution" came from middle ranking German technocrats, often well-educated young men who based their ideas on a detached analysis of the socioeconomic structure of Eastern Europe and were essentially interested in modernization rather than extermination (a view echoed also by the German scholar Rainer Zitelmann, though on different grounds).[9] Browning, however (along with the German historian of foreign and forced labor, Ulrich Herbert),[10] demonstrates that the influence of these technocrats has been exaggerated and, more important, that it is impossible to eliminate ideology as a main motivating factor in Nazi policies, especially since they were so often anything but economically rational. Ideology, that is, came first, even when it proved economically (and, of course, militarily and politically) disastrous.

By the same token, Browning dismisses the main contention of Arno Mayer's book *Why Did the Heavens Not Darken?* according to which the Holocaust was a by-product of the failure of the German attack on the Soviet Union, rather than a goal on its own right.[11] Browning questions most of the major arguments presented by Mayer. He shows that mass killing of Jews began long before there were any signs of a slowdown in the Blitzkrieg campaign; he disproves Mayer's curious idea that more Jews died of "so-called 'natural' causes" than by direct killing; he corrects Mayer's inaccurate description of the emergence of the death camps, showing that they were anything but the result of an afterthought sometime in the winter of 1941–42 and that in fact they were already in preparation the previous fall. Finally, he criticizes Mayer for failing to take Hitler's racism, and Nazism's "biological politics," seriously, arguing that they were essential to National Socialism.

Up to this point Browning's study clearly shows the merits of thorough and conscientious archival work, as well as the advantages of eschewing grandiose theories and sensational statements. Yet in the third and last part of his book we are faced with the limitations of this approach, some of which can also be found in several other works discussed below.

Browning begins this part with an attempt to understand the minds and motivations of German bureaucrats involved in mass murder and concludes that, while they did not initiate genocide from below (as "functionalists" would have it), they also did not receive explicit orders from above (as "intentionalists" would argue). Rather, they reacted to the bureaucratic and administrative environment as they understood it, reading the signals just as any relatively intelligent bureaucrat would do in any bureaucratic system. The "Final Solution," says Browning, was implemented mainly by "moderate," "normal" bureaucrats, not by the zealots, and the shift toward unprecedented mass murder was experienced by these individuals as anything but radical, the final step being another increment, at the end of a series of policies leading "logically" to that conclusion.

In a similar vein, the next chapter examines the role of German doctors in initiating "public health" policies in the occupied territories and their relationship to anti-Jewish measures. Adding to the recent discussions on German doctors in the Third Reich,[12] Browning demonstrates once more, using specific examples, the "logic" of the medical bureaucrats involved in mass murder, who allowed hundreds of thousands of Jews to die of epidemics brought about by overcrowding, malnutrition, lack of sanitation, and shortage of medical supplies, legitimizing their indifference by the argument that diseases related to such conditions were inherent to Jews. Moreover, this "scientific" logic, which made possible a more efficient, scientific execution of the "Final Solution," was so solid that even postwar trials often failed to undermine it, and many doctors associated with "euthanasia" and the "Final Solution" continued to pursue their careers in the Federal Republic.

These two discussions by Browning clearly illustrate the extent to which various sectors of German society became involved in the machinery of extermination. Yet they fail to confront the most important question raised by the Nazi phenomenon: How does a modern state transform itself into a murder organization? For this purpose, a more daring leap of the mind may be called for, both upward and inward: First, by generalizing such empirical findings into a larger explanatory system (as, for instance, Hannah Arendt had done with such remarkable insight, notwithstanding inaccuracies of detail and ideological bias), and, second, by delving deeper into the psychology of one's protagonists (as, say, Robert Lifton has done). Such investigations of both the "higher" and "deeper" spheres of human action and mind may yield profoundly disturbing conclusions, for they tend to bring our own world, indeed our own selves, closer to the Nazi universe than we would like to concede. What they tell us about the bureaucratic state, about lawyers, doctors, soldiers, technocrats, and so forth, is so frightening that we tend to ignore their relevance for our current civilization; consequently, if we happen to be scholars of the Holocaust, we prefer to confine ourselves to the period in question.[13] But, of course, we should be the first to know what this attitude may lead to.

This problem is most clearly demonstrated in the last chapter, Browning's horrifying tale of Reserve Police Battalion 101, which has been published in book form in an expanded version.[14] This is a detailed investigation of the process whereby relatively older policemen were turned into mass murderers, not by coercion or indoctrination but simply by repeated involvement. This study both qualifies apologetic arguments about lack of choice (for the men were allowed not to take part in the shootings) and implicitly criticizes arguments (such as my own) about the importance of ideological motivation (because of their age, these policemen were presumably less susceptible to Nazi ideology than the young combat soldiers I studied).[15]

Yet precisely because it deals with such crucial issues, Browning's study of these "ordinary men" is not wholly satisfactory. Does he imply that anyone could be made into a mass murderer, no matter his education, social background, political convictions, and so forth? If so, then the conclusions he draws about human nature and the modern state are so devastating as to merit more serious discussion. Without wishing to dispute this here, I would point out, however, that one would like to know more about the training and education of the Hamburg policemen Browning studied. Were they brought up and molded in the same fashion as, say, New York or London police officers in the 1930s? Or were there (as I would argue) some elements in their environment that made them quite receptive to Nazi policies? Conversely (though admittedly this objection properly applies to the book rather than the article at the end of the collection discussed here), one would have liked a more sustained discussion of the implications of the Federal Republic's failure to punish these killers and especially of their continued presence as regular policemen in postwar Hamburg. What does this tell us about the nature of law enforcement in West Germany between 1945 and the late 1960s? Indeed, what does it tell us about the modern state's police in general and about its predilection to serve any regime and enforce any law by any means allowed it at any given moment?[16] Finally, what does all this tell us about the plight of the individual law-abiding citizen, when the law and its enforcers turn out to be criminal?

In a state of upheaval, chaos, and unprecedented violence, the status of crime itself becomes dubious. Hollywood depictions notwithstanding, during the Second World War there was a progressive blurring of boundaries between such notions as heroism and barbarism, patriotism and betrayal, sacrifice and fanaticism, justice and vengeance, legality and criminality. The Weimar Republic's legal establishment adjusted to the Nazi system of terror and, twelve years later, adjusted once more to the Federal Republic; apparently few laws had to be changed (with the obvious exception of some overtly racist legislation such as the Nuremberg Laws), and hence adjustment in both cases was quite smooth. Furthermore, while the victors took the unprecedented step of trying the vanquished according to principles of international law (which have never been applied since, and not for lack of appropriate opportunities), they also set out to "denazify" Germany but ended up by legitimizing the continued presence in the FRG of former Nazis. Even in the few cases where German courts found themselves compelled to try some of the more repellent criminals of the previous regime, they merely furnished a unique example of victors' justice being more just than that of the vanquished, since those finally convicted were let off with truly ludicrous sentences.

One instance of the deadly effects of such blurring of boundaries is sketched in David Engel's *Facing a Holocaust*, a meticulous documentary study of the Polish exile government's policies toward the Jews, and a sequel to his 1987 book *In the Shadow of Auschwitz*.[17] Even from the perspective of five decades of political cynicism it is difficult to believe the extent to which the Polish leaders in exile, while leading a bitter struggle against the Nazis, retained their antisemitic sentiments and, indeed, seemed to find at least one positive aspect about the Nazi occupation of their homeland—namely, that they were ridding Poland of the Jews.

Claude Lanzmann has been attacked for unfairly portraying the Poles as having been almost as bad as the Germans, using as evidence interviews with a few ignorant, not to say stupid, peasants still living in the vicinity of death camp sites. Whatever the merits of this criticism, Engel's documentation (and, one may add, his detached evaluation) of the Polish political leadership's stance on the "Jewish Question" is quite devastating. Indeed, according to Engel, even when the Polish exile government did act on behalf of the Jews (as when after years of prevarications it finally issued a call to Poles to help the Jews), this step was motivated by the traditional antisemitic (and unfortunately for the Poles totally false) assumption that the Jews wielded great international influence and would thus repay Polish concern for their fate by persuading the United States and Britain to support the Polish government's territorial claims.

There is little doubt that the gentile population of Poland also suffered terribly during the German occupation, that many Poles fought with great courage against the Nazis, that relatively few collaborated (not least because the Germans did not seek collaborators among them), and, finally, that there were Poles who did actively assist Jews in spite of the grave danger to themselves and their families. But as Engel's study shows, the boundaries between resistance to occupation and assistance to murder are depressingly vague. Not only were Polish policy-makers reluctant to act on behalf of their Jewish citizens and, indeed, refused to see them as possessing the same rights as ethnic Poles, they also viewed the Jews in the "Free World" as enemies whose interests were wholly contradictory to those of Poland but who might have to be pacified or dealt with diplomatically only because of their alleged power.

Engel does consider the fact that much of the initial information on the unfolding of the "Final Solution" came from Polish sources, and he notes that some of the financial assistance to the Jews of Poland was channeled through Polish agencies on the ground, though even in this case there seems to have been resistance to collaborating with the Jews. He also concedes that it took a tremendous mental effort even for Jewish political leaders in the West and in

Palestine to realize that the Germans were in fact practicing genocide. But when all is said and done, it is difficult to maintain one's detachment on being presented with evidence according to which the Polish exile government began publicizing the fact of genocide against the Jews on Polish soil only when it dawned on its members that the Poles might be next in line, and with the hope that if the world turned its attention to Polish Jews (which, it was thought, was more likely than gaining attention for Polish gentiles), then the plight of the Polish gentiles (which, they argued, was just as bad as that of the Jews) would also be noticed.

Hence, few Poles (or at least few of their political leaders) seem to have lamented the destruction of a centuries-old Jewish civilization on Polish soil. While they wanted both to be liberated from Nazi occupation and avoid being occupied by their prospective Soviet liberators, they also wanted to be rid of the Jews, one way or another. Postwar Poland would have to solve its "Jewish Problem," these officials thought, and they expressed fears that in spite of the Nazi murder campaign too many Jews would be left behind once the Wehrmacht was finally pushed out. Indeed, at the end of the war numerous Poles complained that too many Jews *were* left, and those who returned for their property were often greeted with violence that claimed the lives of hundreds of survivors.[18] This is just one more example of the blurring of boundaries and the confusion of distinctions mentioned above. Liberation meant very different things to many different people. The Poles wished to be liberated not only from the German occupation and the looming Soviet domination, but also from the remaining Jews, even if some ninety percent of Poland's prewar Jewish population had already been murdered. The Jews, on the other hand, experienced liberation in an essentially different manner from their liberators, the "Free World," and subsequent generations; though liberated, the survivors were not free, neither psychologically, nor, in many cases, politically—a sentiment well reflected, for instance, both in Primo Levi's account of his own liberation and, even more powerfully, in his very last essays.[19] This sense of imprisonment within the memories of their experiences felt so strongly by the survivors will be discussed in greater detail in the third section and epilogue of this chapter. For the moment, however, let us examine another crucial factor in the phenomenon of modern genocide: its remarkable capacity rapidly to transform itself into what appears to its makers and observers (and in a very different sense also to its victims) as a normal, or at least unavoidable, and in not a few cases even profitable condition.

II. As a Matter of Fact

For some, liberation was less ambiguous than for others. They were freed from a disturbing, though not wholly unwelcome, presence in their midst, one they had accepted as a matter of fact in the changed circumstances of their lives, learning to accommodate themselves to it and suffering by and large only minor discomforts while at times making a neat profit. Once it ceased to exist in its previous capacity, it was likewise quickly erased from memory as a matter of fact. The concentration camp Mauthausen, by the town of the same name, is explored as a concrete reality in the lives of the population in Gordon Horwitz's excellent *In the Shadow of Death*, but this is a tale that can just as well serve as a metaphor for the essence of the "Final Solution" or, for that matter, for most other atrocities in human history, for it is a story of a secret crime carried out publicly, of an enormity committed regularly, on an everyday basis, in broad daylight, and yet considered and perceived as a secret that no one saw, no one heard, no one remembers.

Horwitz's sensitive study provides us with much insight into an aspect of the Holocaust that up to now has received little rigorous treatment, namely, the role of the bystanders in genocide. Rejecting both the apologetic argument that most people knew nothing or little of the mass murders executed by the Nazis, and the generalizing (and therefore meaningless) assertion that everyone was to blame (all the Germans, all the Poles, all the gentiles), Horwitz illustrates how the life of a quiet, backwater Austrian community became deeply enmeshed in a variety of ways and on several levels in the routine activity of the concentration camp, from delivering food supplies to employing inmates on farms, from watching behind half-closed curtains as the prisoners struggled along the main street to refusing shelter and food to escaped prisoners, if not actually hunting them down with shotguns and pickaxes.

In the Shadow of Death (the word "shadow" seems a popular choice in titles of Holocaust histories) is very well written, well researched (using both primary and secondary sources, oral histories, and interviews), and quite horrifying. Those of us who have accepted the more comforting aspects of Arendt's "banality of evil"—namely, that the Holocaust was at least carried out by a bureaucratic, industrial, "neat" killing machine—are here compelled to confront the sheer brutality of the camps, their sadism and depravity, unimaginative perhaps, indeed anything but original, yet nauseating and terrifying all the same. The concentration and death camps could be both: brutal and efficient, employing medieval tortures and state-of-the-art gas chambers. And, like so many previous evils, they could be—indeed they almost by definition had to be—just far enough from the eye to prevent protest and just close enough to provoke fear. Camps such as Mauthausen dehumanized not only their inmates and guards but also the bystanders, by making them into accomplices in the atrocity through fear and humiliation, profit and prejudice, indifference and guilt.

Horwitz makes us realize not only that it was impossible to live next to a concentration camp without having a pretty good idea of what was happening in it, just as it was impossible to run a concentration camp without some civilian community in the vicinity to sustain it, but also that in such situations people were very much faced with choices as to how they should act, even if at the time, as well as subsequently, they normally refused to admit this both to others and themselves. He shows that in some, unfortunately few instances, members of the community did try to assist the inmates, whether simply by looking at them with compassion or leaving them some food along their route, or even sheltering those who escaped. Interestingly, and very much unlike conditions in the East, those caught helping inmates either were not punished at all or were punished only lightly. This does not mean that risks were not involved, but it does illustrate that the choice for some human action was present, and that those who ignored it made a choice nevertheless, since passivity meant complicity with the killers.

Collaboration could be interpreted in various ways. Dr. Renno, a member of the medical staff in charge of the "euthanasia" operations in the gas chamber of Castle Hartheim, near Mauthausen, stated after the war that "The notion that a state could pass a law that was illegal was beyond my conception, particularly as people of station and name accepted the euthanasia program" (p. 63). Dr. Renno was devoted not only to a certain concept of legality but also to some interesting ideas regarding his professional duties. Accordingly, he expressed reluctance to perform "mercy killing" by gas since "he had not studied medicine in order to turn on the gas spigot" (p. 63). This kind of psychological makeup, described in detail by Robert Lifton,[20] made doctors prefer either to cause death by "medical means" (such as lethal injections) or have someone else turn on the gas while they fulfilled the "professional task" of deciding who was fit for the gas chamber. As Horwitz observes, no matter whether the men and women who staffed the murder castle liked their duties, they all performed with zeal and efficiency. The option of "bureaucratic resistance," whereby covert administrative obstruction hampered the implementation of genocidal policies without appearing as overt resistance, so successfully employed by the Italians,[21] seems to have never occurred to these diligent administrators, even as the air became thick with the stench of burning bodies. Instead, they preferred to concentrate on their specific tasks and claim ignorance of, and no responsibility for, anything that happened beyond their individual area of activity. This, of course, left only a small number of men who were actually doing the killing, and who often had no idea for what purpose they were performing their odious task but assumed that their supervisors (who had no hand in the killing) did. Again, this is a microcosm that reflects the vast machinery of genocide as a whole. Similarly, the inhabitants of the town by the castle smelled the stench of the crematorium, saw the fumes, indeed were confronted daily with human remains on the street, yet none of them were willing to admit that they were living right next to a murder factory. By the same token, when the population of Mauthausen was confronted face to face with brutality to inmates of the camp, people calmed their consciences by arguing that the prisoners, who hardly looked human, must have done something unspeakable to have ended up in a concentration camp. To be sure, people also feared that anything they might do to help the inmates could land them in the same spot. The prisoners, in contrast, felt quite invisible when they encountered the townspeople, for the latter did not acknowledge their presence, did not recognize them as human beings. Dehumanized by the bystanders during the affair, they were repressed and forgotten as quickly as possible once it was over.

A few episodes in Horwitz's powerful book illustrate the psychological processes at work among the bystanders. When American aircraft bombed one of the concentration camps in the Mauthausen complex the inhabitants nearby felt relieved, almost grateful for this error in identifying a target, for now, they claimed, the U.S. Air Force was also killing inmates. Worse still, when a few hundred desperate Soviet prisoners of war tried to escape from the camp, they were chased by the whole community, from Hitler Youth teenagers to elderly *Volkssturm* members. As Horwitz points out, once the barriers had fallen, all pretense at ignorance or detachment was gone and the population went after the inmates with almost greater relish than the SS troops themselves. Finally, when the camp was evacuated in a series of horrifying death marches, few of the inhabitants in the communities along the way ventured to help, although by now they could no longer claim ignorance of the atrocities taking place right below their front windows.

This is largely a tale of human cowardice, indifference, and depravity. The few instances of heroism are drowned in that typical combination of barbarity and pettiness. It is difficult indeed to retain a belief in the nobility of the human spirit after closing this book. Nor does it have a happy end, for the community of Mauthausen has shown great reluctance to be remembered as the home of one of the most notorious concentration camps in a long list of man-made hells. It is consequently a good example of the Austrian attitude toward the memory of the "Nazi occupation," so well embodied by Kurt Waldheim, whose 1986 speech marked the beginning of a new but not a better era, forty years after the fall of Greater Germany (of which Austria was part): "What really bothers me is that this [Jewish] congress tries to ruin the reputation of a whole generation and makes all these people bad people. . . . We were not criminals but decent men who faced a terrible fate" (p. 186).[22]

The people of Mauthausen accepted the camp as a matter of fact. Waldheim's assertions of innocence, decency, and duty were also a matter of (distorted) fact. Raul Hilberg, who has done more than any other single scholar to compile and analyze the facts of the Holocaust, devotes his recent book, *Perpetrators Victims Bystanders*, to a series of individual and group portraits of people involved in the "Final Solution." Hilberg writes in a detached, almost matter-of-fact style. He tells the most chilling stories without, so to speak, even raising his voice. And indeed, close to two-thirds of the book examines the casual manner in which the killers killed and the observers observed. Even when writing on the victims, Hilberg often presents them as exhibiting a growing sense of fatalism. Only a minority rebelled against this seemingly inevitable destiny in several exceptional ways.

Hilberg argues that Adolf Hitler formulated his ideas on Jews only in 1919, and then remained fixated on them for the rest of his life. Stressing Hitler's immense popularity, he points out that the Führer's importance for understanding the Third Reich derives from his indispensability for the Nazi system. Though he could not have carried out the Holocaust single-handed, Hitler was essential for its realization. Indeed, Hilberg asserts that the decision on the "Final Solution" came from Hitler, after a period of germination and indecision that began in the final planning stages for "Barbarossa" in March 1941 and ended in the fall of that year, when the first preparations for the construction of death camps were set into motion and after the *Einsatzgruppen* had already killed hundreds of thousands through mass shootings in the USSR.

Hilberg also does not accept the assertion that genocide was merely a bureaucratic, administrative process, although it was very much that too. Officials of the SS such as Eichmann employed a great deal of initiative and will, the absence of which would have crippled the murder apparatus. Furthermore, the machinery of destruction depended to a large extent on the functionaries of the previous regime. Here too we find how easily senior administrators were mobilized to organize mass murder and, what is just as disturbing, how easily they got off at the end of the war, some reaching top administrative positions in the Federal Republic, many reaching a ripe old age. At the same time, for these top officials organizing genocide was only a minor part of their responsibilities, and, considering their long previous and subsequent careers, the Holocaust was never an important part of their lives.

Among the newcomers, Hilberg notes the predominance and success of Austrians, especially in the SS; careerists who often continued their rise within the bureaucracy without difficulty beyond 1945; the so-called negative elite, the dregs of society who formed the personnel of the concentration camps; and, perhaps most troubling, a large number of intellectuals, academics, and professionals who manned both the mobile killing units and the administrative posts of the Reich Security Main Office, men with secure and respectable positions who joined these murder organizations out of conviction. Of course, for some it was not easy to adapt to the killing right away, but Hilberg sketches a few cases that demonstrate, in a manner similar to Browning's study, how these men grew accustomed to the murder of men, women, and children within a relatively short span of time.

Hilberg is also interested in the process of "medicalized killing" by physicians who transformed themselves from healers to killers by viewing themselves as society's surgeons and considering some other categories of people as viruses that must be exterminated for the health of the social organism. Doctors sterilized some 400,000 mostly "Aryan" Germans and killed a further 100,000 in the euthanasia campaign. They were then made into the cadre for the establishment of the death camp network of Belzec-Sobibor-Treblinka, where some 1.5 million people were killed with carbon monoxide gas. Doctors were also involved, as we have seen, in the administration of ghettos and in propounding theories on Jews as carriers of disease. Best known, of course, were the medical experiments performed by doctors on concentration camp inmates, which apparently helped them legitimize their role as "real" scientists rather than merely instruments of murder. As has been shown, quite a number of these doctors also went on to successful careers in postwar Germany.[23] The same holds true for the lawyers who played a crucial role in each and every stage of Nazi Jewish policy, from prohibitions of marriage and sexual contacts to expropriation and finally to legalizing murder.[24]

In writing about the German perpetrators, Hilberg evokes in us the feeling that these actions were perceived as quite normal. Nowhere does he exclaim that there was something insane in this general participation of people of all social and educational backgrounds in mass, useless, idiotic murder on an unprecedented scale. People were, more or less, going about their usual business, whose character had, admittedly, changed somewhat, but not to such a degree that they could not carry out their specific duties with their accustomed efficiency. Participation in the murder of the Jews seemed a matter of course also to some other nationalities conquered (or "liberated") by the Wehrmacht. Among them the Balts and the Ukrainians featured most prominently. The involvement of the Baltic police in anti-Jewish actions was on a particularly remarkable scale considering the relatively small population of these three countries. Numbering together only five million people, Estonia, Latvia, and Lithuania nevertheless proved to be a major asset to the SS, assisting it in massacring one of the most ancient Jewish communities in Europe and destroying some of the greatest centers of Jewish learning and civilization.[25]

As for the bystanders, most nations under German occupation showed greater or lesser degrees of indifference to anything that did not touch their own people's immediate existence. In Germany the difference between perpetrators and bystanders was least pronounced, and indifference to the fate of the Jews was only matched by interest in their property and the positions they "vacated." Most of the few thousand Jews assisted by Germans appear to have had non-Jewish relatives. As we saw, in the Baltic countries, as well as in the Ukraine, collaboration in anti-Jewish policies surpassed the dreams of even the most devoted *Einsatzgruppen* commanders. Poland, however, though strongly antisemitic, produced fewer collaborators, since the Germans placed the Poles so low on their own racial and cultural scale that they denied them even the status of Jew hunters. In the West, the murder of close to three-quarters of Holland's 140,000 Jews best illustrates another technique of mass killing, not through persecution or antisemitic pogroms and collaboration but by means of an efficient bureaucratic administration and smooth cooperation between all involved—the Dutch bureaucrats, the Jewish community leaders, and the mass of the Jewish population—this in spite of Dutch acceptance of the Jews as fellow citizens and their willingness to protect many of them on an individual basis.

Genocide as a matter-of-fact event is seen in Hilberg's section on bystanders from many other angles: the observers of atrocities who remained indifferent, claimed helplessness, or made a profit; the messengers whose news of genocide confronted a wall of disbelief, discomfort, passivity; the Jewish agencies outside Nazi-occupied Europe that failed to mobilize the Allied governments; the leaders of England and the United States, who would not present the war as an effort to save the Jews for fear that their populations would perceive that as a cause unworthy of their sacrifice and could only promise that the Jews would be saved as a by-product of an Allied victory; and the churches, which, with few exceptions, did little to dissuade the perpetrators from their actions or urge the bystanders into active opposition.

For the victims, the Holocaust was anything but a matter-of-fact event. And yet, as both Hilberg and several other scholars have shown,[26] the Jewish leadership and large portions of the Jewish population reacted to the Nazi genocide by resorting to the traditional patterns of behavior internalized over centuries of persecution. The vast majority of the Jews, almost to the very end, failed to devise a new manner of reacting to this unprecedented, unimaginable scheme, even after its details were known. Hence the *Judenräte*, or Jewish councils, and especially their leaders, tried to save their communities by satisfying real or imagined German demands; their tragedy was that not only did they fail to save the communities, but they also rendered crucial assistance to the Germans in the organization and administration of systematic destruction.

Only one category of victims, labeled by Hilberg as "unadjusted," consisted of people who could not or would not accept the reality of the Holocaust and turned instead to suicide, hiding, escape, or resistance. It was only they, along perhaps with the exiles, who did not view the attempted genocide as a matter of fact, as an event that must be accepted, that one must learn to "live" with rather than oppose. To this minority belong also those gentiles who not only resisted Nazi occupation but also did what they could to help the victims— again, a small minority. The many horrors we find in Hilberg's pages on the victims have this in common with the other sections of the book, namely, that they are about people who accepted the "logic" of the event. There was, one might say, a horrible, perverse bond between the perpetrators, victims, and bystanders: the vast majority of them perceived the situation in which they found themselves as unavoidable, as a circumstance one had to learn to cope with rather than one that had to be fundamentally transformed, exploded, or destroyed. This was an idiot's tale that no one could undo, a nightmare from which no one managed to wake. And perhaps the most horrifying aspect of it is that it still continues, both in the memories of the victims (and very differently in those of the perpetrators and bystanders) and in its many contemporary offshoots, whether as more recent atrocities or as normalizing interpretations of the past.

III. Competing Memories

There is a widely held assumption among historians that documents are more trustworthy than memory, written evidence is more objective than verbal testimony, and oral history is more dubious than that based on archival findings. Yet as a brief look at the historiography of the Holocaust will show, historians have by now produced so many different and contradictory versions of the event, its causes, course, consequences, and meaning, that we may have to concede that there are certain limits to the extent to which traditional methods of inquiry can enhance our understanding. Conversely, memories of the event, though in some aspects differing greatly from each other, have certain qualities that make them more stable and permanent than any scholarly representation. It is therefore of extreme importance to record and employ such memories in any attempt to comprehend the past, while constantly keeping in mind the problems inherent in these sources.

One striking aspect of the Holocaust is that a large number of what have traditionally been considered trustworthy or respectable historical documents stem from the perpetrators, whereas the victims have left few "official" documents behind. The old dilemma of which documents can be accepted as reliable is particularly acute in this case. Would we prefer the filmic evidence of the *Eighty-First Blow*, which employs mainly contemporary German film material, or that of *Shoah*, which refuses to make use of such "contaminated," biased documentary evidence produced by the perpetrators and instead opts for the "real" *memory* of the event among those who experienced it, both survivors, bystanders, and perpetrators?[27]

Memory is the subject of the last three books to be discussed here. The first is concerned with distortions of memory; the second with the inability of memory to reassert itself; the third with the refusal of memory to go away, and its relentless penetration of the present.

Pierre Vidal-Naquet is a highly respected scholar of ancient Greece who has also been active in contemporary political debates in France ever since the Algerian war.[28] The English translation of *Assassins of Memory* contains a series of essays concerned with the "revisionists," especially those in France, who in recent years have attempted to deny the Holocaust (or deny its importance) and have thereby unleashed several academic and intellectual scandals. The book is a polemical debate in the respected Dreyfusard tradition. The essays are often hard-hitting, their mood is a brew of irony and wrath, and put together they constitute an attempt to discredit and undermine the revisionist thesis both on scholarly grounds (as unfounded and contradicted by the evidence), on logical grounds (as self-contradictory, self-defeating, irrational), on moral grounds (as insidious as well as self-promoting), and on historical-contextual grounds (as belonging to a long tradition of denial and falsification, which, however, has presumably always failed to win out in the end).

Vidal-Naquet's campaign against the revisionists is of course a laudable and courageous act, which should serve as an example for contemporary scholars who commonly shy away from involvement in political debates. Nevertheless, it must be admitted that this specific foray into modern history and polemics is not always successful.

First, the author does not always have a firm grasp on the facts as we know them, which is especially problematic since much of his argument is directed against the distortion of facts (and thereby of memory) by the revisionists. Thus, for instance, Red Army commissars were mostly shot by the army, not gassed along with the mentally ill as part of the "euthanasia" program (p. 14);[29] if Jews did not suffer from a "pariah status" in Weimar Germany (p. 103), the high levels of suicide among them, as noted by Hilberg in the volume discussed here (Hilberg, p. 171), are only one indication of the sense of crisis in that community; and if the debate over the timing of the decision on the "Final Solution" still "continues unresolved" (p. 108), it certainly no longer includes the contention that it was made only at the end of the fall of 1941 following the first major defeats of the Wehrmacht.

Second, some of Vidal-Naquet's articles in this collection suffer from tilting too far toward the polemical/political and thereby abandoning the more careful scrutiny of evidence required (indeed demanded) by a scholar of his stature. It is problematic to blame the revisionists (quite rightly!) for falsifying their evidence and then to say that "the massacre of Dir yassin by men of the Irgun and Stern gang (April 9 and 10, 1948) can be compared with Oradour, not Auschwitz" (p. 16). Quite apart from his choice of words ("Stern gang" was the term used by the British colonial ruler in Palestine for LEHI, the acronym of *Lohamey Herut Yisrael*, "Fighters for the Liberation of Israel"; using the British name is like calling the PLO the Arafat gang), it is preposterous to compare Dir Yassin with Oradour (though not *as* preposterous as comparing it with Auschwitz). Oradour was only one of tens of thousands of villages and towns wiped out by the German army as part of a general policy of murder and subjugation; it is remembered chiefly because it happened in France, where this policy was far less common than in the East. Dir Yassin is remembered so well because it was an exception and has rightly remained a blot in Israel's history. Moreover, when another massacre took place in Kfar Kassem in 1956, the perpetrators were tried by an Israeli court and sentenced to prison terms, and a new supreme court ruling on the right (and duty) of soldiers to disobey unlawful orders was passed and incorporated into Israeli martial law.[30] It is difficult to imagine Nazi courts trying the members of the SS division *Das Reich* for having killed French civilians in Oradour, whether during the war or after its conclusion.[31] Moreover, one cannot ignore the extent to which Dir Yassin has served German apologists in retrospectively blaming the Jews for the outbreak of the Second World War and all the misfortunes that have happened to Germany ever since. Thus, the German postwar Nazi leader Erwin Schönborn wrote an open letter to President Sadat following his visit to Israel, in which he asked him not to speak with Begin, "the mass murderer of Dir Yassin," since Israel, "the thorn in the Arab flesh," was not only "the eternal enemy [Todfeind] of all the Arabs," but also that of Germany. Hence, "Auschwitz and 'Yad Vashem' are symbols of the great lie—Dir Yassin is the bloody reality on the path of the state of Israel."[32]

Vidal-Naquet also makes some problematic assertions regarding Germany. Claiming, for instance, that one "extreme example of a 'revisionist' literature" is the argument that the "historians who have disseminated the *'official* image of Auschwitz . . . are all Jews, which would explain the partiality of their works'" (p. 123),[33] he ignores the fact that this argument has been made by far less "extreme revisionists," such as the highly respected scholar Martin Broszat,[34] and in a milder form also by Ian Kershaw.[35] Indeed, Arno Mayer, with whose views Vidal-Naquet seems generally to sympathize, has similarly complained about Jewish domination of Holocaust studies and the consequent overemphasis on the fate of the Jews to the detriment of other persecuted groups.[36]

There are several other examples of such inaccuracies. But the main difficulty with Vidal-Naquet's essays stems rather from an essential flaw in their form and line of argument. In the preface to his book the author claims that "one can and should enter into a discussion *concerning* the 'revisionists'. . . . But one should not enter into debate *with* the 'revisionists'" (p. xxiv). Perhaps it is possible to maintain the boundary between the two, but I am afraid that much of the text reads very much like a debate *with* his foes—indeed, an angry exchange that robs his arguments of much of the force they might have had if he had resisted the temptation to polemicize with people who, as he well knows, are no partners for discussion.[37]

Some aspects of Vidal-Naquet's book are both intriguing and closely related to Alain Finkielkraut's *Remembering in Vain*. Vidal-Naquet himself quite candidly reproduces a text that he had signed on October 17, 1961, comparing what he calls an anti-Algerian "pogrom" to the deportations to Auschwitz (p. 128). Though he now realizes the folly of that statement, his subsequent attempts "to situate colonial war crimes in relation to those of the Nazis" have not been much more successful. Thus, he has meanwhile also had to retract his 1972 statement that the French commander of Algeria, General Massu, was "less guilty than Eichmann and more guilty than Klaus Barbie," since, as he admits in the present volume, at the time he was unaware of Barbie's role in sealing the fate of the children of Izieu (pp. 129–30). Vidal-Naquet's difficulty was, of course, compounded by the attempt of Klaus Barbie's defense lawyer Jacques Vergès to shift the focus from, in Vergès' words, "only a crime committed by some Germans against some Jews" to "a crime that is far more serious, far more current, and far more frightening for the future: the crime committed by imperialism against the peoples struggling for their liberation" (cited on p. 132).

Barbie was the first person in France to be tried for "crimes against humanity," and it is the larger implications of his trial that form the focus of Finkielkraut's brilliant and terse essay. This is a truly polemical piece, whose major defect may be said to be its excessive brevity. One wishes Finkielkraut had written a little more, though one admires him for being able to say so much, and to say it so clearly, with so few words.

Finkielkraut finds the decision made in Nuremberg to institute a concept of "crimes against humanity," "the criminal exercising of the power of the state," a momentous judicial event, since it recognized for the first time that men acting within the legality of their state can nevertheless be tried as criminals. At the same time he stresses that precisely because of the scale of the crimes, "the executioners, taken one by one, all appear insignificant," as was indeed the case not only with Barbie but also with Eichmann. All the more reason to bring them to justice, he insists, since "the notion of crimes against humanity is, precisely, to reestablish the link between man and the crime . . . to recall, by treating the *cogs* in the Nazi apparatus as *persons*, that service to the state does not exonerate any civil servant in any bureaucracy, nor any engineer in any laboratory, from his responsibility an an individual" (p. 8).

Yet Finkielkraut laments the failure of civilization to institute an international judicial body for dealing with crimes against humanity, and while he accepts the unique features of the Holocaust, he does not agree that they should justify lack of action against other crimes against humanity that have meanwhile occurred. Conversely, he insists on maintaining the distinctions made at Nuremberg that defined what "crimes against humanity were" and on not allowing that concept to be misused.

These are not only legalistic distinctions; they also have to do with what Finkielkraut calls "the competition of memories" (p. 19). Finkielkraut has little doubt that the initial silence of the so-called "racially deported" (i.e., the "mere" victims of the Nazis, as opposed to the "politically deported," i.e., the heroes of the Resistance) after the war "was not because they were unable to speak . . . but because no one wanted to hear them. Beware the pathos of the ineffable!" (p. 18).[38] This has been changing, not least because while the children of the Resistance fighters are simply their children, the children of the Jews are Jewish—that is, they retain the quality for which their parents were persecuted. But the war of memories continues, to the extent that the court was compelled to rule that crimes against Resistance fighters would also be included in the definition of crimes against humanity. This, as Finkielkraut explains, eliminated the distinction between those who were tortured for what they did and those who were tortured and murdered for what they were. For the author, "It is not the same thing, to be an enemy and to be a hunted quarry. In the first case, the world is still a world, for one is still the master of one's choices. Even in the absence of freedom one is still free to give or not to give meaning to one's life . . . one can attest to one's humanity through action" (p. 22). Because of this essential difference Finkielkraut also dismisses the distinction between Jews who revolted and Jews who followed the directions of the Nazis as one of resistance versus collaboration, because both these terms meant something essentially different for Jews and non-Jews.[39]

Finkielkraut's aim is especially to explode the distinction drawn by Vergès between the extermination of the Jews, merely a "crime of local interest, a drop of European blood," and the "ocean of human suffering." By claiming that the genocide of the Jews "offended only the consciousness of white people," Vergès turned the trial in Lyons into a mockery of the Nuremberg Trials and nullified, according to Finkielkraut, the important finding in Nuremberg—"that humanity *itself* was mortal" (pp. 25–26). For while it was possible until the Third Reich to claim that man was mortal but civilization marched forward, that nations could commit crimes but that humanity was still constantly progressing, at Nuremberg it was conceded that the *victims could no longer be chalked up to progress.*" "The human race," insists Finkielkraut, "had been forever impoverished by the destruction of the world of European Jews" (pp. 28–29). Because the Nazis "broke all bonds of humanity" in what they claimed and believed to be "the service of mankind," it became impossible to believe "in the grandeur of a collective destiny," and it was realized in 1945 that "men are not the *means*" of humanity, "but that humanity is their responsibility, that they are its *guardians.*" Hence, humanity can die, for it is at the mercy of men, and they can commit crimes against it, even murder it altogether (pp. 30–31).

Barbie's lawyers, however, chose to attack that very notion that the Holocaust was a crime against humanity, arguing that the memories and lamentations of the West have nothing to do with them—the Algerian, Congolese, and French-Vietnamese lawyers who set themselves up as the spokesmen of the "Third World." Not only have the whites oppressed all other races; they also expect these races to pity them for *their* disaster, which is not the business of the truly oppressed.

Finkielkraut finds a close similarity between this tactic and the tradition of left-wing anti-Dreyfusism, namely, the argument by the French left during the Dreyfus trial that since it was taking place among the privileged classes the whole affair was of no concern to the oppressed (but progressive) working class. Similarly, as the genocide of the Jews happened among the oppressors, the enemies of Man, there was no reason for humanity (and those in charge of its progress) to mourn its victims (pp. 33–34). And, since the "Third World" is the herald of progress, those perceived as its enemies are the logical successors of Nazism: the Americans in Vietnam, the French in Algeria, the Israelis in the West Bank. Thus, Barbie's defense chose to "accuse Jewish pain of obstructing the world's memory" and to present "former slaves or former victims of colonialism as victims of 'the conspiracy of the remnants of Zion'" (p. 36).[40] By this amazing *coup de main*, Barbie's defense made the real Nazi no longer relevant to humanity, while presenting the alleged opposers of progress as Nazi and therefore as worthy of being wiped out and exterminated.

This "emotional confusion" in the trial both expanded the definition of crimes against humanity to inhuman actions of any sort, on the one hand, and made possible the exclusion of those crimes (such as the Cambodian murder campaign) that could not be ascribed to the West, on the other hand. This was further complicated by the insistence of Nuremberg that the definition of crimes against humanity be limited to those inflicted during wartime (motivated by the opposition of nations to intervention in their domestic affairs), as well as by the absence of an international criminal court that could implement the UN pledge of 1948 to punish genocide. Hence "Genocide becomes an internal affair, its punishment reduced (when it takes place) to a purge, and one is thus left with the very situation that one sought to correct: the breaking up of the human race into a multitude of states" (p. 55–56).

Consequently, argues the author, "Emotional thought surrendered to totalitarian thought, reintroduced under the guise of antiracism by Barbie's defenders" (p. 56)—a bitter paradox if ever there was one. For Finkielkraut, the greatest achievement of the post-1945 era *could* have been a release from totalitarian thought, that longing for the idyll of tomorrow and the consequent exclusion or elimination of the enemies of today in the name of the future. It *should* have returned us to the era of *Polemos*, the recognition that institutionalized conflict is the basis of democracy. But instead of the discredited homogeneity of the community of blood, people opted for what Hannah Arendt has called "the excessive closeness of a brotherliness that obliterate[s] all distinctions" (p. 59).[41] And this excessive emphasis on love and brotherhood negates the principle of conflict against those who seek to abolish it, and makes for an exclusively moral division of the world into "them" and "us." This is the disappearance of politics, the urge for "purging the world of all profundity and indeterminacy . . . the dizzying simplicity of its good sentiments" (p. 60). If Thomas Mann defined National Socialism as the desire for a simple folktale,[42] Finkielkraut attacks contemporary discourse for making "antiracism play the same role that the Stalinist vulgate assigned to class struggle" and charges that "by invoking the *shoah* with indecent smugness . . . the aspiration to the simple folktale has today depoliticized political debate, has transformed culture into pious images, and, with no concern for the truth, has reduced the unmasterable multitude of mankind to an exultant face-to-face confrontation between Innocence and the Unspeakable Beast" (pp. 60–61).

Courageously refusing to accept current intellectual fashions, Finkielkraut's essay is nevertheless profoundly melancholy, and as such it reflects the spirit of cultural pessimism characteristic of our age which, in turn, has striking similarities with the mood that prevailed at the turn of the previous century. Hence, when he laments the tendencies "to transform history, in its entirety, into a children's story" (p. 73), he could well be speaking of the 1890s. The Holocaust, he might have said, is being rewritten as a meaningless idiot's tale.

His fear of this process prompted Finkielkraut to oppose televising the trial proceedings, as that would have banalized the horrifying testimonies related by the witnesses into another feature of entertainment, to be watched, as he says, while munching an apple. Yet he agrees that forcing these testimonies into people's homes might have prevented four million Frenchmen from voting for Le Pen, who claimed that the existence of the concentration camps was not "revealed truth" since "historians debate these questions" (p. 70). It is with these testimonies, as recorded for the Fortunoff Video Archives for Holocaust Testimonies at Yale University and analyzed with great sensitivity and understanding by Lawrence L. Langer in his book *Holocaust Testimonies*, that we come full circle to the facts of the matter yet remain within the realm of memory, of confused, bewildering personal tales, whose meaning and significance is doubted even by those who are daily compelled to relive them.

Two elements in this remarkable book stand out clearly. The first is that it is memory that makes the facts of the Holocaust (such as those so well analyzed by Browning) belong uniquely to that event and not to any other conceivable historical occurrence. This can be grasped only from the personal accounts of the survivors. No other historical source can replace these "ruins of memory"; nothing can bring us closer to comprehending (and realizing our inability fully to comprehend) the experience of the victims and thereby the essence of the event.

Second, however, is the horrifying realization, precisely through these tormented, shattered recollections, that the event lacks all coherence, that it has left a vacuum both in the minds of the survivors and in the history of humanity, that it was, indeed, meaningless, that it has signified nothing, taught us nothing, brought us no profound truth or clarity. It has left a gaping, black, empty hole.

This is a profoundly disturbing finding. The thought that such immense destruction of lives could have left things precisely as they were before appears as the act of a mad wizard.[43] How is it possible that everything was for nothing, all the suffering and bloodshed and loss? We rebel against the thought, we scramble for meanings and interpretations, at times we feel that perhaps something has been learned, at least some lesson that will help us prevent a recurrence of the event. But when we read Langer's book we are thrown back into the void. If Finkielkraut's is a melancholy contemplation on the intellectual condition of our post-Holocaust world, Langer's is an acute analysis of the psychological landscape of our society, both of the victims and of the amorphous interviewers, these shadows moving behind the camera, whose questions and comments, fears and anxieties, disbeliefs and embarrassed silences make us realize that nothing has been learned.

The victims too are groping for meaning. But they repeatedly find themselves hampered both in explaining their experiences to others and, what is worse, in understanding them themselves, for this condition of bewilderment creates a constant inner conflict between the post-event-self, seeking to understand, and the in-event-self that could not understand then and therefore cannot transmit any meaning into the future.

This book ought to have an instantaneously humbling effect on anyone who has ever resorted to generalities and platitudes about the Holocaust. Yet this is by now such an ingrained habit that, while the author criticizes the vocabulary of "redeeming" and "salvation" used in popular representations of the Holocaust (pp. 1–2), he too occasionally slips into a similar mode, calling on us to "embrace the legacy of these testimonies, which bear witness to the simultaneous destruction *and* survival of European Jewry" (p. 38). A jarring note—especially following Langer's assertion that many of the survivors feel dead or still trapped in their Holocaust existence or, indeed, fear they are transmitting this very feeling on to their own children. Nor would I know how to "embrace the legacy" of such memories. Can we embrace the nightmare of another who, on waking, realized that the nightmare was reality?

Langer divides his book into several chapters, though many of the themes he introduces in one chapter reappear later on. In "Deep Memory" he tries to understand the sense of disconnection between the memory of the experience and the knowledge that it was actually experienced by the same person who remembers it now. This is made doubly difficult for the viewer of the videotaped interview, because, as Langer says, "the testimonies are not based on common experience or an imaginable past." Hence, "we need to search for the inner principle of *in*coherence that makes these testimonies accessible to us" (pp. 16–17). This means that while the survivors are searching for a connection with their own past (person), the viewer is trying to follow them on their often crooked path into an incoherent past. Meanwhile, the survivors constantly ask themselves "whether *any*thing can be meaningfully conveyed" in view of "the difficulty of narrating, from the context of normality *now*, the nature of the abnormality *then*" (pp. 21–22). The difficulty of reaching into this "deep memory" also has to do with "*un*heroic gestures" (p. 26) and the effort needed by both the survivor and the viewer to accept that moral distinctions crumble under the immense weight of the event. Perhaps even worse, the testimonies reveal that "the *prepared* will or intelligence was not necessarily more effective," and hence that courageous acts, instead of ending in rescue, could bring about catastrophe. Much as we resist this notion, we find that often "belief in choice betrayed the victim and turned out to be an illusion" (pp. 32–33).

In "Anguished Memory" Langer attempts to delve deeper into the problem of the "divided self," the difficulty of perceiving the reality of the story *as* reality, a barrier felt even by the survivors themselves, who often claim not to be able to believe their own stories. Using Maurice Blanchot's terminology,[44] Langer notes that in the face of the "impossible real" all of us, with the exception of the survivors, have an "un-story" to tell, that which "escapes quotation and which memory does not recall." The survivors' "effort to recapture through memory what, because of the impossibility of its content, has already (for us) fallen outside memory, risks estranging the audience they seek to inform." Langer finds Blanchot's statement that "the disaster always takes place after having taken place" a precise definition of oral testimony, and accepts his conclusion that consequently "there cannot possibly be any experience of it." Hence, according to Langer, anguished memory "imprisons the consciousness it should be liberating," because the survivors in these oral testimonies are concerned primarily with "a sense of the past in the present" (pp. 39–40). But unlike the ancient Jewish commemoration of liberation from slavery,[45] *that* past, which will not go away, is at the same time firmly rooted in its own specific context of destruction. It is ever present, yet it cannot be cut loose from its annihilating environment, it cannot be instrumentalized (p. 48). Survivors who had lost families and rebuilt their lives after the war are often imbued with a sense of having already died once and of having transmitted that sense to their new families (pp. 49–50).

Langer acutely notes that if for us, perhaps, silence would be better, because it would spare us the pain of speaking about the Holocaust, that is not the case with the survivors, for whom *not* telling their story would not ease the pain of the remembered experience. As one witness says, "I feel my head is filled with garbage; all these images, you know, and sounds, and my nostrils are filled with the stench of burning flesh . . . and we have these . . . these double lives" (pp. 52–54). Indeed, some of the testimonies reveal a memory of desperate attempts to remember what normality had been, and how far away normality seemed, and the memory of those attempts makes present normality appear all the more fragile and insecure (p. 55). Hence, just as Finkielkraut has insisted, the refusal of witnesses to speak is rooted in the "belief that the very story you try to tell drives off the audience you seek to capture," and in "the further suspicion that the story you tell *cannot* be precisely the story as it happened. Reluctance to speak has little to do with *preference* for silence" (p. 61). Typically, when one survivor claims that she was saved through "luck" and "stupidity," her interviewers insist that what *actually* saved her was "pluck" and "guts," which seems to them the "desired" interpretation (p. 64).

The "uncomfortable" issues raised by witnesses are explored in the next chapter, "Humiliated Memory," the uncovered details of which, contends Langer, "dispute the claim still advanced by many commentators that the invincible human spirit provided an armor invulnerable to Nazi assaults against the self" (p. 77). In fact, "humiliated memory" "forces us into an unnatural relation with the past, because the 'knowledge' it imparts crushes the spirit and frustrates the incentive to renewal" (p. 79). For while we, as well as the survivors, long for a narrative with a closure, "Humiliated memory is defeated by its own efforts to rescue itself from the cul-de-sac of . . . uncompensated and uncompensatable loss," and the attempt to transform "personal stories of unredeemable atrocity back into triumphal accounts of survival" are shown to be futile, ending without closure, or at least without one "that feeds on the need for the realization of prior ethical ideals" (pp. 109–110).[46]

The problem is accentuated by what Langer calls "Tainted Memory," whereby the witnesses themselves "are bewildered by the disequilibrium between the impromptu self, which followed impulse in order to stay alive" (even if its actions were contrary to "normal" ethical norms), "and memories of the dignified life that was the goal of their prewar existence and continues as their aim today" (p. 140). As one witness says: "No no, everything that happened destroyed part of me. I was dying slowly. Piece by piece. I built a new family. . . . Life was one big hell even after the war. So you make believe that you go on. . . . You can't be normal. As a matter of fact, I think that we are not normal because we are normal" (pp. 140–41). Another witness insists that the story "can only be told . . . but it cannot be felt, it cannot be experienced. *I* cannot even experience it" (p. 142). Yet Langer quite rightly points out that "guilt, both as label and concept, is totally inadequate and indeed misleading as a description of the internal discomfort of surviving victims," since here we have no conventional loss of innocence, but one for which the victims can find no principle of rationalization in either time or memory: "Nothing exists to redeem the moment they recall, and to their dismay, nothing exists to redeem them as they recall it" (p. 144).[47] Hence "Tainted memory, memory of that impromptu self unrecognizable even through the act of mental memory, is a monument to ruin rather than reconstruction." This is, indeed, as Langer puts it, "one of the most melancholy legacies in the subtexts of these testimonies" (pp. 145–46).

In the last chapter of his book, "Unheroic Memory," Langer assaults the mythology and clichés that have evolved around human behavior in the Holocaust. For him, "The pretense that from the wreckage of mass murder we can salvage a tribute to the victory of the human spirit is a version of Holocaust reality more necessary than true" (p. 165). The enormity of the crime creates our need (as spectators) for heroism. But it is precisely this "chronicle of atrocities" that undermines our attempt to "normalize" the event. Yet it would be absurd to feel "rescued and consoled" by such notions, "which seek to restore us to the world of the familiar, of personal honor and family unity," for this would have to rely on the assumption that "the destruction of European Jewry signified little more than a temporary foray against the bulwarks of civilization." The testimony of the witnesses, insists Langer, teaches us the *impossibility* of reconciliation, and thus we are compelled to accept "that an unreconciled understanding has a meaning and a value of its own, one of the most disruptive being that violence, passivity, and indifference are *natural* and *unsurprising* expressions of the human will under certain circumstances" (pp. 167–68).

In stark contradiction to accepted notions of liberation, Langer points out that for many survivors survival was synonymous with *deprival*, as they realized that they were the only ones left of their families and communities and, moreover, that they themselves had not only lived through, but also "died through," the event. He similarly rejects the simplicity of the vocabulary of heroism during, and recovery after the event, which in no way corresponds to the manner in which the Holocaust, and its memory, is reflected in the testimonies. Attempts to rejoice at the prospect of the future are constantly undermined by the memory of the past, which in the camps constituted a loss of continuity with the future, a condition in which "there is no tomorrow" (pp. 172–73). In Langer's powerful phrase: "Two clocks dominate the landscape of Holocaust testimonies, a time clock (ticking from then to now) and a space clock (ticking from there to here)" (p. 174). Here the vocabulary of survival is insufficient, since the victims had to bend all their efforts to *staying alive*, from one moment to the next, without a thought of the future, because, as one witness says, the future meant tomorrow, and tomorrow meant death (p. 175). Hence liberation does not bring happiness, and survival is paid for by the loss of the *memory* of innocence. As one witness put it: "I've got something always in the back of my mind which is like a double existence. . . . I live life before and life now [and that life before] is something entirely different from what we have now, and I don't think I can ever forget that" (p. 189).

Langer concludes that "the Holocaust does little to confirm theories of moral reality but much to question the reality of moral theories." Thus, the testimonies of the survivors, the stories of individual psychology, are linked with the larger moral context of the event. It is not only the survivors who cannot be liberated from the Holocaust. For Philip K., the Holocaust is "my skin. This is not a coat. You can't take it off." But it is not only his personal prison, for he knows that "we have lost. We'll never recover what was lost. We can't even assess what was lost. . . . The world lost. . . . And yet we won, we're going on." The victory is survival. But, as Philip K. concludes, "there are as many ways of surviving survival as there have been to survive" (p. 205).

IV. Epilogue: Satan's Playground

For most of his post-Auschwitz life, Primo Levi tried to fulfil the task he had set himself of preserving the truth and memory of the Holocaust and deriving a humanistic, positive message from its horrors. Increasingly disturbed by the distortions of both history and memory, apology and representation, fiction and imagination, Levi fought an unrelenting battle for truth and humanism, and against lies and denial. He also appears to have fought an increasingly hopeless battle against himself. For while he saw attempts at relativizing the Holocaust as pernicious (and these, as he well knew, date back to the event itself, rather than being a new idea of the 1980s as their recent proponents have claimed), his own doubts about the possibility of either explaining the event, representing it truthfully, or indeed drawing any positive conclusions from it for the future of humanity seem to have grown just as the chronological distance from Auschwitz increased. Levi insisted that the history of the Third Reich could be "reread as a war against memory, an Orwellian falsification of memory, falsification of reality, negation of reality,"[48] and he asked himself with growing insistence whether "we who have returned" have "been able to understand and make others understand our experience?"[49] His humanistic, positivistic urge compelled him to answer this question affirmatively, or at least to stress the potential of a positive reply. But his experience, his interaction with the world and with his innermost self constantly defied that resolution. Levi rejected arguments, such as the Italian film director Liliana Cavani's, that "We are all victims or murderers, and we accept these roles voluntarily."[50] Indeed, he juxtaposed this position with the attempt of the Nazis "to shift onto others— specifically, the victims—the burden of guilt, so that they were deprived of even the solace of innocence," and their assurance that "We, the master race, are your destroyers, but you are no better than we are; if we so wish, and we do so wish, we can destroy not only your bodies but also your souls, just as we have destroyed ours."[51] Yet Levi was increasingly beset by precisely that pessimism and ambiguity exploited by those he condemned, the relativizers and the representers of the Holocaust as a general human condition. Observing the case of Rumkowski, the autocratic elder of the Lodz ghetto, he concluded that "we are all mirrored in Rumkowski, his ambiguity is ours, it is our second nature, we hybrids molded from clay and spirit. His fever is ours, the fever of Western civilization that 'descends into hell with trumpets and drums'." Indeed, he wrote, we, like Rumkowski, "come to terms with power, forgetting that we are all in the ghetto, that the ghetto is walled in, that outside the ghetto reign the lords of death, and that close by the train is waiting."[52]

This Pascalian image of humanity, this extension of the "concentrationary universe" to the whole of humanity, is the disturbing note struck by Levi in his last essays, one that denies the truth of liberation and insists on the perpetual imprisonment of us all in the madness of mutual destruction. "In the majority of cases," he writes, "the hour of liberation was neither joyful nor lighthearted. For most it occurred against a tragic background of destruction, slaughter, and suffering . . . which seemed definitive, past cure. . . . Leaving the past behind was a delight for only a few fortunate beings . . . almost always it coincided with a phase of anguish."[53] When, upon returning from Auschwitz, Levi was told by a friend that his survival was the work of Providence, rather than, as he maintained, the result of chance, he became filled with doubt: "I might be alive in the place of another, at the expense of another; I might have usurped, that is, in fact, killed. . . . The worst survived, that is, the fittest; the best all died." "I felt innocent," he writes, "yes, but enrolled among the saved and therefore in permanent search of a justification." Levi's friend told him that he had survived to bear witness, and "I have done so, as best I could." And yet he was haunted by "the thought that this testifying of mine could by itself gain for me the privilege of surviving . . . because I cannot see any proportion between the privilege and its outcome." After years of writing and reading others' testimonies, Levi concluded that "we, the survivors, are not the true witnesses," but rather "an anomalous minority" that "did not touch bottom." The dead "are the rule, we are the exception."[54] But while this was a cause for shame, among the victims there was a greater "remorse, shame, and pain for the misdeeds that others and not they had committed, in which they felt involved, because they sensed that what had happened around them and in their presence, and in them, was irrevocable." Hence his terrifying conclusion that this enormity could "Never again . . . be cleansed; it would prove that man, the human species—we, in short—had the potential to construct an infinite enormity of pain, and that pain is the only force created from nothing, without cost and without effort."[55]

It must be stressed that shame is not guilt. Levi feels shame, for himself, for the survivors, the victims, the perpetrators; for humanity. Most of all, he fears for the world. For the Holocaust "happened, therefore it can happen again: this is the core of what I have to say." His humanistic instinct tells him that "Satan is not necessary," but he acknowledges that "many signs lead us to think of a genealogy of today's violence that branches out precisely from the violence that was dominant in Hitler's Germany." While "even in the midst of the insensate slaughter of World War I there survived the traits of reciprocal respect between the antagonists, a vestige of humanity toward prisoners and unarmed citizens," under Nazism the "destruction of a people and a civilization was proven to be possible and desirable both in itself and as an instrument of rule." And since then he writes, "Many new tyrants have kept in their drawers Adolf Hitler's *Mein Kampf*: with a few changes perhaps, and the substitution of a few names, it can still come in handy."[56]

This is the terrible message of the most humanistic of all survivors; that if there is any meaning to this tale, if there is anything to be learned from all the facts and memories, reconstructions, and interpretation, it is only this: that "Satan is not necessary," not because, as Levi so hopelessly wishes, humanity can do without violence, but rather because having once played the Devil's game, it is now doomed to play it over and over again, in an endless variety of locations and forms. For the moral of the idiot's tale is that murder is already in our midst.

Intellectuals on Auschwitz: Memory, History, and Truth

When I came / From Circe at last . . . / No tenderness
. . . nor pity . . . / nor . . . wedded love . . . / Could
have conquered in me the restless itch to rove/And
rummage through the world exploring it, / All
human worth and wickedness to prove. / So on the
deep and open sea I set/Forth . . . / I and my fellows
were grown old and tardy . . . / . . . that none should
prove so hardy / To venture the uncharted distances
. . . / 'Brothers,' said I . . . / Think of your breed; for
brutish ignorance / Your mettle was not made; you
were made men, / To follow after knowledge and
excellence.' . . . / Then we rejoiced; but soon we had
to weep, / For out of the unknown land there blew
foul weather, / And a whirlwind struck the forepart
of the ship; . . . / And over our heads the hollow seas
closed up."[1]

The urge to write this chapter can be traced back to several causes. A number of scholarly/polemical discussions on the difficulties with memory and forgetting, representation and commemoration of the Holocaust prompted me to attempt to articulate my thoughts on the subject and clarify to myself what it was that so disturbed me in those seemingly reasonable and detached ruminations.[2] Teaching a course on the Holocaust brought me once more face to face with the familiar, yet still jarring realization that neither teachers nor students, nor for that matter anyone who had either experienced it or studied it from some geographical or chronological distance could quite grasp the essence of the Holocaust or make it understandable to others.[3] Always remaining from without, on the margins of experience and comprehension, one was never actually speaking of the thing itself, one never dared (or found oneself unable) to put one's finger on the heart of the matter. Was this due to the elusive nature of the matter, or to the fears aroused in us by the prospect of direct confrontation? This predilection for the indirect or oblique approach could also be observed in some scholarly gatherings and subsequent publications, whether they consisted of the more down-to-earth variety of scholars or of those more inclined toward contemporary literary criticism.[4]

Finally, there were some texts by survivors, and especially those by Jean Améry and Primo Levi.[5] It was the immense gap between their thoughts on the experience and phenomenon of Auschwitz and those of the intellectual and academic community that suggested a deeper and more complex relationship, indeed, a multifaceted obstacle or disturbance, whose presence was being felt but not fully acknowledged, and whose origins and implications might reveal to us some failure in communication and understanding, an emotional block springing from an abyss of anxiety, that must be investigated, however little hope we may have of reaching its roots and exposing it fully to light.

In the larger background I have detected in myself a growing unease with the postwar and, more recently, the so-called postmodern representations of the Holocaust (and by implication also of fascism, war, and numerous other forms of violence), as well as with the choice of focus, tone, and methodology evident in the literary-intellectual discourse on Auschwitz and in the new (or not so new) historiographical trends emerging especially, but by no means exclusively, from Germany. Conversations with survivors (many of whom have only lately become capable of speaking about their experiences), on the one hand, and recent manifestations of right-wing, xenophobic sentiments in Germany, on the other, along with the intensification of political abuses of the Holocaust in commemoration and demagogy, have greatly contributed to the urge to investigate the links between these seemingly unrelated phenomena that nevertheless all had one theme in common—namely, mass, industrial murder in the heart of Western civilization. Indeed, the experience of simultaneously teaching a course on German history demonstrated how difficult it was to bridge the gap between *that* and Auschwitz. Yet I have been plagued by the constant, nagging inability to point out what was the reason for my unease, what was actually wrong with the recent treatment of the Holocaust, and what were the alternatives. If there was one common denominator here, I felt, it was the widespread fascination, indeed the obsession, with perversity and obscenity, inhumanity and criminality, aggression and horror. Yet this was no fanatic fascination, no savage obsession; rather, it revealed a strange, but not wholly unfamiliar mixture of cool aesthetic pleasure and mild nausea at being confronted (or choosing to be confronted) with a highly stylized form of these phenomena, recreated on the page or in the studio in a manner assured to make them appear attractive, stimulating, *interesting*.[6] This was disturbing: an obsession with fascism and all its attributes whose psychological and intellectual motivations bore an uncanny resemblance to those that had accompanied the phenomenon itself.

The following cannot claim to be anything more than some reflections by one who until recently has avoided writing directly on the Holocaust. Belonging to a generation born after the event, I do not claim to profit from this biological coincidence as Helmut Kohl and many of his younger compatriots have done. Indeed, I am conscious of being anything but unscathed by the Shoah, whether personally, intellectually, politically, or morally. Moreover, I clearly realize that I cannot hope to understand the heart of darkness any better than the next person, and that every attempt to illuminate it must confront the horrifying tendency of the event to pollute and swallow any ray of light. Nevertheless, for us there is only the trying. By posing some questions and tying together some issues, I hope to point toward new paths of inquiry both regarding the Holocaust itself and its impact on our present intellectual, moral, and political predicament. Indeed, I believe that a critique of the intellectual discourse on and the historiography of the Holocaust can extend far beyond the limits of the death camps and encompass the general problems we face today in writing on the history of humanity and in seeking to distil its meaning for our own culture and society. For however small our individual contribution may be, this is, or should be, the task of the intellectual.

I. The Surfeit of Memory and the Uses of Forgetting

There seems to be a new trend, which at a second glance proves to be a rather old one, to remove the Holocaust from our view (or at least shift it aside a little) with the argument that it obscures our perception and prevents us from a more vivid understanding of the real issues and cardinal problems of the epoch in which we are living.[7] This view distinguishes itself from what is claimed to have been the dominant argument, or, rather, persuasion previously—namely, that the Holocaust is an ineffable, incomprehensible, and therefore somewhat ahistorical event. According to an extreme version of this view, the Holocaust is precisely that, a vast sacrificial act somehow meant to purge the world of evil by exercising it to the greatest conceivable degree; the Jewish people sacrificing itself for the ultimate good of humanity, just as Jesus had done two thousand years before; a sort of insanely (or Godly) logical circle finally closed, necessarily containing some kind of message to humanity and civilization, even if we wretched humans may not yet be capable of deciphering its meaning.[8] Conversely, the critics of this eschatological view contend with some degree of complacency that although they can sympathize with its proponents, they themselves apply more rational, scientific, and detached instruments to explain and put into perspective this historical event just like any other.[9] The Holocaust, then, is being pulled apart by two contending camps, either as a core event of the twentieth century, if not indeed of Western civilization or even humanity as a whole, with the tragic Jewish fate as its centerpiece, a culmination of (anti-Jewish) persecution throughout the ages and of the unfolding of divine will;[10] or as a block that distorts and obscures our view of the past and our hopes, plans, and dreams of the future, that relegates all other barbarities and achievements to a secondary place, that overemphasizes the Jewish experience, human depravity, and ineffable (divine or Satanic) forces, that is backward, theological, emotional, nationalist, narrow-minded, and finally anti-humanistic, and which therefore must absolutely be removed.[11]

Removed where? To forgetfulness. Not to be repressed, but instead to be consciously, rationally put into its proper context and perspective, with the appropriate scholarly tools ensuring us of good judgment, minimizing the weight of emotion and sensation, giving everyone their just historical due.[12]

Yet, strangely, there is a measure of impatience precisely among the proponents of the balanced and detached scholarly approach. This impatience is

reflected both in the speed with which they would like to bring about that transformation of approaches they so persuasively propagate, and in their tendency
to oversimplify the views they contend to be confronting. For their opponents
are neither made of one mold, nor, for that very reason, can they be removed
by the allegedly opposing arguments of scholarship, balance, and objectivity.
Indeed, by presenting the other side as a monolithic body of opinion (or emotion), the proponents of the contextualized view are themselves paradoxically
forced together and—mostly very much against their will and better judgment—are found sharing their scholarly abodes with very strange bedfellows
indeed.[13]

Another characteristic of the discussion is that both survivors and scholarly critics seem to feel the urgency of their approaching demise. This of course
brings to mind other aspects of the relationship between time, age, and death
in confronting the Holocaust: arguments concerning the chronological distance
between crimes committed and judgment handed down as regards the perpetrators; the effect of time on retelling their experiences, or, conversely, on their
inability to go on living and consequent acts of suicide, as regards the survivors; the political legitimation time seemingly brings to German politicians,
identity, and aspirations; and the effects of historical distance on scholarship.
But, at this point, historians seem to be torn between the scholarly benefits of
time, on the one hand, and its far less merciful effects on the individual. And
it is here that we find that some of the most eloquent promoters of forgetting
belong to the generation of both the perpetrators and the (more often than
not potential) victims, that is, to those who presumably still retain vivid personal memories of the period.[14] Hence we, who cannot remember, are urged
to recognize the merits of forgetting by those who cannot forget—all this with
a sense of urgency springing from the realization that soon they will no longer
be there to remember and may themselves thereafter be forgotten.[15]

Now the argument of the surfeit of memory is problematic on a number of
counts. For one thing, it seems to follow too closely on the heels of other sensationalist theses, such as the pronouncement of the end of history and the
assertion regarding the arrival of the post-national age, both of which must now
come to terms with the melancholy restaging of pre-1914 nationalist, ethnic,
and religious hatreds and passions. The same can be said about the strange
revival of the idea of forgetting, so common immediately after the affair, at a
time when it at least had the merit of helping both Jews and Germans to go
about the business of reconstructing their lives;[16] for now, very few people
remember anyway. It is only among select communities that memory, both
personal and historical, still plays a major role, and it is to them that one should
address oneself, rather than to some general audience that does not remember what it is being asked to forget. If there is a surfeit of memory, if there is a
need to forget, it is in three communities, namely, the relatively limited intel-
lectual/academic, often Jewish and left-liberal community in the United States;
the much wider scholarly, intellectual, media, and political circles in Germany;
and the corresponding, and perhaps locally even more influential groups in
Israel.

To claim that there is a surfeit of memory of the Holocaust in the United States is highly debatable. Most Americans have only the vaguest possible notion of what the Holocaust was about.[17] Indeed, Americans are arguably the least well-informed people in the West on the Holocaust, Nazism, or, for that matter, the history of this (or any other) century. The Holocaust has also played a relatively minor role in American politics and foreign policy, though in this case it was given ample rhetorical consideration. Neither the decision to rearm Germany nor the decision to support Israel militarily have anything more than the most tenuous connection with the former's Nazi past and the latter's status as the political representative of its victims. Hence I would argue that it is wholly gratuitous to call for a new campaign of forgetting as regards a community notorious for the weakness of its historical memory.

When speaking of the Jewish community in the United States, the picture is naturally very different. However, even here I would argue that one has to differentiate between various groups. The Jewish orthodox community is neither influenced by any of the debates on memory and forgetting, nor does it seek an explanation for the Holocaust. On the other extreme, it would seem that not a small portion of the Jewish-American population feels only very loosely tied to Jewish experience and history, and is generally just as ignorant of the European past as the gentiles. This leaves us with the intelligentsia, a group whose discourse is really directed to its own members, the international scholarly and intellectual community, and most specifically to Germans and Israelis. As such, I feel that this discourse must be examined together with similar discourses in Germany and Israel, as well as among scholars of the period and intellectuals involved in writing on it.

The debate on the Holocaust tends to make use of a large number of commonly accepted but often either inaccurate or false assumptions. In what follows, I will therefore try to point out some problems relevant to the question of memory and history, forgetting and repressing, political abuse and commemoration, in Germany and Israel. I will then turn to the question of the representation of the Holocaust and to the scholarly, literary, and philosophical discourse on this theme.

II. The *Historikerstreit* and the Importance of Memory

The German historians' controversy has been relegated to the status of a "mere" political debate without any scholarly merit.[18] I would like to argue that the wider implications and repercussions of the *Historikerstreit* can only now be properly understood. Leaving academic rivalries and party politics aside, the deep-seated motivations and sentiments of German scholars manifested in the debate can now be seen to have had a major impact both on the discourse on history, memory, and identity in Germany and on the historical reevaluation of Nazism and the Holocaust. In another sense, the *Historikerstreit* clearly demonstrated the inability to make precisely those distinctions between detached scholarly pursuits, ideological persuasion, and personal memories and experience that some (if not most) of its participants had demanded.

Unlike the United States, Germany is a nation in which memory and history have always played a major role, at least since the beginning of the previous century. For a national culture so deeply attached to history the events of 1933–45 are obviously a seemingly insurmountable obstacle in the way of reconstructing both personal and national identity, both the political organization of the country and the scholarly analysis of past and present. Hence the calls for a more contextualized view of Hitler's regime presented in the mid-1980s as heralding a new approach to the past were in fact anything but new; the comparisons of German barbarism with other nations' brutalities and atrocities were current even in the Third Reich itself, serving as a legitimizing element and generating even greater destructive and nihilistic passions.[19]

Memory, as we all recognize, is elusive and ambiguous. Politicians have always relied on the shortness of people's memories. When some German scholars claimed less than ten years ago that it was time to cease treating the Third Reich as consisting first and foremost of Auschwitz, and that one should turn to other, no less important aspects of this period, an impression was created that indeed up to that point most historians had concerned themselves with the "Final Solution" to the exclusion of everything else.[20] Yet the same arguments were heard twenty years previously, despite the fact that even then a large body of research on many other facets of the Nazi regime already existed, while the scholarship on the Holocaust, especially in Germany, was anything but predominant or particularly impressive.[21] The wish to shift the emphasis was therefore not based on a real need to cease an obsessive preoccupation with the "Final Solution," but rather on the personal discomfort, the scholarly difficulties, and the political/ideological implications of coming to terms with this phenomenon in the first place. There was here once more an impatience with the necessity of confronting what one wished to do away with, rationalized by the perceived need to stop doing what had in fact been done only to a very limited degree in the past.

Many German historians involved in the *Historikerstreit* had very vivid memories of the period they now wished to historicize. They had internalized the period and now, in their late middle-age, those events came back to haunt them. They wished to understand that past, for, after all, those still were, at least in the biological sense, the best years of their lives. And yet they did not wish the history that was so much part of their formative years to consist only of the darkest aspects of Nazi rule, those very aspects to whose study they themselves had contributed so much. Thus, they turned to the more positive sides of the period: to resistance, nonconformity, finally to everyday life.[22] This direction of research was initially motivated or legitimized by the worthy aim of doing away with the conservative presentation of the Nazi regime as a brutal dictatorship ruled by a criminal clique with no relevance for German society or history as a whole. However, it soon transpired that once we investigate the experience of the common man and woman, we discover that even during abnormal times most people continue to live normal lives. The conclusion to be drawn could have been, of course, that this was precisely what was abnormal in Nazi society—namely, that people continued their normal existence under a terroristic and murderous regime whose actions were wholly or partly known to most people. But this was not always the conclusion drawn by these scholars; rather, some saw in their findings proof of some form of resistance to the regime, that is, that by living normally, people had refused to adopt the ideological fanaticism urged on them by the regime, and even, at times, made demands on the regime (such as the workers),[23] refused to carry out some of its orders (such as Catholic school teachers),[24] or adopted some forms of youthful nonconformity such as listening and dancing to forbidden music.[25] That this sort of resistance did not seem at any point to threaten the regime—indeed, that in most cases the same people who "resisted" also collaborated—was of course recognized, and yet one was left with a much more positive impression of German society under Nazism. And, naturally, when speaking of the *Alltagsgeschichte* of the simple German citizen, one did not speak of the "concentrationary universe" erected by the regime elsewhere.[26] Thus, a separation of existences was created; there was German history and there was the history of the victims of Nazism, or, as it was perceived both by Germans and Jews, Jewish history. Similarly, there was German memory (finally repossessed, to his own satisfaction, by Edgar Reitz in his film *Heimat*),[27] and there was Jewish memory (brought to us through Claude Lanzmann's *Shoah*). Moreover, while German memory got its due, often via the most respectable academic circles and most gifted artists, Jewish memory was condemned by both German and non-German, often also Jewish, scholars as constituting a sentimental, mythical obstruction to the understanding of the past.[28]

The repercussions of the *Historikerstreit* can be seen, for instance, in certain recent works by some younger German scholars who had no personal exposure to Nazism. Interestingly, however, they seem to have picked up and further developed ideas first proposed by their older colleagues. Among the more controversial is the theory that presents the Nazi regime as a modernizing agent in German history.[29] This is not the same argument raised some two decades ago—that the destruction brought on Germany by Hitler's war had compelled material and social reconstruction on a new and much more modern basis.[30] Rather, this is a positive view of some elements of Nazism, its industries, its social policies and legislation, its technological obsessions, its mobilization of women, and so forth. This relates to the recent appeals for a different periodization of German history, according to which the dates 1933–45 are obviously mere indications of political and military events, whereas most Germans would have considered the period between 1929–49 as much more crucial to their existence.[31] For, while the victims of the regime were naturally concerned with the political periodization, the majority of Germans remember the past as divided into the bad years of 1929–35 (economic depression and unemployment), the good years of 1935–41 (economic expansion and conquest), the catastrophe of 1941–49 (military defeats and economic devastation), and finally the economic miracle of the 1950s.[32] This division has the added merit of stretching into the present, as the argument is raised that the time has arrived to turn Germany's economic might into political clout.

To be sure, the modernizing theory of Nazism consistently ignores the most obvious contribution of the Third Reich to modernization, namely, mass, industrial murder. For while the Nazi contribution to the formulation of postwar German social policies, for instance, is debatable, the example given by the Nazi regime as to the ability of a modern state to destroy human lives with the same techniques used by modern industry, employing the bureaucratic apparatus readily available to any modern state, is one that can hardly be ignored. Because although history may not repeat itself, it is rare that anything introduced to human history is not used again. Whether the Holocaust was unique or not in terms of its precedents is one question; whether it will remain so is quite another.

The modernization theory, which has other aspects to it referring to the decision on the "Final Solution" that cannot be discussed here,[33] very much concerns German memory of, as well as wishful thinking on, the past. Memory and history are here closely bound, and we can extricate one from the other only with extreme care, if we do not wish to distort the outcome of the operation. For this reason, too, arguments regarding the surfeit of memory in Germany must come to terms with recent political events in that country. For while there is, of course, a memory of Nazism in Germany, what that memory consists of is quite a different matter. If some view Nazism as a past to be forgotten, perhaps because they remember its reality all too well, others would like to resurrect it because, lacking a personal memory of its horrors, they have reconstructed it in their minds as something horribly fascinating, anarchic, nihilistic, as well as containing the magic formula of bringing full employment, freedom from foreign influence, and national pride. How could some German youngsters today have constructed such an image of Nazism for themselves? Is this the kind of past that won't go away, that will keep haunting Germany (and its victims)?

Hence the calls for separating memory and history are based on a far too simplistic presentation of the issues involved.[34] First, because as historians we should know that memory plays a role in everything we do, think, or write, just as it did for the subjects of our research. Second, because the critics of memory do not in fact want to do away with it, but rather recommend a different *kind* of memory, of different *subjects*, and remembering in different *ways*. Hence the debate is in fact not at all on more or less memory, but on the politics of memory. And once in the realm of politics, arguably anyone's politics is as good as anyone else's: some people want to remember Jews and concentration camps, others want to remember German soldiers and their defense of the West against Bolshevism; some study memory through personal accounts, others distribute questionnaires, others still conduct studies of oral history; some speak of collective memory, some of national memory, some of personal memory. Thus the manner in which we speak of memory betrays our political beliefs, just as our political beliefs are molded to a large extent by our memories.

III. Israel, Commemoration,
and the Normalization of Jewish Existence

The contention that Israel is strongly preoccupied, to some degree even obsessed, with the Holocaust, is undeniably true. Indeed, one could hardly expect things to be otherwise, considering the percentage of people living in Israel who have either personally experienced the Shoah, or whose family members survived the camps or perished in Nazi-occupied Europe. The question to be asked is, rather, how have the memory and history of the Holocaust, and the memory and history of Israel intermingled, and what are the results of this (potentially explosive) mixture? Clearly, this issue entails a wide array of psychological, sociological, and cultural dimensions, and retains a strongly emotional quality. Hence the simplistic portrayal of Israel as a society whose whole political culture and cultural identity are based on a manipulative commemoration of the Holocaust is somewhat off the mark. The argument that Zionism had found its legitimation in Nazism, that Israel owes its existence to the "Final Solution," that Israeli literary production offers a monolithic view of the proud, fighting Israeli as opposed to the Diaspora Jews who went like sheep to the slaughter, itself springs originally from assertions made by Israeli critics of what seemed to them the established view in that country in the 1960s, and even they had ignored quite different trends among the preceding literary generation. By now, the critics themselves are strongly identified with the political establishment and are in their turn under sustained attack from a younger generation of writers, poets, and playwrights.[35]

In point of fact, the obsession with the Holocaust in Israel has taken very different forms, especially over the last twenty-odd years. In a wide array of literary and artistic representations, Israelis have traced the complex, often disturbing connections between the Jewish experience in Europe and the Israeli experience in the Middle East. While in the past the dominant image was of the heroic Israeli, fighting against overwhelming numbers, and dying with a gun in his hand and the words "it is good to die for our land" on his lips, more recently the Israeli soldier has been represented as an occupier of another people (and in some of the more extreme versions made to appear as the equivalent of the Nazi), while the Palestinians have been portrayed as a persecuted and suppressed minority (with the implication, often adopted by the Palestinians themselves, that they are the contemporary equivalents of European Jewry).[36]

Conversely, the growing interest in the prewar Jewish existence in Europe finds increasing expression in Israeli intellectual life, literary representations, film, and university courses.[37] This of course reflects doubts about Israeli identity, as well as indicating the perceived need to connect Israel's short past with the much deeper roots of Jewish existence in Europe.[38] The early, so-called "synthetic" image of the Israeli, that heroic, handsome (somewhat Aryan-looking) youth who "was born from the sea,"[39] has been greatly complicated by growing anxiety about the present, skepticism about the future, and a sentimental longing for a vision of an idealized past. This has also been the occasion for, as well as one of the causes of, the meeting between grandchildren and grand-parents, the new willingness of the elderly to remember, and the new interest awakened in the young to listen to those memories. Hence the self-perception of young Israelis is ambivalent and in constant flux, as they view themselves both as rebels against a vanished past and as strongly, inseparably (and increasingly less unwillingly) rooted in it, both as descendents of a persecuted minority in Europe and presently as oppressors in their own land.[40] This is not a comfort-able, complacent attitude; rather it breeds tension, anger, frustration. But it does not reflect a simple, one-sided view of one's existence and makes for an inti-mate connection between memory and history, image and reality.

Nor can one accept the simplistic view of Israel as the epitome of the memorializing society, a nation that claims for itself a monopoly over the memory of the Holocaust as manifested in the Yad Vashem memorial and exhibit. For while the commemoration of the Day of Holocaust and Heroism (the official name of the Day of the Holocaust in Israel) has always been con-tentious in Israel, the Jewish state could hardly afford not to officially com-memorate the murder of European Jewry.[41] Moreover, here too one should note that the Israeli media, scholars, and intellectuals have recently subjected previously held beliefs to a harsh critique, stressing the blindness of the *Yishuv* (the Jewish community in Palestine before the foundation of the state of Israel) to events in Nazi-occupied Europe, and shedding light on the reception of the survivors in Palestine, who were perceived by the public as "typical," cowardly Diaspora Jews whose main task must be to become rapidly socialized by means of repressing their past and assuming a new, "healthy" Israeli identity.[42] Just as the cult of the heroic Israeli has been greatly modified, so too has that of the heroes of the Holocaust. Recently the notion of heroism has been extended to include not only armed resistance, but also the very fact of enduring the most inhuman conditions.[43]

To be sure, Israeli youths are constantly exposed to a discourse on the Holocaust that serves as part of their identity-formation. This may create an image of humanity, history, and survival one would have preferred to be able to deny, yet it is unavoidable. Hence the point is to observe modifications in this discourse, rather than simply see it as an excess of memory, memoriali-zation, and consequently biased history. The fact that this is indeed happen-ing gives one room for hope, particularly if we consider the fact that a society one of whose central historical experiences is an event such as the Holocaust cannot be entirely "normal."

Normality is the other side of the coin. Here we reach another, Israeli-centered discourse that is deeply rooted in turn-of-the-century Zionism and has miraculously survived the crucial events of this century without shedding some of its more pernicious aspects. Paradoxically, precisely because this view pre-sents the Diaspora Jew and the Israeli in radical opposition to each other, it is actually based on a complete avoidance of the Holocaust and its meaning. As such, although by now it is anything but a generally accepted opinion, it is of some interest in tracing the interplay of history, memory, and image in Israel.[44]

Zionism, like many other nationalist movements in the previous century, had to present a highly negative picture of the conditions it wished to transform so as to win adherents to its own ideology. For Zionism, this was the "abnormality" of Jewish existence in the Diaspora. This position was quite clearly related to the antisemitic rhetoric of the period. The Jew was presented as economically and socially parasitic, intellectually and physically degenerate, historically doomed. Borrowing both from the sociobiological and the Marxist discourses of late nineteenth-century Europe, the Zionists too spoke of the need to change both the material condition of the Jews and their physical constitution, to renew them mentally and biologically, to make them into a healthy race in mind and spirit, body and economic occupation.

Thus, Zionism strove to "normalize" the existence of the Jews by the creation of a national state. The notion of normalcy insinuates that the social and cultural life of the Jews in the Diaspora was "abnormal." It even seems that the Zionist image of the Jew confirmed antisemitic perceptions. Indeed, early Zionism accepted the seeming inevitability of antisemitism as inherent to the condition of statelessness. The affinity between antisemitic movements and Zionist intentions to concentrate the Jews in their own land made possible an ad hoc cooperation in the 1930s between Zionists and the Nazi regime concerning immigration from Germany to Palestine.[45] Moreover, among some Israeli intellectuals the early Zionist view of the "degenerate" Jews of the Diaspora persists to this day.[46] This perpetuation of an imagery that supposedly legitimizes the new, "normal" Jew in his homeland is clearly the result of both ignorance of the consequences such images had only fifty years ago and of a remarkable insensitivity produced by an unrelenting adherence to a political agenda. That such images are not the product of right-wing, revisionist circles, but rather of the Left, gives reason to pause before sketching a simplistic view of the effects of memory and its political abuses.[47] Let me repeat that this is not the predominant view, but rather one of several that are competing with each other in a society and a cultural environment still trying to come to terms with the events of the Holocaust and their meaning for Israeli existence.

Thus, memory and history, politics and prejudice, still play an important role both within Israeli society and in attitudes toward Israel and Jews abroad. The point is therefore not to appeal for a diminished preoccupation with memory, because such appeals will not and cannot have any effect on communities such as those of Germany and Israel that are understandably still obsessed with the past, but rather to try and understand what the interrelationship between memory and history is both on the personal and political level, as well as in scholarship and representation. For it is only by grasping the complexity of this phenomenon that we can enhance our insight into the political and cultural scene and perhaps begin to formulate our own intellectual and political response.[48]

IV. Representation and its Discontents

Ever since the end of the Second World War intellectuals have debated whether the Holocaust is at all representable, what are the motivations behind various representations of Auschwitz and to what extent such representations constitute an abuse of the historical truth and memory of the event. It has been said that figures such as Jean Améry, Primo Levi, and Paul Celan constantly wrote on their experiences so as to be able to (literally) keep body and soul together, and that finally their resistance broke down, leading them to suicide.[49] Yet this assertion hardly does justice to these figures or, for that matter, to many other survivors. Indeed, it seems to me to make a false distinction between those who write so as to rid themselves of a burden that otherwise would make their existence impossible and those who feel charged with a moral mission and direct their writing at the public. I see no reason to privilege one over the other. Writers who tend to be more inward-looking may well reflect on their personal experiences and question the understanding of such experiences and their wider implication both by themselves and by others; they can thereby fulfil also a social and moral function without becoming necessarily politicized. As for Levi and Améry (and in a different way also Celan), they stated quite unambiguously that the reason for their writing and the cause of their increasing despair had to do just as much with the political reality of the post-Holocaust world, perceived by them as constantly repeating at least some aspects of their own experiences in Auschwitz, as well as with the manner in which the horrors they had undergone were represented by artists, intellectuals, and politicians.[50] This is the important point: it was what happened after the Holocaust, when it became clear to the survivors that Auschwitz had not been the horror to end all horrors, but only signalled the beginning of a seemingly endless cycle of similar horrors (to which humanity was adapting itself with remarkable speed), which caused them such bottomless despair. And it was the newly emerging trends in representing their experiences in the Holocaust, which they saw not merely as being unfair to them, but perhaps more important as reflecting some fascination with extremity and with artificially recreating the most horror-filled situations so as to be able to observe them from the safety of one's armchair, that made them realize the extent to which Auschwitz was anything but the end, indeed merely the beginning of a new age.[51]

Jean Améry's collection of essays *At the Mind's Limits* consists not only, as the subtitle would suggest, of "contemplations by a survivor on Auschwitz and its realities," but is rather a series of melancholy ruminations on the situation of the intellectual as uprooted exile, as concentration camp inmate, and as a postwar voice feeling increasingly detached from the contemporary intellectual and cultural scene. It is, to my mind, the latter that is most painful and troubling, because Améry *wants* to communicate his experience, *wants* to draw conclusions from it and transmit them at least to the intellectual community, yet finds himself progressively isolated, misunderstood, marginalized, and finally rejected as a remnant of a past everyone is already trying to remold into a much more convenient, appropriately streamlined cast, one that would reflect the preoccupations of the postwar generation.[52] Many years after Auschwitz, Améry knows that millions of people are still suffering and dying in the most horrible ways all over the globe, and it is that which he cannot accept, the fact that Auschwitz and all its horrors did not even have the effect of mitigating the lot of posterity.

Anyone who reads Primo Levi's *Survival in Auschwitz* (an unhappy English rendering of the original Italian, *Is This a Man?*) should have no difficulties in recognizing that it *is* possible to represent the Holocaust. Having read several scholarly texts on the "Final Solution," my own students both in the United States and Israel agreed almost unanimously that it was only through Levi's memoir that they came close to understanding the experience of the individual in Auschwitz. And yet Levi himself was increasingly critical of his own account. As he wrote in his last published essays, *The Drowned and the Saved*, he had described life in the *Lager* from the position of one of the privileged, for it was only the privileged who had any chance at all of surviving.[53] Hence the vast majority, the "real" inmates who lacked any privileges, remained unrepresented. Moreover, Levi's late ruminations on Auschwitz are far darker and more ominous than the memoir written shortly after his return to Italy. In his essay "The Intellectual in Auschwitz," Levi comes to grips with Améry's forbidding visions of past and present. Intellectually, he refuses to agree with Améry, for during most of his post-Auschwitz existence Levi maintained an optimistic view of humanity. One must, and one could, retain one's humanity. This was the secret to survival, even if Levi's experience itself had given ample reason to qualify his belief. One must, and one could, learn from Auschwitz, draw the right conclusions (only, though, by knowing what happened there—hence the task Levi had set himself as informant) and thereby bring more humanity to the world. And one must not despair. Levi strongly objected to Améry's suicide, not on the personal level, but on the intellectual/moral one, that is, he rejected Améry's causes for despair. Yet his own late essays betray the same sort of despair, both concerning the veracity and fairness of his own depictions of the experience, the transmission of his experience in Auschwitz to a younger, uncomprehending generation, the political realities of the present, and, not least, the manner in which his experience was being represented.

Levi is very much concerned with what he has called "the gray zone," the regions where victims were also collaborators and where perpetrators could also show some signs of humanity. He looks into the "gray zone" with the eye of the humanist, he tries to derive comfort from the human element to be found even in the most brutal conditions, yet we somehow feel that the effect is quite the opposite. For as Levi himself says, the worst crime committed by the Nazis was to make the Jewish *Sonderkommandos* do their work for them in the gas chambers. Does Levi find a flicker of humanity even in the heart of darkness, or does he reveal the potential of barbarism even in the most humane? Initially, immediately after his release, his belief in humanity seems to have been greater than forty years after the event. What does this tell us about our reception of the survivors, our understanding of their existence, and the nature of the world we have built for ourselves with the benefit of knowing its barbaric potentials?

Whereas Levi and Améry do show that some sort of representation of the Holocaust is possible, there is little doubt that they rebel against much of what they see around them in postwar Europe. Levi clearly distinguished between his "gray zone" and Liliana Cavani's *The Night Porter* (1974). For him, the SS man who had shown a momentary compassion for the girl who survived the gassing is, nevertheless, a mass murderer who should be executed. He rebels against the allegedly intellectually stimulating zone of crime and sexual perversion, attraction and repulsion, subjugation and submission, so often exploited by filmmakers, and achieving such intellectual (and not so intellectual) popularity precisely due to its "dangerous" subject. This, to him, is abuse of the experience.[54]

There exists now a huge industry concerned with the representation of the Holocaust and its periphery, fascism, Nazism, and war, testifying to the morbid attraction to and fascination with the worst epoch in contemporary history. Our modern, or as some would have it, postmodern sensibilities seem no longer to be satisfied with simple, unambiguous images, and the alleged beauty of fascism, for which it itself had laid claim with such insistence, attracts the makers of filmic images and their viewers alike precisely because of the knowledge that behind that beauty lay the depths of horror and depravity. Hence such films as Luchino Visconti's *The Damned* (1969), Pier Paolo Pasolini's *Salo—The 120 Days of Sodom* (1975), Bernardo Bertolucci's *1900* (1976), Lina Wertmuller's *Seven Beauties* (1976), Hans Jürgen Syberberg's *Hitler, a Film from Germany* (1977), Rainer Werner Fassbinder's *Lili Marleen* (1981), and many more.[55] These are works whose message is as ambiguous as the sentiments they evoke in their viewers. They exploit our own mean instincts and then seem to blame us for possessing them; they fill us with anger, disgust, and frustration, yet we do not take our eyes off the screen. They shame and morally disarm us by making us accomplices to evil, at least as bystanders once removed. And they also sell very well since they possess the further ambiguous characteristic of attracting both intellectuals and professional peepers, both those of fine aesthetic sensibilities and individuals who like viewing brutalities, perversions, pain, and rape. They do not tell us much about the human experience under fascism, but rather about our own potential of being drawn to it. They are very much part of a relatively recent tendency toward detached, amoral, nonjudgmental, complacent, and yet highly dangerous morbid curiosity about extremity.

Yet this is not to say that the Holocaust is unrepresentable. Granted, memory can be abused. The German filmmaker Edgar Reitz vowed to undo the theft of German history allegedly committed by the American television series *Holocaust* and to "give it back" to his countrymen.[56] Hence his film *Heimat* (1984) spends sixteen hours telling us (or the Germans) what the *German memory* of the past is; predictably it hardly even mentions the Holocaust. Conversely, the French-Jewish filmmaker Claude Lanzmann produced his own eight-hour reconstruction of the Jewish memory of the Holocaust, in which he intentionally avoided using any German newsreels or other film material of the period, which obviously formed no part of the Jewish memory and presented the Jews as the Germans saw and remember them—as subhuman, faceless living or dead corpses.[57] Lanzmann's *Shoah* (1985) sets out to prove both the existence of the Holocaust as an historical event and as one that still lives on in the memories of all who were involved in it.[58] This is not a documentary, just as Levi's *Survival in Auschwitz* is not an autobiography. For these works reveal the immense importance of memory and show that the artificial distinction made between a so-called sacrilizing memory and a scientifically oriented history is invalid.

This was, of course, clearly recognized by both perpetrators and victims. For the accounts written during the Holocaust by *Lager* inmates were the very essence of the struggle between Nazism, which strove to annihilate both the Jews and their memory, and the victims, who refused to allow their memory to perish along with their physical existence. Such personal accounts are still being written today by survivors who had not been able either to verbalize or write down their experience until late middle-age. These too are representations, often filled with ruminations about human existence in the camps, belief in God, friendship and barbarism, selfishness and betrayal, sacrifice and loyalty.[59] No historian of the period, no one who seriously wishes to fathom human psychology or to understand the experience of humanity in this century, can afford to ignore them.[60]

Yet it is precisely for this reason that prose fiction on the Holocaust seems rarely to have the same effect as memoir literature and appears at best contrived, at worst cheap and sensationalist. For somehow fiction and imagination seem unable to confront what the Germans called "the arse-hole of the world"—Auschwitz, a place even those who had been there, both victims and perpetrators, kept describing as unimaginable.[61] If anything, *this* is the issue, much more than memory, for the historian is also called on to use his or her imagination, and the impossibility to imagine creates a block not easily overcome without precisely that distancing mechanism referred to by German historians who have "pleaded" for a historicization of the Third Reich.[62] Perhaps we can remember the unimaginable, but we cannot imagine it. It is precisely for this reason that we depend on other people's accounts, indeed, that we will not even begin to understand what we strive to clarify without constantly referring to those borrowed, tortured, at times inhumanly distorted memories.

The argument on the unrepresentability of the Holocaust was voiced in conjunction with one of the greatest single poems of the century. When Adorno asserted that poetry after Auschwitz was barbarism, the poem he appears to have had in mind was Paul Celan's *Todesfuge*.[63] Perhaps only those who have heard Celan reading this poem aloud can perceive the extent to which its relentless rhythm and stark imagery seem to recapture the whole experience of the death camp, the crazy logic of the extermination, the horrifying irony of installing the "chosen people" as smoke in the sky, this insane world of music and bloodhounds, of beauty and ashes, of total, endless, unremitting despair.

And yet Celan himself seems to have found his poem too coherent, too "poetic," too musical; it was taught in German schools as a good example of a poetic fugue; it was set to music; it did not, for him, recapture the essence of the unimaginable industrial annihilation, without any traces, of millions.[64] It is therefore his later poem, *Engführung* that wholly dispenses with any imagery, rhythm, balance, but is as disjointed, disoriented, verbally crippled, emotionally inexpressible as the memories of the survivors. It is a cry of pain, despair, boundless sorrow, which must remain mute because it is confronted with the wasteland of ashes and an indifferent world. Listening to Celan read this poem in Jerusalem, just a year before his suicide, one cannot forget the broken voice repeating "Asche, Asche Asche," for here one confronts not a surfeit of memory, not even a limit of representation, but the despair of not being able to remember, of trying to hold onto remnants of words spoken long ago, objects touched, feelings aroused, and yet constantly returning to the ashes. A world destroyed, turned into ashes, can never suffer from too much memory. That its representation—the true, impassioned attempt to resurrect it in words and images—cannot wholly succeed is testimony to the fragility of that memory and to the condition of what is being remembered, for it is blown away with every gust of wind.

V.   Denial, Relativism, Truth:
The Fruits of Morbid Curiosity

The French revisionist Robert Faurisson is an extreme case. His denial of the existence of the gas chambers is so preposterous that one would tend to shrug it off as irrelevant. But the fact is that the discussion on the question of the existence of gas chambers has become one of major importance not only regarding the murder of the Jews, but concerning the very nature of truth and its historical reconstruction. One might similarly reject offhand the application of theories of relativism to Auschwitz. But that too would be an error, for in Auschwitz the truth, as constructed by Western civilization, was shattered. Hence it is by applying whichever theory of historical explanation we consider useful and accurate to Auschwitz that we can test its validity. If we accept that Auschwitz happened in history, then theoretical generalizations that do not apply to it cannot apply anywhere else. If we do not accept that Auschwitz happened in history, then there is no reason to believe that anything else did.

Faurisson has argued that he had "tried in vain to find a single former deportee capable of proving to me that he had really seen, with his own eyes, a gas chamber."[65] This statement, as the philosopher Jean-François Lyotard has written, is based on the crazy logic that "in order for a place to be identified as a gas chamber, the only eyewitness I will accept would be a victim of this gas chamber; now, according to my opponent, there is no victim that is not dead; otherwise, this gas chamber would not be what he or she claims it to be. There is, therefore, no gas chamber."[66]

We are thus faced with a question of truth. Was there or was there not a gas chamber? Faurisson asserts that it did not exist, and we have to prove that it did. And in order to do so as historians, we need witnesses. Yet the very nature of the gas chamber makes witnesses a logical impossibility.

This is an issue of extreme importance and urgency. It confronts the historical profession, it confronts the intellectual, indeed, it confronts any human being with the peril of losing all control over the truth, of not being able to distinguish between what is false and what is true, of plunging into a dangerous abyss of an openended relativity, wherein there is no objective reality, but a multitude of subjective views, all legitimate. The historian Pierre Vidal-Naquet recognized this danger in his debate with Faurisson when he argued that although "everything should necessarily go through to a discourse . . . there was something irreducible which, for better or for worse, I would still call reality. Without this reality, how could we make a difference between fiction and history?"[67]

But can we make that difference? Vidal-Naquet, after all, called his own book on the subject *Assassins of Memory*, not of history.[68] And in the above-cited passage, we actually sense some despair, coming as it does from a distinguished scholar of antiquity who knows as well as (if not better than) most of us that truth is a highly ambivalent notion and that it can be reconstructed by the historian only on the most tenuous level. Is memory an integral part of history? Is history based on, or does it constitute at least a search for, truth? Is it, or should it be, an attempt to reconstruct reality? And how do we cope with a historical phenomenon in which one group of people consciously attempted to erase the memory, and therefore the history, of another group? Simon Wiesenthal writes that SS men in the *Lager* used to mock them by saying that "even if some proof should remain and some of you survive, people will say that the events you describe are too monstrous to be believed."[69]

Now we do have much evidence, both German and Jewish, as well as witnesses. But we cannot have testimonies of the gas chambers, from within, while they were operating. And if Faurisson's assertion may appear to us preposterous, Levi's admission, cited above, that he was not a true witness, for the true witnesses all perished, should be taken more seriously. So where is the truth? Even if we accept Levi's account of the labor camp as truthful, it does not tell us much about the gas chambers. And even if we accept the testimonies of the only survivors of the Chelmno death camp, they too, though they were inmates of the death camp, had never been inside an operating gas chamber, otherwise they would not have survived.

Faurisson does not claim that there is no truth, but rather that we need witnesses to establish it. And while Carlo Ginzburg, for instance, has argued that historians must rely even on the evidence of a single witness, and not insist on two,[70] the case we are confronted with is one of no witnesses at all. But there is another argument that has a direct bearing on this issue. For even after significantly modifying his position, most likely because he has clearly understood its implications when applied to the Holocaust, Hayden White has asserted that "There is an inexpungeable relativity in every representation of historical phenomena."[71]

At first glance, it is difficult to disagree with this position. Obviously, our choice of language, just as much as our choice of subject, point of view, our historical context, our own memories and education, and a whole series of other factors influence the way in which we write on an historical event. The question is, however, whether that event exists independently of our own reconstruction of it, and whether any reconstruction of an event is equally legitimate. Now while White finds the denial of the Holocaust "as morally offensive as it is intellectually bewildering,"[72] if he wishes to be consistent with his theory, there is no reason to reach that conclusion, for one could emplot the history of the Third Reich with the Holocaust taken out, or at least greatly modified;

indeed, there are quite a number of such instances, whether in German school books that speak of the "persecution" of Jews by the "Nazis" or in films such as *Heimat*, which simply leaves the story of the Holocaust to others. If one is to argue that some kinds of emplotment are admissible and others are not, then one must propose some criteria in order to make that judgment.[73] Those can be criteria belonging to the realm of truth or to the realm of morality (and they are not mutually exclusive). But if one argues that all historical representation is relative, then one would be hard put to apply such criteria. Nor is it clear why certain modes of emplotment would be unacceptable, especially if we do not make a distinction between facts and interpretation, truth and lies, reality and image.[74]

Returning to the gas chambers, the question arises as to how we would emplot that phenomenon. We could tell it from the point of view of the victim, which might be imaginary (because the victim actually died) and yet factually accurate (this is done, for instance, in Schwarz-Bart's *The Last of the Just*). We might emplot it from the point of view of the Jewish *Sonderkommando*, some of whose members had actually survived to tell the tale; but we might also tell it from the point of view of the SS men present. Their view of their actions would be very different from that of the victims or the work-team, but it would be their reality and their understanding of what they were doing, their truth. Would we then be allowed to judge their representation of their actions against some objective reality?[75]

In his infamous speech in Posen in 1943 Heinrich Himmler told an assembly of SS officers that by their extermination of the Jewish people they had written a glorious page of German history, which, however, would never be recorded.[76] This would therefore constitute a fact that would never be admitted to have existed, a reality to be erased, a memory to be forgotten. This assertion brings me back to the unease I expressed at the opening of this chapter. The difficulty stems first and foremost, perhaps, from the realization that our own intellectual efforts to come to terms with the amorphous nature of reality can play so easily into the hands of those who have no qualms about producing realities of the most horrific nature and then claiming that they had never taken place.

Relativism has two other peculiar links. First, the issue of relativization. This is not to say that the relativists seek to relativize or that the proponents of historicization in Germany, who have been accused of trying to relativize Auschwitz, are in any way relativists. In fact, nothing could be farther from the truth, especially in the latter case. And yet, both schools, though without any visible direct ties, are part of the same intellectual discourse. If previously we found it immensely difficult to understand Auschwitz simply because of the nature and dimensions of the event itself, we are now faced with a new situation, whereby the event keeps slipping away from us either by being relativized as unoriginal, not central, not a focus of identification, indeed as a block to understanding both past and present; or by being given a relativistic treatment, whereby it can be remembered, imagined, and emplotted in so many different but equally acceptable ways that even if we would never deny it, at the same time we cannot say that one representation of it is more valid than another because the event is not recuperable as such.

Second, we are faced with a growing and highly disturbing fascination with extremity. This is linked both with relativism, due to the tendency of such theories to try and test their validity against extreme situations, and with the kind of fascination with violence that had triggered such extremities in the first place. The connection is also one of mood, or temperament. This is not an impassioned, engaged fascination, but rather a detached curiosity, devoid of any powerful emotion, a kind of peeping into the void from a safe theoretical distance, without risking even one's reputation, let alone physical injury. Finally, there seems to be a connection between this intellectual curiosity about extremity and the rise of violence and extremism in the West. For the fantastic realism of cinematic images, simultaneously purged of all real pain to the viewer, vivid and yet detached, arranged in such aesthetic forms so as to attract even the more feeble hearted, cannot fail to produce some reaction. And, as a quick glance at publishers' lists of books will reveal, intellectuals and academics are just as fascinated with death, suffering, perversion, and depravity.

We are thus faced, as I understand it, with several false dichotomies. One is the argument that an event cannot be proved to have taken place if no one who had experienced it directly, with his or her own eyes, can testify to it. This is the dichotomy between event and non-event. Another dichotomy is between naive realism and interpretation.[77] It is based on the contention that there are only two choices between a blind and uncritical belief in facts and a wholly skeptical view that refuses to accept them as anything more than previous interpretations. The last is between truth and relativity. The assumption is ultimately that the event took place and yet at the same time it did not. It did, in the sense that it can be emplotted in innumerable ways. It did not, in the sense that no one emplotment is better or, rather, more truthful, than another. If the event has no objective reality, then it is free to transform itself into whatever we may like.

It is here that I find myself beset by extreme unease. As historians, I believe we all know, or should know, that we can never achieve true objectivity, nor could we hope to discover true objective reality in the past. Obviously the past was, and is, made of numerous truths and realities, and it is highly difficult to distinguish between them, just as it is difficult for us to distinguish between our own motivations in studying a certain period in a certain manner. Obviously, there are numerous ways of telling the story of a murder, and those depend on the witnesses as much as on the person reconstructing the event. But a murder has taken place; we did not construct it in our imagination. In that sense, it is not relative. Moreover, it is important to adjudicate who was responsible (which is the real point of Akira Kurosawa's 1950 film *Rashomon*, of course).[78] The historian cannot escape the responsibility of acting as judge in this context.[79] And if we are told about it by way of a joke or informed that it did not happen, although we know that it did, or if we are told that the question of responsibility is so multifaceted as to defy definition, when we suspect that this position is evasive or duplicitous, then we have a right, indeed a duty, to be morally outraged both as historians and as human beings. Perhaps, too, we should examine whether we have ourselves made it possible for such assertions to be made. Perhaps what we believed to be interesting, intellectually stimulating, even playful, when applied to an extreme case proves to be morally dubious. And then, perhaps, we should admit that we had made an error, and that if our theory does not work here, it can no longer be called a theory, and might have to be discarded, or at least radically modified.

Proponents of relativism and indeterminacy often claim to be fighting a war of liberation against the tyranny of a totalizing discourse (in complicity with the authoritarian elements of society). Thus it has been argued that if we do not accept relativism, we are bound to end up as determinists. I believe that is wrong. Indeed, as Isaiah Berlin wrote more than twenty years ago, "Both [determinism and relativism] have, at times, succeeded in reasoning men or frightening men out of their most human moral or political convictions in the name of a deeper and more devastating insight into the nature of things."[80]

Hence, since relativism lacks a commitment to truth and morality and does not allow choice, it contains an element of cynicism; and while humanity is based on choice, relativism makes every argument allegedly possible. What is at stake is therefore not only what intellectuals say about the Holocaust, but how they view history and by extension how they perceive humanity. In this sense, the question of whether the gas chambers existed or not is vital, for if this can be doubted, or if it is a relative issue open to multiple emplotments, then everything is. Hence the question is not one of the limits of representation, but the limits of truth. If historians, as intellectuals, concede their moral neutrality, then they will finally concede their intellectual, political, and moral irrelevance. Thereby they will also abuse their function as educators, reconstructors of the past, and serious critics of the present. I do not see why historians or, more generally, intellectuals should doubt their role as critics of society, as representatives of a moral view, as persons seeking the truth and exposing lies. They must do so carefully, with integrity, with critical self-reflection, recognizing their weaknesses and limitations, remaining open to criticism, to new ideas and new evidence. But once they surrender their claim for truth, they will end up serving those who will never be afraid of claiming the truth for themselves.

Let me conclude by way of some general remarks. I do not pretend to offer some new approach to the study of the Holocaust or to either the historical, literary-critical, or literary discourse on it. I do believe, however, that the issue is serious enough to merit consideration by any historical approach or literary theory that claims universal applicability. It is serious both because of the nature of the thing itself and because of its implications for the world in which we live.

By and large, none of us can really come to terms with the fact that modern civilization had been capable of perpetrating such an enormity. The conclusions to be drawn are so frightening, the anxiety into which we would plunge is so paralyzing, that we simply must, as indeed we have done, think of our culture, tradition, civilization, with Auschwitz taken out. At the same time, however, I feel that when attempting to generalize about modern human experience and nature, one cannot afford to begin by a general theory and then see whether it conforms with the evidence from the Holocaust. For the obvious result of this would be either a significant modification of the theory or the assumption that Auschwitz does not belong to, or teach us anything about, humanity. On the other hand, I do not believe that we should generalize the Holocaust in a manner that would block all other avenues of human understanding and experience. Western civilization, even the twentieth century itself, consists of more than the Holocaust. If Auschwitz is central, indeed, if it signifies a "break of civilization,"[81] it nevertheless must not be allowed to obscure our vision completely.

There has been a great deal of criticism of institutionalized memory, represented either by certain individuals or institutions. Some aspects of this phenomenon are clearly lamentable, especially in cases where professional rememberers make a material and moral profit from peddling their memories. In other cases this is problematic, but both inevitable and not wholly negative. A museum of the Holocaust may not be the most appealing idea to many of us. And yet, depending on the organization and didactic message of such institutions (and they all have one), I do not think we can a priori disapprove of them, for the simple reason that apart from a minuscule minority among even the more educated sectors of Western society, most people know hardly anything about the event and are not likely to take the trouble to learn about it in the future. If even a small minority does become exposed to some kind of well-arranged museum exhibit, that may not be so bad after all. For although I personally believe that knowledge about the past does not at all necessarily prevent its recurrence, I also would claim that thinking about the future without a keen awareness of the past is even more perilous. This is, after all, one of the reasons why many of us have studied history.

But I do object to the assumed moral superiority of survivors (very few of them make such claims, of course, but it is that minority that is heard most loudly). I believe that the experience and memories of survivors give them insight not only into the event itself, but also into some aspects of human behavior and psychology, into the potential of each of us and into the potential of human society to create hell on this earth. However, though it is difficult to say, I do not think that the experience of Auschwitz gives one moral superiority, both for the reasons raised by Levi (that is, that the survivors often belonged to the "privileged," and those were not necessarily morally superior to those who perished), and because in many other areas of human experience and creativity Auschwitz had absolutely nothing to teach us. Hence, while we must take into account what survivors tell us about human behavior, we must also remember that this is a partial view, formed under the most extreme conditions. It is a warning, but it is not a whole picture of human action and potential.

It is partly for this reason that the artificial separation between those who study modern European history and those who study Jewish history or, even more precisely, the history of the Holocaust, is lamentable. Because just as the Holocaust was part of the European experience, so too Jewish history was part of European history. The way we study history now tends to separate the two, so that the Jews are kept out of the general stream of history, and the general stream of history is seen as having had nothing to do with the Jews. So too with the Holocaust. Just as Auschwitz was part of a general European scene, so too Jewish history does not simply lead to Auschwitz and therefore consist mainly of it.

Teaching a university course on the Holocaust has made me realize how important it is to expose young people, of whatever nationality, to this central event of our century. But the fact that one could teach Holocaust history in one class, and German history in another, with very few overlaps, made me understand once more that we are perpetuating an unfortunate and in some ways dangerous process.[82] Auschwitz must not be made into the focus of Jewish existence, for it is a black hole that sucks everything beautiful and hopeful into its void. By the same token, however, no member of Western civilization may study his or her history without knowing that one of its potentials was, indeed, Auschwitz.

III

The Aesthetics of Murder:
Visual Representations
of Evil

War, Memory, and Repression: Alexander Kluge and the Politics of Representation in Postwar Germany

The most serious act of expropriation occurs when a person is deprived of his or her own history. With Holocaust, the Americans have taken away our history. . . .

The Jews, since time immemorial "people who go away" [*Weggeher*], fit well into this American culture, a culture that only seeks to expand and to compete in all areas, whose very own language is competition.[1]

We'll never recover what was lost. We can't even assess what was lost. Who knows what beauty and grandeur six million could have contributed to the world? Who can measure it up? What standards do you use? How do you count it? How do you estimate it?[2]

In Alexander Kluge's 1979 film *The Patriot*, Gabi Teichert, a German history teacher, spends much of her time digging for the past, its images, memories, artifacts, fairy tales. She digs and digs and digs, and as she does so we cannot avoid thinking that neither the action, nor the tool associated with it, nor even the German word used to describe this action can remain innocent in a post-Nazi, post-Holocaust world. In Germany, we should know, a spade is no longer just a spade. It is the weapon of the men of the *Arbeitsfront* (Labor Front), featured so vividly and frighteningly in Leni Riefenstahl's film *Triumph of the Will* (1935), shouldering their spades like rifles, precisely as Gabi Teichert does in *The Patriot*, and crying out for Germany in the most moving scene of Riefenstahl's film. It is the weapon of the workers in the Nazi labor organization, *Organisation Todt*, who make an appearance in Kluge's film in excerpts from authentic documentaries of Aryan "spade-workers" building the Reich's new *Autobahnen*, accompanied, of course, by Wagnerian themes.

Excessive digging, when used as a metaphor for an obsession with the past, may be related to a passionate need either to uncover the truth or to bury it.

Now in German, "digging" and "burying" are closely related: *graben, begraben*. The second central character in Kluge's film, the commentator, remarks: "*Sie haben gegraben und gegraben, sie haben die Märchen erforscht*" ("They have dug and dug, they have researched fairy tales"). But in the Germany of the 1980s it called for a special effort to hear this phrase, and to view this scene, without immediately associating it with Paul Celan's poem *Todesfuge* (*Death Fugue*), whose highly visible public status in the Federal Republic could hardly be disputed, and whose emphasis on the motif of graves and digging is absolutely crucial: "*wir schaufeln ein Grab in den Lüften* (We shovel a grave in the air) . . . *lässt schaufeln ein Grab in der Erde* (has them shovel a grave in the ground) . . . *stecht tiefer ins Erdreich* (jab the earth deeper) . . . *stecht tiefer die Spaten* (jab your spades deeper) . . .*dann habt ihr ein Grab in den Wolken* (you'll have a grave then in the clouds) . . . *er schenkt uns ein Grab in der Luft* (he grants us a grave in the air)."[3]

In Kluge's film, however, the graves belong to German soldiers and citizens, the spades are for history teachers, and history is a uniquely, purely German affair, purged of any recognizable foreign elements. Yet, as Gabi Teichert vehemently argues, the available history books must be changed, because they do not enable her to teach positive history. This is so, she says, since the history they describe is not positive, and history books are, in her words, the "end product" of history. Hence history itself must be changed, so that the books can be rewritten. In this way Kluge, through Gabi, anticipates the *Historikerstreit* by seven years. In 1986 Michael Stürmer, historian and political advisor of the German Chancellor Helmut Kohl, wrote that "in a land without history the future is controlled by those who determine the content of memory, who coin concepts and interpret the past," since "in a country without memory anything is possible."[4]

The past, therefore, is there not only to be dug out and rediscovered, but also to be glued together, restored, recreated from those fragments brought to the surface by the busy spades wielded by such well-meaning teachers of history as Gabi Teichert. But since most of the past will remain buried, either because we can no longer uncover it, or because we covered it up by this incessant digging, the reconstruction will necessarily be a collage, whose parts (already preselected by the digger) have been arranged in one of many possible alternatives. And Kluge's selection and pasting of those selected fragments, rather than changing the past, recreates it as a saga of suffering and pain, a melancholy cycle of death without redemption, of silent natural beauty and anonymous catastrophe, of individual purity and integrity in a cracked, distorted, meaningless universe. Because Kluge's apparently haphazard bricolage is in fact based on a careful selection of the material, it both introduces some *neglected* themes of the German past and simultaneously *neglects* those elements that might threaten his preferred representation of that past. For Kluge's film is indeed a masterpiece of memory and repression.[5]

Neglected themes are just as important in this collage-like reconstruction of the past as those that are present. Perhaps the most evocative, because the most subtle, is Kluge's use of the music that accompanied Alain Resnais' 1955 film *Night and Fog* (*La nuit et brouillard*). Whereas in the latter the music was composed to serve as a melancholy background to scenes of the *Holocaust*, in the former it is played while showing scenes from *Germany's* lost wars. That is, while in *Night and Fog* the music accompanies pictures of the *Jewish* victims, in *The Patriot* it serves as a lament for the *German* victims of history, the fallen soldiers of a thousand years of German misfortune. It has been suggested that this (unacknowledged) recruitment of Resnais' musical theme is an attempt *not* "to exclude Auschwitz from the patriotic *Trauerarbeit* (work of mourning)."[6] It may be argued, however, that this is, in fact, Kluge's *answer* to Auschwitz (or to *Holocaust*, the American television series, broadcast in the FRG in 1979),[7] which is never mentioned in this work of mourning, since the subjects of this mourning are the Germans, and only the Germans. Hence we can say that from Kluge's point of view, whereas *Night and Fog* limited itself to the victims *of* the Germans, *The Patriot* devotes itself to the Germans *as* victims. This too is in uncanny anticipation of the Bitburg controversy over President Reagan's portrayal of German soldiers as victims of Nazism.[8] Kluge's film, strewn as it is with German corpses, is also a film *not* strewn with the corpses of their victims.

But then the question is, of course, are we dealing with the past or with its *memory*? If the latter, then there is little doubt that Kluge (just like Edgar Reitz in his 1984 film *Heimat*)[9] made a film about the German collective memory of the war, even if in his postmodern rendition of that past, it *appears* as nothing more (or less) than a bricolage of images from which we as viewers can pick and choose. This convenient notion of Germany as victim, bemoaned, quite ironically, in 1981 by the historian Andreas Hillgruber, who by 1986 had come round to the view that (German) historians *must* identify with the fate of the German soldiers who protected the Reich from the Red Army in 1944–45,[10] is derived from the natural inclination to remember the retreats and debacles of the last two years of the war, and to repress the preceding years of conquest, destruction, and subjugation of others that were the direct cause of that eventual "German Catastrophe."[11]

Kluge's film is closely related to other representations of the past, and especially of the Second World War and the Nazi era, in many other ways. Several important postwar German films have given us some insight into their directors' own perception, and their understanding of their protagonists' perception, of the enemy, the victor, the occupier, the other. In many of these films, such as, most prominently perhaps, in Rainer Werner Fassbinder's 1979 *The Marriage of Maria Braun*, this figure is represented by a large, good-hearted, naively exploitative, and not particularly intelligent black GI.[12] In Kluge's film the notion of Germany as the victim of amorphous, not to say mysterious forces of history and destiny (and romantic terms, distorted and popularized by Hitler and Goebbels, such as *Schicksalsgemeinschaft*, or community of fate, and *Schicksalskampf*, or battle of destiny, come readily to mind in this context), is given another perspective in the only appearance of concrete enemies. Here we see an excerpt from a contemporary newsreel, featuring the smiling, naive, cigarette-smoking and obviously uncomprehending crew of an American bomber, just back from what the (German) commentator (Kluge) describes as "18 hours of destroying Germany," and now off to a good night's sleep.

The war, then, at least in Kluge's film (as in Fassbinder's *The Marriage of Maria Braun* [1979], Helma Sanders-Brahms' *Germany Pale Mother* [1980],[13] and many more) is first and foremost about the destruction of Germany, mainly from the air. "We must not forget that the RAF cremated 60,000 people in Hamburg," announces the commentator (in Kluge's voice), where, we are told, Gabi Teichert's parents *would* also have perished, had they not been away in the country that day. And inevitably we think of the millions burned by the Nazis who *could not* have "gone away to the country that day." But Kluge does not seem to suffer from the same chain of associations, or, perhaps more likely, precisely because the same thought occurs to him and to his assumed audience, he provocatively and quite consistently makes absolutely no mention at all of the victims of the Germans. Instead, by emphasizing such terms as incineration and cremation (of Germans), he both strives to create an implicit parallel between the German victims and the victims of Germany, and to deny making it by scrupulously insisting on the absence of the latter from his film, in full knowledge, one presumes, of their presence in the minds of his viewers. By this point Gabi Teichert's history (and Kluge's history of Teichert) looks increasingly troubling, and disturbingly familiar, since while symbolizing the rebellion against the official, bureaucratic, hypocritical version of the past, her own tales of bygone days begin to shift more and more in a similar direction, filled as they are with a combination of self-pity, one-sidedness, and repression. Is her (and by extension Kluge's) quest for a rearrangement of the relationship between history, memory, and forgetting the herald of a new understanding of the German past, or is it merely a new, highly stylized and artistically original rendition of the old, tired, almost pathetic (mis)representation and repression, the refusal to take up individual responsibility and the ready assignment of blame to demonic figures and anonymous historical and apocalyptical forces?[14]

Although it uses postmodern techniques of collage, and while it eschews narrative and supposedly abandons the notion of a uniform perspective, *The Patriot* is in fact neither free from romantic sentimentality nor purged of a series of rather common (not to say commonplace) underlying assumptions regarding the sense and meaning of German history. This reminds one of similar contradictions between the implicit claims made by a work of art through the form it assumes and the eventual implications of both form and content (or, if we like, of both the content of their form and the form in which their content is represented).[15] Günter Grass's *The Tin Drum* comes to mind here, where sentimental, romantic views of the past are never totally obscured by the book's predilection for grotesque characters and surrealist situations.[16] Kluge's apparently disjointed film similarly finds the time for long, melancholy shots of the German countryside, which finally come to rest on a lonely tree near Kaliningrad, the former Königsberg, a tree that, we are told, does not mind the change of this (ancient German) town's name and identity, and yet, almost unintentionally, evokes a feeling of longing and sadness over a loss, indeed a kind of quietly desperate *Sehnsucht* that by definition cannot be fulfilled. Here again we cannot but think of the long shots of the Polish forest in Claude Lanzmann's 1985 film *Shoah*, which are intended not to make us wish for a lost primeval existence, or to evoke memories of youthful nature hikes, but rather to contrast the silence and beauty of the forest with what is hidden under its canopy of leaves, namely the remnants of millions of cremated bodies murdered in modern death-factories. Kluge does not tell us the circumstances under which (Kant's) Königsberg was transformed into (the faceless Russian) Kaliningrad. In this film on the history of the Germans he is concerned neither with the fate of the 20 to 25 million Russians who paid the price of Germany's lost war, nor with the vast tracts of land first occupied, then destroyed, by the Germans.[17] To be sure, Lanzmann too does not say directly why he subjects us to long views of a forest. But in both cases we know the reason; while the former wants us (as Germans) to think of the loss and *repress* its context, the latter demands that we (as members of the human race) *relate* the loss to its context, that we remember, as the Hebrew poet H. N. Bialik wrote, that "The sun shone, the acacia bloomed and the slaughterer slaughtered."

The central theme of Kluge's work reflects a wide variety of Germany's cinematic, literary, and rhetorical treatments of the Nazi past; namely, man's helplessness against the forces of fate and history, man's lack of choice, and the senselessness of action against destiny.[18] This manner of reasoning has often enough served to justify passivity, cowardice, and collaboration in the past, and has formed the basis for numerous subsequent apologetics. In a time when the analogy between Soviet Russia and Nazi Germany is once more quite common, it is of some interest to compare, for instance, such works as Siegfried Lenz's *The German Lesson*, Heinrich Böll's *Billiards at Half-Past Nine*, and Günter Grass's *Cat and Mouse*, with Vasily Grossman's *Life and Fate*. The protagonists of the German novels are caught within an historical web they can neither escape nor resist: a blind and unremitting fate, whose representatives are either the faceless *Ledermantel*, the Gestapo agents, or the stupid, repelling, and generally unpopular SA members and party officials. Little attempt is made to understand the appearance and popularity of Nazism, or the psychology of its supporters, and yet the impression is created that there was no way of stopping the evil this regime embodied, and hence that the only resistance possible was a kind of "inner immigration," which is also (justifiably) seen as suspect (at least by Grass and Lenz, while some of Böll's heroes are of a more saintly quality, such as Leni in *Group Portrait with a Lady*). Conversely, Grossman, who as a journalist during the war worked for Soviet propaganda, manages in this later book (whose publication was banned in the USSR) to combine the historical breadth and psychological depth of the great nineteenth-century Russian novels with elements of social realism and communist optimism. This is a novel about a horrible, murderous fate; yet one that an array of protagonists fight with and against, and which, at least in small part, they can still change. Here the mean, frightened, and opportunistic are treated with some sympathy and understanding by the author (with the exclusion of the German enemy); indeed, the reader occasionally senses that the author has taken a liking to one of his characters of whom in principle he totally disapproves (as is of course the case with many of Dostoevsky's protagonists). Hence, despite Grossman's personal fate, as well as his nation's (both Russian and Jewish), turning out to have been far worse than that of the German authors and *their* nation, the author of *Life and Fate* succeeds in recreating a vast panorama of the war in Russia, where man and fate can interact and grapple with each other in the face of domestic and foreign oppression, where the authority of anonymous forces is not supreme, and where action can have meaning even in the darkest of times. Moreover, Grossman personally proved that repression of the memory of the past, disturbing as it may be, cannot and should not be allowed, even at the cost of one's own creative life.[19]

Kluge's (and many of his contemporaries') view of man's helplessness against fate also bears comparison with the long tradition of Jewish preoccupation with man's helplessness against evil, going back to the Biblical rebellion against God's passivity in the face of injustice, whose modern, pre-Holocaust expressions strangely anticipated that ultimate "Final Solution." Thus, while Kluge is well within the German romantic tradition, the poem by Bialik, *On the Slaughter*, written in the wake of the Kishinev pogrom of 1903, is well within the Jewish tradition of *kinot*, or lamentations. Here the poet refuses to accept the order of the world, and rebels against both fate and belief: "And if there is justice— let it appear at once! / But if after I have been destroyed under the heavens / Justice will appear/May its throne be forever eradicated! / And the heavens rot with eternal evil." At the same time, Bialik realizes that once evil *has* been committed, action against it is meaningless: "And cursed be the man who says: Avenge! / No such revenge—revenge for the blood of a little child / Has yet been devised by Satan."[20]

But the blood is another's blood, and Kluge's history, anticipating the kind of history promoted by the revisionists of the *Historikerstreit*, is wholly and unreservedly *only* German history, assertively denying the need to consider anyone else's history or the relationship with it. It is one-sided not only in its evocation of the victims, but also in remembering beauty, creativity, knowledge, life. The commentator in *The Patriot*, that is, Kluge's own voice, tells us of the "simpler times" of the Middle Ages. But Kluge's view of that period in his nation's history neglects to mention the Jews, who both reached new cultural heights in Germany, *and* were massacred by the tens of thousands in the course of the Crusades, precisely during those simpler times.[21] For Kluge, the Jews are *not* part of German history, neither then nor later, while the Middle Ages *are* part of a German romantic dream, one that perforce excludes both "foreigners" and massacres, since it is neither a nightmare nor a history lesson; instead it is the kind of history lesson Gabi Teichert hopes to be able to teach and cannot, because the precondition for that would indeed be changing history itself.

Not untypically for the German representation of the Nazi past, the only "atrocity" in *The Patriot* is an excerpt from an apparently authentic newsreel showing the execution of so called "Werewolf" fighters (underground German resisters to the Allies)[22] in spring 1945, "among them some juveniles," as the commentator explains, as well as a Wehrmacht officer charged with having ordered the execution of two American prisoners of war. The remarkable, one might even say brutal, absence of any other atrocity is so emphatic as to suggest that it is not motivated merely by the insistence on focusing strictly on German history (and the genocide of the Jews was apparently part of Jewish, not German history), but also by an urge to provoke questions *about* this absence, questions that would then presumably be answered by reference to the film's own interpretation of history. The Nazis might have murdered well over a million Jewish children, but *that* tale belongs to a different history, a different collage, with whose recounting this filmmaker, or for that matter, most other German filmmakers and writers, do not feel themselves to be charged, leaving it to those who can later be said to have lacked the necessary objectivity to deal with such an emotional matter.[23] In the meanwhile, however, we are urged to remember that German juveniles were also executed, that the German people were also subjected to atrocities, even if they were often quite active in bringing such (far more limited) atrocities on themselves. Thus, the dead soldier Wieland, fallen in Stalingrad, whose knee is the third central character in the film, is indeed shown for a moment as having once, as a youth, been a Nazi follower or supporter. But the commentator hastens to reassure us with the curious assertion that poor Wieland had simply "found himself in the wrong history." Presumably, in a better history, such as the one Gabi Teichert is digging for, he would have been a better man.[24]

History, indeed, is not made *by* people in this film, it *happens* to them. "What is to be done?" asks the commentator as he takes us on a visit to Lenin's home. But he has no answers. The war, says the knee, was at least work and toil—in any case, from the knee's point of view. Perhaps, the knee observes, it is better to think of what *not* to do. But even here it does not suggest the obvious: that it might have tried *not* to work, *not* to toil, *not* to march and to kick and to kill. Moreover, the very structure of *The Patriot* both implies and subtly evokes a passive view of history in the viewers. The absence of plot has the effect of suspending our critical faculties, privileging pathos over insight, empathy over understanding. The cinematic technique employed by Kluge (i.e., the film's structural rhetoric) whereby disjointed images, haphazard flashes, seeming lack of control, disorder, and unpredictability replace narrative, persuades us even more effectively than its verbal rhetoric of the complete lack of human agency in the affairs of humanity.

This position is not unique to Kluge, of course. History as a force to which individuals are subjected, rather than a context in which they actively participate, plays a major role in German representations of the Nazi past, just as the State has for several generations played a major role in German views of the present. Both are seen as agencies independent of human choice and action; and because they have the capacity to suppress the individual, the individual in turn is at least compensated by the ability to deny responsibility for his or her actions, as well as to repress their memory, since, according to this interpretation, neither the action nor its memory are *really* one's own, but merely an extension of the anonymous powers of historical fate and political control.

The only memory over which one can still retain ownership, according to this view, is the memory of one's dreams, whose content is apparently free from state control and history's arbitrary flow. And the memory of dreams is, after all, already twice removed from reality, and therefore thrice from personal involvement and responsibility.[25]

Post-World War I films were often concerned with the memory of the event, and the manner in which both the war and its memory had molded the present.[26] One intriguing motif (not free from Judeo-Christian metaphors) was that of the dead soldiers rising up from their graves to remind the living of the atrocity committed in the war and prevent them from repeating it in the future. This theme was exploited, most powerfully perhaps, in Abel Gance's two versions of *J'accuse* (1918/1937),[27] and has returned, in a more subtle form, in Bertrand Tavernier's 1989 film *La vie et rien d'autre* (*Life and Nothing But*), where the dead soldier returns through the memory of his wife and mistress, while public memory of the dead is buried with meaningless pomp in the tomb of the unknown soldier.[28] Clearly, the fear of collective amnesia haunts the memory of the two world wars, whose most distinct feature was the introduction and ruthless implementation of mass industrial killing.[29] Yet in Germany collective amnesia assumes particular prominence, since, more than anywhere else, German memory and repression are closely related; the urge to forget and the passion for (selective) remembering are both disproportionately powerful. To be sure, this is very much Kluge's main concern, and yet what troubles him most is the fear that the suffering of the *soldiers*, not the death and destruction they had *inflicted* on others, might be forgotten. Indeed, he seems to feel that the only way to stress the fate of the former is precisely by repressing that of the latter. In this Kluge cannot claim to be unique, nor can he pretend that his battle for history is a lonely one. In fact, since *The Patriot* was made, we have witnessed a concerted attempt to confront the perceived danger of collective amnesia by means of disseminating the notion of German victimhood, indeed of recreating an appropriately organized and selected memory of Germany's history that makes for a more cozy and confident interaction with the past, whose burden is no longer perceived as an obstacle to be overcome.[30]

Stalingrad, which has obsessed Kluge throughout his career,[31] is an interesting case in point, since in recent years German scholars, and well as the media and the general public, have become increasingly fascinated with this horrifically bloody *Entscheidungskampf* (decisive battle).[32] One indication of this has been the negotiations between the municipality of Volgograd, as Stalingrad is now named, and the *Volksbund Deutsche Kriegsgräberfürsorge* (the Organization for the Care of German War Graves, which is connected to the German government), over the reconstruction of cemeteries for the 150,000 German soldiers buried there.[33] There is also a plan by the Austrian government to erect a monument to commemorate its own 50,000 soldiers who are said to have fallen in Stalingrad. The Germans and Austrians seem willing to pay handsomely for this right to commemorate the men who destroyed Stalingrad, while the Russians may well accept the deal since they sorely need the money. Meanwhile the children of Volgograd try to make ends meet by selling remnants of soldiers' items on the black market as the corpses, buried in shallow graves dug into the frozen ground of 1942–43, keep resurfacing every thaw, as they have done for the last fifty years, and each year some of the children are killed or maimed by stepping on mines and unexploded shells. Kluge, whose obsession with the battle, the suffering, the extremities of existence experienced in Stalingrad parallels many of his compatriots' fascination with this grim event, never raises the simple question: what were German soldiers doing there in the first place, why did they march 1,500 miles to Stalingrad, and how many Russians paid with their lives not only to kick them out, but also simply because they were Russians (i.e., Slavs, Bolsheviks, Jews, "Asiatics," "Mongols," and so forth) occupied by the soldiers of the Third Reich?[34]

It has rightly been suggested that "Kluge's intertextual approach to history may . . . have the effect of ultimately dehistoricizing the past by dislocating historical images and text fragments," with the result that "undeniably forceful dependencies and contingencies . . . remain simply excluded."[35] And there is little doubt that the context of the bits and pieces of which Kluge's film is composed, the *Zusammenhang* (as Kluge would prefer to call it) on which all these historical images and text fragments are dependent, is the war of murder, destruction, and genocide waged by Germany against most of the rest of the world.[36] Moreover, when speaking about Gabi Teichert's search for positive history, it is well to remember that even in defeat Germany made its victims pay a much heavier price than its own people. This context, so much in the background, not merely of the film, but of the German postwar reality as such, is not at all remarked on by either the director of *The Patriot* or by his gloomy protagonist. It also receives little space in most other cinematic and literary representations of the German past produced in postwar Germany, and is not accepted as a historical fact by most German molders of public opinion, with the exception of some scholars and intellectuals whose own position has been significantly eroded since the new revisionist trend of the mid-1980s and the reunification of Germany with all its social, political, and economic tensions.[37] It is important to note that while most official, intellectual, and scholarly pronouncements in Germany are likely to find an occasion to condemn the Holocaust (carried out, as the official phrase runs, "in the *name* of the German people," not by it), the same cannot be said about the memory of the war and the facts of its reality. Hence, once "Auschwitz" is taken out of the picture, war becomes everyone's hell and suffering, shame and guilt, sorrow and pity.[38]

It is difficult, perhaps unfair, to charge works such as Kluge's with ignoring the "context" and not providing all the facts, since this type of postmodern representation is based on a notion of "critical realism" aiming at an "alternative organization of experience." Kluge's film, just like Hans Jürgen Syberberg's *Hitler, a Film from Germany*, refuses to employ the images of Nazism that had already been used and abused by the Nazis themselves, and have since been recirculated over and over again in cheap television series, comic books, yellow magazines, dust jacket photographs, and so forth. Such works dismiss the notion that there was only one reality of the Third Reich that we can either accept or reject, admit or repress, feel responsible for or remain indifferent to. Hence Kluge, like many of his contemporary intellectuals, wants to do away with what he perceives as the artificial separation between fiction and fact, since it does not take into account the "coexistence of fact and desire in the human mind." The difficulty with this assertion is that when speaking of *that* specific German past, the refusal to distinguish between fact and fiction is highly convenient for those to whom the "burden of the past" appears too overwhelming and is just as welcome for those who never accepted they had any burden to carry in the first place. This of course is not necessarily the conscious intention of such a view of reality, past, and memory; but *ignoring* this consequence must certainly be intentional, since it is all too clear for anyone who has had anything to do with German sensibilities of the past.

This blurring of the distinctions between fiction and reality, fact and legend, endows the discussion about German history with the quality of a "winter tale." By balancing fact and desire we are in a position to end up, as does Kluge, with only those facts we desire, discarding such details that stand in the way of whichever memory, history, representation, dream, interpretation or fairy tale we wish to maintain. To be sure, Kluge's technique of collage claims or even sincerely hopes to provide us with the materials from which we can construct our own narrative; that is, it liberates us from the tyranny of a preordained, authoritative version of the past. And yet within the universe of the film the materials provided are necessarily limited and carefully selected, just as they are in any literary or cinematic work. If we are to reconstruct the past strictly with the materials we are given by the director, then we can do so in only so many ways, and can erect only so many alternative versions of the past. If we prefer different reconstructions, plots, and narratives, we must either be supplied with other materials or borrow whole alternative versions from other representational or historical universes. This is so, for instance, in the case of what has come to be called the "concentrationary universe," for which no material whatsoever has been provided by Kluge. Similarly, on the basis of Kluge's bricolage, it would be impossible to construct any sort of narrative of the Russian suffering under German occupation, whereas any representation of the suffering of German soldiers in the Russian campaign, or of the German civilian population's predicament under the Allies' strategic bombing, can draw on a rich supply of images from Kluge's assorted materials. Hence, representations of the victims of Germany must necessarily be constructed as *narratives of absence* in the German memory of the war, forming an important *missing* element, a void that tells us perhaps just as much about intention and desire, subconscious and willed perception of the past, as do the materials Kluge and many other filmmakers and novelists *have* strewn in our path.[39]

Kluge's postmodern preference for fragmentation and dispersal, and his rejection of narrative, unity, and intelligibility, leave the question of origins unanswered, perhaps, indeed, in his view, unanswerable.[40] Yet origins are a main concern for anyone who "digs" for history, especially German history, and even more so when it is written, reconstructed, or represented in a post-Nazi, post-Holocaust Germany. "How could it have happened?" was the question asked again and again after 1945, even if the "it" to which the question referred was not always the same (Nazism, war, defeat, genocide).[41] The quest for the origins of Nazism, the war, the "Final Solution," has exercised the minds of numerous scholars and intellectuals of all persuasions. Yet the trend to obscure, deny, or transfer the origins is as present today as it was half a century ago. The origins can be transferred to another location, such as Stalinist Russia, Marxism, Communism;[42] they can be denied, for instance, by speaking of Nazism as having had no roots in German history, culture, politics, but rather having been imposed by a clique of criminals and opportunists (who by implication came from the outside and therefore had their origins elsewhere);[43] they can be obscured, by denying the whole notion of origins in history, indeed by arguing that just as there is no clear distinction between fact and fiction, so too there is no way to distinguish between cause and effect.[44] It can further be argued, as is actually implied, I believe, in such works as Syberberg's *Hitler* and Kluge's *The Patriot*, that in the cosmological scheme of things, as well as in the universe of the individual's mind and psychology, the question of historical origins of such events as the rise of Hitler to power or the decision on the "Final Solution" is either too minute to be worth considering or too distant to concern the "little man."[45] This can be a philosophical, or historiosophical stance, or the view of an artist, a filmmaker, a writer. Possibly, at least in part, it is even quite true. Yet it is a disturbingly convenient perception of a disturbingly inconvenient past and, what is even more troubling, it is a view that tends to be adopted more readily than anywhere else by German manufacturers of artistic representations.

Thus, Kluge's bizarre ability to anticipate the future is in fact part of a trend, since just as he, Fassbinder, Syberberg, and some others had anticipated the *Historikerstreit*, so too the historians involved in that debate unfailingly anticipated German reunification. Perhaps this was more than mere anticipation, but was rather both the consequence of a keen insight into the *Zeitgeist* and a measure of the influence public intellectual and scholarly debates have had on the political process. Let us remember that one of the major issues raised in the 1986 historians' debate referred to the origins of the Holocaust, or rather to what had been the "original" on which the "extermination of the Jews" (*Judenvernichtung*) was modeled (the answer being, of course, the Gulags).[46] The question of origins is crucial, whether or not we accept the very notion of origins and originals in history, since a German past *devoid* of origins (or whose evil aspects always derive from *foreign* origins) is a past that can be constructed in any way we like.[47] Moreover, a past used to challenge the present (the past Gabi Teichert is seeking) is as potentially openended as it may be intentionally narrow in focus. Kluge's *Zusammenhang*, for instance, though it reflects his respect for history as the work of his ancestors, is radically different from the linear historical narrative he associates with Hollywood films (and in *this* context there is little doubt that the film *Holocaust* belongs to the type of historical representation he wishes to eschew). Rather, it is a collage-like structure where, due to the absence of (explicit, but not implicit) narrative, past and present, victim and perpetrator, cause and effect, guilt and innocence blur together in a bricolage claiming to be reconstructible according to the desire of the viewer, but in fact open to manipulation by the supplier of the images on the screen. And, since this is a *German* bricolage, with *German* history as the center, composed of *German* materials and expressing *German* interests, memories, and repressions, one can hardly be surprised by the resulting reconstruction.[48]

While Kluge blurs the distinction between fact and fiction, image and reality, the stubborn matter of the past he is trying to come to terms with, the resistance afforded him and his contemporaries in postwar Germany by the enormity of the past calls for an even more radical treatment. Hence memory too is employed. But unlike the use made of memory in Lanzmann's *Shoah*, which is *about* the memory and the presence of the Holocaust both in the past and present precisely because it is remembered, for Kluge memory is a dream, and dreams are by definition unreal (if they do not happen to have been dreamt by Chuang Tzu who, on waking from a dream in which he had been a butterfly, could not decide whether he was a butterfly dreaming he was Chuang Tzu or Chuang Tzu who had dreamt he was a butterfly).[49] Memory is an oppressive capacity for thoughtful postwar Germans, as it is for many Jews. But the confusion between our ability to remember our dreams, and our supposed predilection to dream our memories, implies in this case the allegedly fictive quality of any memory and justifies the presentation of remembering as an act of selection and hence of selective memory (or its selective representation) as equally legitimate. And once we are allowed to select our memories (at least in the public sphere) they do indeed tend to become much less oppressive, especially for those whose unselected memories may still haunt them by evoking feelings of guilt and shame or pain and sorrow.

Selection is another one of those terms whose meaning was contaminated in the Holocaust. Selective remembering perpetuates that selection. Lanzmann presents one kind of memory; Kluge (and Reitz, Fassbinder, Grass, Böll, Lenz, etc.) another.[50] Moreover, postmodern representations such as Kluge's also base themselves on selective quotation from history (rather than memory), since they in any case reject both the reality of and the necessity for a history *"wie es eigentlich gewesen."* And, admittedly, one would be hard put to affirm the existence of such an entity in the late twentieth century. Yet selection is a matter of choice, and our choice of who would live and who would die, which elements of history will appear on our page and which will be consigned to (at least relatively) eternal obscurity, is to some extent conscious, and as such is an expression of our liberty. Hence when Kluge employs this concept, originally expressed by Walter Benjamin,[51] we can say with some assurance that he does not select *those* quotes from *that* history that Benjamin might have cited had he been given the opportunity to do so by those who had selected him *out* of his intellectual and physical environment. Kluge's view of the past, therefore, is based on a cosmological yet fragmented perspective, in which the details do not matter but the (selected) details are all that matters.

The greater evil in the background is rarely approached directly in German representations of the Nazi past. We read about rumors, we see shadows, we are told about fear and silence and distant horrors. It is, after all, no wonder that the series *Holocaust* had such a traumatic effect on the German public (and was so strongly resented by the German intellectual community); it was, quite ironically, the first direct (if a Hollywood representation of any reality can be called that) confrontation of Germans with the reality of the Holocaust. The reaction of filmmakers such as Kluge and Reitz, however, was not to concede that the time had arrived for Germans to attempt a representation of their perspective of the *Jewish* Holocaust, but rather, that Germans must win back their past from the Hollywood studios that had stolen it from them and create their own representation of the *German* past, even of the *German* catastrophe.[52]

Hence only at one point does Kluge hint at some other, greater evil in the background. Since his is a search for German history, Kluge finally comes to rest in the sphere of the fairy tale. "Jacob and Wilhelm Grimm," tells us (Kluge) the commentator, "dug intensively into German history. They dug and dug and found fairy tales. Their content: how a people spends 800 years working on its wishes." Having evoked the constant digging (with all its above-noted linguistic and cultural connotations), and having guided us to the hair-raising fairyland of Germanic lore, Kluge introduces us to an elderly scholar of fairy tales (a typically German contradiction in terms that serves Kluge both to poke fun at German academics and undermine the notion of a scholarly reconstruction of the past). This particular expert is preoccupied, of all things, with the legal aspects of fairy tales, and his interest, along with the general thrust of the Grimm Brothers' grim tales, brings us for the first and only time into the domain of murder. The tale of the wolf and the seven little goats, says the expert, is all about "a curious mass murder," or rather, as he hastens to correct his not entirely innocent slip, it is "a mass murder with a curiously happy ending." This is the only time in the film that this term makes an appearance, uttered not by the otherwise quite wordy commentator, but rather by a mildly ridiculous scholarly figure speaking with solemn severity about the legal aspects of fairy tales. But our comical expert does have a few more words to say on the subject. In discussing another fairy tale, he notes that the twelfth fairy was a murderer, indeed, was rather more than a *Schreibtischmörderin* (i.e., a desk murderer à la Eichmann) since she gave a *direct order* that the princess would die on being pricked by a thorn; but the thirteenth fairy, the scholar tells us with visible relief, "*macht die Sache wieder gut*" or, as the English language subtitle has it, "undoes the evil." Mass murder, bureaucratic, banal evil, even the (in)famous *Wiedergutmachung*, are all encapsulated in the magical world of legend. And what of the law? The expert has an answer ready for this question too. In considering the legal aspects of the tale about the king who had ordered the murder of his sons so that his only daughter could inherit the kingdom, he says the king was in the right since he was king, and as such his actions were the law of the land. Which must make coming to terms with the past, especially in the world of fairy tales, that much easier.

In the real world, the German legal profession made coming to terms with the past, as well as the present, indeed much easier than one might have expected. Only recently, following the ludicrously light sentences given to neo-Nazis for violent crimes against foreigners, Berlin's chief prosecutor claimed that "our system is blind in the right eye."[53] But this is no news for those acquainted with the history of justice in Germany. Since the publication of a major study on this issue a few years ago, we know that German judges and legal experts collaborated to an extraordinary degree with the regime, indeed helped it erect a seemingly legal system that carried out its wishes to the letter and beyond. And, what is arguably even worse, we find that this system was neither purged after the war, nor did its key officeholders fundamentally change their opinions, with the inevitable consequence that they protected not only their own colleagues from prosecution, but also many other former Nazis, by fabricating the most elaborate legal arguments in their favor. On reading this study, one is struck by its fairy-tale quality, in spite of the hard evidence it is based on, since it is almost incredible that the Federal Republic was founded on the legal system of the Third Reich, and that all these years the legal profession had succeeded in disseminating the outrageous legend that it had been a pillar of justice, reason, and resistance to the regime.[54] One wonders to what extent a fairy tale past (the only one Germany had apparently been able to come to terms with) can act as a guide to action in a newly independent future; or, in Kluge's terms, where does one draw the line and make the distinction between a realistic appraisal of the present and a selective memory of the dream of a fictive past? Is all representation fairy tale, and, if so, at what point do we wake up from the dream?

To be sure, the possible analogy between fairy tales and Kluge's film lies in its (unrealized) potential for irony and self-reflexivity. This could be an important element in any attempt to "come to terms" with, or "overcome" the past, and it is no wonder that many German cinematic and literary representations have tried to employ it, though few with any measure of success. Kluge's film, to my mind, highlights the limitations of such works.[55] Its structure may well be postmodern, yet its message, due to its selection of materials, is not. This is anything but a self-reflexive work, and it does not (at least consciously) subvert its own argument or put its own enterprise into question. Indeed, it lacks precisely that quality of self-irony that could have enriched its texture and liberated it from the charge that it is, ultimately, a disturbingly self-obsessed, apologetic work. As such, it is an outstanding example of the failure of German intellectuals to face up to the task of representing the repressed memories of an evil, but by no means ineffable past.

Chambers of Horror:
The Reordering
of Murders Past

UNLESBARKEIT dieser Welt. Alles doppelt.	UNREADABILITY of this world. Everything doubled.
Die starken Uhren geben der Spaltstunde recht, heiser.	The powerful clocks agree with the ruptured hour, hoarsely.
Du, in dein Tiefstes geklemmt, entsteigst dir für immer.[1]	You, jammed in your innermost, rise from yourself forever.

I. Clean Empty Uniforms: War Exhibited

As a child growing up in Israel in the 1950s and 1960s, I was fascinated by war machines. I would spend hours putting together plastic models of fighter planes and bombers, war ships and aircraft carriers. I would paint them with the appropriate camouflage colors, stick to them the various national insignia, then hang them from the ceiling or arrange them on top of a chest of drawers. My room was a virtual battlefield complete with barbed wire and tanks, charging soldiers and destroyers bristling with guns. At night the immense firepower surrounding my bed calmed my spirit and infused my child's dreams with images of heroism and sacrifice. By the time I was fourteen years old, I probably knew more about the different types of war machines in both world wars and thereafter than many of the soldiers who had been subjected to their destructive powers; I was certainly more comfortable with reciting the qualities of aircraft and ships than with the algebra and geometry my teachers tried in vain to pump into my head.

Growing up in a self-made miniature battlefield has its drawbacks. Protected from the perils of an uncertain environment behind my paper-clip barbed wire, I grew restless, yearning for new, real adventures beyond the four walls of my room. Once I left, there was no turning back. Going out with girls suddenly became much more fascinating than putting together a "Flying Fortress." By the time I was conscripted, my plastic models had been packed away, reappearing occasionally only as broken fragments in the hands of my younger kin.

In Israel at that time there were no war museums. War was all too close and present for it to be enclosed in buildings preserving its memory. It still had a long and bloody future ahead of it. As youngsters we would watch the military parade of the Day of Independence, as the tanks roared down the street and the planes performed aerial acrobatics in the sky. When France delivered the *Mirage* III to the Israeli air force, I drew it countless times in my school books; its delta wings, its pointed nose: it was such a beautiful machine. But time rushed on, and soon I too was in uniform, training for war, and, it so happened, also for the Independence Day parade. That was spring 1973. A few months later the Yom Kippur War broke out. Once more, the battlefields were littered with corpses and broken war machines, and even I could not glue them together again.

The first war exhibit I saw was in London in the late 1960s. The air was filled with the Beatles ("love, love, love"), the boulevards glistened with miniskirts, and French students were reported to be rising against *le général*, de Gaulle. The Imperial War Museum seemed very distant from all that. I was impressed, of course. The museum had even more models of war machines than I did, and they were larger, indeed life-sized. They were the real thing. Or almost. Because even then, just as I turned thirteen, I was troubled by the strange emptiness of those huge halls cluttered with endless machines and puppets dressed in uniforms. It was all so lifeless, silent, clean.

I remember landing for the first time in Munich, many years later, when I began to do research for my dissertation. The bus taking the passengers from the aircraft to the terminal was accompanied by an armored vehicle. By then I had spent many hours in precisely the same vehicle in the Sinai Peninsula. But the German APC was different: I had never seen it so clean before, so shiny and fresh. It looked strikingly similar to my old plastic models. It surely could not harm a fly. (Yet it was manned by German soldiers sent to protect me from Arab terrorists: I could not help but ponder the irony of it all).

The great European war museums, such as the one in London and the Hôtel des Invalides in Paris, are vast, intimidating, yet also strangely sentimental displays of the remnants of a bygone age. Like the great cathedrals of France and England, we may no longer share the values and ideals they had represented to past generations, yet we flock to them in ever increasing numbers as part of a tourist industry that moves millions upon millions of people across national frontiers each summer, re-enacting a population migration that easily dwarfs the Germanic, Tartar, and Mongol invasions put together. These are icons of past greatness, an endless array of items put together in more or less tasteful displays that, taken as a whole, reflect one of the most characteristic components of Western civilization: its obsession with and relentless utilization of war and violence stretching over two millennia of human history. If the great cathedrals serve as the symbol of the secular power of Europe's spiritual institutions, the great war museums embody the sacralization of violence, the aestheticization of war, the glory of soldiering. Conquest and subjugation, massacre and destruction, suffering and pain, are all neatly reordered in glass cases and glittering suits of armor, informative plaques, and laundered, lovingly ironed uniforms. Children and adults alike seem to find them almost as fascinating as dinosaurs.

War museums are dependent on the contents of their displays. The idea of creating an antiwar war museum has of course been entertained in the past, but it is as difficult to achieve as the making of an antiwar war film. The curators may express deeply felt antiwar and anti-militarist sentiments, but if they are to put together plastic representations of war, they inevitably attract a public often more interested in the qualities and aesthetics of these tools of war than in the antiwar subtext that may infuse the arrangement of such artifacts. It is far more difficult plastically to represent the senseless slaughter and suffering of war than to set up the machines that actually do the killing. We may know that a machine gun from the Great War had mowed down thousands of men; yet we examine it, trying to figure out its mechanism, moved by the knowledge that it is a *real, authentic* piece of the past, handled by soldiers long dead and buried. It brings us closer to the past, but that past we feel ourselves close to is cleansed of precisely those elements that made it so horrific. Quite apart from the fact that war museums often have to rely on government support and funds, and are therefore dependent on the manner in which governments would like to portray the national past, they are encumbered by precisely those elements that attract the public to them: they display the tools, not the destruction wreaked by those tools.

Some years ago an attempt was made to create a new kind of war museum. The *Historial de la Grande Guerre* in Péronne, France, is located next to some of the bloodiest battlefields of Europe where, especially in the Great War, millions of Frenchmen, Germans, and Englishmen fought and died. This modern structure seems to defy the imposing buildings of traditional war museums, thereby presumably also rejecting their claim to an imperialist past, while its location near the endless cemeteries of the war implies its more intimate links with the dead soldiers rather than with the governments that had led them to the slaughter. The designers of the *Historial* have attempted to oppose the glorification of war and soldiering implicit in traditional exhibits by laying the uniforms of the various armies and arms in shallow, grave-like craters on the floor, rather than using them to dress puppets standing in heroic or "realistic" postures as is customary in conventional displays. The museum also makes excellent use of video monitors, where a constant stream of documentary film material is shown, bringing the visitors closer to the "reality" of the war and its historical context. Yet even these innovative organizational ideas and technological additions fail to overcome the inherent logic of museums devoted to war. The neatly pressed uniforms on the floor seem to have come directly from the manufacturer. Indeed, all that is needed is a troop of volunteers to put them on and march directly to the battlefields surrounding the museum. The mortars and machine guns, grenades and rifles, all seem in perfect working condition, and curious visitors examine them as they would in any other war museum. The documentary film material includes, as it invariably would, all kinds of films, some uplifting, others shocking and disturbing, all seen before and endlessly reproduced since that first bout of industrial killing without any noticeable effect on people's willingness to do it all over again. Indeed, the curators of the museum seem themselves to have been torn between their abhorrence of war and their fascination with the specific events of 1914–18. It is still, in their minds, a "great" war, great both in its destructive energies and its impact on future generations, in its horror and its fascination. One comes out of the museum feeling that despite its visible intention to demystify both the war and its plastic displays, it has nevertheless once more neatly ordered the slaughter, rearranging it in an interesting, original, aesthetically pleasing manner. What this exhibit has in common with the chaos and confusion, stench and suffering, senselessness and devastation of the event itself remains a moot point.[2]

It is by visiting the surroundings of the museum that one is confronted with the incongruity of the *Historial*. Not the commemorative monuments, but the innumerable rows of graves, the jarring contrast between the silent, beautiful landscape and the corpses on which the lush vegetation feeds, the (transmitted) memory of the hell that these rolling hills once were for their inhabitants.

To be sure, it is thanks to such museums, to documentary films, to accounts and histories, memoirs and novels about the war that we see the silent landscape with a different eye, that we read into it the suffering and death that had dominated it for four years at the dawn of our century. But then I ask myself, what would these soldiers, buried here in the Somme, have made of the *Historial*? Would it have reminded *them* of their experiences? Would they have recognized *themselves* there? Would it have seemed to be at all about *their* war?

I cannot say. Veterans of wars are often thankful that the governments which had sent them to kill and be killed take the trouble to commemorate their suffering and their comrades' sacrifice. But then such commemoration is not intended merely to thank the survivors and the dead, but to justify the killing and the dying and create the psychological preconditions for yet another war. Can a war museum avoid this peril? Can we prevent young people who visit the *Historial* from secretly wishing to handle one of the machine guns, throw one of the grenades, put on one of the neater, more attractive uniforms, distinguish themselves in battle by killing their enemies and saving their comrades? Can we depict war without glorifying it?

Perhaps there is no answer to these questions. But there is clearly a link between the games children play with toy guns, the guns soldiers handle as toys, and the attraction of both children and adults to weapon displays in museums. There is something at work here that turns our rational antiwar sentiments into fascination with the artifacts of war, that transforms our abhorrence of organized violence into a much more complex curiosity concerning the potentials of human nature, our own very private nature, in conditions of danger and extremity. Can we openly confront these questions without exposing ourselves to the obvious perils of this discourse? Is it best simply to ignore, or to suppress in ourselves, sentiments and unspoken desires of which our rational mind surely disapproves? Can it be that by invoking war and violence we are already opening the way for its imitation by those who will read into our well-meant depictions precisely the opposite meaning, who will be fascinated by what we had hoped they would find repellent? Is there, indeed, a side in us too that contains this dangerous tendency, which had in fact been at the core of our preoccupation with these questions from the very start?

Standing on a hill overlooking one of the most murderous battlefields of the war, I think back to my plastic airplanes and warships, tanks and aircraft carriers. I remember the feel of the uniform on my body, I sense the power of the machine gun shaking my frame as it spat out hundreds of rounds. I remember the filthy bundles of uniforms, mixed with burned flesh and black blood, and the smell of putrefaction. Exhilaration and disgust, fear and pride, anger and compassion. There are no antiwar war museums. If war could not make men turn against it, clean empty uniforms certainly cannot. At best, they will remind some of us of the sorrow and the pity of it all.

II.   Shooting War: The Price of Glory

When we were teenagers, we would encourage every villain gunned down by the hero in the innumerable Westerns we watched by calling out: "Now you can pick up your paycheck and go home!" Perhaps that was our way of distancing ourselves from the killing, or, rather, from our pleasure of watching it on the screen. After all, we all knew that we would soon be soldiers ourselves. Many years and several wars later, I find myself returning to that juvenile reaction and all the pleasure and anxiety it expressed. War films are precisely about this: taking part in violence twice removed, empathizing and distancing simultaneously. And here the difference between antiwar war films and straightforward cinematic representations of violence is often quite tenuous.

The paradox of antiwar films is that the closer they come to "actual" battle and its (for many often exciting) horrors, the less effective they are in evoking antiwar sentiments. Conversely, the farther they stray from the event of battle itself, and the more they portray the effects of war as mediated through the (often civilian) casualties of war, the more effectively they drive home their antiwar message and the less they tend to create in their viewers a sense of fascination with fighting or, indeed, the kind of catharsis not untypical of representations of violence. Even the most explicitly antiwar war films, if they are to have any effect, must evoke in us empathy for at least some of the soldiers, who will invariably be portrayed as victims. Only films that preserve a distance from the fighting, exploring the experience of war obliquely, through the eyes of its non-soldier victims, and most especially focusing on the fate of children, the most innocent of all war casualties, liberate us from the polluting effects of that all-too-common uplifting, though horrified excitement of battle, and force us to confront war's destructive reality and its contaminating social and cultural consequences. Yet another, very different technique of building up a distance between the experience of battle and its deeper implications is to approach the event as an act of remembering, either through direct or transmitted memory. While direct memory authenticates itself by the assertion of having been "actually there," transmitted memory assumes a much greater distance, weaving together and reworking the conjunction of imagined personal memories and a past collective experience, and seeking thereby to excavate the core of war's physical and psychological devastation.

The inherent contradictions of antiwar war films were already apparent in the first talking movie ever made in this genre, Lewis Milestone's celebrated *All Quiet on the Western Front* (1930). Significantly, both the Nazis and the German army censors who successfully fought to get it off the screen, and the film's supporters in Germany, were reacting to its alleged "realistic" portrayal of the war. Yet Milestone had seen the war only in film footage and still photographs in the United States. The film's perceived "realism" therefore largely reflected the already pervasive popular view and filmic images of the war rather than its reality. This was, and probably still is, the main reason for its immense success. No wonder that stills from the film, shot in California a whole decade after the end of the war, were subsequently included in picture albums supposedly providing a "graphic" representation of the "reality" of the front, alongside numerous other photographs of "battles" actually staged behind the line by soldiers temporarily pulled out of the trenches.[3]

The public did not seem to mind that this "realistic" film was made by people who had never seen the war; it flocked to it in great numbers. Yet the film's explicit antiwar message had as little effect on the viewers as many other, far less successful films made in the 1920s and 1930s. Indeed, in many ways we may say that it had precisely the opposite effect, Nazi fears notwithstanding. To be sure, *All Quiet* did convince many youngsters that war should be fought only for a "good" or a "true" cause. Not surprisingly, however, when the time came American and German, British and Russian (and to a far lesser extent also French and Italian) soldiers were supplied with precisely the kind of cause they thought they needed to go and kill or be killed at the front. Hugely successful as a war movie, *All Quiet* did rather poorly as an antiwar film.

Milestone's greatest innovation was his recreation of a "realistic" battlefield atmosphere; his filming techniques were subsequently emulated by a long row of filmmakers interested far more in box-office returns than in disseminating antiwar sentiments. The battle scenes, after all, are neither for or against war; claiming to represent reality itself, they depict a murderous, yet intensely exciting moment, one many young viewers seem to have wanted to experience themselves, assuming of course that they would survive to tell the tale. Experiencing battle for the first time as spectators rather than participants, "feeling" themselves as part of the event while simultaneously sitting safely in the cinema, viewers had the illusion that they would indeed survive the real thing just as they had survived (and enjoyed) its screened images. In film the moment of danger and exhilaration is deprived of its most crucial element: man's personal encounter with death. Hence the continuing intoxication, the desire to experience it again.

The propagandists of war rapidly learned that only a few minor changes were needed to transform battle scenes such as those of *All Quiet* into an evocation of the glory and virtues of war. Filmmakers all over the world realized that "realistic" battles on the screen made for large audiences. Indeed, the film's preoccupation with violence, even if intended to portray it as something to be avoided, is mirrored in the growing, rather than diminishing fascination with violence in the media. The 1979 German television version of *All Quiet* serves as a good example, mobilizing as it did all the recent techniques of hyperrealistic representations of human destruction and mutilation, without, however, achieving the psychological effect of the original. The public had by then become quite used to such cinematic simulations of violence. The spectators knew, as did my friends and I twenty years ago, that while this all "looked" completely real, it was mere pyrotechnics: the dead actors would pick up their paychecks and go home happily ever after.

There is thus no telling what effect realistic representations of violence may have, whatever their intended message. While the cinematic portrayals of 1914–18 made some people want to avoid another war at all cost, it made others yearn to participate in it, and convinced others still that the best way of avoiding its destructive consequences was to perpetrate it on others. The ironies of such realistic cinema were well reflected in the fate of Lew Ayres, the main protagonist of *All Quiet*, whose strong identification with his role made him into a pacifist, causing him to confront highly unsympathetic American officials when the United States went again to war.[4] While some of those officials might well have empathized with Ayres' cinematic persona ten years earlier, much of the American public seems to have concurred with the Nazi and German army censorship view of the film: not as an antiwar production, but as an anti-German one. Moreover, along with many other post-1918 representations of war, the film had the ambivalent effect of making the soldiers into victims. Morally, at least, the soldiers came out quite well from the slaughter they had perpetrated, even if physically and mentally it had ruined them.

The cacophony of sophisticated weapons and puerile characters that has become the staple of post-1945 cinematic representations of war and violence doubtlessly indicates the inability or at least lack of will of the popular media to confront the reality of mutual human destruction. Recognizing the huge profits to be reaped from the public's fascination with simulated violence, and constantly enhancing this fascination by providing the viewers with ever more graphic images, this vast industry's focus on box-office returns has had an immensely insidious influence on (especially young) people's perceptions of conflict, killing, and suffering. Whether presented in the guise of fighting criminals, doing war against the forces of evil, pursuing what is "right and just," or frankly celebrating violence and destruction, such films have created and catered to an audience addicted to aestheticized and desensitized images of human aggression and depravity.

A few productions have nevertheless attempted to confront this phenomenon while remaining within the parameters of the genre of antiwar war films that assures filmmakers of box-office success. In the United States the occasion for such films was not surprisingly the Vietnam War, which provided both a rich imagery of concentrated violence and created greater public receptivity to antiwar sentiments. The relative popularity of such films, however, may have as much to do with their fantastic, hyperrealistic reconstructions of destruction as with their implicit message; in this sense, they are very much part of the tradition that began with *All Quiet*.

Probably the most outstanding example of this new/old genre is Francis Ford Coppola's *Apocalypse Now* (1979), precisely because it is not about the Vietnam War at all, but rather about Joseph Conrad's *Heart of Darkness*, interspersed with scenes from Michael Herr's *Dispatches*.[5] This is a film about a man's journey to the innermost depths of evil and perversion, of good intentions turned into human and moral corruption. By exposing the evils of colonialism, Conrad had also anticipated our own century's wars of destruction and genocide. Conversely, Coppola's movie is concerned with the manner in which technological, industrial war has polluted American society and spread its poison to the farthest reaches of humanity. That the making of the film itself actually introduced more of the same to the regions in which it was shot is merely one more indication of the apparently unstoppable, insidious penetration of all that is corrupt in Western civilization, cleansed of its better aspects, into whichever part of the world it turns its attention to.[6] *Apocalypse Now*'s Wagnerian helicopter assault on a Vietnamese village is not an attempt to portray the war "realistically," but an evocation of that dangerous combination of technology and mythology so typical of our modern wars ever since 1914. Nevertheless, the ruthless brutality of these scenes may well have appealed to viewers otherwise unconcerned with what they tell us about the relationship between modernity and annihilation. Similarly, Kurtz's "penal colony" in the jungle is precisely that "black hole," that "anus mundi" which has become the perpetual potential of our civilization's mix of hope and despair, good intentions and violent means. Yet many viewers might have associated the closing episodes of the film with the representations of evil and monstrosity characteristic of popular horror films, especially attractive in this case since the monster was played by Marlon Brando. Hence *Apocalypse Now* brings to mind Graham Greene's "quiet American" both through the character of Captain Willard (based on Conrad's Marlow) and by the ambiguity of its appeal to the American audience. This uncomprehending, optimistic college graduate set upon repairing a world he is busily and conscientiously destroying, is more than a mere literary trope: he is still with us today, charged with such improbable tasks as "nation-building" and "peace-making" in Somalia and Kuwait, Haiti and Panama, followed wherever he turns by ever larger television crews, whose technological sophistication is matched only by their superficial intellects and profound ignorance of that which they allegedly represent on our screens.

Coppola's film thus typifies the constraints of this genre by its uneasy balance between celebrating and condemning human violence and corruption. Michael Cimino's *The Deer Hunter* (1978) exemplifies the other problem of the genre, the theme of the soldier as victim. Rejecting both heroization and demonization, Cimino looks at the war as it is brought home to the distant American towns from which the soldiers had sailed off to contain what they were told was the incarnation of evil (and to assert their masculinity), and to which some of them returned as physical and psychological wrecks. There are no important battle scenes here, just human suffering and disintegration, social and mental. Dislocated from their homes, the soldiers can never wholly reintegrate, unable to transmit or understand their own experience in an alien world they had believed they could master. The devastating effects of war are of course not merely personal, since quite apart from the destruction of another land (never successfully depicted in American films, and thereby manifesting a long-term inability to empathize with the "enemy"), the war and its survivors bring back home a sense of frustration and cynicism, anger and helplessness, suspicion and alienation, which may well be at the root of the present public mood in the United States. There is a great deal of self-pity in this film, and a celebration of the suffering, victimized soldier at the expense of his own victims who are indeed somewhat crudely dehumanized in scenes of torture and brutality. Here too we can recognized themes already present in *All Quiet*, where the instruments of destruction are seen as its main targets. Hence even these two films, not least because they remain within the parameters of antiwar movies directly concerned with war and soldiers, reveal the limitations and ambiguities of this approach. They can be seen as antiwar works, but they can just as easily be accepted by those merely fascinated with violence and sympathetic to the fate of its perpetrators.

Whatever their shortcomings, *Apocalypse Now* and *The Deer Hunter* signified the beginning of America's coming to terms with the price of war and its destructive effects on its own society, even when fought in far-off places by men whose compatriots hastily marginalized on their return. But precisely because of their ambivalent attitude toward violence and victimhood, and the manner in which they were received and perceived by both critics and the moviegoing public, it is also no wonder that this beginning was not followed by much more in the subsequent decades. The popular imagination preferred Rambo-like depictions of war, while slightly more subtle tastes opted for such films as Oliver Stone's *Platoon* (1986) and Stanley Kubrick's *Full Metal Jacket* (1987), which returned to the pseudo-realistic representation of battle, mobilizing now the evermore sophisticated techniques of hyperrealism to camouflage their psychological superficiality and inability to confront the meaning and significance of modern war for our civilization.[7] Here bodies are torn to shreds, blood flows in endless torrents, sound effects make the audience "feel" the "reality" of battle, and minds are numbed by scene after scene of violence and destruction. And when it is all over people leave the cinema with the same sense of complacent gratification evoked by any horror or pornographic film. Noise and gore replace understanding, and the cameras perform the same task in the studio they were expected to perform on the landing beaches in Somalia: bring to us the "reality" of war while obscuring its meaning. Heads roll in newsreels from Sarajevo as they do in Hollywood reenactments of past battles; they seem to have little to do with our own.

Can we then conclude that it is impossible to make antiwar films? I think not. Films, after all, can be more subtle and richer in imagery and meaning than museums. But I doubt whether it is possible to make antiwar war films without conceding the fascination they may exert on at least some of the viewers. Nor, I believe, can antiwar films limit themselves only to this particular agenda. This is to say, just as the antiwar message cannot exist independently of a wider view of human affairs, so too an antiwar film will not be effective without offering a more comprehensive, albeit more ambiguous critique of both its own cinematic universe and of the social context in which it is made.

This genre of antiwar films, in which war is seen as both consequence and reflection of a deeper social and cultural malaise, found powerful expression in Jean Renoir's masterpiece *The Grand Illusion* (1937). Here battle is not depicted, and the boundaries between victim and victimizer, hero and villain are frequently blurred. Instead of making the viewers complicit in the excitement and brutalization of battle, Renoir urges them to share his melancholy view of the crumbling, hypocritical, yet somehow also more decent and dignified old codes of behavior in favor of the new, brutally sincere, and sincerely brutal norms, where physical survival is paramount, and anything that stands in its way must be eliminated. Not everyone dies in this film, and those who do are not imbued with the romantic vision of Remarque's "lost generation." The dead die because what they represent has already perished, that same chivalrous ethos that had brought about the slaughter and thereby sealed its own fate. Renoir, who in principle has no sympathy for the aristocracy and the old officer corps, empathizes with them precisely because they are on the way to becoming an extinct species. Conversely, the living survive because they are the natural inheritors of the post-1918 world. They are the fittest, those who are tough enough to withstand the destruction and dull enough not to be perturbed by its horrors, and those who are sufficiently clever to shelter from the destruction and sufficiently adaptable to find a niche in the new, far more ruthless and chaotic reality of postwar society. Renoir can sympathize, even empathize with them; yet he cannot help revealing his own nostalgia for the "world of yesterday," lost in a typically unnecessary, foolhardy, spectacular act of chivalry.

The Grand Illusion is a successful antiwar film precisely because it is not *about* war, but about the effects of war on human society, and because it is not only about its own antiwar sentiments, but about a larger view of humanity, a view that while ideologically favoring the emergence of a new society can also lament the disappearance of the old. It is, in brief, truly antiwar because it empathizes with humanity and refuses to accept the dehumanizing effect of war it so well portrays. In rejecting the dark forebodings and anxieties so characteristic of interwar representation, *The Grand Illusion* can be accused of naiveté; and because it eschewed depicting the carnage of the front, it did not have the same box-office success as *All Quiet*. By 1939, however, Renoir had grown increasingly pessimistic, and his portrayal of European society on the eve of another world war was far more bitter and cynical. The film that expressed this mood, *The Rules of the Game*, is the epitome of an antiwar movie with war left completely out, though always present in the background. It is a biting critique of a society geared to murder, though the guns are almost always directed only at animals. If we needed any proof that antiwar films can indeed be made, this is certainly one of the best examples. Yet its impact was and remains minimal. Acknowledged as a cinematic masterpiece, Renoir's last interwar film was a total failure in France, and is viewed today only by a few film lovers. The future, it seemed already then, belonged to the great antiwar war movies, whose message could be comfortably set aside in favor of an ample supply of battlefield heroism and comradeship, action and sacrifice (even if in vain).[8]

Nevertheless, this genre of antiwar films with the war left out did not wholly vanish. Indeed, perhaps precisely because the Second World War had claimed so many more civilian victims than its predecessor, several filmmakers chose to investigate its effects and condemn its devastation by evoking the experience of children, the truly innocent victims of conflicts between adults. One remarkable example of this genre is René Clément's *Forbidden Games* (*Jeux interdits*, 1952). The only war scene in this film is brief, brutal, and composed merely of a column of civilian refugees strafed from the air by German aircraft. The rest of the film concentrates on the deadly games played by war children, traumatized by loss of parents and the general chaos, want, and despair of war and destruction, fear and anxiety. In depicting the brutalization of children in the dehumanizing environment of war and devastation, *Forbidden Games* is related both to Andrei Tarkovsky's *My Name Is Ivan* (*Ivanovo detstvo*, 1962), and to Elem Klimov's more recent *Come and See* (*Idi i smotri*, 1985), though the latter especially is less subtle and far more ruthlessly realistic. Clément achieves what few filmmakers have done before or after; with great sensitivity and an uncanny understanding of children he shows us the war through their eyes, and what we see is so frightening that we step back in horror. Here it no longer matters who is fighting whom and for what cause, since what the war does to the children must (although of course it fails to) make us decide once and for all never to make war again. It is a deeply pacifist and humanist film, quiet and gentle, yet always threatened by the limitless violence lurking just beyond the horizon. Louis Malle's *Au revoir les enfants* (*Goodbye Children*, 1987) is surely part of that tradition, though it is much more about the victims of the victims, Jewish children among the French. Malle's children lead an apparently normal life in the midst of defeat and occupation, until the moment an outside power indicates that they are not all the same after all, that some can remain children and others must become victims, some may live and some must die. Clément's children play burial games, just like many other children, but the context in which these games are played, and their increasing obsession with them, gradually make us realize that the adult world has introduced death to their thoughts and has thereby robbed them of their childhood and consequently of part of their humanity.

Children will remember war very differently from adults, just as soldiers' memories will differ from those of civilians, men's from women's, victims' from perpetrators'. Personal memories will never wholly correspond to society's collective memory of war. Yet although individual memory is acknowledged to be subjective, it nevertheless will often make a claim for authenticity, since it is a mental record of a person's actual involvement in a past event. Hence the tendency for overlap between authenticity, subjectivity, and realism. Edgar Reitz's film *Heimat* (1984), for instance, claimed both to be an "authentic" depiction of life in one German village between 1918 and 1982, and at the same time asserted that it was concerned with the memory, not the reality of the events. In this sense, it is a film about authentic (yet imagined) memories, not about authentic (and largely documented) reality. This type of authenticity enabled *Heimat* to avoid precisely those inconvenient issues that the protagonist of Michael Verhoeven's cabaret-like production *The Nasty Girl* (*Das Schreckliche Mädchen*, 1990) persistently raised to the consternation of her own community, whose "authentic" memories had very little to do with the reality of the past. Similarly, Wolfgang Petersen's *The Boat* (*Das Boot*, 1982) was presented as a realistic depiction of war as seen through the eyes of one German submarine crew during the Second World War. In fact, however, by decontextualizing Germany's war and reconstructing its memory as an "authentic" reflection of past reality, the film strives to relativize that very specific war as merely one more example of the old truism that war, any war, is hell, and that therefore all soldiers, including those in Hitler's service, are victims. Thus, selective (and convenient) memory is recreated as harsh realism, and that fabricated realism is then used as a measuring rod for other memories that contradict it.

The tension between memory and authenticity, past reality and present concerns, is insightfully explored in Harriet Eder's and Thomas Kufus' innovative film *My War* (*Mein Krieg*, 1989/90). This is a view of the war as it was filmed by six Wehrmacht soldiers and amateur photographers, and simultaneously a view of the war by these same six men, now elderly and respectable citizens of the Federal Republic, as they show their films to the directors and reminisce on their war experience. Hence we are provided not only with a peculiar angle of the war as a quasi-touristic adventure, but also with a unique sort of oral history whereby the speaker is constantly confronted with his own records of his past. It is this combination of private film material, mostly kept hidden in sealed closets and drawers since 1945, with the comments made by the very men who had filmed these scenes, this confrontation between record and memory, youth and old age, dangerous adventure and cozy middle-class existence, reality and nostalgia, that makes this into a compelling, and not unambiguous journey along the tenuous frontiers between subjective perceptions and objective historical events, empathy and condemnation, revelation and suppression.

My War is about *their* war, not ours. Whatever films such as *The Boat* may claim, *their* war was not only hell; there were many good moments in it, and some horrors. Most of all, it happened to them when they were young, hopeful, adventurous. Did their experience make them oppose war? Does our exposure to *their* war make us reject war altogether? Just as the film is about subjective experience and memory, so too are our reactions. Films concerned with "real" memories and oral histories, like much of the scholarship on this issue, provoke ambivalent and contradictory reactions, dependent largely on one's own subjective view of the events remembered. Are these men potentially our parents and grandparents, or their potential murderers? Do we empathize with them, or do we feel rage that they had been allowed to reach comfortable middle age and complacently reminisce about "their" war, which is not ours?

Photographic images of Germany's war in Russia have previously consisted mainly of films shot by Wehrmacht propaganda companies.[9] This is of course highly problematic material, not least because it tends either wholly to ignore the criminal aspects of the Russian campaign, or to represent the victims as insidious *Untermenschen*, thereby perpetuating a distancing between the observer and the hardly human forms of the murdered. But in recent years pictorial images from another source have become increasingly available. German soldiers marched into battle equipped not only with orders to murder people belonging to a wide array of political and "biological" categories, but also with their own private cameras. Consequently we now have numerous photographs of Wehrmacht troops photographing their own atrocities, hangings of women, children, and youths, mowing down by machine gun fire of alleged partisans, mass executions by *Einsatzgruppen*. Though forbidden by the Wehrmacht authorities, soldiers could not desist from this "war tourism," and their broad smiles when observing the torture and murder inflicted on their victims have thus remained forever imprinted on our minds thanks to their own photographic obsession.[10]

My War makes no use of propaganda films, but neither does it contain any convincing material on the barbarous nature of the war. In this sense it is not about "their" war as they had experienced (or perhaps even remember) it, but about that selected portion of these former soldiers' films and memories they would like to present as "their" war. Hence this is not merely a subjective view, but a representation of willfully selected subjectivity, or at least of unconscious selection, that tells us as much about the person remembering by what is repressed as it does by what is revealed. The gaps and absences in these amateur films are thus as crucial as the images they have preserved. The edited or unfilmed scenes whose absence we sense while watching the film are the real core of its authenticity: the authenticity of annihilated images.

My War is a film about the filtered memories of real men and the distorted filmic images of real events. As such, it is not an antiwar film, but one about the ambiguity of memory and the uncertainty of authenticity. Conversely, Bertrand Tavernier's *Life and Nothing But* (*La vie et rien d'autre*, 1989) is a film about the authenticity of imagined memories, and the ability of cinematic images to recapture the true core of a past reality that still informs much of our own civilization. It is also an antiwar film *par excellence*, demonstrating once more that truly antiwar films cannot portray battle, but only its deeper consequences for the world that inherits its destruction. Watching Tavernier's film, we no longer believe that the dead actors will simply pick up their paychecks and go home once the shooting is over. The dead in this film are as numerous, and as dead, as the inhabitants of Europe's boundless war cemeteries. For this is a film about the memory of the war, the true and the false, and therefore it is also a film about the authenticity of representation. Yet it is not a self-referential work, nor a postmodern one. Its structure is simple—indeed conventional—and it is the context of the events it confronts, and the deep irony it gradually reveals, that make us realize that beneath its unpretentious facade lies concealed a deeply pessimistic and subversive message.

Life and Nothing But is one of the best films ever made on the industrial killing of 1914–18. No shots are fired in the film, no soldiers charge into a hail of machine-gun bullets. Almost all the soldiers in this film are corpses. The few survivors are preoccupied with identifying and burying their innumerable dead comrades. Mostly we see civilians, who have come to look for their dead. They no longer hope to find them alive; merely finding them would suffice. But the scale and nature of the killing has made that difficult too. Burial is a privilege not many receive. As the plot develops, we realize that two women searching for the dead are after the same man—the same dead man. As they secretly compete for his as yet undiscovered corpse, the authorities launch their own search for the unknown soldier, who is to be buried with great pomp and ceremony under the Arc de Triomphe. The authorities obviously do not want an identifiable corpse, yet they nevertheless want to make sure that it is appropriately representative of their (national) view of all other unidentifiable and identifiable corpses: that it is French, white, male, and that it had once belonged to a soldier. And in the midst of it all is an officer whose task is to identify and register the dead for their families, and to find the right candidates for the tomb of the unknown soldier.[11]

At the center of Tavernier's film is a tunnel blown up by the retreating Germans as a train was passing through it. The families of the soldiers entombed in the tunnel are gathered outside, occasionally entering the tunnel or waiting for items brought out by the search party and rejoicing when they can recognize them as belonging to their dead soldiers. This is an inverse Pascalian universe; here humanity is perched at the mouth of a tunnel of death, threatening to explode at any moment, and every once in a while someone goes in, bringing out a meaningless remnant of a life extinguished long ago.[12] It is this tunnel of horrors, this path into the hellish underworld of industrial killing, that any antiwar film must traverse. Now that the fighting is over, let us at least count the bodies before we recommence the shooting.

III. On Heroes and Villains: The Holocaust in Hollywood

One of the most important (and problematic) aspects of the film *Schindler's List* is that by choosing Oskar Schindler's story as the focus of his representation of the Holocaust, Steven Spielberg implies that even in the heart of darkness, even within sight of the death camps, the option of hampering the Nazi murder machine never wholly disappeared. This is not to say that the *victims* could or should have done more to save themselves; rather, the film rightly stresses that at any given point during the Holocaust, both bystanders and perpetrators were always faced with the choice of collaborating in, passively observing, or actively resisting mass murder, and that resistance could come in a variety of ways, and could be meaningful, even if it meant saving only a handful of victims. Hence the film qualifies the widespread view of the Holocaust as an inherently inevitable, fateful, unstoppable event, one over which human agency had no control, except for its dubious capacity for bringing it to an apocalyptic end.[13]

Schindler is therefore the proof that a single individual, even under the most adverse circumstances, could and did save lives. The painful question is, of course, why were there so few Schindlers, why was his case so extraordinary? And, in the present context, what are the implications of making a film about such a unique case?

The choice of Schindler is crucial not only because he saved Jews, but because he had none of the qualities normally associated with such "righteous Gentiles." An unsuccessful, common crook before he installed himself in the heart of the "Final Solution," Schindler is a true Brechtian character, who sets himself against a state of much worse (but officially "legal") criminals, a man who wishes to profit from evil but also enjoys undermining it, a potentially mediocre character who precisely thanks to his far from respectable qualities can become a saint in this world turned upside down. To be sure, as Schindler admits in the film, the war was the best thing that ever happened to him, but eventually he applies his newly won riches to save the people who enabled him to win them. Finally impoverished, Schindler's real profit is the innocent lives he has saved.

The juxtaposition between the crook and the criminal context in which he operates underlines Schindler's mirror image, the "decent" man who becomes a criminal under the same circumstances. This in turn subverts the Hollywood convention of a cinematic world neatly divided between good and evil. Yet Schindler can exist on the Hollywood screen because he somehow manages to straddle these two modes, that of the cynical, pessimistic, corrupt, wholly un-American hero, whose moral qualities can only shine in the midst of evil; and that of the tough, rough, undisciplined, yet incorruptible and supremely courageous hero of the classic American Western, who is however similarly motivated into action only when faced with truly bad guys.

Spielberg therefore complicates the popularly accepted tale of the Holocaust as neatly divided into victims, perpetrators, and bystanders. Schindler belongs to none of these categories, yet potentially he could fit into any one of them. Initially a bystander hoping to profit from other people's misfortune, he can at any time choose to join the perpetrators; and, since he elects to help the victims, he stands a good chance of becoming one himself. Because he chooses to act, and because he thereby assumes a new identity, Schindler belies the assertion that his (bystander) world had denied one the freedom of choice and the choice of identity.

Spielberg retains admirable control over his film for much of the time, largely avoiding the kitsch and sentimentality that have plagued many other movies in this genre. The combination of pseudo-newsreel qualities with on-location shots and historical characters populates a (fictive) segment of the Holocaust with living human beings and thereby makes for greater empathy with the protagonists than any "real" documentary. And by stressing the sheer brutality and sadism of the "Final Solution" as it was experienced by the victims, Spielberg has filmed some of the most haunting moments in any cinematic representation of the Holocaust. This, however, brings us to some of the inherent problems of films that try to confront the genocide of the Jews.

Being a Hollywood production, *Schindler's List* inevitably has a plot and a "happy" end. By ending the film with an emotional catharsis and a final humanization of his hero, Spielberg compels us to consider the compatibility of the conventions and constraints of American cinema with the profound rupture of Western civilization at the core of the Holocaust.

The film's penultimate scene banalizes both Schindler and the context of his actions. For only the Schindler who precedes this scene, that do-gooder crook who gets a kick from helping Jews and fooling Nazis, that anarchist underworld character with a swastika badge who enjoys his cognac and cigars even under the shadow of Auschwitz, that trickster who befriends a sadistic concentration camp commander, that failure of prewar and postwar normality who relishes the mad universe of the SS where he is king, only that man could have saved the Jews in quite that manner. This Schindler could not, and did not, break down. Nor was the world in which he operated an appropriate setting for sentimental scenes.

The measure of the film's success is that it was watched by large numbers of people who had very little previous knowledge of the Holocaust. Yet this may also mean that *Schindler's List* and all that it depicts will remain the only version of the Holocaust to which much of the public will become exposed, and one, moreover, whose authority as a true reconstruction of the past is reinforced by the fact that it is based on an "authentic" story. This extraordinary tale is therefore transformed into a representative segment of the "story" as a whole, obliterating thereby the fact that in the real Holocaust most of the Jews died, most of those sent to the showers were gassed, and most of the Germans either collaborated with the perpetrators or remained passive bystanders. Consequently, the film distorts the reality of the Holocaust by leaving out that most common and typical feature of the event—namely mass industrial killing.

Post-Holocaust public taste makes two major requirements for representations of the past. First, a "human" story of will and determination, decency and courage, and final triumph over evil. Second, an "authentic" story that, however, is retold according to accepted conventions of representation. To be sure, these two demands contradict each other, since authentic stories rarely conform to conventional representations and even less frequently culminate in the triumph of good over evil. After all, as far as the vast majority of the Holocaust's victims were concerned, evil did indeed triumph. In order to overcome the "unconventional" character of the Holocaust and thereby appeal to the viewers, Spielberg must tell a story that is both authentic and conventional. Yet within the context of the Holocaust, this tale is so unique as to be untrue in the sense of not reflecting (or even negating) the fate of the vast majority of victims who were in fact swallowed up in an unprecedented, and therefore (at least as far as Hollywood conventions are concerned) unrepresentable murder machine. Spielberg therefore tells an "authentic" story that (almost) never happened.

Spielberg's is an evil we can live with, made in Hollywood, that can be defeated by skill and perseverance, willpower and determination. It leaves out the millions who were in no way inferior to the survivors, yet drowned nevertheless. Salvation through personal gifts has no place in the Holocaust, just as it is pernicious to argue (at least as long as one is not a survivor) that the worst survived while the best perished. But such troubling facts would confuse the film's moral agenda and undermine its symmetry, casting doubt on the authenticity of Schindler's case as representative of anything but itself, making the genocide unbearable to contemplate and profoundly shaking our belief in the viability of civilized post-Auschwitz existence. It is this that Primo Levi, Paul Celan, and Jean Améry understood with ever greater urgency in the years following their personal survival: that the stories told by the saved distort the past, not because they are not authentic, but because they exclude the stories of the majority, who drowned not for lack of will to survive, but due to a combination of circumstances in which individual will and skills rarely played an important role, and chance was paramount.[14]

Schindler's List brings us the promise of human decency arising even from the darkest souls and the greatest depths of evil. Everything the Holocaust had actually destroyed, both material and spiritual, is reconstituted (on the screen) by Spielberg, with the same wave of a magic wand we have come to expect from his earlier films. By claiming to provide us with an authentic picture, the screen does what it has always done best: it creates a dream world of glimmering images that hovers momentarily over the debris of reality and then remains in our minds as a comforting tranquilizer. We do not feel the pain, ergo, the pain is no longer there.

Hollywood has been known to conjure up cinematic worlds of intense evil; but such worlds must remain temporary cinematic fantasies, lest they cease to entertain and consequently repel rather than attract audiences. Their success relies precisely on the assumption that they are totally different from the reality beyond the theatre walls. Hence the relief felt by audiences when they return to the street, the expectation of which is at the very root of enjoying the fantasy indoors. Yet Nazism was no fantasy; there was no "outdoors." Nor did the inverted world it had created simply go up in smoke in 1945, either for the survivors, or for the perpetrators, or for human civilization as whole, which has never healed from this horrific surge of modern barbarism. But all this, of course, has no room in a Hollywood production.

Conventionally, the image of a Hollywood hero is enhanced by a diminution of all other characters, apart, of course, from the villain he confronts. Hence we find Schindler (crook turned saint) and Göth (the embodiment of evil) towering both physically (as tall, handsome Aryans) and personally (as clearly etched, strong characters) over a mass of weak, featureless Jews. The potential victims thus largely serve as a mere background to the epic struggle between the good guy and the bad guy. Moreover, the representation of Jews in *Schindler's List* disturbingly evokes the kind of stereotypes Nazism had thrived on, as they haggle over loss and profit while their brethren are being tormented and starved, sell their wares during mass in a Catholic church, vacate huge apartments, hide diamonds and gold in their bread. Jews in this film do not compare well with Schindler's initially detached, cynical posture, transformed in front of our eyes into a courageous, noble stance.

Hollywood's convention of providing sexual distraction to the viewers also plays a disturbing role in the film. Most troubling is the shower scene, since that mass of attractive, frightened, naked women, finally relieved from their anxiety by jets of water rather than gas is more appropriate to a sadomasochistic film than to its horrifying context. That this "actually" happened is, of course, wholly beside the point, for in most cases it did not, and even when it did, the only spectators to have derived any sexual pleasure from observing such scenes were the SS. Spielberg thus makes the viewers complicit with the SS, both in sharing their voyeurism and in blocking out the reality of the gas chambers.

The inherent problems of a "realistic" portrayal of Nazi brutality and sadism were exemplified by a minor scandal in northern California, where a group of high school students reacted to some of the most violent scenes in *Schindler's List* in a manner reminiscent of audience participation in Rambo-style movies. Youths in present-day America associate "graphic" depictions of death and violence in film with entertainment, while simultaneously being exposed to a great deal of actual violence on the streets and in the news media. Hence, while people shot in reality are said to die "just like in the movies," violence in the cinema both entertains and furnishes examples for actual acts of violence on the street. Spielberg's "graphic" portrayal of Nazi sadism was therefore "normalized" as part of a genre to which it ought not to belong (though in a paradoxical, perverse way it nevertheless does), and the students compared these scenes both to other cinematic representations of violence, and to their own very real experiences. As one of them said: "My man got busted in the head just like that last year."[15]

To be sure, no film can recreate an inhuman reality. We cannot blame *Schindler's List* for not showing people actually being gassed, but only for showing them *not* being gassed; we cannot blame it for not showing the emaciated bodies of concentration camp inmates, but only for showing us the attractive, healthy naked bodies of young actresses, whose shorn hair strangely resembles current fashions. It is precisely because of the inability of cinematic representation to authentically recreate a distorted reality that the claim of authenticity—and the sense of the viewers that they are seeing things as they "actually were"—is so troubling. Perhaps we should condemn outright any attempt to represent what the Nazis called "the asshole of the world," where the actual process of dehumanization and murder was practiced on a daily basis. But if we believe that it *is* necessary to make cinematic representations of the thing itself, to show not only the forest grown over the death camp but also the death camp in operation, to record not only the survivors' memories but also the circumstances they remember, then we must accept the limitations of the genre and (some of) the price that may have to be paid.

The debate over *Schindler's List* has raised the question about which genres are most appropriate to cinematic representations of the Holocaust. Should we prefer documentaries to fiction? Is memory the most immediate, sincere, and authentic element in reconstructing the event? And how does film relate to other, non-cinematic forms of representation?

Agnieszka Holland's *Europa, Europa* (1991), similarly based on a true story, shares with *Schindler's List* the quality of being both "authentic" and at the same time too extraordinary truly to represent the fate of most Jews in the Holocaust. The relative popularity of Holland's film was also related to its adventure-like, fantastic, intense plot, and to the consequent tension it creates between its unbelievable tale and the knowledge that it did in fact (more or less) happen. By and large, however, *Schindler's List* has coped better with the dilemmas of such cinematic fiction, both because it contains less kitsch and is more controlled in tone and content, and because it dares to come much closer to the heart of the Nazi genocidal enterprise. Spielberg is less concerned with the incredible fate of a single individual (victim), and more (if insufficiently) with that of the multitude of victims and the circumstances of their murder (or salvation). Schindler's Jews are doubtlessly exceptional, but far less so than Holland's wonder kid. Moreover, by constantly stressing individual ingenuity, imagination, courage, and cunning, *Europa, Europa* distinguishes to an even greater extent than *Schindler's List* between its resourceful hero and his less gifted six million brethren. In this sense too Spielberg's film is a less false, more honest rendering of human fate in the Holocaust.

While acknowledging the dilemma of audience familiarity with graphic violence in popular films, the question remains as to how film can represent the truly unique element of the Holocaust, the industrial killing of millions in the gas chambers, recognized as such even by Holocaust deniers, who precisely for that reason try to negate its reality. Can we resolve the inherent tension between exposure to barbarity and trivialization, ignorance and distorted knowledge, distancing and indifference, objectivity and false understanding, inhumanity and pornography?

Some would argue that only documentaries can resolve these dilemmas. Yet this genre depends, of course, not only on the nature of the documentary material, but just as much on selection, editing, presentation, and commentary, all of which are extraneous to the document itself. *Night and Fog* (1955) might well have neglected to mention the Jews as the main victims of the Nazi death camps because Alain Resnais wanted to prevent his viewers from blocking out the enormity of the Holocaust by seeing it as an event that concerned only other, non-French human beings. Nevertheless, this decision introduced a major distortion of the historical record to a film commonly considered a documentary, and therefore an "objective" representation of the past. Resnais' failure to differentiate between concentration and death camps was similarly related to the implications of distinguishing between political and "biological" victims of the Nazis in postwar France. But in rightly trying to present the Holocaust as a universal problem, Resnais recreated it as an amorphous, ahistorical event, where both perpetrators and victims are ill defined, guilt is too widely dispersed to be specifically attributed, and anxiety in the face of evil replaces demands for practical action.

While the use of contemporary material tends to reinforce the argument of authenticity in documentaries, the circumstances under which such film material was originally shot may strongly undermine its value as "objective" evidence. Nazi film crews clearly intended to confirm the propagandistic image of the regime's victims as subhumans, and thereby create horror, disgust, fear, or detachment, but certainly not empathy in German viewers. Amateur films and photographs of victims similarly reflect the prejudices and morbid curiosity characteristic of Wehrmacht troops.[16] Even films shot by the liberators inevitably show the victims as horribly emaciated, only quasi-human creatures. Precisely because it masquerades as an "objective" representation of "reality," documentary film material may therefore have an even more insidious effect than "authentic" fiction, for it can never be wholly purged of its original context, and will always retain some of the qualities that had made it useful to those who had initially produced it. Indeed, in making documentaries on the Holocaust, directors must take into account that the detachment, revulsion, even outrage felt by their viewers may be at least in part a reflection of the pernicious impact of those Nazi representations of the victims they recycle in their own films.[17]

If Holocaust documentaries may dehumanize the victims and desensitize the viewers, making them emotionally complicit in the crime (at least as bystanders and onlookers), perhaps only the victims' own memory of the event can liberate us from the dilemmas of "authentic" fictions and polluted documents. This is clearly the position of Claude Lanzmann, whose film *Shoah* (1985) both resists a Hollywood-type narrative, and scrupulously avoids any contemporary documentary material. Lanzmann has argued that the only way to make a film on the Holocaust is to invent a wholly new genre. While *Schindler's List* is for Lanzmann a melodrama, a work of kitsch that uses the destruction as a background for the heroic story of Schindler, he describes *Shoah* as a dry and pure work, avoiding personal stories, and creating a mold that can encompass the destruction of the Jewish people as a whole. Implicit in Lanzmann's critique is the argument that *Shoah* is the only possible cinematic rendering of the Holocaust.[18]

Yet Lanzmann's is a flawed masterpiece. Far from being "dry and pure" as its maker would have us believe, and although it may not tell personal stories, *Shoah* is highly biased, reflecting its director's intensely personal, national, and ideological prejudices, and finding expression in his style of interviewing, his editing technique, and the content of his comments. Lanzmann has admitted that he had eliminated numerous witnesses because they were too weak.[19] In fact, he seems to have sought witnesses strong enough to testify at some length and coherence, yet sufficiently "weak" to finally break down in front of the camera under the incessant pressure of his questions, thereby eliciting in his viewers precisely that catharsis he finds so objectionable in Spielberg's film. Lanzmann's ruthlessness as an interviewer, though it makes for an extraordinary film, is also highly disturbing, for his obsession with *Shoah* (both the film and the event) makes him treat survivors as mere human documents, rather than human beings. Hence the almost uncanny lack of empathy in a man who has devoted much of his life to making a film on the memory of the destruction, and the mutilated lives of the saved, the last carriers of that memory.

Nor is Lanzmann in search of the "truth" of the Holocaust, for his obsession with the complicity of the Polish population in the destruction is matched by his almost total lack of interest in his own compatriots (in stark contradiction to that other masterpiece of French documentary cinema, Marcel Ophuls' 1969 film *The Sorrow and the Pity*). And because of Lanzmann's concern with memory, this last omission is especially striking in view of the role which the memory of Vichy (and its repression) has recently been shown to have played in postwar France.[20]

We do not need to accept Lanzmann's apparent belief that his is the only possible *film* on the Holocaust in order to agree that only one *such* film can be made. *Shoah*, the film, is indeed unique.[21] But if we believe that one must make more films on the Holocaust, then they will perforce have to be different. One alternative that shares some common features with Lanzmann's enterprise is the project of recording survivors' testimonies on videotape carried out in the United States and Israel. In one sense, these are an even "purer" form of memory reconstruction, and are an immensely important source for understanding both the reality and the memory of the Holocaust.[22] But in another sense, this is no alternative at all, since if *Shoah* was watched by relatively limited audiences,[23] these videotaped interviews are essentially oral documents intended only for scholars, and can therefore not be expected to have any direct impact on the general public.

In this context we might note that non-cinematic forms of representing the Holocaust display many of the same characteristics we have seen in film, both in their public perception and as far as their own inherent qualities and limitations are concerned.[24] Thus, we find a tendency to privilege memoirs or personal accounts over fiction, and scholarship over museums. Moreover, this ranking exhibits the same tensions we have noted above between limited exposure and distortion, imposed both by the nature of the medium and the greater scope for bias and prejudice in the more popular genres.

Even more crucially, claims for "authenticity," "realism," and "objectivity" are just as prevalent and problematic in these forms of representation as in film. Museums, which purport to present a dispassionate array of "authentic" artifacts, actually impose a more or less coherent and didactic narrative on their displays by means of their selection, organization, captions, and so forth. Yet in the presence of "real" objects visitors are hampered from uncovering the subtext that actually orders such plastic reconstructions of the past.[25] Survivors' memoirs too, quite apart from questions of authenticity, are not always free from melodrama and manipulation of emotions.[26] Nor is historical scholarship immune to prejudice and bias, leaving aside the built-in limitations of every historical text that impose on it a process of selection, evaluation, directions of inquiry, allegiances to subdisciplines, and personal interest and style. Historical texts can offer highly distorted representations of the past without appearing to diverge from the format and conventions of established scholarly practice. Moreover, when given the right exposure in the mass media, the authority of the historian may play a major role in popularizing false or partial reconstructions of the past. Indeed, the lay public is most likely to be exposed to those historical interpretations least likely to offer a reliable representation of the past, and yet would be prone to take precisely such stories at face value because they would be presented as the culmination of scholarly research. For while contemporary historians are increasingly aware of the tenuous nature of their claims for objectivity, much of the public still maintains considerable faith in them as judges and interpreters of the truth, at least as far as the past is concerned.

By recognizing the limitations of historical scholarship as a means of public enlightenment, on the one hand, and the widespread public ignorance of the past, on the other, it might behoove us to conclude that we can ill afford to dismiss a relatively well conceived and produced, though flawed, cinematic representation of the Nazi genocide of the Jews, which has managed to reach a far wider public than any other such venture since the television production *Holocaust* (1978). Indeed, though far inferior to *Schindler's List*, that mini-series is a good example of the positive effect even mediocre films may have if they appear at the right time and in the right place. The impact of *Holocaust*, especially in Germany, was by and large salutary, the biting criticism of the German intelligentsia and the complaint that Hollywood had stolen Germany's history from the Germans, notwithstanding.[27]

Since as scholars we are rarely in a position to prevent the proliferation of objectionable popular representations of the past, but do have an interest in creating greater public awareness and knowledge of the Holocaust and other crimes against humanity, we might as well try to influence the media by constructive criticism or involvement, rather than dismiss anything that does not meet our expectations. I, for one, find that of all the Oscars recently awarded, both Spielberg's film and Oskar Schindler the man have deserved it most. And speaking of Oskars, I am reminded of Oskar Matzerath, the protagonist of Günter Grass's *The Tin Drum* and of Volker Schlöndorff's eponymous 1979 cinematic rendering of the novel.[28] The similarities between the two characters are quite striking. Both thrive only in times of war and terror: Schindler makes a fortune and becomes a hero, Matzerath remains an eternally beautiful three year old whose appearance and glass-shattering voice protect him from all harm. Both are destroyed by peace and normalcy: Schindler fails in business, loses his fortune, drinks, and lives on "his" Jews, despised by his own countrymen; Matzerath is transformed into an ugly dwarf and ends up in an insane asylum. And yet I still prefer Oskar Schindler, the man and the film, if only because, when all is said and done, the man had saved real people, and the film, despite all its faults, made an attempt to represent the evil of the time and the valiant efforts of one man to oppose it. The dwarf, Oskar Matzerath, could only destroy. And, since he is only a metaphor, he was never much good at saving people anyway.

IV. Plastic Holocausts: Making It Better

Driving from the fertile plain by the sea on the old pre-state road, by agricultural settlements and former British army barracks, up the reforested mountains (the burned-out hulls of armored cars that tried to break through to the besieged city in 1948 still by the roadside), then quite suddenly within sight of Jerusalem, I cannot help thinking that if there is any site in the world where a Holocaust memorial and museum should stand, it is right here, in this ancient symbol of unity and discord, faith and fanaticism, hope and despair, where the Jewish people was formed as a nation and whence the universal message of Christianity first began its long journey into the world, creating the vast, rich civilization that finally turned on its origins in Auschwitz.

It is a cool, rainy day. The dust has washed off the cypresses, and the rocky slopes are bright with moisture as the sun briefly reappears behind the racing clouds. From this spot it is not difficult to imagine the troubled millennia of the surroundings, the countless stories every stone seems to contain, the forebodings of a future that still, as always, mixes promises of salvation and prophesies of doom. The cafeteria is still empty, smelling of Turkish coffee and poppy-seed cakes. Only a few tourist buses are parked outside. Has it already been twenty years since I last visited Yad Vashem as part of the "education week" in the army?

Yad Vashem is of course a national institution, and as such was set up to serve many purposes, some of them quite contradictory.[29] It is Israel's official memorial of the Holocaust and therefore is based on the assumption that the Jewish state is the only political entity that can appropriate the memory of the attempted genocide of the Jews as part of its own self-definition and legitimation. All visiting foreign dignitaries are taken there (although a recent Foreign Ministry decision, indicative of the changing political climate in Israel, has struck the obligatory visit off the official protocol), along with school children, soldiers, policemen, trade union members. The state of Israel is thus seen as both the consequence and the panacea: the visitor should come out with the thought that had there been a Jewish state before the Holocaust, genocide would not have occurred; and since genocide did occur, there must be a state. But also that just as the state can be traced back to the Holocaust, so too the Holocaust belongs to the state: the millions of victims were potential Israelis, just as the Israelis are the offspring of the survivors. And more: that all Israelis are potential victims, in the past, the present, and the future. Hence the tie is not only historical, personal, ideological; it is also projected into the future, the bond that ties all Israelis to each other as survivors of a catastrophe still living on the brink of an abyss. Only unity, determination, a knowledge of past disasters, and a commitment to preventing their recurrence can keep out the forces of evil. We, the Israelis, are totally different, having metamorphosed ourselves into a new/old breed, bridging the two millennia between the Israelites and the citizens of Israel, a living contradiction of the interim of exile and humiliation. Yet we are also the sons and daughters of the murdered, and it is their image that must always shine darkly in our minds as we contemplate our own existence, fight our wars, make our peace. Yad Vashem tries to provide a simple, clear message; but it is part of an ambiguous history, and therefore its own message is filled with the contradictions of our time.

Yad Vashem is very much the setting, the purpose(s), the context. It is also an important research and documentation center, though this too is not wholly free of the politics of its environment. The site contains some impressive structures, such as *Ohel Yizkor* (Memorial Tent), a vast concrete slab set on a heap of stones, evoking a combination of the Biblical *Gal'ed* (commemorative mound), *Ohel Mo'ed* (tabernacle or God's tent), and a modern bunker (intended to preserve memory, but also, unintentionally perhaps, associating the fate of unarmed European Jewry with the military might of Israel and its self-proclaimed task of protecting the Jews). The exhibit itself, however, has the strange quality of many other 1950s Israeli museums, kibbutz and municipal memorial halls, school exhibits. One is reminded of Greece, the contents of whose unmovable ruins in their majestic setting were transported to the museums of younger, richer members of Western civilization. Yad Vashem cannot boast the architectural design and extensive holdings of the United States Holocaust Memorial Museum in Washington, D.C., nor the electronic sophistication of the Simon Wiesenthal Center's Beit Hashoah Museum of Tolerance in Los Angeles. It contains some photographs, a slide show, a film, a few "authentic" requisites, mainly partisans' weapons. Though a national institution, it is a poor man's exhibit. Its power is derived from both its location and the event it commemorates.

Yet the Holocaust occurred elsewhere. The camps are scattered throughout Central and Eastern Europe. Hence the location is significant in a different way from that of antiquity's remains. Athens, after all, is a site of former greatness, a monument to humanity's past achievements (robbed by modern empires). Auschwitz is a site of recent murder, still richly sown with the ashes of millions of victims.[30] Ancient rulers used to put up columns on the sites of their victories. But the Holocaust was humanity's greatest defeat. Can this devastating debacle at the end of what we like to think of as millennia of progress be commemorated where it happened? Or should it be remembered where the tortuous journey to Auschwitz began? Or, perhaps, as has been argued by the legitimizers of the Washington museum, the Holocaust should be made part of the New World, integrated into the fabric of American aspirations and optimism, not in order to qualify them, but rather to be qualified itself, as a terrible, but by no means fatal road accident on the highway to a better future?

Curiously, although its reveals an "intentionalist" ordering of the past, Yad Vashem's reasoning, both as manifested in the captions, and as an institution of political importance, is "functionalist." We move through the traditional historical chronology of German antisemitism, the rise of Nazism, to the death camps. But much space is devoted to the bureaucratic, "banal" aspects of genocide. And, of course, Yad Vashem is very much intended as a functional site, to teach and to warn, not merely to remember and to mourn, to prove the necessity of the state to others, not only to remind them of its tragic legacy. Yet the ambiguity of the "lessons" of the event seems to have informed the organizers of the exhibit. It is, of course, like all plastic representations of the past, didactic, but its demagogy is uncertain of its own message, and is thus less blatant and deterministic than might be expected, fearful, perhaps, of imposing too clear and one-sided a reading on an event that defies easy explanations. To be sure, Yad Vashem leaves little room for non-Jewish victims of Nazi genocidal policies, and expresses some reservations regarding their status as victims on a par with the Jews. Similarly, the *Judenräte* (Jewish Councils) are hardly mentioned, in an obvious attempt to avoid controversy in a site devoted to the unity of the victims, just as the Warsaw Ghetto rebellion is given great prominence (and German losses appear somewhat exaggerated), as is appropriate to a national museum that seeks to trace the beginnings of the Israeli transformation of Jewish identity from "abnormal" subjugation and defenselessness to "normal" statehood and military defiance. And, of course, the exhibit ends with a clear Zionist message, according to which the "natural" culmination of the Holocaust was the *Ha'apala* (the illegal immigration to Palestine) and the establishment of the State of the Jews.[31] Nevertheless, one does not come away from the museum with a sense of triumph, nor with a feeling that this reordering of the past has liberated its future, our present, of ambiguity and doubt.

This is manifested most clearly by the visitors, who infuse this strangely dusty, seemingly improvised exhibit with meaning and emotion, as they interact with each other, with the artifacts, the monuments, even the surrounding nature. For nature here, though so different from the sites in which the genocide took place, is somehow not alienating, nor in stark contradiction to the indoor exhibit. One does not exit onto a busy street, cramped with sights of grandeur and poverty relentlessly rubbing against each with that ruthless energy of modernity, as in Washington or Los Angeles. One is in an ancient, somehow forgiving landscape, though heavy with portents of the future and memories of shattered hopes, of new construction and crumbling remnants, a multiplicity of faiths and indefatigable animosities. Soldiers discreetly weeping, old men and women murmuring in Yiddish, French nuns and German tourists, organized groups from New Jersey and school children from Tel Aviv. Descending from the buses, they all seem alike, off on some joyous expedition. Exiting from the exhibit, they become, just for a moment, part of the setting, subdued, slowly moving on the hilly path from one structure to another, outlined against the cloudy sky.

Two recent additions to Yad Vashem exemplify the different modes of evoking memory through plastic representations. The Children's Memorial is a modern conceptualization of the traditional Jewish memorial candle: reflected in numerous mirrors within an enclosed space, through which the visitors wind their way in almost total darkness. It is a moving, yet somewhat disturbing experience, not only because the visitors' preoccupation with finding their way in the dark distracts them from the fragile, flickering lights around them, but

also because the structure is so completely alien to its environment, the mate-
rialization of a sophisticated idea artificially latched on to this stony hill. It seems
to belong to another world, neither to children, nor the mountains of Jerusalem, but to a cold, modern, glass and steel metropolis: Los Angeles, or Washington. Emerging from the darkness, adjusting with difficulty to the bright light
outside as the sky finally clears and the sun rapidly dries the rocks, one is struck
by the incongruity of the memorial with all that is around it. The children, one
feels, had they been allowed to live, would have played outside; but they are
locked inside this chamber of reflected lights, while the adults wind their away
amongst their souls, claustrophobically staring at their feet, anxious to find the
exit from the tomb and return to the real world.

Not so the last, remarkable memorial, *Emek Hakehilot* (Valley of the Communities). About a mile from the main structures of Yad Vashem, this rocky
labyrinth dug into the mountainside is made of narrow, steep-walled paths, onto
which the names of all Jewish communities destroyed by the Nazis are carved.
There is no easy way out of the labyrinth, and one must walk down these silent
alleys, surrounded by names of dead, faraway places, many of which have since
revived and gone back to normality, no longer aware of or willing to remember their vanished prewar populations, torn out of them in a massive surgical
operation: Vienna and Berlin, Riga and Warsaw, Odessa and Lodz, Vilna and
Minsk, on and on. Above the sky is now luminous blue, the tough Jerusalemite
bushes are sprouting on the bare rock face, and bunches of delicate cyclamens
peer from under the stones. There is a place in Spain called the *Ciudad
Encantada*, the enchanted city, a valley known for its strange rock formations
created by natural erosion. *Emek Hakehilot* is the enchanted site of the souls
murdered in the Holocaust: the earth is bare and ancient, the plants are fresh
and wild, the sky is bright and transparent.

The parking lot has meanwhile filled with buses. The kiosk is now surrounded by tourists clamoring for memorabilia. As I drive down the mountain
back to the fertile plain by the sea, a soft rain begins to fall. The radio reports
bombs and deaths, peace negotiations and threats of violence. The spell is gone:
nothing is new under the sun, the world follows its course.

During a coffee break in a conference in Washington in 1993, one of the participants announced that he had just returned from a visit to the United States
Holocaust Memorial Museum, upon which another colleague asked: "Well, did
you like it? Did you like the Holocaust?"

If there is a need for a Holocaust museum, and I know that many, including
myself, have had grave doubts about the idea of plastic representations of the
Holocaust, then the museum in Washington is arguably the best that we can
hope for, some specific reservations notwithstanding.[32] The location, even if it
carries very different associations from those of Jerusalem, is highly symbolic:
a museum of the Holocaust in the capital of the United States, far from the
sites of the genocide, in a country the vast majority of whose population was
neither directly nor indirectly touched by the event, has the potential of universalizing the Holocaust as a phenomenon of major significance for human

civilization as a whole. The location also ensures that the museum will be visited by very large numbers of people.

There are problems, however, with universalizing the Holocaust.[33] Does it mean that the genocide of the Jews "belongs" to all of humanity and, if so, in what way? Does it imply a shared *responsibility* for the Holocaust, and, if so, in what sense? Does it signify that genocide is a perpetual potential in human civilization, or that the "Final Solution" was merely one of many other mass murders in history? More specifically, is the museum intended to commemorate and remember the murder of the Jews, or does the murder of the Jews serve merely to evoke the many other murders before and after? What is the position of the Jews, and what is the position of the United States, vis-à-vis the genocide? If the Jews are the victims, is America the savior? If modern civilization is the context, where does the United States fit in? If the Jews are the main subject of the museum, what about all other ethnic and cultural minorities (or majorities) in the increasingly diverse American society, where a growing awareness of muticulturalism is increasingly confronting fears of fragmentation and calls for a return to old and trusted "Christian" values?

The question is, indeed, *why* a Holocaust museum in the United States? Is it because America perceives itself as the land of the free, the liberator of oppressed minorities, the crusader of human rights? Does it reflect the power and influence of the Jews? Or is this the result of specific foreign and domestic political circumstances and interests, some of which are still present, others that played a role in the decision to build the museum but have since been forgotten or have lost all relevance?

The point is not that these questions must be answered (there are as many answers as there are points of view and prejudices), but rather that they could be, and have been asked, and that while some of them may indicate the beneficial effects of the museum, others hint at the potentially insidious interpretation of the whole undertaking, and still others reveal the manner in which the museum can be used to obscure certain pernicious aspects of that very society in which it was erected. Like all important cultural institutions, the Holocaust Memorial Museum is not only about memory and its commemoration: it is about the politics of the present and about an interpretation of the past that seeks either to legitimize, or to criticize, the present. If the past is a foreign country, then in the museum we walk through an exhibition of photographs and artifacts put together by those who had toured that country and wish to tell us about it. But what they tell us is *their* impressions of that foreign land, not what that land *actually* is or was, even if some of the "natives" were enrolled in the planning and organization of the exhibit. And *their* impressions become *ours*, especially those of us who do not have access to other sources of information and comparison. And having been "there" (in the museum, not the past it represents), we now think we *know*, because we *saw* and *felt* it, and on the basis of that "knowledge" we can also reevaluate, or reconfirm, our perceptions of our own society, and of ourselves. Do we and our present-day society become more familiar, or more foreign to ourselves after this visit to a (representation of a) strange and forbidding region? Do we look

at ourselves and our neighbors with different eyes, or do we find relief in stepping out to a familiar environment, whose dangers and benefits are known to
us? Are we *comfortable* with the stark differences between here and there, then
and now, and do we want to maintain them, at least in our minds, or can we
perceive the potential similarities?

Stepping out of the museum we (if "we" are not foreigners) know the zones
of plenty and power, of danger and poverty. We know that the color of our
skin and the shape of our eyes *matters*, just as much as our income and place
of residence. But *this* is not as bad as *that*. And, by and large, at this point in
time, the victims are different. Is the museum then a warning, or does it serve
the purpose of catharsis, of showing us the worse to tell us that *nothing* is as
bad as *that*, and therefore that everything is better, and we all, the rich and
the poor, the persecuted and the persecuter, should be relieved that at least
that is over? Does the museum, therefore, have a galvanizing or a debilitating
effect? Does it subvert or legitimize? Does it accuse those who can no longer
be punished and acquit those who are still among us, even ourselves?

Inside the building, however, we are transported to another world. The
remarkable physical structure of the museum serves the purpose of evocatively
housing the exhibit exceptionally well. To be sure, we are guided to the ultimate horror by the same, seemingly unavoidable plastic rhetoric characteristic of all conventional Holocaust exhibits. Although the captions, written in
consultation with some of the best scholars in the field, provide more depth,
they too do not commit themselves to any controversial interpretation of either
the causes or the nature of the genocide. We move through the rise of Nazism
to the persecution of the Jews, the boycotts and violence, the concentration
camps and racial laws, *Kristallnacht* and the deportations, finally the ghettos
and the death camps. Relatively little space is devoted to the role of science in
furthering and legitimizing the murder of undesirable human beings, or to the
part played by the legal profession in sanctioning and legalizing genocide.
Hence the Holocaust in this museum is very much a German affair, its victims
are mainly Jews, and the perpetrators are mainly identifiable Nazis. This is not
far from the truth, of course; but it is a strangely comforting narrative, since
Germany has been evidently transformed (as its government hoped to be
allowed to show in another section of the museum), the Nazis are presumably
no longer with us, and antisemitism is supposedly restricted now to a few
marginal fanatics. In this sense, the Holocaust keeps happening only within
the confines of the museum, and we, the visitors, are safe from its implications
by the very fact that we can only see it exhibited as an historical event. Since
by now most visitors to the museum were born after the event, they may well
come out with the sense that terrible things had happened in the past, in some
cases even to their own relatives, but that these concern them only as historical facts, not as related in any direct manner to their present society.

This impression is enhanced by the optimistic, uplifting ending of the
exhibit. Just like Spielberg's *Schindler's List*, the museum concludes with scenes
of newly arrived survivors in Palestine. Zionism was, it seems, the appropriate
answer to Nazism. And since Nazism is gone, and the State of Israel is alive

and well, we no longer have any reason to worry (though according to this logic "we," if we are Jews, should either live in or support Israel, that is, be Zionists of one kind or another). *That* genocide, in any case, has been mastered.

To be sure, the Holocaust museum in Washington is very much an expression of a difficult dilemma. An alternative narrative might have been at least as problematic, if not indeed much worse. There was, as we know, a great deal of pressure on the organizers of the museum to include in it many other groups persecuted by the Nazis, as well as groups, ethnic or political, persecuted and murdered before and since. This might have made it into a museum of genocide, or persecution, rather than a museum of the Holocaust. But such a solution might have both relativized the Holocaust in the sense intended by the revisionists of the *Historikerstreit* and created a host of political debates on sensitive issues. Does one include Native Americans, or Armenians, or Kulaks? Does one include the millions murdered in colonial wars, from Algeria to Vietnam, Latin America to Africa? And what about slavery? Is genocide only physical elimination, or should we also include cultural genocide, or marginalization of homosexuals, suppression of women, abuse of children, infanticide, and female circumcision?

There can be no doubt that a single museum cannot and most probably should not even try to provide room for all that. Just like courses in world history, by attempting to teach everything, it would have ended up by teaching nothing, or, worse still, by creating a sense of knowledge in people who would actually remain as ignorant as before, their minds merely splattered with a few disparate, unconnected, unexplained, and decontextualized images, and hence even more open than before to abuse by savvy manipulators of opinion and emotion. Therefore, problematic as this narrow focus on the genocide of the Jews may be, it is nevertheless preferable to this alternative, especially because, when all is said and done, the "Final Solution" was indeed unlike any other event, even in a human history of great savagery and cruelty, endless massacres, and genocides. This does not make it any "better" or "higher," but merely suggests that there may be some specific lessons that we could draw from this event, particularly since they might have a direct bearing on our present condition. Yet I would argue that these lessons are not presented by the Washington museum, and that this absence is neither accidental nor insignificant.

The genocide of the Jews was very much a modern phenomenon. Genocide has occurred many times in the past, but this kind of industrial killing had only one clear precedent—the Great War—with the important qualification that while the latter was directed by soldiers at soldiers, the latter was carried out by technicians and bureaucrats against a whole people, with the explicit aim of killing each and every member of that "race" in an efficient, well-organized, industrial manner. This could be achieved only by a highly modern, disciplined, bureaucratic state, in which people had respect for law and order, science and technology. That is, the crucial precondition for the genocide of the Jews was a modern state, just like the Western industrialized states in which we now live, and whose basic features so many of us would like to see being exported to other parts of the world that do not yet benefit from them and are therefore neither as "civilized" nor as economically efficient as our own societies, being instead poor, prone to political disorder and violence, and suffering from epidemics, famine, and an allegedly general condition of savagery and brutality.

If there is any single lesson to be drawn specifically from the Holocaust, it is that precisely our own society, our political and economic institutions, as well as mass and individual psychology, contain the potential of another *such* genocide. Yet this is a lesson we wish *not* to draw, and certainly one that a state-funded, public institution, cannot emphasize; because it is not only profoundly disturbing, but also highly subversive. And no state would allow the erection of a major cultural institution devoted to subverting its very essence right in the heart of its own center of power.

While avoiding sensitive current political issues, the museum strives to underline the historicity of the event it exhibits through the authenticity of its artifacts, requisites, and documentary records. A great effort was made to bring numerous "authentic" artifacts of the Holocaust to the exhibit: barracks from Auschwitz, a freight car used for deportations, the victims' shoes and shorn hair. Clearly, this is meant to bring the visitors closer to the "reality" of the event and simultaneously to repudiate the challenge of the deniers of the Holocaust. And yet the result is rather to create a false sense of "reality" while trivializing the genocide. Walking through a clean, somewhat rickety freight car, staring at a pile of old shoes, inspecting the symmetrical wooden bunks of a concentration camp (strangely reminiscent of camping sites, such as those once inhabited, perhaps, by the ardent German youths of the *Wandervogel*) does not bring us "closer" to the filth and stench, brutality and fear, death and cruelty that was the Holocaust; it makes us merely empathize with what is *not* the thing itself, but merely its nicely reordered reproduction. These "authentic" artifacts are no more related to the reality of the Holocaust than the reconstituted Puritan settlements in New England or the fake traditional farm houses in the Black Forest; the similarity is as deceptive (and heart-wrenching) as that between a busy barber shop and the mounds of rotting victims' hair in the museum's cellars.

The most powerful aspect of the museum is to my mind the documentary material constantly shown in its numerous video monitors. Despite the problems of using such film material discussed above, seen within the setting of the museum these images continue to haunt the mind long after leaving the building, even if one had been exposed to most of them many times in the past. Moreover, the distancing that this massive exposure to dehumanized victims may facilitate is attenuated to some extent by that remarkable exhibit of pictures taken from a single Jewish town *before* the disaster. Precisely these photographs of normal human beings as they had lived shortly before they were turned into victims do not allow us to think of the mountains of corpses in the monitors as somehow unrelated to our own existence. For we too soon return to our normal homes and families, jobs and colleagues, loves and friendships. But unlike the inhabitants of that town, we may remember that the distance between normality and barbarity is a very short one—indeed, sometimes only a few blocks away, or within reach of our television remote control, or in our own hearts and minds. Thus, while charting a careful, uncontroversial, politically safe course, the Holocaust Memorial Museum in Washington nevertheless sends a different, though muted and indirect message: that the past is still with us, not merely as memory, but as a very real, perpetual peril.

Holocaust museums seem to offer two narrative options: one that presents Zionism as the ultimate answer to Jewish persecution by host gentile nations; another that argues in favor of toleration and understanding for cultural and ethnic minorities. The first is a nationalist narrative, the second a humanist one. These are not mutually contradictory messages, but they do reflect the social and intellectual environment in which they tend to be disseminated. What they have in common, however, is their insistence on ignoring such aspects of the genocide of the Jews that relate it to precisely those present political and socioeconomic conditions one would rather maintain, even if they clearly acted as major factors in generating and perpetuating industrial killing. Moreover, while the bureaucratic, legal and scientific establishment of the modern state was crucial to the realization of genocide, and nationalism has often stood in the way of tolerance, the insistence of cultural and ethnic minorities on their own unique rights and privileges has also been known to serve the cause of conflict and hatred, both domestic and foreign. Zionism has by now had its history of suppressing "minorities" and "indigenous" populations. By the same token, multiculturalism has played a role in the fragmentation of American society, basing itself as it does on group identity and exclusion, rather than on the multicultural individual who may therefore belong to more than one group at any given time.[34] Tolerance of groups can lead to intolerance of individuals who refuse wholly to identify themselves with the group, expressing thereby their unwillingness to chose between the various components of their identity and rejecting the totalizing demands of monopolizing group identities. Groups (ethnic, cultural, religious), it must be recognized, are rarely satisfied with being "tolerated"; they will inevitably seek hegemony over their members, and not infrequently also hope to hegemonize the rest of society by dominating those other groups of which it might be constituted.

The Simon Wisenthal Center's Beit Hashoah Museum of Tolerance in Los Angeles is in the heart of what might be called the epitome of a postmodern metropolis. Flying across vast, empty stretches of plain and desert, one finally descends into that narrow strip of land between the forbidding mountains in the east and the ocean in the west, densely populated by people of every race and creed, a teeming Tower of Babylon where the mere mention of nationalism could provoke a major conflict. This is the land of (in)tolerance, of sleepy smiles and riots, fantasy villas and wretched poverty, endless factories of cinematic illusions and multitudes of desperate, illegal "aliens." This is the (displaced?) heart of the American dream, that impossible combination of Christian Love and the armed citizenry, of the melting pot (pressure cooker?) and ethnic particularism, of sharing and togetherness in the face of unbelievable social and economic divides. What is needed to avoid another Holocaust (or LA riot), argues the museum, is tolerance. All we need to do is tolerate, nay, love each other, and then we can return to our respective slums or villas wholly transformed, accepting of our fate and fortune. Prejudice, we are told, was at the root of genocide, hence we must eliminate prejudice (not its causes) and all will be well. Not a change of material realities, but a change of heart, not a transformation of the conditions that perpetuate frustration and violence, but a transformation of our perception of these conditions. Just as the medieval Catholic Church had insisted that man's station in society was divinely ordained, and that all that was needed was love and acceptance, so too the Simon Wiesenthal Center accepts the conditions that breed prejudice while calling for the replacement of prejudice with love. If the 1960s celebrated love as a transforming social force, the 1990s seem to celebrate love (of oneself, one's group, one's nature) as an antidote to social upheaval in the face of potential explosion. Ironically, this museum, which attempts to find a relationship between present intolerance and past genocide of the Jews, interprets the past through a Christian prism of infusing matter with spirit, allowing things to remain precisely as they are while simultaneously arguing that they have been transformed in their essence through love (and faith). The possibility that love, or at least human dignity and mutual respect, can only be created through a change in the material conditions of humanity, does not seem to occur to the organizers of the Hall of Tolerance.

Human dignity and respect may well also have to do with the fundamental assumption made by the museum, according to which American youths are incapable of taking in any complex, let alone verbal or written messages, but are only receptive to visual imagery whose technological sophistication is only matched by its immense intellectual poverty. Indeed, the basic notion of this museum is that emotion and image, slogans and crude simplifications must replace comprehension and contemplation, thought and analysis. But even here the museum cannot sustain a consistent point of view, since while urging the visitor to "feel" the events it plastically (and electronically) displays, it also condemns such manipulators of public opinion as Hitler and Stalin for mobilizing people's emotions to evil ends. Hence utilizing emotions for positive purposes is good, and for negative ones is bad. Who is responsible, one of the highly didactic displays asks, and immediately furnishes us with the answer: evil leaders, fanaticized followers, indifferent masses. That is, those who "feel" too strongly and those who do not "feel" enough. And what about us, the spectators? What exactly are we asked to feel, and how strongly?

The message of tolerance is therefore useful because it makes for emotional catharsis without demanding any action on the part of the visitor. What is, after all, the political agenda of tolerance? Are we to tolerate everyone and everything, or can we concede that some people, some things, some regimes, are intolerable, and must be opposed, even destroyed? We empathize with a vague category of victims, possibly or potentially including ourselves, we "feel" for them, but all we are called on to actually do is to tolerate each other (should we then tolerate the perpetrators or should we fight them?). In a society whose members are legally equal, tolerance is merely a psychological, mental process. We are "moved" by sights of intolerance, but we are not asked to make any concrete move to put an end to them. Civil rights having been achieved, as the museum shows in a brief, not particularly informative, but very "moving" film, what is left to accomplish is Love—not adjustment of the socioeconomic system so as to reflect the goals of that great, but now moribund movement, nor even analysis of the roots of the problem. Indeed, we might conclude that precisely this call for inactive, passive tolerance legitimizes our acceptance of conditions of glaring inequality and injustice, so long as we learn to love each other.

A recent perceptive analysis of the Simon Wisenthal Center by Nicola Lisus and Richard Ericson has pointed out that the "emotions factory" it creates exerts a "creeping surrealism" on the visitor.[35] Memory and history are misplaced in favor of an electronically generated, ahistorically oriented emotional catharsis. Although critical of this approach, the authors concede that in our "post-Gutenberg-galaxy" there is "no obvious escape" from this type of representation, since "We are a generation weaned on the sensual forms and 'sensual surrealism' of television." Hence, they write, the "managers of the Museum are at least putting television power to good use," even if the museum's assumption that television experiences can be directly translated into understanding and "genocide prevention" is as problematic as the underlying contention that the Holocaust was a product of intolerance, and that therefore tolerance will inevitably prevent its recurrence. The inherent difficulties of this type of representation are clearly manifested in the museum's attempt to provide the visitor with a false sense of what Lisus and Ericson call a "free flicker" environment, while actually determining the available images and thereby manipulating the audience. This is of course not unique to the museum, but is characteristic of any "flicker environment," since, as television viewers know, in that universe we are always imprisoned in a false freedom of identical images. Hence, if we accept the museum's assumption of a "post-Gutenberg-galaxy," we must perforce accept electronic manipulation. Indeed, while the museum attempts to adapt itself to the imagined intellectual capacities and tastes of the so-called MTV generation, we might ask whether it is in this sense a "microcosm of larger society," or rather merely a reflection of an *image* of our society, disseminated by the producers of images who have a keen interest in both preserving this image and making it into a reality. Should we accept the museum's assertions regarding the alleged "limited attention spans of the Nintendo generation," or is it the makers of Nintendo who would like to create this mentality by making us believe that it already exists?

The main peril of such television education is of course its reliance on the senses and emotions and its neglect of the intellect.[36] This is especially disturbing in view of the fact that emphasis on emotion rather than intellect was the central trope of fascism, both in manipulating the masses and in describing the "other," the "Jew," as being the exact opposite of this view, a person with a destructive intellect and a total inability to empathize. The museum's attempt to connect "the personal to the political through sensual means," as Lisus and Ericson so aptly put it, is thus especially troubling because of its affinity with theories of mass manipulation propounded by Hitler and Goebbels. Indeed, while the museum has rightly been accused of neglecting the bureaucratic aspects of the Holocaust, it should also be noted that prejudice, intolerance, and a distorted perception of reality *were* essential preconditions to the success of fascism. The "industry of death" was created and administered not only by "rationality and cold intellect, separated from emotion." Rather, for the Nazis it was the Jews who were the representatives *par excellence* of the "cold intellect" that fascism had set itself up against.

Lisus and Ericson conclude that by inviting the audience to participate in a spectacle of the real, the spectacle replaces the real, and becomes "a real without origin or reality: a hyperreal."[37] This is a crucial observation, since a simulated Holocaust converts the event into a mere image in a museum which can be "experienced" and discarded at will. By trying to make the audience "feel" the event, the museum extracts it from its historical context, negating its past reality altogether. By faking the event, even if with the intention of telling the truth, the museum creates an imaginary lie. Signs are added to make fabricated artifacts comprehensible that did not exist in reality, actors read out testimonies to make them sound "more real" than when they were read by the actual witnesses themselves. Finally, the whole spectacle is made "better," more comprehensible, indeed more "useful" as a guide for the future, than the reality on which it is supposedly based.

In this sense the museum may have a much more pernicious effect than even Lisus and Ericson seem to think. By making for an unreflective emotionality rather than understanding, by privileging pathos over knowledge, and basing its representation on stark oppositions, the museum assumes a mentality in the public which it in fact helps to create and perpetuate. Moreover, it obscures not only the bureaucratic character of the Holocaust, but also the fact that while the makers of genocide and their supporters were themselves driven by images they perceived as reality, it was science and technology, celebrated in the museum, that were an inherent part of envisioning and implementing Auschwitz. Hence the emotions factory of Nazi propaganda was essential for the technological factory of death; trying to grasp this complexity by a hyperrealistic emotions factory via a hypertechnological environment seems not merely to make for a misunderstanding of the past but also for a perpetuation of its potential future perils.

Notes

Abbreviations

AHR	*American Historical Review*
AJC	*American Jewish Committee*
AJHG	*American Journal of Human Genetics*
AJSR	*Association for Jewish Studies Review*
BA-MA	Bundesarchiv-Militärarchiv (Freiburg, Germany)
CEH	*Central European History*
EHQ	*European History Quarterly*
FAZ	*Frankfurter Allgemeine Zeitung*
FR	*Frankfurter Rundschau*
GPS	*German Politics and Society*
GSR	*German Studies Review*
H&M	*History and Memory*
HJFRT	*Historical Journal of Film, Radio and Television*
HR/RH	*Historical Reflections/Réflexions Historiques*
HT	*History Today*
HWJ	*History Workshop Journal*
JCH	*Journal of Contemporary History*
JMH	*Journal of Modern History*
JSS	*Journal of Strategic Studies*
LBIY	*Leo Baeck Institute Year Book*
NYR	*New York Review of Books*
NYT	*New York Times*
NYTBR	*The New York Times Book Review*
P&P	*Past and Present*
POQ	*Public Opinion Quarterly*
RDS	*Research on Democracy and Society*
RHR	*Radical History Review*
SWCA	*Simon Wiesenthal Center Annual*
TAJ	*Tel Aviver Jahrbuch für deutsche Geschichte*
TNR	*The New Republic*
TNY	*The New Yorker*
VfZ	*Vierteljahrshefte für Zeitgeschichte*
W&S	*War and Society*
YVS	*Yad Vashem Studies*

Introduction

1. Pascal, *Pensées* (Harmondsworth, 1984 [1966]), XII. "Beginning" (183), p. 82.

2. On the current debate in the United States, see, e.g., R. J. Herrnstein and C. Murray, *The Bell Curve: Intelligence and Class Structure in American Life* (New York, 1994); J. P. Rushton, *Race, Evolution, and Behavior: A Life History Perspective* (New Brunswick: N.J., 1994); and S. W. Itzkoff, *The Decline of Intelligence in America: A Strategy for National Renewal* (Westport: Conn., 1994). See also the following reviews of these books: J. DeParle, "Daring Research or 'Social Science Pornography'?" *The New York Times Magazine* (October 9, 1994): 48ff; M. W. Browne, "What Is Intelligence, and Who Has It?" *NYR* (October 16, 1994): 3, 41, 45; J. Holt, "Anti-Social Science?" in OP-ED, *NYT* (October 19, 1994); "Race," *TNR* (October 31, 1994): whole issue; "Letters," *NYTBR* (November 13, 1994): 3, 75; A. Ryan, "Apocalypse Now?" *NYR* (November 17, 1994): 7–11; C. Lane, "The Tainted Sources of 'The Bell Curve'," *NYR* (December 1, 1994): 14–19.

3. See most recently H. Friedlander, "Step by Step: The Expansion of Murder, 1939–1941," *GSR* 17/3 (1994): 495–507. See also *infra*, Chapter 3, note 61.

4. I also owe thanks to Mr. Lewis Bateman, who first suggested to me the idea of putting my articles together in a book.

5. Apart from works cited *infra*, Chapter 1, see also V. G. Kiernan, *The Duel in European History: Honour and the Reign of Aristocracy*, 2d ed. (Oxford, 1989), and K. McAleer, *Dueling: The Cult of Honor in Fin-de-Siècle Germany* (Princeton, 1994).

6. See, in this context, I. Buruma, *The Wages of Guilt: Memories of War in Germany and Japan* (New York, 1994). For more on the Japanese case, see J. W. Treat, *Writing Ground Zero: Japanese Literature and the Atomic Bomb* (Chicago, 1995).

7. See the somewhat different interpretation in E. Barkan, *The Retreat of Scientific Racism: Changing Concepts of Race in Britain and the United States between the World Wars* (Cambridge, 1992).

8. Remarks made by Professor George Mosse in the conference "Lessons and Legacies," Dartmouth College, October 1994. In this context see also P. Gilory, *"There Ain't No Black in the Union Jack": The Cultural Politics of Race and Nation* (Chicago, 1987).

9. This is of course the main argument of Z. Bauman, *Modernity and the Holocaust*, 2d ed. (Ithaca, 1991).

10. See, e.g., J. E. Doneson, "Is a Little Memory Better Than None?" unpublished paper (1994).

Chapter 1

1. Homer, *The Iliad*, 35th ed. (Harmondsworth, 1985), pp. 73–74. This is a much revised version of an article by the same name originally published in *H&M* 1/2 (1989): 99–122. I wish to thank the editors of the journal for permitting me to reprint it here.

2. J. M. Esmonds (ed.), *Elegy and Iambus*, 4th ed. (Cambridge: Mass., 1961) 1: 73–75.

3. Xenophon, *The Persian Expedition*, 14th ed. (Harmondsworth, 1986), p. 88.

4. Arrian, *The Life of Alexander the Great* (Harmondsworth, 1958), p. 104.

5. Esmonds, *Elegy*, pp. 75–77.

6. Xenophon, *Expedition*, p. 270.

7. Arrian, *Alexander*, pp. 35–36.

8. Esmonds, *Elegy*, pp. 75–77.

9. Xenophon, *Expedition*, p. 180.

10. Arrian, *Alexander*, pp. 39–41.

11. Virgil, *The Aeneid*, 2d rev. ed. (Harmondsworth, 1959), pp. 13, 27–28; Livy, *The Early History of Rome*, 8th ed. (Harmondsworth, 1974), pp. 34–35.

12. Josephus, *The Jewish War*, 3d rev. ed. (Harmondsworth, 1985), pp. 197, 236; Caesar, *The Conquest of Gaul*, 12th ed. (Harmondsworth, 1976), pp. 113, 210; Dio Cassius, *The Roman History* (Harmondsworth, 1987), pp. 52–57. See also the fascinating account of mutiny, defeat, and victory during the Roman wars against the Germans, in Tacitus, *The Annals of Imperial Rome*, rev. ed., (Harmondsworth, 1985), pp. 43–89.

13. On arguments for and against the stirrup hypothesis, see P. Contamine, *War in the Middle Ages*, 5th ed. (Oxford, 1989 [1980]), pp. 179–84; the author ultimately takes up the position of an evolution in medieval warfare due to the gradual adoption of the stirrup and the growing use of the couched lance. The case for a more revolutionary change under the Merovingians was made by L. White, *Medieval Technology and Social Change* (Oxford, 1962), pp. 1–38. See also W. H. McNeill, *The Pursuit of Power* (Oxford, 1983), p. 20; J. Keegan, *A History of Warfare* (New York, 1994), pp. 285–86, and more generally on Greek, Roman, and medieval warfare, ibid., pp. 237–98.

14. *The Song of Roland*, 25th ed. (Harmondsworth, 1984), pp. 187–89.

15. *The Nibelungenlied*, rev. ed. (Harmondsworth, 1982), pp. 37–38.

16. *The Quest of the Holy Grail*, 9th ed. (Harmondsworth, 1982), p. 149.

17. Froissart, *Chronicles*, rev. ed. (Harmondsworth, 1985), p. 37.

18. Ibid., pp. 88–92, 134–35, 137–39.

19. J. Keegan, *The Face of Battle*, 2d ed. (London, 1976), pp. 79–116.

20. McNeill, *Pursuit*, p. 83. See also on the early use of artillery in Keegan, *Warfare*, pp. 319–34; and a detailed exposition in Contamine, *Middle Ages*, pp. 193–207.

21. For more on the ideological, political, military, and technological aspects of the military revolution in Europe and its aftermath, see G. Parker, *The Military Revolution: Military Innovation and the Rise of the West, 1500–1800* (Cambridge, 1988); B. M. Downing, *The Military Revolution and Political Change: Origins of Democracy and Autocracy in Early Modern Europe* (Princeton, 1992); J. A. Lynn (ed.), *Tools of War: Instruments, Ideas, and Institutions of Warfare, 1445–1871* (Urbana, 1990).

22. On this, see especially A. Forrest, *Soldiers of the French Revolution* (Durham, 1990); J. A. Lynn, *The Bayonets of the Republic: Motivation and Tactics in the Army of Revolutionary France, 1791–94* (Urbana, 1984); R. Cobb, *The People's Armies: The armées révolutionnaires* (New Haven, 1987); G. L. Mosse, *The Nationalization of the Masses: Political Symbolism and Mass Movements in Germany from the Napoleonic Wars Through the Third Reich*, 2d ed. (Ithaca, 1991).

23. J. Ellis, *The Social History of the Machine Gun*, 2d ed. (London, 1987).

24. N. Perrin, *Giving Up the Gun: Japan's Reversion to the Sword, 1543–1879* (Boston, 1979). See also Keegan, *Warfare*, pp. 40–46; M. Adas, *Machines as the Measure of Men: Science, Technology, and Ideologies of Western Dominance* (Ithaca, 1989), pp. 357–65.

25. McNeill, *Pursuit*, Chapters 3–4, 6–8.

26. J. Stevenson, *British Society 1914–45* (Harmondsworth, 1984), pp. 46–53, 60–64.

27. Keegan, *Battle*, pp. 217–18.

28. Stevenson, British Society, p. 49. On the effect of Europe's colonial wars on several "exotic" countries, see D. B. Ralston, *Importing the European Army: The Intro-*

duction of European Military Techniques and Institutions into the Extra-European World, 1600–1914 (Chicago, 1990). On how the Europeans viewed those "others," see Adas, *Machines*. On the relationship between the individual and history as reflected in the modern novel, the importance of war in literary representation, and the crucial role of 1914, see N. Chiaromonte's brilliant *The Paradox of History: Stendhal, Tolstoy, Pasternak, and Others*, 2d rev. ed. (Philadelphia, 1985).

29. J.-J. Becker, *The Great War and the French People* (Leamington Spa, 1985). See also E. J. Weber, *The Nationalist Revival in France, 1905–1914* (Berkeley, 1959).

30. R. Graves, *Goodbye to All That*, 2d ed. (New York, 1957), p. 67.

31. Becker, *Great War*, pp. 40–41.

32. Ibid., p. 30.

33. P. Fussell, *The Great War and Modern Memory* (Oxford, 1975), p. 19.

34. T. Mann, *The Magic Mountain*, 11th ed. (Harmondsworth, 1979 [1924]), pp. 712–16.

35. E. Jünger, "In Stahlgewittern," in *Sämtliche Werke*, 18 vols. (Stuttgart, 1978 [1920]), 1: 11.

36. J. H. Johnston, *English Poetry of the First World War* (Princeton, 1964), pp. 10–16, cited in Ellis, *Machine Gun*, p. 144.

37. R. Haigh and P. Turner, *Not For Glory* (London, 1969), p. 41, cited in Ellis, *Machine Gun*, p. 135.

38. M. Middelbrook, *The First Day on the Somme* (New York, 1972), p. 138.

39. M. Ferro, *The Great War 1914–1918*, 2d ed. (London, 1987), p. 90.

40. Middelbrook, *First Day*, p. 185.

41. A. Farrar-Hockley, *The Somme* (London, 1966), p. 193, cited in Ellis, *Machine Gun*, p. 136.

42. Middelbrook, *First Day*, p. 170.

43. Ibid., p. 147. For some powerful photographic documentation, see J. Ellis, *Eye-Deep in Hell: Trench Warfare in World War I*, 2d ed. (Baltimore, 1989). An excellent portrayal of British troops, with a great deal of oral testimony, is D. Winter, *Death's Men: Soldiers of the Great War*, 2d ed. (Harmondsworth, 1985).

44. See esp. E. J. Leed, *No Man's Land* (Cambridge, 1979).

45. R. Wohl, *The Generation of 1914* (Cambridge: Mass., 1979).

46. P. Lubbock (ed.), *The Letters of Henry James*, 2 vols. (New York, 1920), 1: 384, cited in Fussell, *Modern Memory*, p. 8.

47. Fussell, *Modern Memory*, p. 179.

48. Ferro, *Great War*, pp. 85–86.

49. Ibid., p. 97.

50. Fussell, *Modern Memory*, p. 115.

51. Ibid., p. 116.

52. W. J. Mommsen, "German Artists and Intellectuals and the Meaning of War, 1914–1918," unpublished paper (1994), p. 1.

53. Ibid., p. 33.

54. In this context, see M. Geyer, "Professionals and Junkers: German Rearmament and Politics in the Weimar Republic," in *Social Change and Political Development in Weimar Germany*, ed. R. Bessel and E. J. Feuchtwanger (London, 1981), pp. 77–133.

55. C. Carrington, "Some Soldiers," in *Promise of Greatness*, ed. G. A. Panichas (London, 1968), p. 157, cited in Fussell, *Modern Memory*, p. 115.

56. I do not wish to imply here that there was not a "good cause" in 1939–45. Quite the contrary, I am convinced that defeating Nazi Germany was not only a "good cause,"

but crucial for the physical and cultural survival of millions of people, whatever the cost. It is important to stress, however, that those who fought on the other side were no less (and perhaps even more) convinced that theirs was the "good cause."

57. M. Howard, *War in European History*, 2d ed. (Oxford, 1977), pp. 116–35.

58. R. A. Beaumont, *Military Elites*, 2d ed. (London, 1976).

59. V. R. Kiernan, *European Armies from Conquest to Collapse* (Bungay: Suffolk, 1982), pp. 208–26. See also A. Horne, *A Savage War of Peace: Algeria 1954–1962*, 2d ed. (Harmondsworth, 1985); D. Porch, *The French Foreign Legion*, 2d ed. (New York, 1992); J.-P. Rioux, *La guerre d'Algerie et les français* (Paris, 1990). The most impressive cinematic representation of chopper cavalry tactics is the Wagnerian scene in Francis Ford Coppola's *Apocalypse Now* (1979).

60. See A. Silver, "Democratic Citizenship and High Military Strategy: The Inheritance, Decay, and Reshaping of Political Culture," *RDS* 2 (1994): 317–49; and R. Brubaker, *Citizenship and Nationhood in France and Germany* (Cambridge: Mass., 1992), p. 145.

61. See, e.g., R. J. Lifton, *The Nazi Doctors: Medical Killing and the Psychology of Genocide* (New York, 1986); R. N. Proctor, *Racial Hygiene: Medicine Under the Nazis* (Cambridge: Mass., 1988); M. H. Kater, *Doctors Under Hitler* (Chapel Hill, 1989); A. D. Beyerchen, *Scientists Under Hitler: Politics and the Physics Community in the Third Reich* (New Haven, 1977); T. Powers: *Heisenberg's War: The Secret History of the German Bomb* (New York, 1993); M. Burleigh, *Germany Turns Eastwards: A Study of Ostforschung in the Third Reich*, 2d ed. (Cambridge, 1989).

62. For painting, see, e.g., R. Hughes, *The Shock of the New: Art and the Century of Change*, 2d ed. (London, 1981), esp. Chapters 1–2; J. Rye, *Futurism* (London, 1972); K. Lucic, *Charles Sheeler and the Cult of the Machine* (Cambridge: Mass., 1991). As for films and fiction, suffice it to mention here Fritz Lang's *Metropolis* (1927) and Franz Kafka's *In the Penal Colony* (1919) as two of the most evocative works on the horror and fascination of the machine in the interwar period. In a very different, but related vein is Ernst Jünger's *Der Arbeiter* (1932). The striking scene in the American film *All Quiet on the Western Front* (1930), in which a single burst of machine-gun fire decimates a whole line of attacking Frenchmen, filmed, as it were, through the sights, is also part of this fascination with, and fear of, the power of killing machines. See F. Kafka, "In der Strafkolonie," in *Sämtliche Erzählungen*, 16th ed. (Frankfurt/M., 1980); S. Kracauer, *From Caligari to Hitler: A Psychological History of the German Film*, 2d ed. (Princeton, 1974 [1947]), esp. pp. 149–50; E. Jünger, "Der Arbeiter: Herrschaft und Gestalt," in *Sämtliche Werke*, 18 vols. (Stuttgart, 1981 [1932]), 8: 9–317. Also: J. W. Chambers II, "All Quiet on the Western Front (1930): the Antiwar Film and Image of the First World War," *HJFRT* 14/4 (1994): 377–411; and M. Eksteins, "War, Memory, and Politics: The Fate of the Film *All Quiet on the Western Front*," *CEH* 13/1 (March 1980): 60–82. One of the best post-1945 films on the Bomb is Stanley Kubrick's 1963 *Dr. Strangelove*; Joseph Heller, *Catch-22* (New York, 1961), is an appropriate literary example of post-1945 sensibilities regarding the horrors and insanity of modern warfare.

63. H. Barbusse, *Under Fire: The Story of a Squad (Le feu)* (New York, 1917 [1916]); E. M. Remarque, *All Quiet on the Western Front*, 12th ed. (New York, 1991 [1928]); N. Mailer, *The Naked and the Dead* (New York, 1948); M. Herr, *Dispatches*, 3d ed. (London, 1978).

64. G. Chapman, *A Passionate Prodigality* (London, 1933), p. 277, cited in J. M. Winter, *The Great War and the British People* (Cambridge: Mass., 1986), p. 292.

65. H. Höhne, *The Order of the Death's Head: The Story of Hitler's SS*, 2d ed.

(London, 1981 [1966]), pp. 409–10; B. Wegner, *Hitlers Politische Soldaten: Die Waffen-SS 1933–1945* (Paderborn, 1982), pp. 25–75, esp. 65–66; R. G. L. Waite, *Vanguard of Nazism: The Free Corps Movement in Postwar Germany, 1918–1923*, 2d ed. (Cambridge: Mass., 1970 [1952]), esp. pp. 22–30; K. Theweleit, *Männerphantasien*, 2 vols., 2d ed. (Reinbeck bei Hamburg, 1987 [1977]), with some excellent examples also of the soldier as (part of) machine (*Ganzheitsmaschine Truppe*), ibid., 2:154–58, and as individual (*Die Einzelteilganzheit "Stahlgestalt"*), ibid., 2:158–62. See also Ernst von Salomon, esp. *Die Geächteten* (Berlin, 1930), *Die Kadetten* (Berlin, 1933), and *Der Fragebogen* (Hamburg, 1951).

66. In this context, see also P. Fritzsche, "Machine Dreams: Airmindedness and the Reinvention of Germany," *AHR* 98/3 (1993): 685–709; and idem., *A Nation of Fliers: German Aviation and the Popular Imagination* (Cambridge: Mass., 1992).

67. See R. G. L. Waite, *Hitler: The Psychopathic God*, 2d ed. (New York, 1993 [1977]), between pp. 160–61, and background of this portrait, which Hitler chose as his official painting for 1938, ibid., pp. 101–102. See also J. W. Baird, *To Die for Germany: Heroes in the Nazi Pantheon*, 2d ed. (Bloomington, 1992).

Chapter 2

1. Barbusse, *Under Fire*, pp. 154–56. The second section of this previously unpublished chapter is based in part on my "'The Nation in Arms': Germany and France, 1789–1939," *HT* 44/9 (September 1994): 27–33. The third section employs (and revises) some ideas originally presented in my "Martyrs' Vengeance: Memory, Trauma, and Fear of War in France, 1918–1940," *HR/RH* (forthcoming). I would like to thank the editors of these journals for allowing me to use these publications in this chapter. I am also grateful for the comments on earlier versions of these papers presented at the Council for European Studies in 1992, and at the Rutgers Center for Historical Analysis in 1994.

2. The most vivid medieval depiction of Death and Hell I can think of is the cycle of wall frescoes by a fourteenth-century artist in the cemetery (*Camposanto*) located in the *Piazza del Duomo* in Pisa, Italy, comprising "The Triumph of Death" and "The Last Judgement and Hell." Quite appropriately, while most of the frescoes there were destroyed in a fire caused by artillery shelling in 1944, Hell survived. One of the most remarkable portrayals of hell in modern literature is, of course, the preacher's sermon in James Joyce's *A Portrait of the Artist as a Young Man*, 7th ed. (London, 1982), pp. 110–15, originally published in 1916, the same year that Barbusse's *Le Feu* first appeared: "Hell is a strait and dark and foulsmelling prison, an abode of demons and lost souls, filled with fire and smoke . . . the prisoners are heaped together in their awful prison . . . the fire of hell . . . is a neverending storm of darkness . . . amid which the bodies are heaped one upon another without even a glimpse of air. . . . The horror . . . is increased by its awful stench. All the filth of the world, all the offal and scum of the world. . . . Imagine some foul and putrid corpse that has lain rotting and decomposing in the grave, a jellylike mass of liquid corruption . . . devoured by the fire of burning brimstone and giving off dense choking fumes of nauseous loathsome decomposition . . . multiplied a millionfold and a millionfold again from the millions upon millions of fetid carcasses massed together in the reeking darkness, a huge and rotting human fungus. . . . And . . . the fires of punishment torture the spirit with the flesh. . . . In hell all laws are overturned: there is no thought of family or country, of ties, of relationships. The damned howl and scream at each other, their torture and rage intensified by the presence of beings tortured and raging like themselves. All sense of humanity is forgotten."

3. On the literature of the world wars, as well as other forms of representation, see, e.g., Fussell, *Modern Memory*; M. Eksteins, *Rites of Spring: The Great War and the Birth of the Modern Age*, 2d ed. (New York, 1989); S. Hynes, *A War Imagined: The First World War and English Culture* (New York, 1991); R. Taylor, *Literature & Society in Germany, 1918–1945* (Sussex, 1980), esp. Part 1; M. Richler (ed.), *Writers on World War II: An Anthology* (New York, 1991); P. Fussell, *Wartime: Understanding and Behavior in the Second World War*, 2d ed. (New York, 1990); P. Virilio, *War and Cinema: The Logistics of Perception* (London, 1989). On representations of the Holocaust, see, e.g., L. Langer, *The Holocaust and the Literary Imagination* (New Haven, 1975); S. D. Ezrahi, *By Words Alone: The Holocaust in Literature* (Chicago, 1980); D. G. Roskies, *Against the Apocalypse: Responses to Catastrophe in Modern Jewish Culture* (Cambridge: Mass., 1984); A. H. Rosenfeld, *A Double Dying: Reflections on Holocaust Literature*, 2d ed. (Bloomington, 1988); J. E. Young, *Writing and Rewriting the Holocaust: Narrative and the Consequences of Interpretation*, 2d ed. (Bloomington, 1990); idem., *The Texture of Memory: Holocaust Memorials and Meaning* (New Haven, 1993); S. Lewis (ed.), *Art Out of Agony: The Holocaust Theme in Literature, Sculpture and Film* (Montréal, 1984); I. Avisar, *Screening the Holocaust: Cinema's Images of the Unimaginable* (Bloomington, 1988); D. LaCapra, *Representing the Holocaust: History, Theory, Trauma* (Ithaca, 1994); S. Friedlander (ed.), *Probing the Limits of Representation: Nazism and the "Final Solution"* (Cambridge: Mass., 1992); and the remarks in idem., *Reflections of Nazism: An Essay on Kitsch and Death*, 2d ed. (Bloomington, 1993), pp. 98–99.

4. And those who have, like Hannah Arendt, were heavily censured for doing so. See H. Arendt, *Eichmann in Jerusalem: A Report on the Banality of Evil*, rev. ed. (New York, 1977 [1963]); and comments by S. Ettinger, *Modern Anti-Semitism: Studies and Essays* (Tel-Aviv, 1978 [Hebrew]), pp. x–xi; T. Segev, *The Seventh Million: The Israelis and the Holocaust* (New York, 1993), pp. 357–60.

5. These attitudes of numerous European Jewish communities are treated by R. Hilberg, *The Destruction of the European Jews*, 3 vols., rev. ed. (New York, 1985), 3: 1030–44; L. Yahil, *The Holocaust: The Fate of European Jewry*, 2d ed. (New York, 1990), pp. 186–224 (esp. 199–200), 329–35, 546–72; on revolts, pp. 457–98 (by Israel Gutman); L. S. Dawidowicz, *The War Against the Jews, 1933–1945*, 2d ed. (New York, 1986), pp. 341–53.

6. I am well aware that another crucial instance of this process is the mass killings by Stalin's regime. See, e.g., R. Conquest, *The Great Terror: A Reassessment* (New York, 1990); idem., *The Harvest of Sorrow: Soviet Collectivization and the Terror-Famine* (New York, 1986). This case does not receive substantial treatment in this book (although it is referred to in several discussions), partly because of my own deficiencies, and partly because the Great Purges and Collectivization did not represent industrial killing to the same extent as either the Holocaust or the Great War (though even according to the most conservative estimates, the number of their victims was astonishing), but rather a combination of traditional forms of brutality, bureaucratic callousness (and inefficiency), pathological tyranny, and a revolutionary notion of "purging" society in order to improve it, largely inherited from the French Revolution (which itself was informed by earlier Christian urges to "purify" humanity). While the relationship between the "Gulags" and Auschwitz has been the center of a major controversy, waged mainly around E. Nolte, "Between Historical Legend and Revisionism? The Third Reich in the Perspective of 1980," and his "The Past That Will Not Pass: A Speech That Could Be Written but Not Delivered," both now in *Forever in the Shadow of Hitler? Original Documents of the Historikerstreit, the Controversy Concerning the Singularity of the Holocaust* (Atlantic Highlands: N.J., 1993), pp. 1–15, 18–23, I

remain critical of this comparison, as I was at the time of the controversy. For a longer discussion, see *infra*, Chapter 5. See also E. Nolte, *Three Faces of Fascism: Action Française, Italian Fascism, National Socialism* (New York, 1969 [1963]), where the author presented a very different view of the origins of Nazism, as the subtitle clearly indicates. For somewhat similar reasons I also do not discuss the Armenian genocide, which was, it must be emphasized, very much part of the Great War and formed a point of reference for all consequent discussions of genocide and attempted legitimations thereof. See R. G. Hovannisian (ed.), *The Armenian Genocide in Perspective* (New Brunswick, 1986); L. Kuper, *Genocide: Its Political Use in the Twentieth Century* (New Haven, 1982), Chapter 6.

7. Lynn, *Bayonets*, p. 56. See also Forrest, *Soldiers*, pp. 75–76.

8. Apart from discussions in the two books cited above, see also I. Woloch, "Napoleonic Conscription: State Power and Civil Society," *P&P* 111 (1986): 101–129; J. P. Bertaud, "Napoleon's Officers," *P&P* 112 (1986): 91–111; idem., *The Army of the French Revolution: From Citizen-Soldiers to Instruments of Power* (Princeton, 1988); D. D. Bien, "The Army in the French Enlightenment: Reform, Reaction and Revolution," *P&P* 85 (1979): 68–98; S. E. Van Holde, "State Building and the Limits of State Power: Conscription in Napoleonic France," unpublished paper (1992); A. Grab, "Army, State, and Society: Conscription and Desertion in Napoleonic Italy (1802–1814)," *JMH* 67/1 (1995): 25–54.

9. J. J. Sheehan, *German History, 1770–1866*, 2d ed. (Oxford, 1993), p. 295.

10. Ibid.

11. Ibid., p. 309. For a general discussions of the Prussian reforms, see ibid., pp. 291–310, and H. Rosenberg, *Bureaucracy, Aristocracy, and Autocracy: The Prussian Experience 1660–1815*, 2d ed. (Boston, 1968 [1958]), pp. 202–28; more specifically on the military reforms, see G. A. Craig, *The Politics of the Prussian Army, 1640–1945*, rev. ed. (Oxford, 1978 [1955]), pp. 37–53. See also H. Kohn, *Prelude to the Nation-States: The French and German Experience, 1789–1815* (Princeton, 1967).

12. C. von Clausewitz, *On War*, ed. M. Howard and P. Paret, 2d ed. (Princeton, 1989), pp. 87, 606, and the introductory essays to this volume by P. Paret, M. Howard, and B. Brodie, pp. 3–58; Sheehan, *German History*, p. 232. Also see P. Paret, *Clausewitz and the State: The Man, His Theories, and His Times*, 2d ed. (Princeton, 1985); idem., "Clausewitz," in *Makers of Modern Strategy: From Machiavelli to the Nuclear Age*, 2d ed. (Princeton, 1986), pp. 186–213; M. I. Handel (ed.), *Clausewitz and Modern Strategy* (London, 1986), esp. Part 3; R. Aron, *Clausewitz: Philosopher of War*, 2d ed. (New York, 1986), esp. Part 4; J. L. Wallach, *The Dogma of the Battle of Annihilation: The Theories of Clausewitz and Schlieffen and Their Impact on the German Conduct of Two World Wars* (Westport: Conn., 1986).

13. Generally on the liberation of Prussia and the consequent Reaction in Germany, see Sheehan, *German History*, pp. 310–23, 391–450; more specifically on the Prussian army, see Craig, *Prussian Army*, pp. 53–81.

14. Generally on Restoration France, see A. Jardin and A.-J. Tudesq, *Restoration & Reaction, 1815–1848*, 2d ed. (Cambridge, 1988); more specifically on the French army, see D. Porch, *Army and Revolution: France 1815–1858* (London, 1977).

15. On France, see M. Agulhon, *The Republican Experiment, 1848–1852* (Cambridge, 1983), esp. pp. 56–62; F. de Luna, *The French Republic Under Cavaignac, 1848* (Princeton, 1969). On Germany see H. Schulze, *The Course of German Nationalism: From Frederick the Great to Bismarck, 1763–1867* (Cambridge, 1991), esp. pp. 5–31; T. S. Hamerow, *Restoration, Revolution, Reaction: Economics and Politics in Germany, 1815–1871*, 2d ed. (Princeton, 1966), Part 2.

16. For background on both armies, see M. Howard, *The Franco-Prussian War: The German Invasion of France, 1870–1871*, 2d ed. (London, 1981), pp. 1–39. On Napoleon's France, see A. Plessis, *The Rise and Fall of the Second Empire, 1852–1871*, 2d ed. (Cambridge, 1987); and more specifically on the army, R. Holmes, *The Road to Sedan. The French Army 1866–70* (London, 1984). On Germany, see Sheehan, *German History*, pp. 853–911; G. A. Craig, *Germany, 1866–1945*, 2d ed. (New York, 1980), pp. 1–37; on the army, idem., *Prussian Army*, pp. 82–216.

17. For a discussion of German militarism, see G. Ritter, *The Sword and the Sceptre: The Problem of Militarism in Germany*, 4 vols. (Coral Gables, 1972); and, more generally, V. R. Berghahn, *Militarism: The History of an International Debate, 1861–1979* (London, 1981).

18. Among the many books on this subject, see esp. F. Fischer, *War of Illusions: German Policies, 1911–1914* (New York, 1975); V. R. Berghahn, *Germany and the Approach of War in 1914*, 2d ed. (New York, 1993); and more generally, H.-U. Wehler, *The German Empire, 1871–1918* (Leamington Spa, 1985); V. R. Berghahn, *Imperial Germany, 1871–1914: Economy, Society, Culture and Politics* (Providence, 1994).

19. Generally on the war of 1870–71, see Howard, *Franco-Prussian War*. On the French side, see R. Tombs, *The War Against Paris: 1871* (Cambridge, 1981); A. Horne, *The Fall of Paris: The Siege and the Commune, 1870–71*, 2d ed. (Harmondsworth, 1987).

20. On German leagues, see R. Chickering, *We Who Feel Most German: A Cultural Study of the Pan-German League, 1886–1914* (Boston, 1984); G. Eley, *Reshaping the German Right: Radical Nationalism and Political Change after Bismarck*, 2d ed. (Ann Arbor, 1991); M. S. Coetzee, *The German Army League: Popular Nationalism in Wilhelmine Germany* (New York, 1990). On officer recruitment, see D. Bald, *Vom Kaiserheer zur Bundeswehr. Sozialstruktur des Militärs: Politik der Rekrutierung von Offizieren und Unteroffizieren* (Frankfurt/M., 1981), esp. p. 21. On the French army, see D. B. Ralston, *The Army of the Republic: The Place of the Military in the Political Evolution of France, 1871–1914* (Cambridge: Mass., 1967); D. Porch, *The March to the Marne: The French Army, 1871–1914* (Cambridge, 1981).

21. On French recruitment policies, political crises, and civil-military relations, see R. D. Challener, *The French Theory of the Nation in Arms* (New York, 1955); J.-D. Bredin, *The Affair. The Case of Alfred Dreyfus* (New York, 1986); E. Weber, *Peasants into Frenchmen: The Modernization of Rural France, 1870–1914* (Stanford, 1976); idem., *Nationalist Revival*; J. H. M. Narducci, *The French Officer Corps and the Social Role of the Army, 1890–1908* (Bellevue, 1981); G. Krumeich, *Armaments and Politics in France on the Eve of the First World War: The Introduction of Three-Year Conscription, 1913–1914* (Leamington Spa, 1984). On German extremism, pacifism, and the military, see S. Volkov, *The Rise of Popular Antimodernism in Germany: The Urban Master Artisans, 1873–1896* (Princeton, 1978); R. Chickering, *Imperial Germany and a World Without War: The Peace Movement and German Society, 1892–1914* (Princeton, 1975); M. Kitchen, *The German Officer Corps, 1890–1914* (Oxford, 1968). On socialism, see M. Drachkovitch, *Les socialismes français et allemands et le problème de la guerre, 1870–1914* (Geneva, 1953); C. E. Schorske, *German Social Democracy, 1905–1917: The Development of the Great Schism*, 2d ed. (Cambridge: Mass., 1983).

22. On Imperial Germany's war aims, see F. Fischer, *Germany's Aims in the First World War* (London, 1967); H. W. Gatzke, *Germany's Drive to the West: A Study of Germany's Western War Aims During the First Wold War* (Baltimore, 1950). On earlier colonialist initiatives, see W. D. Smith, *The Ideological Origins of Nazi Imperialism*, 2d ed. (New York, 1989), pp. 32–40; H. Pogge von Strandmann, "Domestic Ori-

gins of Germany's Colonial Expansion under Bismarck," *P&P* 42 (1969): 140–69. On French imperialism and colonialism, see J. J. Cooke, *New French Imperialism, 1880–1910: The Third Republic and Colonial Expansion* (Hampden: Conn., 1973); C. M. Andrew and A. S. Kanya-Forster, *The Climax of French Imperial Expansion, 1914–24* (Stanford, 1981); R. G. Brown, *Fashoda Reconsidered: The Impact of Domestic Politics on French Policy in Africa, 1893–1898* (Baltimore, 1970).

23. H. Kohn, *The Idea of Nationalism: A Study in its Origins and Political Background* (New York, 1944), p. 16, defines nationalism as "a state of mind, permeating the large majority of a people and claiming to permeate all its members," which "recognizes the nation-state as the ideal form of political organization and the nationality as the source of creative cultural energy and of economic well-being." Cited in D. Kaiser, *Politics and War: European Conflict from Philip II to Hitler* (Cambridge: Mass., 1990), p. 307. More specifically, see M. Hughes, *Nationalism and Society: Germany, 1800–1945*, 2d ed. (London, 1989); H. Lebovics, *True France: The Wars Over Cultural Identity, 1900–1945* (Ithaca, 1992).

24. On France, see J.-J. Becker, *Comment les français sont entrés dans la guerre* (Paris, 1977), and idem., *Great War*. On Germany, J. Kocka, *Facing Total War: German Society, 1914–1918* (Leamington Spa, 1984); G. D. Feldman, *Army, Industry and Labor in Germany, 1914–1918*, 2d ed. (Providence, 1992). On Britain, Winter, *Great War*. See also M. R. Higonnet et al. (eds.), *Behind the Lines: Gender and the Two World Wars* (New Haven, 1987).

25. For a vivid pictorial account of the Great War, see J. Winter, *The Experience of World War I* (New York, 1989).

26. Mann, *The Magic Mountain*, p. 716.

27. On pre-1914 European war planning, see J. Snyder, *The Ideology of the Offensive: Military Decision Making and the Disasters of 1914*, 2d ed. (Ithaca, 1989). For an excellent survey of the whole period of total war, see Kaiser, *Politics and War*, pp. 269–414.

28. On interwar military planning, see B. R. Posen, *The Sources of Military Doctrine: France, Britain, and Germany between the World War*, 2d ed. (Ithaca, 1986). On the German army and its military, political, and ideological preparation for war, see W. Deist et al. (eds.), *Das Deutsche Reich und der Zweite Weltkrieg*, Vol. 1, *Ursachen und Voraussetzungen der deutschen Kriegspolitik* (Stuttgart, 1979); idem., *The Wehrmacht and German Rearmament* (London, 1981); K.-J. Müller, *The Army, Politics and Society in Germany, 1933–45: Studies in the Army's Relation to Nazism* (New York, 1987); M. Messerschmidt, *Die Wehrmacht in NS-Staat: Zeit der Indoktrination* (Hamburg, 1969), parts 1–3; A. Seaton, *The German Army, 1933–45* (London, 1982), Chapters 1–4; M. Cooper, *The German Army, 1933–1945: Its Political and Military Failure* (London, 1978), Chapter 8. On French civil-military relations and the Maginot Line, see P. C. F. Bankwitz, *Maxime Weygand and Civil-Military Relations in Modern France* (Cambridge: Mass., 1967); R. J. Young, *In Command of France: French Foreign Policy and Military Planning, 1933–1940* (Cambridge: Mass., 1978); J. M. Hughes, *To the Maginot Line: The Politics of French Military Preparation in the 1920s* (Cambridge: Mass., 1971); J. Nobécourt, *Une histoire politique de l'armée*, Vol. 1, *1919–1942: de Pétain à Pétain* (Paris, 1967); J. Bodin, *Les officiers français: Grandeur et misères, 1936–1991* (Paris, 1992), Chapter 1. On the Red Army, see M. von Hagen, *Soldiers in the Proletarian Dictatorship: The Red Army and the Soviet Socialist State, 1917–1930*, 2d ed. (Ithaca, 1993); J. Erickson, *Stalin's War with Germany*, Vol. 1, *The Road to Stalingrad*, 2d ed. (London, 1985), pp. 27–76; idem., *The Soviet High Command: A Military-Political History, 1918–1941* (New York, 1962); J. Hoffmann, "Die Sowjet-

Notes to Pages 41 to 44 ■ 197

union bis zum Vorabend des deutschen Angriffs," in *Das Deutsche Reich und der Zweite Weltkrieg*, Vol. 4, *Der Angriff auf die Sowjetunion* (Stuttgart, 1983), pp. 38–97.

29. Wohl, *The Generation of 1914*, Chapter 2 (on German youth), and Chapter 1 (on French youth).

30. On French propaganda in the Great War, see Becker, *Great War*, Chapter 2; on emerging criticism and opposition, ibid., Chapters 4, 13–16; specifically on writers, Chapter 11 (G. Colin). See also F. Kupferman, "Rumeurs, bobards et propagande," in *14–18: Mourir pour la patrie* (Paris, 1992), pp. 211–20; P. Fridenson (ed.), *The French Home Front, 1914–1918* (Providence, 1992). On the soldiers' mutiny not long after Barbusse's account was published, see G. Pedrocini, *Les mutineries de 1917*, 2d rev. ed. (Paris, 1983). For oral accounts by French soldiers, see P. Miquel, *Les hommes de la Grande guerre* (Paris, 1987).

31. T. Mann, *Betrachtungen eines Unpolitischen*, 2d ed. (Frankfurt/M., 1956 [1918]).

32. On pacifist and antiwar movements, see S. E. Cooper, *Patriotic Pacifism: Waging War on War in Europe, 1815–1914* (New York, 1991); F. L. Carsten, *War Against War: British and German Radical Movements in the First World War* (Berkeley, 1982); N. Ingram, *The Politics of Dissent: Pacifism in France, 1919–1939* (Oxford, 1991); R. Evans, *Comrades and Sisters: Feminism, Socialism and Pacifism in Europe, 1870–1945* (New York, 1987).

33. Barbusse, *Under Fire*, pp. 3–4. Compare with L. Barthas, *Les carnets de guerre de Louis Barthas, tonnelier, 1914–1918* (Paris, 1992); M. Bloch, *Memoirs of War, 1914–15*, 2d ed. (Cambridge, 1988); S. Audoin-Rouzeau, *Men at War, 1914–1918: National Sentiment and Trench Journalism in France During the First World War* (Providence, 1992). For an account of the deadliest battle of the Great War, see A. Horne, *The Price of Glory: Verdun 1916*, 2d ed. (Harmondsworth, 1978).

34. On the veterans and wounded of the Great War in the interwar years, see R. W. Whalen, *Bitter Wounds: German Victims of the Great War, 1914–1939* (Ithaca, 1984); A. Prost, *Les anciens combattants, 1914–1940* (Paris, 1977).

35. For German tendencies to identify Jews with shirkers during and after the Great War, see D. E. Showalter, *Little Man, What Now? Der Stürmer in the Weimar Republic* (Hamden, 1982), esp. pp. 17–19. See also G. L. Mosse, *Germans & Jews: The Right, the Left, and the Search for a "Third Force" in Pre-Nazi Germany*, 2d ed. (New York, 1971), Chapters. 5–7; S. Gordon, *Hitler, Germans, and the "Jewish Question"* (Princeton, 1984), Chapters. 1–2. 1920s France expressed mainly abhorrence of war, though fascism did spread for a while. The 1930s saw a rapid growth of antisemitism, and Jews were blamed for both the last war and for conspiring to cause another. See S. Bernstein, "La paix inachevée," and J.-F. Sirinelli, "La génération du feu," in *14–18*, pp. 279–311; A. Chebel d'Appollonia, *L'Extrême-Droite en France: De Maurras à Le Pen* (Brussels, 1988), pp. 127–224; M. Winock, *Nationalisme, antisémitisme et fascisme en France* (Paris, 1990), pp. 374–96; R. Schor, *L'Antisémitisme en France pendant les années trente* (Brussels, 1992); J. Mehlman, *Legacies of Anti-Semitism in France* (Minneapolis, 1983).

36. See *supra*, Chapter 2, n. 65.

37. Remarque, *All Quiet*, pp. 113–14.

38. Ernest Hemingway wrote that "when a man is still in rebellion against death he has pleasure in taking to himself one of the Godlike attributes; that of giving it. This is one of the most profound feelings in those men who enjoy killing." *Death in the Afternoon* (New York, 1960), p. 233, cited in T. Des Pres, *The Survivor: An Anatomy of Life in the Death Camp* (New York, 1976), p. 206. This is true only in the sense

that fear of death promotes killing; it is not true that this phenomenon is limited to those who enjoy killing, at least not to those who openly admit their pleasure. All soldiers who kill in war are motivated, at least in part, by precisely this fear. Conversely we may say that in war many soldiers *discover* the pleasure of killing; some will rebel against that pleasure (and become pacifist); others will yearn to perpetuate it (and become fascist). Remarque belongs to the first category; Jünger to the second; Barbusse and Céline seem to have derived absolutely no pleasure from killing, yet one became a revolutionary-pacifist, the other a genocide-inciting fascist.

39. See, e.g., B. Hüppauf, "Langemarck, Verdun and the Myth of a New Man in Germany after the First World War," *W&S* 6/2 (1988): 70–103. For a profile of Hitler's early supporters, see T. Abel, *Why Hitler Came into Power*, 2d rev. ed. (Cambridge: Mass., 1986); P. H. Merkl, *Political Violence under the Swastika: 581 Early Nazis* (Princeton, 1975). For early fascism in France, see R. Soucy, *French Fascism: The First Wave, 1924–1933* (New Haven, 1986). For the cult of the fallen soldier, see G. L. Mosse, *Fallen Soldiers: Reshaping the Memory of the World Wars* (New York, 1990); K. S. Inglis, "Entombing Unknown Soldiers: From London and Paris to Baghdad," *H&M* 5/2 (1993): 7–31. On faith and commemoration in France, see A. Becker, *La guerre et la foi: De la mort à la mémoire, 1914–1930* (Paris, 1944); idem., "From Death to Memory: The National Ossuaries in France After the Great War," *H&M* 5/2 (1993): 32–49. More generally on intellectual attitudes, see P. Ory and J.-F. Sirinelli, *Les Intellectuels en France, de l'Affaire Dreyfus à nos jours* (Paris, 1986), Chapters 4–5; J.-F. Sirinelli, *Intellectuels et passions françaises: Manifestes et pétitions au XXe siècle* (Paris, 1990), Chapters 2–5. Also see J. Miller (ed.), *Voices Against Tyranny: Writings of the Spanish Civil War* (New York, 1986).

40. For an early discussion of post-1945 violence, see H. Arendt, *On Violence*, 2d ed. (New York, 1970).

41. See, e.g., Jünger, *Der Arbeiter*.

42. E. Jünger, "Die Totale Mobilmachung," in *Sämtliche Werke*, 18 vols. (Stuttgart, 1980 [1930]), 7: 119–142. See also S. D. Denham, *Visions of War: Ideologies and Images of War in German Literature Before and After the Great War* (Bern, 1992), esp. pp. 99–130; idem., *"Die jüngste Jüngerei*: Is Ernst Jünger Finding a Place in the German Pantheon?" *GPS* 22 (1991): 60–73; P. Fritzsche, "Landscape of Danger, Landscape of Design: Crisis and Modernism in Weimar Germany," in *Dancing on the Volcano: Essays on the Culture of the Weimar Republic*, ed. T. W. Kniesche and S. Brodemann (Columbia: S.C., 1994), pp. 29–46.

43. E. Jünger, "Kirchhorster Blätter," in *Sämtliche Werke*, 18 vols. (Stuttgart, 1979), 3: 360 (January 13, 1945): *"Der gute Junge. Von Kind auf war es sein Bestreben, es dem Vater nachzutun. Nun hat er es gleich beim ersten Male besser gemacht, ging so unendlich über ihn hinaus."* Jünger's son, to whom he refers always as Ernstel, was arrested in February 1944 for allegedly saying that Hitler would have to be hanged before Germany made peace; released several months later (apparently due to his father's efforts and connections), he enlisted in an armored unit and was killed on November 29, 1944, at the age of 18, by a bullet in the head in the course of a reconnaissance action in the marble mountains of Carara in central Italy. E. Jünger, "Das Zweite Pariser Tagebuch," in *Sämtliche Werke*, 18 vols. (Stuttgart, 1979), 3: 223, 228, 232, 245, 249–52; *Kirchhorster Blätter*, pp. 305, 322, 337–38, 344. Jünger found his son's diary, which carried the motto: *"Der kommt am weitesten, der nicht weiss, wohin er geht."* Ibid., p. 360. The son's company commander, though informed of his "offense," notified Jünger that he had fallen *"Für den Führer."* Ibid., p. 362. We should note, however, Jünger's recollection when visiting Ernstel in prison, *"wie sehr er als Kind*

auf kriegerischen Lorbeer hoffte.... Er wollte sich des Vaters würdig erweisen...."
Pariser Tagebuch, p. 251. Jünger, incidentally, opposed assassinating Hitler, and preferred to have him arrested. Ibid., pp. 242–43.

44. B. Engelmann, *In Hitler's Germany: Daily Life in the Third Reich* (New York, 1986), pp. 238–39.

45. Jünger's reaction to reports of mass killings of Jews is revealing; he cites a poem by Friedrich Georg ("Eure Siege sind verächtlich/Wie die Niederlage"), and on the following afternoon visits a newly opened theater in the Boulevard de Montparnasse, followed by tea. The comment made to him: *"Die Arbeit der Grossen erkennt man an ihrem mathematischen Charakter: die Probleme sind teilbar und gehen auf. Es bleibt kein Rest zurück,"* makes him think of Molière and Shakespeare, not of the "Final Solution." Jünger, *Pariser Tagebuch*, pp. 175–77 (October 16 and 17, 1943).

46. Note his comment: *"Die grossen Zerstörungen unseres Vaterlandes könnten ein Gutes haben, indem sie uns für diese Dinge, die unwiderruflich gestaltet schienen, einen zweiten Beginn setzten. Sie schaffen eine Lage, die die kühnsten Träume Bakunins übertrifft."* Jünger, *Pariser Tagebuch*, pp. 172–73; also see his discussion on the difference between nihilism and anarchism. Ibid., pp. 213–14. While reading Josephus, and greatly admiring him, he comes to the following detached conclusion: *"Es ist merkwürdig, wie wenig Jüdisches diesem Autor anhaftet.... Es Scheint, dass sich das Jüdische schwerer als andere Volkstümer abstreifen lässt, dass aber in den seltenen Fällen, in denen das gelingt, das Menschliche sich zu besonderer Höhe erhebt."* Ibid., pp. 196–97 (December 9, 1943). See also ibid., p. 170.

47. Remarque, *All Quiet*, p. 272.

48. L.-F. Céline, *Journey to the End of the Night* (New York, 1983 [1932]), pp. 7–9.

49. Ingram, *Dissent*, pp. 192–93.

50. Ibid., pp. 318–19.

51. See G. Steiner, "Cat Man," *The New Yorker* (August 24, 1992), pp. 81–84.

52. Nor did these essays create at the time the kind of scandal imputed to them after the war, because, as Michel Winock has pointed out, "in 1930s France, Antisemitism played a respectable role." André Gide wrote that *"Il fait de son mieux, pour qu'on ne le prenne pas un sérieux,"* and argued that if *Bagatelles* was not *"un jeu,"* it would mean that Céline was *"complètement maboul."* Pierre Loewel wrote in *L'Ordre* that *"C'est aussi exactement le type d'ouvrage dont un antisémite intelligent se demanderait si, au fond, il n'a pas été payé par les Juifs."* *Bagatelles* can also not be seen as a result of Céline's hatred of the Popular Front, though he did write there that *"je préférerais douze Hitler plutôt qu'un Blum omnipotent. Hitler encore je pourrais le comprendre, tandis que Blum c'est inutile, ça sera toujours le pire ennemi, la haine à mort, absolue."* Already in the play *L'Église*, written even before *le Voyage*, he alludes to a Jewish conspiracy to take over the world. Winock, *Nationalisme*, pp. 374, 377–78; Louis-Ferdinand Céline, *Bagatelles pour un massacre*, 2d ed. (Paris, 1942), p. 192.

53. See leaflets in Archives Nationales: F^7 13233, 13235, 13239.

54. J. Noakes and G. Pridham (eds.), *Foreign Policy, War and Racial Extermination* (Exeter, 1988), vol. 3 of *Nazism, 1919–1945: A Documentary Reader*, 1049. Another interesting parallel with Hitler is Céline's reaction to his 1936 visit to the USSR, after which he apparently decided that man's misfortune was not grounded in class exploitation but in himself, and that those who concealed this truth (namely, the Bolsheviks, i.e., the Jews), were trying to raise people's hopes while at the same time preparing the worst. Céline similarly presented *Bagatelles* as an act of peace, an attempt to stop a war which would be *"Une guerre pour la joie des Juifs,"* an argument made of course by mass circulation papers such as *Gringoire* and intellectual journals like *Com-*

bat. As Céline wrote in *L'École des cadavres*, "Je n'ai rien découvert. Aucune prétention. Simple vulgarisation, virulente, stylisée." Winock, *Nationalisme*, pp. 380–82.

55. G. Steiner, *In Bluebeard's Castle* (New Haven, 1971), pp. 53–54, cited in Des Pres, *The Survivor*, p. 171.

56. Apart from the examples cited below, see the analysis of oral testimonies in L. L. Langer, *Holocaust Testimonies: The Ruins of Memory* (New Haven, 1991), discussed at greater length *infra*, Chapter 6.

57. K. Hart, *I Am Alive* (London, 1962), pp. 92–93, cited in Des Pres, *The Survivor*, p. 83.

58. E. Wiesel, *Night* (New York, 1969), p. 42, cited in Des Pres, *The Survivor*, p. 84.

59. This is Des Pres' phrase. Ibid.

60. J. S. Newman, *In the Hell of Auschwitz* (New York, 1964), p. 20, cited in Des Pres, *The Survivor*, pp. 84–85.

61. K. Zywulska, *I Came Back* (London, 1951), p. 179, cited in Des Pres, *The Survivor*, pp. 172–73.

62. Fussell, *Modern Memory*, p. 74.

63. R. Weiss, *Journey Through Hell* (London, 1961), pp. 74–75, cited in Des Pres, *The Survivor*, pp. 175–76.

Chapter 3

1. R. Hochhuth, *The Deputy* (New York, 1964), p. 248. I would like to thank the participants of the 17th Annual Conference of the German Studies Association in Washington, D.C., in October 1993, and of the Inaugural Conference of the United States Holocaust Memorial Museum in Washington, D.C., in December 1993, for their comments on earlier (and substantially shorter) versions of this chapter. Thanks are also due to Dr. Michael Berenbaum, Director of the United States Holocaust Memorial Museum, for permitting me to use the paper presented there as the basis for this chapter.

2. See esp. B. Lang, *Act and Idea in the Nazi Genocide* (Chicago, 1990), pp. 3–29; F. Chalk and K. Jonassohn (eds), *The History and Sociology of Genocide: Analyses and Case Studies* (New Haven, 1990); Kuper, *Genocide*.

3. For the first version see, e.g., S. Almog (ed.), *Antisemitism Through the Ages* (Oxford, 1988); L. Poliakov, *Histoire de l'antisémitisme*, rev. ed., 2 vols (Paris, 1991); R. S. Wistrich, *Antisemitism: The Longest Hatred*, 2d ed. (New York, 1992). Somewhere between the two poles, see, e.g., Ettinger, *Modern Anti-Semitism*; J. Katz, *From Prejudice to Destruction: Anti-Semitism, 1700–1933* (Cambridge: Mass., 1980). On the second version see, e.g., H. Arendt, *The Origins of Totalitarianism*, 6th ed. (London, 1986), esp. Part I, pp. 3–120; P. Pulzer, *The Rise of Political Anti-Semitism in Germany & Austria*, 2d rev. ed. (Cambridge: Mass., 1988); M. Zimmermann, *Wilhelm Marr: The Patriarch of Antisemitism* (New York, 1986); S. Volkov, "The Written Matter and the Spoken Word: On the Gap Between Pre-1914 and Nazi Anti-Semitism," in *Unanswered Questions: Nazi Germany and the Genocide of the Jews*, ed. F. Furet (New York, 1989), pp. 33–53. For a brief survey, see P. Girard, "Historical Foundations of Anti-Semitism," in *Survivors, Victims, and Perpetrators: Essay on the Nazi Holocaust*, ed. J. E. Dimsdale (Washington, 1980), pp. 55–77.

4. See, e.g., the excellent study by Bauman, *Modernity*.

5. For a forceful presentation of the Zionist view, see A. B. Yehoshua, *The Wall and the Mountain: The Unliterary Reality of the Writer in Israel* (Tel Aviv, 1989

[Hebrew]). See also D. Porat, *The Blue and the Yellow Star of David: The Zionist Leadership in Palestine and the Holocaust, 1939–1945* (Cambridge: Mass., 1990); A. Shapira, *Land and Power: The Zionist Resort to Force, 1881–1948* (New York, 1992).

6. For a survey of the emancipation of European Jewry, see J. Katz, *Out of the Ghetto: The Social Background of the Emancipation of the Jews, 1770–1870* (New York, 1978). On the relationship of this process to modern antisemitism, see R. Rürup, *Emanzipation und Antisemitismus* (Göttingen, 1975); idem., "Jewish Emancipation and Bourgeois Society," *LBIY* 14 (1969): 67–91; A. Hertzberg, *The French Enlightenment and the Jews: The Origins of Modern Anti-Semitism*, 2d ed. (New York, 1990). On antisemitism and religion, see G. I. Langmuir, *History, Religion, and Antisemitism* (Berkeley, 1990). On Arabs and Antisemitism, see B. Lewis, *Semites and Anti-Semites: An Inquiry into Conflict and Prejudice*, 2d ed. (New York, 1987). For alternative views of history among some German Jewish intellectuals, see S. Mosès, *L'Ange de l'histoire: Rosenzweig, Benjamin, Scholem* (Paris, 1992); and G. Scholem, *On Jews and Judaism in Crisis: Selected Essays*, ed. W. J. Dannhauser (New York, 1976); G. L. Mosse, *German Jews Beyond Judaism* (Bloomington, 1985). For an existentialist treatise on Antisemitism, see J.-P. Sartre, *Anti-Semite and Jew*, 2d ed. (New York, 1976).

7. See *supra*, Chapter 2, note 4, and W. Laqueur, "Hannah Arendt in Jerusalem: The Controversy Revisited," with comments by W. S. Allen and D. Schoenbaum, in *Western Society After the Holocaust*, ed. L. H. Legters (Boulder, 1983), pp. 107–29. Compare also with N. Cohn, *Warrant for Genocide: The Myth of the Jewish World-Conspiracy and the Protocols of the Elders of Zion*, 2d ed. (London, 1970); and Y. Bauer, *The Holocaust in Historical Perspective*, 2d ed. (Seattle, 1980), pp. 30–49. Recent works on Jewish society in early modern and modern Europe include N. L. Green, *The Pletzl of Paris: Jewish Immigrant Workers in the Belle Epoque* (New York, 1986); V. Caron, *Between France and Germany: The Jews of Alsace-Lorraine, 1871–1918* (Stanford, 1988); D. Sorkin, *The Transformation of German Jewry, 1780–1840*, 2d ed. (New York, 1990); M. A. Kaplan, *The Making of the Jewish Middle Class: Women, Family, and Identity in Imperial Germany* (New York, 1991); J. Wertheimer, *Unwelcome Strangers: East European Jews in Imperial Germany*, 2d ed. (New York, 1991); W. O. McCagg, Jr., *A History of Habsburg Jews, 1670–1918*, 2d ed. (Bloomington, 1992); S. Beller, *Vienna and the Jews, 1867–1933: A Cultural History*, 2d ed. (Cambridge, 1990); D. D. Moore (ed.), *East European Jews in Two Worlds: Studies from the YIVO Annual* (Evanston, 1990).

8. One example of a work that minimizes the role of Antisemitism in the rise of Nazism is Gordon, *"Jewish Question"*, esp. Chapters 1–2. For evaluations of the importance of Antisemitism by historians see, e.g., L. S. Dawidowicz, *The Holocaust and the Historians* (Cambridge: Mass., 1981), esp. pp. 22–87; M. R. Marrus, *The Holocaust in History*, 2d ed. (New York, 1989), esp. pp. 9–13; I. Kershaw, *The Nazi Dictatorship: Problems and Perspectives of Interpretation*, 3d ed. (London, 1993), esp. Chapter 5. See also R. Levy, *The Downfall of the Antisemitic Political Parties in Imperial Germany* (New Haven, 1975).

9. This is implied in Kershaw, *Nazi Dictatorship*, pp. 80–81, and stated more strongly in Martin Broszat's correspondence with Saul Friedlander, included in *Reworking the Past: Hitler, the Holocaust, and the Historians' Debate*, ed. P. Baldwin (Boston, 1990), esp. p. 106. See also S. Friedlander, *Memory, History, and the Extermination of the Jews of Europe* (Bloomington, 1993). On German memories of the Third Reich, see L. Niethammer (ed.), *"Die Jahre weiss man nicht, wo man die heute hinsetzen soll": Faschismuserfahrungen im Ruhrgebiet* (Berlin, 1983); D. Bar-On, *Legacy of Silence: Encounters with Children of the Third Reich*, 2d ed. (Cambridge:

Mass., 1991); G. L. Posner, *Hitler's Children: Sons and Daughters of Leaders of the Third Reich Talk About Their Fathers and Themselves* (New York, 1991); A. Heck, *A Child of Hitler*, 2d ed. (Toronto, 1986). On memories of victims and their offspring, see Langer, *Testimonies*; H. Epstein, *Children of the Holocaust: Conversations with Sons and Daughters of Survivors*, 2d ed. (New York, 1988); S. Breznitz, *Memory Fields* (Tel Aviv, 1993 [Hebrew]); I. Kertész, *Without Fate* (Tel Aviv, 1994 [Hebrew. Original Hungarian title: *Sorstalanság*]); H. L. Waterford, *Commitment to the Dead: One Woman's Journey Toward Understanding*, rev. ed. (Frederick: Colo., 1993). On national memories of the Holocaust, see J. Miller, *One, By One, By One: Facing the Holocaust*, 2d ed. (New York, 1990). For a more general discussion, see P. H. Hutton, *History as an Art of Memory* (Hanover: N. H., 1993).

10. I refer here to such prompting from widely differing, yet not unrelated quarters. See, e.g., M. Broszat, "A Plea for the Historicization of National Socialism," in Baldwin, *Reworking*, pp. 77–87; Nolte, *Historical Legend*, and idem., *Past That Will Not Pass*; A. Hillgruber, *Zweierlei Untergang: Die Zerschlagung des Deutschen Reiches und das Ende des europäischen Judentums* (Berlin, 1986); A. Mayer, "Memory and History: On the Poverty of Remembering and Forgetting the Judeocide," *RHR* 56 (1993): 5–20; C. S. Maier, "A Surfeit of Memory? Reflections on History, Melancholy, and Denial," *H&M* 5/2 (1993): 136–152.

11. The most conspicuous instance of this was of course Menahem Begin's pronouncement during the Israeli siege of Beirut in 1982. On the debate in the Israeli press, see Segev, *Seventh Million*, pp. 399–403. Also see M. Zukermann, *Shoah in the Sealed Room: The "Holocaust" in Israeli Press During the Gulf War* (Tel Aviv, 1993 [Hebrew]).

12. See F. Stern, *The Whitewashing of the Yellow Badge: Antisemitism and Philosemitism in Postwar Germany* (Oxford, 1992); M. Zimmermann and O. Heilbronner (eds.), *"Normal" Relations: Israeli-German Relations* (Jerusalem, 1993 [Hebrew]).

13. Reports of growing antisemitism in Russia, as well as in East European countries formerly under Soviet domination, seem to confirm this fear. Nor is the growing tide of neofascist organizations in Central and Western Europe to be ignored; and if it has only made major strides in Italy and to a lesser extent France, it may well represent an extreme version of more widespread public xenophobia in many other countries confronting new economic hardship and the "threat" of foreign immigration. See, e.g., M. Schmidt, *The New Reich: Violent Extremism in Unified Germany and Beyond* (New York, 1993); I. Buruma, "Outsiders," *NYR* (April 9, 1992): 15–19; F. Stern, "From Overt Philosemitism to Discreet Antisemitism, and Beyond: Anti-Jewish Developments in the Political Culture of the Federal Republic of Germany," in Almog, *Antisemitism*, pp. 385–404; and idem., "German Unification and the Question of Antisemitism," with comments by S. Stern, L. G. Feldman, T. Kielinger, and H. O. Bräutigam, *International Perspectives: AJC* (New York, May 1993). Also see J. M. Mushaben, "Going to Extremes: The Politics of Resentment Among 'Unified' German Youth," unpublished paper (1993); and R. Karapin, "Political Opportunities for Right-Wing Violence in Reunified Germany," unpublished paper (1993). For recent debates on citizenship in France and Germany informed by traditional concepts and current extremism, see Brubaker, *Citizenship*, Chapters 7–8.

14. For an attempt to confront some of the issues related to this problem, see Friedlander, *Probing the Limits*.

15. On the origins of the term, see Marrus, *Holocaust in History*, pp. 3–4; Kershaw, *Nazi Dictatorship*, p. 80.

16. Other terms used frequently in Germany to denote the Holocaust are "Final Solution," the official Nazi term for the genocide of the Jews, and "Auschwitz," which stands for the whole industrial killing machine rather than for that specific death and concentration camp, which also contained industrial plants and slave barracks. For those who do not know (or do not wish to know) what Auschwitz was, the term evokes neither genocide nor Jews, but at worst a concentration camp somewhere in the East.

17. P. Haidu, "The Dialectic of Unspeakability: Language, Silence, and the Narratives of Desubjectification," in Friedlander, *Probing the Limits*, p. 279.

18. On the reception of the film "Holocaust" in the FRG, see A. Kaes, *From Hitler to Heimat: The Return of History as Film* (Cambridge: Mass., 1989), pp. 28–35. On film and the Holocaust, see Avisar, *Screening the Holocaust*. Also see E. L. Santner, *Stranded Objects: Mourning, Memory, and Film in Postwar Germany*, 2d ed. (Ithaca, 1993); and G. Koch, *Die Einstellung ist die Einstellung: Visuelle Konstruktionen des Judentums* (Frankfurt/M., 1992).

19. The term "*Vernichtung*," annihilation or destruction, so popular in the Third Reich, is often employed by German historians writing on the period. Though German scholars commonly use inverted commas when employing Nazi terms (such as "Führer," "Third Reich," "Final Solution," etc.), the effect of a stream of publications bearing titles lifted out of Nazi discourse is quite disturbing and may well have consequences for the German reading public very different from those intended by the authors. See, e.g., W. Schneider (ed.), *"Vernichtungspolitik": Eine Debatte über den Zusammenhang von Sozialpolitik und Genozid im nationalsozialistischen Deutschland* (Hamburg, 1991), which raises many other problematic issues on the relationship between modernization and annihilation policies; P. Jahn and R. Rürup (eds.), *Erobern und Vernichten: Der Krieg gegen die Sowjetunion 1941–1945* (Berlin, 1991), which also contains articles on the problematic issue of so called demographic policies in the East; and the Piper Verlag collection *"Historikerstreit": Die Dokumentation der Kontroverse um die Einzigartigkeit der nationalsozialistischen Judenvernitung* (Munich, 1987), which we have already encountered in its English translation, where the term *Judenvernichtung* was significantly changed to "Holocaust." See *Forever in the Shadow*.

20. See A. J. Mayer, *Why Did the Heavens Not Darken? The "Final Solution" in History* (New York, 1988), e.g., pp. vii, 3.

21. See, e.g., J.-P. Azéma, *1940 l'année terrible* (Paris, 1990).

22. See the brilliant treatment of this issue in A. Finkielkraut, *Remembering in Vain: The Klaus Barbie Trial and Crimes Against Humanity* (New York, 1992); also see E. Paris, *Unhealed Wounds: France and the Klaus Barbie Affair*, 2d ed. (New York, 1986); P. Vidal-Naquet, *Assassins of Memory: Essays on the Denial of the Holocaust* (New York, 1992). For similarly revealing French literary treatments of the period, see, e.g., J.-P. Sartre, *Iron in the Soul* (Harmondsworth, 1984 [1949]); M. Tournier, *The Ogre* (New York, 1972); M. Duras, *The War: A Memoir* (New York, 1986).

23. Recently the genocide of the Jews has been compared by one writer to the genocide of the population of the Vendée, though with the intention of showing that the contemporary manipulation of memory may cause us to forget the former as we have, to his mind, forgotten the latter. See R. Secher, *Juifs et Vendéens: d'un génocide à l'autre, la manipulation de la mémoire* (Paris, 1991).

24. On the difficulties of the French with the memory of the period, see H. Rousso, *The Vichy Syndrome: History and Memory in France since 1944* (Cambridge: Mass., 1991). On collaboration, see R. O. Paxton, *Vichy France: Old Guard and New Order*,

1940–1944, 2d ed. (New York, 1975); M. R. Marrus and R. O. Paxton, *Vichy France and the Jews* (New York, 1983). For French scholarship on collaboration and opinion during the "black years" see, e.g., P. Ory, *Les collaborateurs 1940–1945* (Paris, 1976); P. Laborie, *L'Opinion française sous Vichy* (Paris, 1990); H. Amouroux, *Quarante millions de pétainistes, juin 1940–juin 1941* (Paris, 1977). On the memory of resistance, see E. Malet (ed.), *Résistance et mémoire: D'Auschwitz à Sarajevo* (Paris, 1993).

25. See *supra*, notes 5 and 11. It should be noted that within the ultra-Orthodox community the term *shoah* is not used, but rather such terms as *churban, gzerah,* or *pur'anut*—that is, destruction, (evil) decree, and calamity or (divine) retribution, respectively. All relate the Holocaust to a Jewish tradition of describing persecution and pogroms in exile, and therefore make sense of it by inserting it into a familiar, if tragic, context. *Churban* is an especially important term, since it is associated with *churban beit ha'mikdash,* the destruction of the temple, which gives both a religious connotation and a historical meaning to the Holocaust (the destruction of the temple *is* the beginning of the exile), and provides it with a hopeful conclusion, since just as the third temple will be built, so too will the Holocaust presumably be undone. I would like to thank Sam Norich for pointing out to me the importance of this term. Also see the excellent article by M. Halbertal, "Speak, Memory," *TNR* (October 18, 1993): 40–47, esp. p. 45; and Ezrahi, *Words,* pp. 10–15; Roskies, *Apocalypse,* Chapter 2, esp. pp. 41–43.

26. On Israeli attempts to come to terms with the memory of war, see the fascinating study by E. Sivan, *The 1948 Generation: Myth, Profile and Memory* (Tel Aviv, 1991 [Hebrew]); and idem., "To Remember Is to Forget: Israel's 1948 War," *JCH* 28 (1993): 341–59. Further on history, memory, and myth in Israel, see: Y. Zerubavel, "The Politics of Interpretation: Tel Hai in Israel's Collective Memory," *AJSR* 16 (1991): 133–159; and idem., "New Beginnings, Old Past: The Collective Memory of Pioneering in Israeli Culture," in *New Perspectives in Israeli History: The Early Years of the State,* ed. L. J. Silberstein (New York, 1991), pp. 193–215.

27. The best introduction to the historiography of the Third Reich is Kershaw, *Nazi Dictatorship.*

28. See, e.g., W. M. McGovern, *From Luther to Hitler: The History of Nazi-Fascist Philosophy* (London, 1946). See also A. J. P. Taylor, *The Course of German History* (London, 1945). On the demerits of the thesis about German history having "failed to turn," see: D. Blackbourn, "The Discreet Charm of the Bourgeoisie: Reappraising German History in the Nineteenth Century," in D. Blackbourn and G. Eley, *The Peculiarities of German History: Bourgeois Society and Politics in Nineteenth-Century Germany,* 5th ed. (Oxford, 1992), esp. pp. 159–65.

29. See, e.g., M. Fechner (ed.), *Wie Konnte es Geschehen* (Berlin, n.d.). The best known examples of this type of literature are F. Meinecke, *The German Catastrophe,* 2d ed. (Boston, 1963 [1946]); and G. Ritter, *The German Problem: Basic Questions of German Political Life, Past and Present* (Columbus, 1965 [1948/1962]).

30. See, e.g., D. Eichholz and K. Gossweiler (eds.), *Faschismusforschung: Positionen, Probleme, Polemik* (Berlin [East], 1980); K. Kwiet, "Historians of the German Democratic Republic on Antisemitism and Persecution," *LBIY* 21 (1976): 173–98. See also W. Wippermann, "The Post-War German Left and Fascism," *JCH* 11 (1976); O. D. Kulka, "Major Trends and Tendencies in German Historiography on National Socialism and the 'Jewish Question' (1924–1984)," *LBIY* 30 (1985): 215–42; J. Rüsen, "Theory of History in the Development of West German Historical Studies: A Reconstruction and Outlook," *GSR* 7 (1984): 14–18.

31. See, e.g., F. Stern, *The Politics of Cultural Despair: A Study in the Rise of the Germanic Ideology*, 2d ed. (Berkeley, 1974 [1961]); G. Mosse, *The Crisis of German Ideology: Intellectual Origins of the Third Reich* (New York, 1964); W. Laqueur, *Young Germany: A History of the German Youth Movement*, 2d ed. (New Brunswick, 1984 [1962]).

32. For a summary of the Fischer debate see J. A. Moses, *The Politics of Illusion* (London, 1975); J. W. Langdon, *July 1914* (Oxford, 1991); R. Fletcher, "Recent Developments in West German Historiography: The Bielefeld School and its Critics," *GSR* 3 (1984): 451–80. See also H. W. Koch (ed.), *The Origins of the First World War: Great Power Rivalry and German War Aims*, 2d ed. (London, 1977); and Berghahn, *Germany and the Approach of War*, pp. 1–14.

33. On intentionalism, see the pathbreaking essay by T. Mason, "Intention and Explanation: A Current Controversy About the Interpretation of National Socialism," in *Der "Führerstaat": Mythos und Realität*, ed. G. Hirschfeld and L. Kettenacker (Stuttgart, 1981), pp. 23–40. See also C. R. Browning, *Fateful Months: Essays on the Emergence of the Final Solution* (New York, 1985), Chapter 1; idem., *The Path to Genocide: Essays on Launching the Final Solution* (Cambridge, 1992), Chapter 5. The debate on uniqueness relates to the so called *Historikerstreit*. See, e.g., C. S. Maier, *The Unmasterable Past: History, Holocaust, and German Nationalism* (Cambridge: Mass., 1988); R. Evans, *In Hitler's Shadow: West German Historians and the Attempt to Escape from the Nazi Past* (New York, 1989); H.-U. Wehler, *Entsorgung der deutschen Vergangenheit? Ein polemischer Essay zum "Historikerstreit"* (Munich, 1988); D. Diner (ed.), *Ist der Nationalsozialismus Geschichte? Zu Historisierung und Historikerstreit* (Frankfurt/M., 1987); O. D. Kulka, "Singularity and Its Relativization: Changing Views in German Historiography on National Socialism and the 'Final Solution'," in Baldwin, *Reworking*, pp. 146–70. Most recently, see U. Herbert and O. Groehler, *Zweierlei Bewältigung: Vier Beiträge über den Umgang mit der NS-Vergangenheit in den beiden deutschen Staaten* (Hamburg, 1992).

34. On film see *supra*, note 18. Also see S. Sontag, "Fascinating Fascism," and "Syberberg's Hitler," in her *Under the Sign of Saturn*, 7th ed. (New York, 1981), pp. 73–105, 137–65; Friedlander, *Reflections*. On literature, see also J. Ryan, *The Uncompleted Past: Postwar German Novels and the Third Reich* (Detroit, 1983). On recent debates and opinions of German intellectuals, see I. Buruma, "There's No Place Like Heimat," *NYR* (December 20, 1990): 34–43, where he quotes some of Hans-Jürgen Syberberg's most antisemitic diatribes ("We live in the Jewish epoch of European cultural history. And we can only wait . . . for our last judgement at the edge of the apocalypse . . . suffocating in unprecedented technological prosperity, without spirit, without meaning") from his collection of essays, suggestively titled *Vom Glück und Unglück der Kunst in Deutschland nach dem Letzten Kriege*. See also D. Diner, *Der Krieg der Erinnerungen und die Ordnung der Welt* (Berlin, 1991).

35. See esp. F. Neumann, *Behemoth: The Structure and Practice of National Socialism 1933-1944* (New York, 1944).

36. See A. Kaes, "Americanism, Modernity, and the 'Terror of the Machine': On Fritz Lang's *Metropolis*," unpublished paper (1993). Martin Broszat was the leader of the multi-volumed project on everyday life in Bavaria; see the concluding essay in the final volume: M. Broszat and E. Fröhlich, *Alltag und Widerstand: Bayern im Nationalsozialismus* (Munich, 1987); and M. Broszat, *The Hitler State: The Foundation and Development of the Internal Structure of the Third Reich* (London, 1981 [1969]). The other main proponent of functionalism is Hans Mommsen; see esp. his "National Social-

ism: Continuity and Change," in *Fascism: A Reader's Guide*, ed. W. Laqueur, 2d ed. (Harmondsworth, 1982), pp. 151–192. Also see M. Nolan, "The *Historikerstreit* and Social History," in Baldwin, *Reworking*, pp. 224–48.

37. See. e.g., J. Förster, "The German Army and the Ideological War Against the Soviet Union," in *The Policies of Genocide: Jews and Soviet Prisoners of War in Nazi Germany*, ed. G. Hirschfeld (London, 1986), pp. 15–29; and idem., "Das Unternehmen 'Barbarossa' als Eroberungs- und Vernichtungskrieg," and "Freiwillige für den 'Kreuzzug Europas gegen den Bolschewismus'," both in *Deutsche Reich*, 4: 413–47, 908–35.

38. One cannot help feeling that in yet another ironic twist typical this time of the United States, the indigenous peoples of North America were renamed Native Americans only after they were reduced to a harmless, hopeless, and wretched marginal minority. On the Armenian genocide, see *supra*, Chapter 3, note 6.

39. On this issue, see Brubaker, *Citizenship*, Chapter 8. It should be added that minorities from the "Third World" have been under a great deal of both popular and governmental pressure in Germany since unification. See, e.g., Buruma, *Outsiders*. See further in U. Herbert, *Geschichte der Ausländerbeschäftigung in Deutschland 1880 bis 1980* (Bonn, 1986).

40. For a serious study of that genocide, see B. Kiernan, "Genocidal Targeting: Two Groups of Victims in Pol Pot's Cambodia," in *State Organized Terror: The Case of Violent Internal Repression*, ed. P. T. Bushnell et al., (Boulder, 1991), pp. 207–26; and in a comparative mode, idem., "The Khmer Rouge and the Nazis: Parallels and Tangents," unpublished paper.

41. For a comparison between the two dictators, see A. Bullock, *Hitler and Stalin: Parallel Lives* (London, 1991). For nightmarish visions among *Freikorps* members, see Theweleit, *Männerphantasien*. Ernst Nolte hoped to put an end to the debate with his *Das Vergehen der Vergangenheit: Antwort an meine Kritiker im sogenannten Historikerstreit* (Berlin, 1987), which contains, curiously, two interviews with Israeli journalists and an article he wrote especially for an Israeli daily trying to explain his position.

42. As can be seen, in one instance, in Herbert's above-cited work.

43. A good introduction is T. Childers and J. Caplan (eds.), *Reevaluating the Third Reich* (New York, 1993).

44. D. J. K. Peukert, *The Weimar Republic: The Crisis of Classical Modernity* (New York, 1992 [1987]).

45. See, e.g., R. Zitelmann, *Hitler: Selbstverständnis eines Revolutionärs* (Stuttgart, 1987); M. Prinz and R. Zitelmann (eds.), *Nationalsozialismus und Modernisierung* (Darmstadt, 1991).

46. See mainly R. Dahrendorf, *Society and Democracy in Germany*, 2d ed. (New York, 1979 [1965]), pp. 381–96; and D. Schoenbaum, *Hitler's Social Revolution: Class and Status in Nazi Germany 1933–1939* (New York, 1966).

47. The original proposal to "historicize" the social policies of the Third Reich was made in Broszat, *Historicization*. See also C. Sachsse, "A Nazi Welfare State? Structures and Features of National Socialist Social Policy 1933–1945," unpublished paper (1992). A related debate, however, focuses primarily on the extent to which the "Final Solution" was perceived by Nazi bureaucrats as an economically rational measure, aimed at modernizing Eastern Europe. This is the thesis argued by G. Aly and S. Heim, *Vordenker der Vernichtung: Auschwitz und die deutsche Pläne für eine neue europäische Ordnung* (Hamburg, 1991). It has been criticized in U. Herbert, "Labour and Extermination: Economic Interest and the Primacy of *Weltanschauung* in National Socialism," *P&P* 138 (1993): 144–95; and C. Browning, *Path to Genocide*, pp. 59–76,

a book that generally presents a series of theses that effectively demolish the Aly/Heim argument. See also Schneider, *"Vernichtungspolitik"*, which is wholly devoted to a debate on the Aly/Heim thesis.

48. Broszat, *Historicization*; Hillgruber, *Zweierlei Untergang*; M. Stürmer, "History in a Land Without History," in *Forever in the Shadow*, pp. 16–17.

49. See in this context S. Friedlander, "Reflections on the Historicization of National Socialism," in Friedlander, *Memory*, pp. 64–84; and his introduction to G. Fleming, *Hitler and the Final Solution* (Berkeley, 1984), esp. pp. xxxii–xxxiii. Fleming's book, incidentally, is a striking example of intentionalist history.

50. The best known representative of this view is Dawidowicz, *War Against the Jews*.

51. In addition to Fleming, *Hitler*, see E. Jäckel, *Hitler's World View: A Blueprint for Power*, 2d ed. (Cambridge: Mass., 1981 [1969]). The personalizing revisionist view can be found in D. Irving, *Hitler's War* (London, 1977). The standard biographies, all more or less intentionalist (though not particularly concerned with Hitler's role in the Holocaust), are K. Heiden, *Der Führer: Hitler's Rise to Power* (Boston, 1969 [1944]); A. Bullock, *Hitler, A Study in Tyranny*, 2d rev. ed. (New York, 1964); J. C. Fest, *Hitler*, 3d ed. (Harmondsworth, 1982 [1973]). See also W. Carr, *Hitler: A Study in Personality and Politics* (London, 1978); E. Jäckel, *Hitler in History* (Hanover, 1984); I. Kershaw, *Hitler* (London, 1991).

52. See *supra*, note 8; Abel, *Hitler*, pp. 154–65; Merkl, *Political Violence*, pp. 498–527.

53. See esp. M. Broszat, "Hitler and the Genesis of the 'Final Solution': An Assessment of David Irving's Theses." *YVS* 13 (1979): 61–98; and H. Mommsen, "The Realization of the Unthinkable: the 'Final Solution of the Jewish Question' in the Third Reich," in Hirschfeld, *Policies of Genocide*, pp. 97–144. Also see the monographs by K. A. Schleunes, *The Twisted Road to Auschwitz: Nazi Policy Toward German Jews, 1933–1939*, 2d ed. (Urbana, 1990); U.-D. Adam, *Judenpolitik im Dritten Reich* (Düsseldorf, 1972); C. R. Browning, *The Final Solution and the Foreign Office: A Study of Referat D III of Abteilung Deutschland 1940–43* (New York, 1978).

54. See D. Diner (ed.) *Zivilisationsbruch: Denken nach Auschwitz* (Frankfurt/M., 1988). Again it should be noted that this term may imply either an inevitable or at least a perpetual potential for genocide in modern civilization, or, conversely, a turning away from, or against, an otherwise positive progress of humanity toward a "higher" moral ground. Here too the key text is Bauman, *Modernity*.

55. Mommsen, *National Socialism*; and Broszat, *Hitler State*; E. N. Peterson, *The Limits of Hitler's Power* (Princeton, 1969).

56. Arendt, *Eichmann*. This trend was noted already in Dawidowicz, *Holocaust and the Historians*, esp. pp. 22–67, and 152–55. The new interest in Nazi eugenic policies has also tended to downplay antisemitism as such in favor of broader Nazi biological policies that included the mentally and physically handicapped as well as women. See esp. C. Koonz, "Eugenics, Gender, and Ethics in Nazi Germany: The Debate about Involuntary Sterilization, 1933–1936," and D. J. K. Peukert, "The Genesis of the 'Final Solution' from the Spirit of Science," both in Childers, *Reevaluating*, pp. 66–85, 234–52. See also G. Bock, "Racism and Sexism in Nazi Germany: Motherhood, Compulsory Sterilization, and the State," in R. Bridenthal et al. (eds.), *When Biology Became Destiny: Women in Weimar and Nazi Germany* (New York, 1984), pp. 271–96; idem., *Zwangssterilisation im Nationalsozialismus* (Opladen, 1986); C. Koonz, *Mothers in the Fatherland: Women, the Family, and Nazi Politics* (New York, 1986).

57. D. J. K. Peukert, "Alltag und Barbarei. Zur Normalität des Dritten Reiches," in Diner, *Ist der Nationalsozialismus Geschichte?*, pp. 51–61, is critical of *Alltagsgeschichte*. Some historians have, of course, made excellent use of this approach. See, e.g., I. Kershaw, *Popular Opinion and Political Dissent in the Third Reich* (Oxford, 1983); idem, *The "Hitler Myth": Image and Reality in the Third Reich* (Oxford, 1987). For an interesting collection, see K. Bergmann and R. Schörken (eds.), *Geschichte im Alltag—Alltag in der Geschichte* (Düsseldorf, 1982).

58. We have now become used to thinking of "Auschwitz" as an inhuman death machine where there was no room for individual brutality, and of the camps as being relatively insulated from their environment. For a recent excellent study that corrects both these misconceptions, see G. J. Horwitz, *In the Shadow of Death: Living Outside the Gates of Mauthausen* (New York, 1990). On the psychology of those involved in genocide, see also the penetrating study by R. Hilberg, *Perpetrators Victims Bystanders: The Jewish Catastrophe 1933–1945* (New York, 1992). On the indifference of Allied governments to reports on genocide and/or their refusal to believe the veracity of such news, see, e.g., M. Gilbert, *Auschwitz and the Allies* (New York, 1981); B. Wasserstein, *Britain and the Jews of Europe, 1939–1945*, 2d ed. (Oxford, 1988); W. Laqueur, *The Terrible Secret: Suppression of the Truth about Hitler's "Final Solution"*, 3d ed. (Harmondsworth, 1982); W. Laqueur and R. Breitman, *Breaking the Silence* (New York, 1986). See also the disturbing account of Polish wartime policies in D. Engel, *In the Shadow of Auschwitz: The Polish Government-in-Exile and the Jews, 1939–1942* (Chapel Hill, N.C., 1987); and idem., *Facing a Holocaust: The Polish Government-in-Exile and the Jews, 1943–1945* (Chapel Hill, N.C., 1993).

59. Here I tend to agree with Detlev Peukert's arguments in his *Weimar Republic* and *The Genesis of the "Final Solution."* It is quite true, however, that Peukert's heavy emphasis on the "biological politics" of Nazism is open to criticism on two counts: first, it underplays the role of antisemitism and specifically of anti-Jewish policies in the Third Reich; and, second, it generalizes "biological politics" to include much of the West, and thereby minimizes Germany's centrality in the development and implementation of this concept. Peukert's studies also undermine Marxist class analysis and considerations of economic factors in evaluating fascism, and generally imply a complete abandonment of the fascist paradigm. This in turn would make Nazi Germany unique as regards other fascist (or "totalitarian") regimes, on the one hand, and contextualize it as part and parcel of the Western modernist project in general, on the other. Hence this analysis may turn into an apologetic blurring of boundaries and categories. See esp. C. S. Maier, "Foreword," and T. Mason, "Appendix: Whatever Happened to 'Fascism'?," both in Childers, *Reevaluating*, pp. xi–xvi and 253–62, respectively. While I hold that the Holocaust as a specific historical event could not have occurred without the precedent of industrial killing in the Great War and the context of modern Western civilization, I would also insist that it was closely related to specific circumstances in Germany. Hence understanding the context should in no way minimize the specificity of the circumstances.

60. On this process see *supra*, Chapters 1 and 2.

61. See esp. Kater, *Doctors*; Proctor, *Racial Hygiene*; Lifton, *Nazi Doctors*; B. Müller-Hill, *Murderous Science: Elimination by Scientific Selection of Jews, Gypsies and Others, Germany 1933–1945* (Oxford, 1988); idem., "The Idea of the Final Solution and the Role of the Experts," in *The Final Solution: Origins and Implementation*, ed. D. Cesarani (London, 1994), pp. 62–70; P. Weindling, *Health, Race and German Politics between National Unification and Nazism 1870–1945* (Cambridge, 1989); idem., "The Survival of Eugenics in 20th-Century Germany," *AJHG* 52 (1993): 643–49;

H. Friedlander, "Euthanasia and the Final Solution," in Cesarani, *Final Solution*, pp. 51–61; M. Biagioli, "Science, Modernity, and the 'Final Solution'," in Friedlander, *Probing the Limits*, pp. 185–205; E. Klee, *"Euthanasie" im NS Staat. Die "Vernichtung lebensunwerten Lebens"* (Frankfurt/M., 1983); idem, *Dokumente zur "Euthanasie"* (Frankfurt/M., 1985); idem, *Was sie taten—was sie wurden. Ärtze, Juristen und andere Beteiligte am Kranken- oder Judenmord* (Frankfurt/M., 1986). See also G. Cocks, *Psychotherapy in the Third Reich: The Göring Institute* (New York, 1985); idem., "Partners and Pariahs: Jews and Medicine in Modern German Society," *LBIY* 36 (1991): 191–205; M. Burleigh and W. Wippermann, *The Racial State: Germany 1933–1945* (Cambridge, 1991). On the physics community, which might have provided Hitler with the ultimate weapon to "purge" humanity, see M. Walker, *German National Socialism and the Quest for Nuclear Power, 1939–1949* (Cambridge, 1989); and J. Bernstein, "The Farm Hall Transcripts: The German Scientists and the Bomb," *NYR* (August 13, 1992): 47–53.

62. See I. Müller, *Hitler's Justice: The Courts of the Third Reich* (Cambridge: Mass., 1991 [1987]). See also J. Bendersky, *Carl Schmitt: Theorist for the Reich* (Princeton, 1983); D. Diner, "Rassistisches Völkerrecht: Elemente einer nationalsozialistischen Weltordnung," *VfZ* 1 (1989): 23–56. On the legalization of military crimes, see M. Messerschmidt and F. Wüllner, *Die Wehrmachtjustiz im Dienste des Nationalsozialismus*, (Baden-Baden, 1987); and M. Messerschmidt, "German Military Law in the Second World War," in *The German Military in the Age of Total War*, ed. W. Deist (Leamington Spa, 1985), pp. 323–35. Of interest here is also J. Tent, *Mission on the Rhine: Reeducation and Denazification in American-Occupied Germany* (Chicago, 1982).

Chapter 4

1. H.-U. Rudel, *Stuka Pilot*, 2d ed. (Maidstone, 1973 [1952]), p. 189. This is a revised version of an article by the same name originally published in *TAJ* 16 (1987): 325–45. I wish to thank the editors of this publication for allowing me to reprint it here.

2. H. Arendt, "Arbeit macht frei oder wie Deutschland vergass und genas," in *FR* (16 August 1986); English original was published as "The Aftermath of Nazi Rule," *Commentary* 10 (October 1950).

3. Meinecke, *German Catastrophe*.

4. Arendt, *Arbeit*.

5. Nolte, *Historical Legend*; originally published as "Between Myth and Revisionism? The Third Reich in the Perspective of the 1980s," in *Aspects of the Third Reich*, ed. W. Koch (London, 1985). Nolte, *Past That Will Not Pass*; originally published as "Vergangenheit, die nicht vergehen will," *FAZ* (6 June 1986). E. Nolte, "Standing Things on Their Heads: Against Negative Nationalism in Interpreting History," in *Forever in the Shadow*, pp. 149–54; originally published as "Die Sache auf den Kopf gestellt," *Die Zeit* (31 October 1986).

6. The main contributions to the debate are now all to be found in *Forever in the Shadow*, and the German originals in *"Historikerstreit."* See esp. the articles by M. Stürmer, J. Habermas, K. Hildebrand, J. Fest, E. Jäckel, J. Kocka, H. Schulze, H. Mommsen, and M. Broszat.

7. Hillgruber, *Zweierlei Untergang*.

8. Apart from the articles noted above, see also S. Friedlander, "The New German Nationalism: The Debate Intensifies," *Ha'aretz* (3 October 1986 [Hebrew]); idem.,

"A Conflict of Memories? The New German Debates about the 'Final Solution'," in Friedlander, *Memory*, pp. 22–41; and idem., *Reflections*. See also W. Schütte, "Einspruch im Namen der Opfer," *FR* (10 November 1986); Leserbriefe, "Herrgott, welch ein Wahnsinn," *Die Zeit* (28 November 1986); W. Malanowski, "Vergangenheit, die nicht vergehen will," *Der Spiegel* 36 (1986).

9. Nolte writes: "Did the National Socialists or Hitler perhaps commit an 'Asiatic' deed merely because they and their ilk considered themselves to be potential victims of an 'Asiatic' deed? Was the Gulag Archipelago not primary to Auschwitz? Was the Bolshevik murder of an entire class not the logical and factual prius of the 'racial murder' of National Socialism? Cannot Hitler's most secret deeds be explained by the fact that he had *not* forgotten the rat cage? Did Auschwitz in its root causes not originate in a past that would not pass?" Nolte, *Past That Will Not Pass*, p. 22. Nolte's "rat cage" reference makes the following (rather unlikely) analogy: "In George Orwell's *1984* there is a description of how the hero, Winston Smith . . . is finally forced by Big Brother's secret police to deny his fiancée and thus to renounce his humanity. They place a cage containing a half-starved rat in front of his head. The interrogator threatens to open the door, and at that point Winston Smith collapses. Orwell did not invent the story. It can be found in numerous places in anti-Bolshevist literature about the Russian Civil War. . . . It is usually attributed to the 'Chinese Cheka'." Ibid., p. 21. Nolte also insists that "It is a notable shortcoming that the literature about National Socialism does not know or does not want to admit to what degree all the deeds—with the sole exception of the technical process of gassing—that the National Socialists later committed had already been described in the voluminous literature of the 1920s." Ibid., pp. 21–22. And in another article: "Auschwitz is not primarily the result of traditional anti-Semitism and was not just one more case of 'genocide.' It was the fear-borne reaction to the acts of annihilation that took place during the Russian Revolution. . . . [T]he so-called annihilation of the Jews by the Third Reich was a reaction or a distorted copy and not a first act or an original." Nolte, *Historical Legend*, pp. 13–14. Here he also argues that "it is hard to deny that Hitler had good reason to be convinced of his enemies' will to annihilate" and as evidence cites "Chaim Weizmann's statement in the first days of September 1939, that in this war the Jews of the world would fight on England's side," which to his mind "could lay a foundation for the thesis that Hitler would have been justified in treating German Jews as prisoners of war." Ibid., p. 8. Hillgruber's arguments will be documented throughout the second part of this chapter.

10. Hillgruber, *Zweierlei Untergang*, p. 65.

11. Ibid., p. 21.

12. Ibid., pp. 24–25.

13. See, e.g., H. Krausnick and H.-H. Wilhelm, *Die Truppe des Weltanschauungskrieges: Die Einsatzgruppen der Sicherheitspolizei und des SD, 1938–1942* (Stuttgart, 1981); C. Streit, *Keine Kameraden: Die Wehrmacht und die sowjetischen Kriegsgefangenen, 1941–1945*, 2d ed. (Bonn, 1991 [1978]); O. Bartov, *Hitler's Army: Soldiers, Nazis, and War in the Third Reich* (New York, 1991).

14. O. Bartov, *The Eastern Front 1941–45: German Troops and the Barbarisation of Warfare* (London, 1985), pp. 106–41. See also the recent article, H. Heer, "Killing Fields: Die Wehrmacht und der Holocaust," *Mittelweg 36* 3 (June/July 1994): 7–40, employing newly discovered documents in the former Soviet Union.

15. Hillgruber, *Zweierlei Untergang*, pp. 34–35.

16. Ibid., p. 36. Some Nazi party officials are also said by Hillgruber to have conducted themselves heroically, while others failed miserably in their task (to save Hitler's regime), and are consequently condemned by the author. Ibid., p. 37.

17. Ibid., pp. 34–35.

18. Translated as *The Ogre*. The French title refers of course to Goethe's poem "The Erl-King."

19. Hillgruber, *Zweierlei Untergang*, p. 38.

20. Ibid., p. 39.

21. Ibid., p. 44.

22. Ibid., p. 45.

23. Ibid., pp. 46–47. On this issue, see esp. Müller, *The Army*.

24. Ibid., p. 47. On the character of "anti-partisan" operations, see, e.g., Bartov, *Eastern Front*, pp. 119–29. On Bach-Zelewski, see also M. Cooper, *The Phantom War* (London, 1979).

25. Hillgruber, *Zweierlei Untergang*, p. 47.

26. Ibid., pp. 73–74. Thus, according to the author, there were actually two "tragedies": the loss of the Eastern Provinces as a specific German tragedy; and the loss of a "German center" as a European tragedy.

27. Ibid., p. 52.

28. Ibid., p. 53.

29. Ibid., p. 61.

30. Ibid., p. 53.

31. Ibid., p. 62.

32. Ibid., p. 64.

33. Ibid.

34. Ibid., p. 65.

35. Ibid., p. 67.

36. Ibid., pp. 67–68.

37. Ibid., p. 72.

38. Ibid., p. 73.

39. Ibid., p. 74.

40. See, e.g., Bartov, *Eastern Front*, pp. 1–3, and notes 1–3.

41. On anthropologists and philosophers debating this problem, see, e.g., R. Needham, *Belief, Language and Experience* (Oxford, 1972); more specifically, see Bartov, *Eastern Front*, pp. 100–105.

42. Ibid., pp. 36–37. More recently and in greater detail, see Bartov, *Hitler's Army*, pp. 29–58. For the opposing view, see E. A. Shils and M. Janowitz, "Cohesion and Disintegration in the Wehrmacht in World War II," *POQ* 12 (1948): 280–315; M. van Crefeld, *Fighting Power* (Westport: Conn., 1982), pp. 83–87, 163–66.

43. Bartov, *Eastern Front*, pp. 12–21; idem., *Hitler's Army*, pp. 29–58; idem., "Indoctrination and Motivation in the Wehrmacht: The Importance of the Unquantifiable," *JSS* 9 (1986): 16–34.

44. See esp. Messerschmidt, *Die Wehrmacht*; V. R. Berghahn, "NSDAP und 'geistige Führung' der Wehrmacht, 1939–1945," *VfZ* 17 (1969): 17–71; Bartov, *Eastern Front*, pp. 68–105.

45. Berghahn, *Geistige Führung*, pp. 92–99; Bartov, *Eastern Front*, pp. 81–92.

46. See, e.g., M. I. Gurfein and M. Janowitz, "Trends in Wehrmacht Morale," in *Propaganda in War and Crisis*, ed. D. Lerner (New York, 1951), pp. 200–208. See also H. R. Trevor-Roper (ed.), *The Goebbels Diaries*, 2d ed. (London, 1979), pp. 95, 113. Goebbels wrote on March 10, 1945: "All [German] POWs . . . have an almost mystical faith in Hitler. This is the reason why we are still standing on our feet and fighting." Two days later he added: "German troops are showing an unbroken fighting spirit. . . . Hitler represents to them a sort of national myth. . . ." More recently, see Bartov, *Hitler's Army*, pp. 106–78, for indications of the extent to which the troops'

perception of reality was molded by indoctrination. For at least a partial critique of this interpretation, see T. Schulte, *The German Army and Nazi Policies in Occupied Russia* (Oxford, 1989), esp. pp. 1–27.

47. Hillgruber, *Zweierlei Untergang*, p. 65.

48. Ibid., p. 18.

49. Ibid., p. 65. On the obsession with red floods already evident in the memoirs of *Freikorps* members from the 1920s, see Theweleit, *Männerphantasien*, 1: 235–54.

50. Hillgruber, *Zweierlei Untergang*, p. 21.

51. Ibid., p. 25.

52. Ibid., p. 34.

53. Ibid., p. 35.

54. Ibid., p. 38.

55. Ibid., p. 65.

56. Bartov, *Eastern Front*, pp. 68–76.

57. BA-MA, RH27–18/4, 21.6.41.

58. Cited in Streit, *Keine Kameraden*, p. 115.

59. BA-MA, RH26–12/262, 28.12.41.

60. "Mitteilungen für die Truppe, Nr. 116," cited in Messerschmidt, *Die Wehrmacht*, pp. 326–27.

61. See mainly Streit, *Keine Kameraden*; Krausnick, *Die Truppe*; Bartov, *Eastern Front*, pp. 106–41.

62. Hillgruber, *Zweierlei Untergang*, p. 21.

63. See Theweleit, *Männerphantasien*.

64. BA-MA, RH27-18/177, 17.11.41.

65. BA-MA, RH27-18/164, 30.4.43.

66. Rudel, *Stuka Pilot*, comment by D. Brader in the foreword.

67. Ibid., p. 189.

68. H. Guderian, *Panzer Leader*, 3d ed. (London, 1977), p. 461.

69. Ibid., p. 440.

70. *Der Zusammenbruch im Osten 1944/45 als Problem der deutschen Nationalgeschichte und der europäischen Geschichte; Der geschichtliche Ort der Judenvernichtung.*

71. Hillgruber, *Zweierlei Untergang*, pp. 95–96.

72. Ibid., p. 20.

73. Broszat, *Plea*, p. 78. Original German published as "Plädoyer für eine Historisierung des Nationalsozialismus," *Merkur* 435 (1985): 373–85; citation, p. 375. Reproduced in H. Graml and K.-D. Henke (eds.), *Nach Hitler. Der schwierige Umgang mit unserer Geschichte: Beiträge von Martin Broszat* (Munich, 1986), pp. 159–73.

74. Broszat, *Plea*, p. 86; German original, p. 384.

75. Nolte, *Past That Will Not Pass*, p. 21, writes: "When Hitler received news of the capitulation of the 6th Army in Stalingrad in February 1, 1943, he predicted in his briefing that several of the captured officers would become involved in Soviet propaganda: 'You have to imagine, he (an officer like this) comes to Moscow, and imagine the "rat cage." He'd sign anything. He will make confessions, proclamations.'"

76. This was written, of course, before the reunification of Germany. Whatever we have since found out about the GDR, its economy, the role of the *Stasi* in public and private life, the corruption of the regime, and so forth, does not change the fact that life under the former communist system was not comparable to Auschwitz, or Dachau, not even the Warsaw Ghetto. Indeed, recently we have been hearing some nostalgic voices longing for the job security, day-care centers, health service, and relative absence of crime that at least in the memories of disgruntled "easterners" had

characterized the GDR. I doubt if any Russian could be found who misses the Nazi occupation, or a Jew who misses the camaraderie of the "concentrationary universe." In any case, the fact remains that had Stalin acted as Hitler had wished to, the FRG would have had nothing to reunite with but a pile of corpses.

Chapter 5

1. W. Shakespeare, *Macbeth*, rev. ed. (Harmondsworth, 1986), p. 105 (V, v). This chapter is a much revised version of a review article by the same name published in *JMH* 67/1 (1995): 55–82. ©1995 by The University of Chicago. All rights reserved. I wish to thank the editors of this journal for allowing me to reprint it here.

2. The books discussed in this chapter are: Browning, *Path to Genocide*; Engel, *Facing a Holocaust*; Finkielkraut, *Remembering in Vain*; Horwitz, *Shadow of Death*; Hilberg, *Perpetrators Victims Bystanders*; Langer, *Holocaust Testimonies*; Vidal-Naquet, *Assassins of Memory*.

3. I am reminded here of the old woman in Émil Ajar's novel *The Life Before Us* (Garden City: N.Y., 1978), who, whenever she was overwhelmed by depression, would take a yellowing photograph of Hitler from under her mattress, look at it, sigh, and say "Well, at least that's over."

4. Some other recent books that attempt to come to grips with these questions are Friedlander, *Probing*; Baldwin, *Reworking*; Diner, *Nationalsozialismus* and *Zivilisationsbruch*.

5. These schools were originally characterized as such in Mason, *Intention and Explanation*.

6. Typical of this approach is Dawidowicz, *War Against the Jews*. See also Fleming, *Hitler*; and K. Hildebrand, *The Third Reich* (London, 1984), esp. pp. 70–72. Hitler's own *intentions* (as distinct from their documented expression) will probably remain a matter of historical and psychological speculation.

7. For good examples of this school see: Broszat, *Genesis*; Mommsen, *Realization*.

8. See, e.g., G. Aly and S. Heim, "Die Ökonomie der 'Endlösung': Menschenvernichtung und wirtschaftliche Neuordnung," *Beiträge zur Nationalsozialistischen Gesundheits- und Sozialpolitik*, vol. V, *Sozialpolitik und Judenvernichtung: Gibt es eine Ökonomie der Endlösung?* (Berlin, 1987), pp. 7–90; idem., "The Economics of the Final Solution: A Case Study from the General Government," *SWCA* 5 (1988): pp. 3–48; and idem., *Vordenker*.

9. See, e.g., Zitelmann, *Hitler*; Prinz and Zitelmann, *Nationalsozialismus*.

10. Herbert, *Labour and Extermination*.

11. Mayer, *Why Did the Heavens Not Darken?*

12. See *supra*, Chapter 3, note 61.

13. See, e.g., Müller, *Hitler's Justice*; H.-W. Schmuhl, *Rassenhygiene, National-sozialismus, Euthanasie. Von der Verhütung zur Vernichtung "lebensunwerten Lebens," 1890–1945* (Götingen, 1987); G. Aly, P. Chroust, C. Pross, *Cleansing the Fatherland: Nazi Medicine and Racial Hygiene* (Baltimore, 1994).

14. C. R. Browning, *Ordinary Men: Reserve Police Battalion 101 and the Final Solution in Poland* (New York, 1992).

15. Bartov, *Hitler's Army* and *Eastern Front*. It should be noted that many of Browning's policemen belonged to the same generation which furnished the so-called *Alte Kämpfer*, namely the original hard-core of the Nazi party in the 1920s, whose social origins, mentality and convictions have been studied in Abel, *Why Hitler Came into Power*, and Merkl, *Political Violence*.

16. The case of the French police under Vichy should suffice to illustrate this point. See, e.g., Marrus and Paxton, *Vichy France and the Jews*. The crucial text on the relationship between the modern state and genocide is Bauman, *Modernity*. One of my readers has noted that a similar criticism was made by T. Kohut in *Psychohistory Review* (1987) of Lifton's relative lack of interest in the social and cultural background of the Nazi doctors. For a pertinent and incisive critique of Lifton's "doubling effect," rejecting the concept of the perpetrator as a "divided self" in favor of the perpetrator's ability to divide *others* into moral categories and therefore treat them differently without any compunction, see Lang, *Act and Idea*, pp. 48–56. Some of the relevant psychological literature is cited therein, p. 52, n. 16.

17. David Engel, *In the Shadow*.

18. See Wistrich, *Antisemitism*, p. 161; Dawidowicz, *Holocaust and the Historians*, pp. 94–95.

19. P. Levi, *The Reawakening*, 2d ed. (New York, 1987 [1963]); idem., *The Drowned and the Saved* (New York, 1988), pp. 70–71. See also "Clara Greenbaum's Account of the Liberation of Bergen-Belsen," cited in J. Bridgman, *The End of the Holocaust: The Liberation of the Camps* (Portland, 1990), pp. 123–32, for a moving and acute description of an inmate's liberation; and see below discussion of Lawrence Langer's *Holocaust Testimonies*.

20. Lifton, *Nazi Doctors*.

21. See J. Steinberg, *All or Nothing: The Axis and the Holocaust 1941–43* (London, 1990). As is shown in Paul Levine's forthcoming Uppsala University Ph.D. dissertation, this tactic was employed successfully by Sweden's representatives in Budapest. See also his "Sweden's Reaction to the Holocaust in Hungary, March–July 1944," unpublished paper, 1994. I wish to thank Mr. Levine for sharing his work with me and suggesting the useful concept of "bureaucratic resistance." On the peculiarities of the German bureaucratic mentality, see Hilberg, *The Destruction of the European Jews*, 3: 993–1044; Browning, *Path to Genocide*, pp. 125–44.

22. See in this context *Kurt Waldheim's Hidden Past: An Interim Report to the President of the World Jewish Congress*, World Jewish Congress (June 2, 1986); *Pflichterfüllung: Ein Bericht über Kurt Waldheim*, ed. Gruppe "Neues Österreich" (Vienna, n.d.). It should be noted that the savage hunting down of the escaped inmates was related to the apparently widespread assumption that they "were hardened criminals. No one knew that they were soldiers," though the police at least seems to have known better. One official wrote after the war: "That it was a matter of criminals was not believed from the very beginning." In fact, it seems that all, or almost all 495 escapees (out of a total inmate population of 570, remnants of the original 4,700 Soviet officer sent to Mauthausen) were Soviet POWs, though there were some Polish, French, Belgian, and German inmates in the camp as well. Horwitz, *In the Shadow of Death*, p. 132 and note 34.

23. See Klee, *Was sie taten*.

24. See Müller, *Hitler's Justice*.

25. For documents and photographs, see the outstanding collection, E. Klee et al. (eds.), *"The Good Old Days": The Holocaust as Seen by Its Perpetrators and Bystanders* (New York, 1991).

26. See, e.g., Dawidowicz, *War Against the Jews*, esp. Part II; and Yahil, *The Holocaust*, esp. Chapters 13–14, 18–21.

27. On films about the Holocaust, see Avisar, *Screening the Holocaust*.

28. See, e.g., P. Vidal-Naquet, *Les Crimes de l'armée française* (Paris, 1977).

29. See Streit, *Keine Kameraden*; A. Streim, *Die Behandlung sowjetischer Kriegs-gefangener in "Fall Barbarossa"* (Heidelberg, 1981); Bartov, *Hitler's Army*.

30. This has been extensively discussed in Israeli legal, political, and historical literature. See, e.g., N. Safran, *Israel, the Embattled Ally*, 2d ed. (Cambridge: Mass., 1981), p. 329.

31. See M. Hastings, *Das Reich: Resistance and the March of the 2nd SS Panzer Division Through France, June 1944* (London, 1981). The trial was conducted by a French court, and German members of the SS received more severe sentences than French SS volunteers who had the same share in the massacre. On the Malmédy massacre of December 1944 by the Waffen-SS and the trial before a U.S. military court in mid 1946, see J. J. Weingartner, *Crossroads of Death: The Story of the Malmédy Massacre and Trial* (Berkeley, 1979); and on the massacre in Le Paradis in 1940 by men of the SS-*Totenkopf* Division, see C. W. Sydnor, Jr., *Soldiers of Destruction: The SS Death's Head Division, 1933–1945* (Princeton, 1977), pp. 106–107.

32. Cited in M. Zimmermann, "Memory of the War and the Holocaust in Germany—the Place of Israel," in Zimmermann, *'Normal' Relations*, p. 90 (in Hebrew), from H. Broder, *Deutschland Erwache* (Cologne, 1978), pp. 86–87. On Israeli-German relations, see also S. Shafir, *An Outstretched Hand: German Social Democrats, Jews, and Israel 1945–1967* (Tel Aviv, 1986 [Hebrew]); L. G. Feldman, *The Special Relationship Between West-Germany and Israel* (Boston, 1984); and M. Wolffsohn, *Deutsch-Israelische Beziehungen: Umfragen und Interpretationen 1952–1986* (Munich, 1986).

33. Citing the French translation of W. Stäglich, *Der Auschwitz-Mythos* (Tübingen, 1979).

34. Broszat, *Plea*. See also exchange between Broszat and Saul Friedlander in: Baldwin, *Reworking*, pp. 102–34.

35. Kershaw, *Nazi Dictatorship*, p. 80.

36. Mayer, *Memory and History*.

37. For a very different discussion of Faurisson, see J.-F. Lyotard, *The Differend: Phrases in Dispute* (Minneapolis, 1988).

38. In this he is in complete agreement with Lawrence Langer, discussed below.

39. This point too is taken up by Langer.

40. Note the curious similarity between this argument and the remarks in Mayer, *Memory and History*.

41. Citing H. Arendt, *Men in Dark Times* (New York, 1968), p. 30.

42. Finkielkraut is referring here to the French translation of Thomas Mann's "In Defense of Wagner. A Letter on the German Culture That Produced Both Wagner and Hitler," *Common Sense* 9 (January 1940). Interestingly, Mann left Germany on February 11, 1933, a few days after Hitler was nominated chancellor, for a series of lectures on Richard Wagner in Amsterdam and Paris, not knowing that he would see Germany again only sixteen years later. Mann's article "Leiden und Grösse Richard Wagners," one of the pieces in his *Leiden und Grösse der Meister* (1935) was his last publication in Germany until after the war. It can now be read in Vol. 9 of Mann's *Gesammelte Werke* (Frankfurt, 1974). See also R. and C. Winston (eds.), *Letters of Thomas Mann, 1889–1955*, 2d ed. (Berkeley, 1990), pp. 165–66, 301; Taylor, *Literature*, pp. 338–39. Further on the view of German history as a folktale, see *infra*, Chapter 7.

43. Or God. The story of Job is so clearly reminiscent of the testimonies examined by Langer that one wonders why he does not mention it. Job too lost all his family, status, property, was indeed "dead," when God "returned" everything to him. Yet

it is not the same family, property, "life." He is condemned to two lives, just as so many of the survivors, on account of a heavenly act he must not try to understand; that is the condition of his "rehabilitation."

44. M. Blanchot, *The Writing of the Disaster* (Lincoln: N.E., 1986).

45. See Y. H. Yerushalmi, *Zakhor: Jewish History and Jewish Memory*, 2d ed. (New York, 1989).

46. Langer is making use here of Hayden White's essay "Narrativity in the Representation of Reality," in his *The Content of the Form: Narrative Discourse and Historical Representation*, 2d ed. (Baltimore, 1992).

47. Compare with Finkielkraut's notion, discussed above, of the inapplicability of the terms "resistance" and "collaboration" to the victims.

48. Levi, *The Drowned and the Saved*, p. 31.

49. Ibid., p. 36.

50. Ibid., p. 48.

51. Ibid., pp. 53–54.

52. Ibid., p. 69.

53. Ibid., pp. 70–71.

54. Ibid., pp. 82–84.

55. Ibid., p. 86.

56. Ibid., pp. 199–201.

Chapter 6

1. Dante Alighieri, *The Divine Comedy: Cantica I: Hell (L'Inferno)* (Harmondsworth, 1972 [1949]), pp. 235–37 (Canto xxvi). This chapter is a revised version of an article by the same name published in *H&M*, 5/1 (1993): 87–29; I would like to thank the editors of this journal and its publisher, Indiana University Press, for allowing me to reprint it here. For instructive comments on various earlier drafts thanks are due also to David Abraham, Guli Arad, Yehudit and Hanoch Bartov, James Buzard, Saul Friedlander, Paul Holdengräber, Peter Novick, Steve Pincus, Immanuel Sivan, Elona Zucker, and most especially Wai-yee Li.

2. See esp. Mayer, *Memory and History*; Maier, *A Surfeit of Memory?* See also L. Valensi, "Commentary on the Text of Arno Mayer," unpublished paper (1993); and the July 1993 issue of the journal *Esprit*, subtitled "Le poids de la mémoire: Comment transmettre le souvenir? Le pardon dans l'histoire."

3. For pertinent and insightful remarks on the problems and frustrations of teaching the most current and painful issues of the day to undergraduates, see L. Trilling, "On the Teaching of Modern Literature," in his *Beyond Culture: Essays on Literature and Learning*, 6th ed. (New York, 1965), pp. 3–30. More specifically on teaching the Holocaust, see M. R. Marrus, "'Good History' and Teaching the Holocaust," *Perspectives* 31/5 (1993): 1–12; A. S. Lindemann, "Anti-Semitism: A Case for Teaching about the manifestations of Prejudice," *Perspectives* 31/9 (1993): 15–20; J. Petropoulos, "Teaching the Holocaust in an Interdisciplinary Manner: Confronting the 'Holocaust as Hoax' Phenomenon," unpublished paper (1993). See also the March-April 1993 issue of *Esprit*, subtitled: "Métamorphoses du racisme et de l'antisémitisme: L'antisémitisme racial est-il appuru au XXe siècle? Comment peut-on être antiraciste?"

4. Good examples are the conference "The Origins of the 'Final Solution'," held at the Institute of Contemporary History and Wiener Library in London in January 1992, whose proceedings have now been published in Cesarani, *The Final Solution*; and the conference on "Nazism and the 'Final Solution': Probing the Limits of Repre-

sentation," held at the University of California, Los Angeles, in April 1990, whose papers were published in Friedlander, *Probing the Limits*.

5. J. Améry, *At the Mind's Limits: Contemplations by a Survivor on Auschwitz and its Realities*, 2d ed. (New York, 1986); P. Levi, *Survival in Auschwitz: The Nazi Assault on Humanity* (New York, 1959), and esp. his *The Drowned and the Saved*.

6. See, e.g., Friedlander, *Reflections of Nazism*. On Friedlander's sense of unease with recent modes of representation of and discourse on Nazism, see also his recent collection of articles, *Memory, History*, esp. Chapters 4, 6, and 7.

7. See, e.g., Mayer, *Memory and History*, and Maier, *A Surfeit of Memory?* But also, e.g., Primo Levi's comments throughout *The Drowned and the Saved* (1986); Martin Broszat's arguments in his *Plea*; Edgar Reitz's remarks in his *Liebe zum Kino: Utopien und Gedanken zum Autorenfilm, 1962–1983* (Cologne, 1984), p. 102, discussed also in E. L. Santner, "History Beyond the Pleasure Principle: Some Thoughts on the Representation of Trauma," in Friedlander, *Probing the Limits*, pp. 149–50, and in Kaes, *From Hitler to Heimat*, pp. 184–85; Jean Améry's comments in his 1977 preface to *At the Mind's Limits*; and Hannah Arendt's observations in her *Aftermath of Nazi Rule*. See further the arguments raised by Ernst Nolte, Andreas Hillgruber, and Michael Stürmer, in *Forever in the Shadow*. Yet Charles S. Maier, author of *The Unmasterable Past*, and Arno Mayer, author of *Why Did the Heavens Not Darken?* are both perfectly aware of what is at stake when discussing a memory which so many would like to see "go away." It is for this reason that I find their present positions somewhat bewildering. In this context, see also D. J. Goldhagen, "False Witness," *TNR* (April 17, 1989): 39–44.

8. Echoes of this view can be found, for instance, in Steiner, *Bluebeard's Castle*. See also G. Steiner, "The Long Life of Metaphor: An Approach to 'the Shoah'," *Encounter* 68/2 (1987): 55–61. On Jewish history as a tale of constant persecution and martyrdom, see, e.g., Almog, *Antisemitism*; and Ettinger, *Modern Anti-Semitism*; Wistrich, *Antisemitism*. The classic critique of this view is H. Arendt, *Totalitarianism*, part I: "Antisemitism." A literary rendering of it can be found, e.g., in A. Schwarz-Bart, *The Last of the Just*, 5th ed. (New York, 1969).

9. Kershaw, *Nazi Dictatorship*, p. 80, differentiates between the difficulties faced by Jewish historians due to the fact that some of them tend toward "'mystification' and religious-cultural eschatology," and the "perspective of non-Jewish historians," which he finds "inevitably different." More strongly worded are the comments by Martin Broszat, in his correspondence with Saul Friedlander, now in Baldwin, *Reworking*, pp. 102–34.

10. Apart from note 8 above, see also Yerushalmi, *Zakhor*.

11. The contradictions between the various types of criticism of the eschatological view derive from the greatly differing political/ideological camps to which the critics belong; American (and in some cases Israeli) liberals on the one hand, German conservatives or "national liberals" on the other; as well as some radical left-wing circles in Germany and self-proclaimed "postmodern" historians in America.

12. Apart from the Broszat/Friedlander exchange in Baldwin, *Reworking*, and other contributions to that volume, see also Diner, *Nationalsozialismus*.

13. The most obvious case is the disturbing similarity between Arno Mayer's argument in *Why Did the Heavens Not Darken?* and Ernst Nolte's assertions in his *Past That Will Not Pass* and *Historical Legend*. See also Mayer, *Memory and History*, Maier, *A Surfeit of Memory?* and the arguments raised by all revisionist historians of the *Historikerstreit*, such as Joachim Fest and Klaus Hildebrand, in *Forever in the Shadow*. Broszat, who attacked the revisionists in 1986, had actually supplied quite a few arguments for their arsenal in his *Plea*, originally published in 1985.

14. Primo Levi was probably the most acute and honest observer of this problem. See his comments in *The Drowned and the Saved*, pp. 34–35.

15. Arno Mayer and Saul Friedlander, Martin Broszat and Andreas Hillgruber, to name but a few, had all experienced Nazism in one way or another; some as refugees, others as soldiers. Friedlander's *When Memory Comes*, 2d ed. (New York, 1991), demonstrates the acuteness of memory and the impact it has had on one's life; so does Hillgruber's *Zweierlei Untergang*, though in a very different manner. On the latter, see *supra*, Chapter 4. The importance of personal memory for historians writing on periods they themselves had experienced is discussed in the Friedlander/Broszat correspondence in Baldwin, *Reworking*, pp. 123, 129.

16. Repression of the immediate past both in Germany and in Palestine (later Israel) can be documented from a wide array of sources. See, e.g., Engelmann, *Hitler's Germany*, pp. 331–32; and Arendt, *Aftermath of Nazi Rule*. For some elements of Israeli repression, see Sivan, *The 1948 Generation*, and his *To Remember Is to Forget*. On soldiers of the Jewish Brigade confronting Holocaust survivors in Europe, see the novel by Hanoch Bartov, *The Brigade* (New York, 1968), and on confronting them in Israel, his *Shesh Kenafayim le-Ehad* (Each Had Six Wings) (Merhavya, 1954). On the perpetual silence of survivors in Israel, especially vis-à-vis their children, see David Grossman, *See Under: Love* (New York, 1989). For a comprehensive study of the Israelis and the Holocaust, see Segev, *The Seventh Million*.

17. Even the students who participate in my course on the Holocaust, a far more motivated group than the average, mostly admit to knowing very little about the event. This is not to say that there are no groups and organizations in the United States obsessed with the memory of the Holocaust and devoted to its institutionalization. But from a national point of view they seem marginal and of little influence on public opinion, let alone knowledge. In this context, see now the provocative unpublished paper by Peter Novick, "Pseudo-Memory and Dubious 'Lessons': The Holocaust in American Culture," (1995).

18. Richard Evans wrote as early as 1989 that the *Historikerstreit* "has very little to offer anyone with a serious, scholarly interest in the German past. It brings no new facts to light; it embodies no new research; it makes no new contribution to historical understanding; it poses no new questions that might stimulate future work." *In Hitler's Shadow*, p. 118. Similar remarks can be found in the introduction to Childers/Caplan, *Reevaluating*.

19. For numerous citations from soldiers' letters and propaganda material, see Bartov, *Hitler's Army*, pp. 106–78. See also Kershaw, *The "Hitler Myth*," p. 209; Kaes, *From Hitler to Heimat*, pp. 3–35, on German cinema's confrontation with Nazism since 1945; and Friedlander, *Reflections of Nazism*. For interesting observations on the paths of German memory, see L. Niethammer, "'Normalisierung' im Westen. Erinnerungsspuren in die 50er Jahre," in Diner, *Nationalsozialismus*, pp. 153–84, and U. Herbert, "'Die guten und die schlechten Zeiten': Überlegungen zur diachronen Analyse lebensgeschichtlicher Interviews," in L. Niethammer (ed.), *"Die Jahre weiss man nicht, wo man die heute hinsetzen soll": Faschismus Erfahrungen im Ruhrgebiet* (Berlin, 1983), pp. 67–96.

20. Broszat, *Plea*.

21. On such arguments, see, e.g., Améry, *At the Mind's Limits*, Preface to the 1977 edition. Also see D. Diner, "Between Aporia and Apology: On the Limits of Historicizing National Socialism" and "Negative Symbiosis: Germans and Jews After Auschwitz"; A. S. Markovits, "Coping with the Past: The West German Labor Movement and the Left," all in Baldwin, *Reworking*, pp. 135–45, 251–61, 262–75, respec-

tively. K.-D. Bracher's classic *The German Dictatorship: The Origins, Structure, and Effects of National Socialism* (New York, 1970), was originally published in 1969, as was the German original of Broszat, *The Hitler State*; J. C. Fest, *The Face of the Third Reich*, 3d ed. (Harmondsworth, 1979), was originally published in 1963. The publication of A. Speer, *Inside The Third Reich*, 2d ed. (London, 1979) in Germany in 1969 and its widespread popularity, is a case in point, as is Fest's 1977 film *Hitler: Eine Karriere*. None of these works devoted much space to the genocide of the Jews. Conversely, the most important work at the time on the Holocaust was Hilberg's *The Destruction of the European Jews*, published originally in 1961, and one of the most popular was Dawidowicz's *The War Against the Jews*, published in 1975; both were written in the United States, as was G. Reitlinger, *The Final Solution*, rev. ed. (South Brunswick, 1968), originally published in 1953. The shock of German audiences at viewing the film *Holocaust* (1979) testifies to their ignorance. See Kaes, *From Hitler to Heimat*, p. 184. Generally, German scholars contributed a great deal to the historiography of the Third Reich, and initially not much to that of the Holocaust; when they did turn to it, they often treated the subject in a highly controversial manner and in declared opposition to allegedly traditional, non-German, frequently Jewish historians. See, e.g., Adam, *Judenpolitik*; Broszat, *Genesis*; Mommsen, *Realization*.

22. In his correspondence with Friedlander, Broszat writes about his generation (the so-called Hitler Youth generation) that they were "old enough to be affected emotionally and intellectually to a high degree by the suggestivity . . . which the Nazi regime was capable of." After the collapse, they realized that they "had been cheated out of important years of our youth." They were, he argues, "Affected, yet hardly burdened" by their experience. How little burdened they felt is reflected in his assertion in another letter, that the "German historian . . . qua scientist and scholar . . . cannot readily accept that Auschwitz also be made, after the fact, into the cardinal point, the hinge on which the entire factual complex of historical events of the Nazi period turns. He cannot simply accept without further ado . . . that Auschwitz even be made into the decisive measuring rod for the historical perception of this period." Baldwin, *Reworking*, pp. 123 and 116, respectively.

23. See T. Mason, "The Workers' Opposition in Nazi Germany," *HWJ* 11 (1981): 120–37; S. Salter, "Class Harmony or Class Conflict?" in *Government Party and People in Nazi Germany*, ed. J. Noakes (Exeter, 1980). See also my "The Missing Years: German Workers, German Soldiers," in *Nazism and German Society, 1933–1945*, ed. D. Crew (London, 1994).

24. The issue of conformity and collaboration it treated in detail in Kershaw, *Popular Opinion*. See also R. Gellately, *The Gestapo and German Society* (Oxford, 1990).

25. See D. J. K. Peukert, *Die Edelweisspiraten: Protestbewegungen jugendlicher Arbeiter im Dritten Reich: Eine Dokumentation* (Cologne, 1980), and *Inside Nazi Germany: Conformity, Opposition, and Racism in Everyday Life* (New Haven, 1987 [1982]), esp. Chapter 8.

26. See Nolan, *Historikerstreit and Social History*. See also Peukert, *Alltag und Barbarei*. On the writing of separate histories see Diner, *Aporia and Apology*.

27. Kaes, *From Heimat to Hitler*, pp. 163–92.

28. This is most strongly put by Broszat in the exchange with Friedlander, and now in Mayer, *Memory and History*, and more subtly also in Maier, *A Surfeit of Memory?*; and Kershaw, *Nazi Dictatorship*, esp. p. 80. See further in Dawidowicz, *Holocaust and the Historians*, esp. pp. 43–67; and Bauer, *Holocaust in Historical Perspective*, esp. pp. 30–49.

29. Aly/Heim, *Vordenker der Vernichtung*; and idem., "Deutsche Herrschaft 'im Osten': Bevölkerungspolitik und Völkermord," in *Erobern und Vernichten*, ed. P. Jahn and R. Rürup (Berlin, 1991), pp. 84–105; Zitelmann, *Hitler*; and Prinz/Zitelmann, *Nationalsozialismus*.

30. See mainly Dahrendorf, *Society and Democracy*; and Schoenbaum, *Hitler's Social Revolution*. Modernization is no longer viewed positively *as such* by the younger German generation; but as regards Nazism, it is represented as a non-ideological, progressive development.

31. See M. Broszat, K.-D. Henke and H. Woller, *Von Stalingrad zur Währungsreform. Zur Sozialgeschichte des Umbruchs in Deutschland* (Munich, 1988); Graml and Henke, *Nach Hitler*.

32. See Herbert, *Die guten und die schlechten Zeiten*; Niethammer, "*Normalisierung" im Westen*. For the "good years" from the point of view of women see A.-K. Einfeldt, "Auskommen—Durchkommen—Weiterkommen. Weibliche Arbeitserfahrungen in der Bergarbeiterkolonie," in Niethammer, *Die Jahre*, pp. 267–96; and J. Stephenson, "'Emancipation' and its Problems: War and Society in Württemberg 1939–45," *EHQ* 17 (1987): 345–65; idem, *The Nazi Organization of Women* (Totowa, 1981). See also T. Mason, "Women in Germany, 1925–40: Family, Welfare and Work," Parts 1–2, *HWJ* 1 (1976): 74–113 and 2 (1976): 5–32; Koonz, *Mothers in the Fatherland*; R. Bridenthal, A. Grossmann, and M. Kaplan (eds.), *When Biology Became Destiny: Women in Weimar and Nazi Germany* (New York, 1984), part 2.

33. See *supra*, Chapter 5, section I.

34. In this discussion the article by Pierre Nora is often invoked: "Between Memory and History: *Les Lieux de Mémoire*," *Representations* 26 (1989): 7–25. But Nora argues that traditional memory (as exemplified according to him by the Jews) has been destroyed by modernity, and that this explains the current preoccupation *both* with memory and with history, both in scholarship and in other intellectual and artistic representations. This is not something that can be stopped by scholarly argument; it is a reflection of a certain cultural phase of Western society. In this context, see also J. Le Goff, *Histoire et mémoire*, 2d ed. (Paris, 1988).

35. See, for instance, the novels by Grossman, *See Under: Love*, Dorit Peleg, *Unah* (Tel Aviv, 1988); Omer Bartov, *Petihat Tsir* (Border Patrol) (Tel Aviv, 1988). For the monolithic portrayal, see Mayer, *Memory and History*. For comments on and analysis of the Israeli literary corpus, see S. D. Ezrahi, "Revisioning the Past: The Changing Legacy of the Holocaust in Hebrew Literature," *Salmagundi* (Fall/Winter 1985/86), and *By Words Alone*; and Y. S. Feldman, "Whose Story Is It, Anyway? Ideology and Psychology in the Representation of the Shoah in Israeli Literature," in Friedlander, *Probing the Limits*, pp. 223–39. See also Sivan, *The 1948 Generation*, and citations therein. The debate in Israel in the 1960s had to do of course with the impact of the Eichmann trial, the first open confrontation of the Israeli public with the Holocaust. See Segev, *The Seventh Million*, pp. 323–66. See also, most recently, Hanoch Bartov, *I am not the Mythological Sabra* (Tel Aviv, 1995).

36. See, e.g., Yehoshua Sobol's play "Ghetto." Another instance of turning *antisemitism* on its head is the Israeli film *Avanti Popolo*, where an Egyptian prisoner of war, an actor in civilian life (who is in turned played by an actor speaking Palestinian rather than Egyptian Arabic), recites Shylock's speech to a group of jeering Israeli reservists. See also the film *Behind Bars*, in which Palestinian prisoners in a high-security jail are portrayed as ideologically committed and educated freedom fighters, while the Israeli inmates are criminals. Another example of the mythical Arab and the awakening awareness of Israeli corruption is David Grossman's novel *Chiyuch Hagdi* (The Smile of the

Lamb) (Tel Aviv, 1983). See in this context also E. Shprinzak, *Every Man Whatever Is Right In His Own Eyes: Illegalism In Israeli Society* (Tel Aviv, 1986 [Hebrew]).

37. Note the Diaspora museum in Tel-Aviv University (Beit Hatfutsot); the popularity of such authors as Shai Agnon and Beshevis Singer; the novels by Aharon Appelfeld; and works by younger writers trying to imagine a past they had never had (n. 35 above); the popularity of resurrected Yiddish songs, e.g., by the singer Hava Alberstein; recent re-issues and the enthusiastic reception of long-forgotten Jewish "Diaspora" literature, such as David Vogel's *Married Life* (London, 1988), originally published in Hebrew in 1929/30 as *Haye Nisuim*, reissued in Israel in 1986. There also seems to be a growing interest in studying the Yiddish language among Israeli students.

38. While in the past one spoke of an "Israeli culture" or folklore (much of which had been fabricated from foreign influences, such as the *Horrah* dance, which is a combination of Cossack and Beduin *Debka* dance), now the two major ethnic groups, the Ashkenazis and Sepharadis, each pull toward their respective cultures of origin, or at least the memory of what they had been decades ago, accompanied by the more common attraction to American popular culture. The growing popularity of Israeli renderings of Arabic music, on the one hand, and the influence of the new, massive Russian immigration, on the other, have further complicated the cultural scene.

39. As is the hero of Moshe Shamir's novel *Be-mo Yadav: Pirkei Elik* (With His Own Hands: Lessons of Elik) (Merhavya, 1951): "Elik was born from the sea." The handsome Sabra, often assuming a Siegfried-like look, is another of those ironies of national fate and literary imagination, whereby the ideal Israeli unburdened himself from the relics of the Diaspora, and yet used as his model the heroic Gentile (and former persecutor), combined with an idealized vision of Biblical figures.

40. The tendency to view the Diaspora with contempt has been replaced by a sense of curiosity, not least due to the fact that while the older generation had attempted to detach itself from its own (or its parents') European past, the younger generation have no direct knowledge of that past, and therefore derive it either from their own imagination or from tales by their grandparents. Thus the generational conflict between children and parents of the previous generation over the ties with the Diaspora has become a much more sentimental (or imaginary) discourse between grandchildren and grandparents, who often are similarly critical of the fabricated Israeli identity created by the middle generation, and express greater sympathy for the supposedly more "authentic" identity of the grandparents. There is here a strange resemblance with similar generational coalitions in Germany, where the grandchildren find it easier to sympathize with the grandparents (active in the Third Reich) than their parents, who had often rejected their own parents and all that they had stood for.

41. On Yom Hashoah Vehagvurah see, inter al., Young, *Texture of Memory*, pp. 263–81.

42. Porat, *The Blue and the Yellow Stars*; Segev, *The Seventh Million*; Shapira, *Land and Power*. One should follow the debates in the media around the publication of such studies, especially Segev's, to understand the immense interest and pain still aroused by this issue. See also Sivan, *The 1948 Generation*.

43. See, e.g., Yahil, *The Holocaust*, p. 379. For a recent investigation of Israeli icons of heroism, see Y. Zerubavel, *Recovered Roots: Collective Memory and the Making of Israeli National Tradition* (Chicago, 1995).

44. Here I refer especially to Yehoshua, *The Wall and the Mountain*, in which he compares the Wailing Wall and Mount Herzl, i.e. the wall of Jewish memory and faith as opposed to the mountain devoted to commemorating Israel's fallen soldiers and named after the visionary of Zionism. The author expresses his preference for the

Mountain as embodying both nationalism and statehood and physical resistance to the enemy and rejects the Wall, which symbolizes for him blind belief in God and the helplessness of non-fighting Diaspora Jews. See my review of his book, "The Banality of Normality," and his reply, "In Favor of Answers," both in *Iton 77* 113 (1989): 6–10 (Hebrew).

45. Schleunes, *The Twisted Road*, pp. 192–213, which analyzes the *Haavara* agreement that created the financial incentives for the transfer of some 45,000 German Jews to Palestine by November 1938. The impact of Austrian antisemitism on Theodor Herzl has now been thoroughly documented in J. Kornberg, *Theodor Herzl: From Assimilation to Zionism* (Bloomington, 1993).

46. See note 44, above. Another version of the new Israeli identity was popularized especially in the 1950s by the so called Canaanites (*Kna'anim*), whose ideal combined the (imaginary) noble Arab warrior with the (mythical) Biblical Hebraic hero, postulating thereby total rejection of the intervening two thousand years of Jewish existence in the Diaspora; this in turn had roots in the earlier, pre-state *Hashomer* movement, whose members tried to adopt the perceived warlike virtues of the Beduin (they encountered in Palestine) and the Cossacks (they had left behind in Russia).

47. In this context see also the interesting discussion of the Warsaw memorial in J. E. Young, "Biography of a Memorial Icon: Nathan Rapoport's Warsaw Ghetto Monument," *Representations* 26 (1989): 69–106.

48. Further on memory, myth, and commemoration in Israel, see Sivan, *The 1948 Generation*; also see G. Shaked, *No Other Place: On Literature and Society* (Tel Aviv, 1988 [Hebrew]), a critique of an Israeli literary output that is far less certain about the absence of alternatives. And, most recently, Nurith Gertz, *Captive of a Dream: National Myths In Israeli Culture* (Tel Aviv, 1995 [Hebrew]).

49. This opinion was recently expressed in Maier, *A Surfeit of Memory?* But it is a rather common one.

50. Levi writes in *The Drowned and the Saved* that his book "sets itself a more ambitious goal, to try to answer the most urgent question, the question which torments all those who happen to read our accounts: How much of the concentration camp is dead and will not return . . . ?" (pp. 20–21). In speaking of feelings of guilt and shame, and of the suicides among survivors, he also notes that "there is another, vaster shame, the shame of the world," both as regards the Nazi period and other, more recent slaughters, such as in Cambodia. Significantly, but as we now know following the massacres in Bosnia (and even more recently in Chechniya), erroneously, he believes that mass slaughter is unlikely in the Western world because "the Lagers of World War II are still part of the memory of many, on both the popular and governmental levels, and a sort of immunization defense is at work which amply coincides with the shame of which I have spoken" (pp. 85–87). For Levi's criticism of representations of the Holocaust, see his remarks on Liliana Cavani's "Beautiful and false film," referring to her 1974 *The Night Porter* (p. 48). Améry writes in his 1977 preface to *At the Mind's Limits* that the preceding thirteen years "were not good years. One need only follow the reports from Amnesty International to see that in horror this period matches the worst epochs of a history that is as real as it is inimical to reason. Sometimes it seems as though Hitler has gained a posthumous triumph" (p. xvii). On Celan's unease with the public status achieved by his poem *Todesfuge* in Germany, his despair in the face of accusations by Germans that his poetic rendering of the Holocaust was too elegant and took too much pleasure in art, and his inability to express and communicate the horror, perceived by him as a reflection of the world he no longer could share, see J. Felstiner, "Translating Paul Celan's 'Todesfuge': Rhythm and Repetition as Metaphor," and S. D. Ezrahi, "'The

Grave in the Air': Unbound Metaphors in Post-Holocaust Poetry," both in Friedlander, *Probing the Limits*, pp. 240–58, and 259–76 respectively.

51. This of course makes one think of the presumed innocence of the bystanders in the Holocaust, who could also be described as participants, once removed, since passively observing atrocities amounts to complicity. The element of curiosity involved in such passive watching, reflected in much of the documentation of the period, also ties in with our current curiosity in watching either staged horrors or horrific documentaries. See Klee, *"The Good Old Days"*; and interviews made by Claude Lanzmann in "Shoah" with Polish peasants living near death camps. See also his book, *Shoah: An Oral History of the Holocaust* (New York, 1985), pp. 24–40.

52. Levi rejects "the term *incommunicability*, so fashionable in the 1970s, first of all because it is a linguistic horror," and finds it "frivolous and irritating," an expression of "mental laziness." He argues that "silence, the absence of signals, is itself a signal, but an ambiguous one, and ambiguity generates anxiety and suspicion." *The Drowned and the Saved*, pp. 88–89.

53. Levi writes: "The worst survived, that is, the fittest; the best all died." Moreover, he stresses: "we, the survivors, are not the true witnesses. . . . We survivors are not only an exiguous but also an anomalous minority: we are those who by their prevarications or abilities or good luck did not touch bottom. Those who did so, those who saw the gorgon, have not returned to tell about it, or have returned mute, but they are the 'Muslims,' the submerged, the complete witnesses, the ones whose deposition would have a general significance." *The Drowned and the Saved*, pp. 83–84. See also *supra*, Chapter 5, section IV.

54. Levi quotes Cavani as expressing her belief "that in every environment, in every relationship, there is a victim-executioner dynamism more or less clearly expressed and generally lived on an unconscious level." He replies: "I do not know, and it does not much interest me to know, whether in my depths there lurks a murderer, but I do know that I was a guiltless victim and I was not a murderer. I know that murderers existed, not only in Germany, and still exist, retired or on active duty, and that to confuse them with their victims is a moral disease or an aesthetic affectation or a sinister sign of complicity; above all, it is precious service rendered (intentionally or not) to the negators of truth." *The Drowned and the Saved*, pp. 48–49.

55. It is interesting to compare, for instance, Bernardo Bertolucci's *The Conformist* (1970) and István Szabó's *Mephisto* (1981). Whereas the first film creates sympathy with the wretched victim of fascism (who is nevertheless a collaborator and an accomplice to a murder), the second distances itself from the protagonist to a point of creating disgust in the viewer. Moreover, Bertolucci recreates scenes of such aesthetic beauty that even the most horrible events, such as the murder in the forest, retain a dreamlike quality in our memory and do not cause anger or revulsion.

56. See Reitz, *Liebe zum Kino*.

57. In Harriet Eder's and Thomas Kufus' 1990 film *Mein Krieg*, for example, we are shown privately filmed scenes from the war with a running commentary by those who had filmed them made to the filmmakers forty or fifty years after the event. See my review in the *AHR* 97/4 (1992): 1155–57.

58. This relates to the revisionist arguments in France that I will refer to in the next section.

59. The constant theme, for instance, in R. Kraemer, *A Girl Whose Name I Fail to Recall: Notes of a Young Girl During the Holocaust* (Tel Aviv, 1992 [Hebrew]). In this context, see also the extraordinary account by H. M. Kovály, *Under a Cruel Star: A Life in Prague, 1941–1968*, 2d ed. (New York, 1989).

60. American undergraduate students participating in my course on the Holocaust tend to find that Levi's *Survival in Auschwitz* gives them "a feel" for what Auschwitz was like, but distinguish between his account and scholarly texts, which they find more objective, and hence more reliable, even if slightly "boring" or "dry." On the American predilection for objectivity in history, see P. Novik, *That Noble Dream: The "Objectivity Question" and the American Historical Profession*, 2d ed. (New York, 1989).

61. One of the two survivors of Chelmno, returning to the site forty years later, says in Lanzmann's film Shoah: "It is hard to recognize, but it was here. . . . Yes, this is the place. . . . No one can describe it. . . . And no one can understand it. Even I, here, now . . . I can't believe I am here. No, I just can't believe it." Cited in Friedlander's Introduction to *Probing the Limits*, p. 17. See also B. Lang, "The Representation of Limits," in ibid., pp. 300–317.

62. Broszat, "Plea."

63. See Felstiner, *Translating Paul Celan*, and Ezrahi, *The Grave in the Air*.

64. This is discussed in Felstiner and Ezrahi, ibid.

65. Cited in J.-F. Lyotard, *The Differend: Phrases in Dispute* (Minneapolis, 1988), p. 3.

66. Ibid., pp. 3–4.

67. Cited in Friedlander, introduction to *Probing the Limits*, p. 8.

68. See *supra*, Chapter 5, for a discussion of this book.

69. Cited in Levi, *The Drowned and the Saved*, pp. 11–12.

70. C. Ginzburg, "Just One Witness," in Friedlander, *Probing the Limits*, pp. 82–96.

71. H. White, "Historical Emplotment and the Problem of Truth," ibid., p. 37. See Martin Jay's regret at White's retreat from his more radical relativist position, which he characterizes as "a failure of nerve," in Jay, "Of Plots, Witnesses, and Judgements," ibid., p. 98.

72. White, *The Content of the Form*, p. 76.

73. White writes that "Hillgruber's suggestion for emplotting the story of the defense of the eastern front did not violate any of the conventions governing the writing of professionally respectable narrative history. He simply suggested narrowing the focus to a particular domain of the historical continuum, casting the agents and agencies occupying that scene as characters in a dramatic conflict, and emplotting this drama in terms of the familiar conventions of the genre of tragedy." *Historical Emplotment*, p. 42. That is, this is *also* possible, though we may not *like* it. There is nothing wrong in this emplotment *per se*. One can emplot the Wehrmacht troops as heroes or as villains, and there is no obvious reason to accept one and object to the other. For a discussion of Hillgruber's book, see *supra*, Chapter 4.

74. White obviously does not accept the "traditional historical discourse" for which "there is presumed to be a crucial difference between an 'interpretation' of 'the facts' and a 'story' told about them," nor does he see the need for such "notions of a 'real' (as against 'imaginary') story and a 'true' (as against a 'false') story." Ibid., p. 39. Hence, presumably, truth and falsehood are relative: what was true for Höss, commandant of Auschwitz, namely, that the Jews were *Untermenschen*, was not true for Primo Levi. Depending on the circumstances, both could have been right or wrong, and we, as historians, cannot be judges of such moral positions because we too will emplot them according to our own biases. For Nazi emplotment, see M. Broszat (ed.), *Kommandant in Auschwitz: Autobiographische Aufzeichnungen des Rudolf Höss*, 10th ed. (Munich, 1985), by which time the book had sold more than 100,000 copies.

75. White claims that some plot types—e.g., pastoral or comic—are inadmissible. But of course his theory does not provide for criteria of inadmissibility. It seems to me that the "middle voice" he recommends has intrinsic elements of paradox, ambiguity, and irony. But with a kind of sleight of hand he attributes the "middle voice" to Levi, thus linking such elements to a self-critical, reflective moral seriousness. In this sense he wants to retain a margin of uncertainty, but subsumes it as an integral component of self-questioning and self-examination. Put simply, he wants to have it both ways: he tries to remain relativist while claiming moral high ground. It should be added that Nazism has probably been emplotted in all conceivable ways. One especially controversial representation was provided in Hans Jürgen Syberberg's seven-hour film *Hitler, a Film from Germany* (1977). See also G. Steiner, *The Portage to San Cristòbal of A. H.* (London, 1981).

76. See discussion of this in P. Haidu, "The Dialectics of Unspeakability: Language, Silence, and the Narratives of Desubjectification," in Friedlander, *Probing the Limits*, pp. 285–86.

77. White and Jay set up a bogey enemy in the form of the naive realism, positivism, and claim for absolute objectivity of the historian, when in fact any historian knows that his or her craft is only the art of the possible. On this, see the brilliant essay by Marc Bloch, *The Historian's Craft* (New York, 1953).

78. As well as of the original story. See R. Akutagawa, *Rashomon, and Other Stories* (Tokyo, 1952).

79. This seems to me the whole thrust of C. R. Browning, "German Memory, Judicial Interrogation, and Historical Reconstruction: Writing Perpetrator History from Postwar Testimony," in Friedlander, *Probing the Limits*, pp. 22–36, and especially of his *Ordinary Men*, where he reconstructs the crime and places the guilt where it belongs, but not without doing his best to explain the motivation and circumstances of the murders. See also *supra*, Chapter 5.

80. I. Berlin, *Four Essays on Liberty*, 2d ed. (Oxford, 1979), p. 106.

81. See Diner *Zivilisationsbruch*; also Yerushalmi, *Zakhor*.

82. In this context, see the illuminating remarks in Lang, *Act and Idea*, pp. 234–40.

Chapter 7

1. Reitz, *Liebe zum Kino*, pp. 102, 145–46, cited in Santner, *Stranded Objects*, pp. 75, 80. Santner notes that "for some strange reason, Reitz fails to italicize *Holocaust* in his essay." Ibid., p. 178, n. 42. This is a revised version of an article by the same name published in *TAJ* 23 (1994): 59–78. I would like to thank the editors of this publication for allowing me to reprint it here. The original draft of this chapter was an extended comment on an unpublished paper by Anton Kaes, "Memory and War in Alexander Kluge's Critical Cinema," presented at the conference "War, Film, and History," Rutgers Center for Historical Analysis, October 21–23, 1993. I wish to thank Professor Kaes for his most stimulating paper, and for many conversations on cinema and history. Though we disagree on some points, I could not have written this chapter without his important analyses of this and other films, some of which can be found in his book *From Hitler to Heimat*.

2. Testimony of Philip K. (T-1300), cited in Langer, *Holocaust Testimonies*, p. 205.

3. I have used the translation in Felstiner, *Translating Paul Celan's "Todesfuge,"* pp. 257–58. See also the translation by M. Hamburger, *Paul Celan: Poems. A Bilingual Edition* (New York, 1980), pp. 50–53. Felstiner notes that German high-schoolers

sometimes rendered the poem vocally, as part song, and that it was suggested to study fugues in music class and then perform Celan's poem so as "to make the polyphony audible." Ezrahi, *The Grave in the Air*, notes the public status of the poem in Germany, which culminated with its recitation in the Bundestag in 1988 to commemorate the 50th anniversary of *Kristallnacht*, its frequent quotation in film, art, dance, and music, all of which have ultimately made it part of the official ritual of remembrance in Germany. She also draws our attention to the following verse from Primo Levi's *Gedale's Song*: "Our brothers have risen to the sky/Through the ovens of Sobibor and Treblinka / They have dug themselves a grave in the air." Cited from the translation by R. Feldman, *Tikkun* 5/5 (1990), inside cover. It would seem that the term employed by both Levi and Celan, "digging a grave in the air," was commonly used by inmates of death camps.

4. Stürmer, *History in a Land Without History*, pp. 16–17.

5. On memory and repression by the victims, see Langer, *Holocaust Testimonies*; on revisionism and memory, see Vidal-Naquet, *Assassins of Memory*; on memory and justice, see Finkielkraut, *Remembering in Vain*. See discussion of these works *supra*, Chapter 5.

6. Kaes, *Memory and War*. On the music that accompanied *La nuit et brouillard*, composed by Hanns Eisler, see Kaes, *From Hitler to Heimat*, pp. 132–33, who notes that Resnais' film was shown on German television for the first time only in 1978; the film is discussed in ibid., pp. 129–35. On Resnais, see also A. Williams, *Republic of Images: A History of French Filmmaking* (Cambridge: Mass., 1992), pp. 367–73.

7. On the effect of *Holocaust*, the television series, on German viewers and intellectuals, see Kaes, *From Hitler to Heimat*, pp. 30–35. Edgar Reitz, the maker of *Heimat*, claimed that since "The Americans have stolen our history through Holocaust," it was now time for German filmmakers to "take possession of their own history and hence the history of the population to which they belong," which obviously excluded their victims. Ibid., p. 184. See also A. Kazin's foreword to Ezrahi, *By Words Alone*; Avisar, *Screening the Holocaust*, pp. 24, 129–30.

8. Ronald Reagan said: "I think there's nothing wrong with visiting that cemetery where those young men are victims of Nazism also, even though they were fighting in the German uniform, drafted into service to carry out the hateful wishes of the Nazis." *Time Magazine* 17 (April 1985), p. 44. See also G. Hartman (ed.), *Bitburg in Moral and Political Perspective* (Bloomington, 1986).

9. See Kaes, *From Hitler to Heimat*, pp. 163–192. Also see T. G. Ash, "The Life of Death," *NYR* 19 December 1985, who replies to his own question, "What about Auschwitz?" with the fictive (but accurate) retort by the "color filters": "Remember, remember, this is a film about what Germans remember. Some things they remember in full color. Some in sepia. Others they prefer to forget. Memory is selective. Memory is partial. Memory is amoral."

10. I refer, of course, to Hillgruber, *Zweierlei Untergang*. See *supra*, Chapter 4.

11. Even more ironic, perhaps, was the fact that Hillgruber cited Ernst Nolte's definition of the war in Russia as the "*ungeheuerlichsten Eroberungs-, Versklavungs- und Vernichtungskrieg*," of the modern era. See A. Hillgruber, "Erschreckende Beteiligung des Heeres an den Verbrechen," *FAZ* 99 (29 April 1981), p. 10.

12. See also my "The Conduct of War: Soldiers and the Barbarization of Warfare," in *Resistance Against the Third Reich: 1933–1990*, ed. M. Geyer and J. W. Boyer (Chicago, 1994). And Kaes, *From Hitler to Heimat*, pp. 75–103.

13. See discussion of this film in Kaes, *Hitler to Heimat*, pp. 139–60. It is also instructive to look, for instance, through German language textbooks, such as those

handed out to students at the Goethe Institute, where Germany's destruction in the war is illustrated with photographs of ruined cities, while the Jews are simply said to have been persecuted by the regime (photographs not supplied).

14. The most outstanding examples of this genre in the early historiography of Nazism are Meinecke, *The German Catastrophe*, and Ritter, *The German Problem*. A different cinematic treatment of the hypocritical version of the past in Germany is Michael Verhoeven's excellent 1990 film *The Nasty Girl*, which uses the genre of the cabaret already employed in some early German films about the hypocrisy of postwar society and the repression of the past (as well as the presence and continuing success of the perpetrators and supporters of the regime), such as Kurt Hoffmann's 1958 *Wir Wunderkinder*. See also M. S. Kang, Review of *Das Schreckliche Mädchen* (The Nasty Girl), *AHR* 96/4 (1991): 1132–34.

15. Here I have in mind, of course, White, *The Content of the Form*, and esp. the disturbing chapter "The Politics of Historical Interpretation," ibid., pp. 58–82. The thesis of this essay is critiqued in Ginzburg, *Just One Witness*, revised and reaffirmed in White's *Historical Emplotment*, and attacked in turn, this time for not being radical enough, in Jay, *Of Plots, Witnesses, and Judgements*.

16. Grass's predilection for an archaic, romantic past became even stronger in such later novels as *The Flounder*. In somewhat more detail, see my *The Conduct of War*. Volker Schlöndorff's cinematic rendering of *The Tin Drum* (1979) may have suffered less from this tendency, which in Grass is highly verbal (though accompanied by such visions as the last charge of the Polish cavalry). But Schlöndorff's film *Der Fangschuss* (1976) based on Marguerite Yourcenar's *Coup de Grâce*, shares with the author, and even enhances, a taste for romanticizing and aestheticizing violence, cruelty, and perversion. See also T. Corrigan, *New German Film: The Displaced Image*, rev. ed. (Bloomington, 1994), pp. 55–73. I agree with Ryan, *The Uncompleted Past*, pp. 42–69, that there is a clear continuation between Thomas Mann's *Doctor Faustus* and Grass's *The Tin Drum*, but I disagree with her much more favorable evaluation of the latter, whose ambiguity, personified by the eternally beautiful blue-eyed child who drums his way through the Third Reich (a grotesque version of Hitler's self-representation as "the drummer") only to become a repulsive, morally degenerate, and at least officially mad dwarf under the Federal Republic, has much in common with Mann's attraction (expressed for the first time long before Hitler arrived on the scene) to the romantic combination of genius, madness, and evil, which incidentally also explains the attraction of so many other German intellectuals to what they perceived as the essence of Nazism.

17. On the conduct of the German army and other Nazi agencies in Russia, see: Streit, *Keine Kameraden*; A. Dallin, *German Rule in Russia 1941–1945: A Study of Occupation Policies*, 2d ed. (London, 1981); Krausnick/Wilhelm, *Die Truppe des Weltanschauungskrieges*; Schulte, *The German Army and Nazi Policies*; Bartov, *Hitler's Army*.

18. This tendency is examined in Ryan, *The Uncompleted Past*. See also my *The Conduct of War* for the contemporary and postwar notion of lack of choice.

19. H. Böll, *Billiards at Half-Past Nine* (New York, 1962); idem., *Group Portrait with Lady* (New York, 1973); G. Grass, *Cat and Mouse* (New York, 1963); S. Lenz, *The German Lesson* (New York, 1972); V. S. Grossman, *Life and Fate: a Novel* (New York, 1985). Other great examples are, for instance, Mikhail Bolgakov, Isaac Babel, and from a very different perspective, Alexander Solzhenitsyn.

20. This is my own translation. See original and an alternative translation in T. Carmi (ed.), *The Penguin Book of Hebrew Verse* (Harmondsworth, 1981), pp. 512–

13. The notion of revenge against the Germans after the Holocaust was a central issue among Jews from Palestine who volunteered to the British army and formed the Jewish Brigade, and is the focus of the novel by Hanoch Bartov, *Pits'ei Bagrut* (The Brigade): "We're here for blood revenge. A single wild Jewish revenge. Just once like the Tatars. Like the Ukrainians. Like the Germans . . . we'll go into one city and burn it . . . Why should it just be us remembering Auschwitz? Let them remember the one city that we'll destroy." But of course apart from some acts of revenge against SS officers by a small minority, none of this took place. See Segev, *The Seventh Million*, pp. 140–52, and citation from Bartov on p. 147. See also discussion in Ezrahi, *By Words Alone*, pp. 114–15, 126–27, on Bartov, and pp. 101–102, 123, on Bialik. For an incisive discussion, see B. Lang, "Holocaust-Memory and Revenge: The Presence of the Past," unpublished paper (1995).

21. See, e.g., Almog, *Antisemitism*, part 2: "Christian Europe"; Poliakov, *Histoire de l'antisémitisme*, vol. 1, part 4: "L'Europe Chrétienne."

22. On the "Werewolf" and German youths, see G. Rempel, *Hitler's Children: The Hitler Youth and the SS* (Chapel Hill, 1989), pp. 244–50. See further in A. Rose, *Werwolf 1944–1945: Eine Dokumentation* (Stuttgart, 1980); C. Whiting, *Hitler's Werewolves: The Story of the Nazi Resistance Movement 1944–1945* (New York, 1972).

23. On the question of to whom does the history of the Holocaust, and the history of Germany, belong, see esp. Broszat, *Plea*, Friedlander, *Reflections*, and the correspondence between the two, all in Baldwin, *Reworking*, pp. 77–134. Also see Kershaw, *Nazi Dictatorship*, esp. Chapters 1, 5, 8, 9. Most recently, see O. Bartov, "Wem gehört die Geschichte? Wehrmacht und Geschichtswissenschaft," in *Vernichtungskrieg: Verbrechen der Wehrmacht 1941–1944*, ed. H. Heer and K. Naumann (Hamburg, 1995)

24. Kluge refers here to Christian Morgenstern's poem, *The Knee*: "In war one time a man was shot/They shot him through and through./His knee alone was in one piece,/As if it were a holy relic./Since then: A knee walks lonely through the world./It's just a knee, that's all." The fallen Wieland says: "I must clear up once and for all a fundamental error: that we dead are somehow dead. We are full of protest and energy. Who wants to die? We speed through history, examining it. How can I escape history that will kill us all?" Kaes, *From Hitler to Heimat*, p. 112. See also Santner, *Stranded Objects*, pp. 153–55.

25. In fact there is no reason to think that dreams are any freer from outside influence than our wakeful consciousness; they merely react to this influence differently. The relationship between memory and place has exercised the imagination of numerous twentieth-century writers and filmmakers, such as, e.g., Marcel Proust and Ingmar Bergman. On the relationship between collective memory and place, see Nora, *Between Memory and History*; and idem. (ed.), *Les Lieux de mémoire*, vol. 1: *La République*; vol. 2: *La Nation* (Paris, 1984 and 1986). The issue of *Representations* 26 (1989) is wholly devoted to "Memory and Counter-Memory." The original conceptualization of "collective memory" was proposed by Maurice Halbwachs in the interwar years. See his *On Collective Memory* (Chicago, 1992).

26. Jean Renoir's masterpieces, *The Grand Illusion* and *The Rules of the Game*, Lewis Milestone's *All Quiet on the Western Front*, and G. W. Pabst's *Westfront 1918*, stand out especially. See A. Sesonske, *Jean Renoir: The French Films 1924–1939* (Cambridge: Mass., 1990); J. Buchsbaum, *Cinema Engagé: Film in the Popular Front* (Urbana, 1988); Eksteins, *All Quiet on the Western Front*; Chambers, "*All Quiet on the Western Front*".

27. For a still picture of the final scene in *J'accuse*, see Prost, *Les Anciens Combattants*, between pp. 96–97. See also M. Ferro, *Cinéma et Histoire*, rev. ed. (Paris, 1993), esp. Chapter 11: "Y a-t-il un cinéma antimilitariste?"

28. See also M. L. Pereboom, review of *La vie et rien d'autre*, AHR 97/4 (1992): 1153–55. This film created a stir in France, with some scholars accusing Tavernier of having besmirched the memory of the Great War and the honor of its fallen soldiers. French preoccupation with the memory of the Great War was recently also indicated by the success of Jean Rouaud's novel *Les champs d'honneur* (Paris, 1990). On memories of the next war (and the Holocaust), see Robert Bober's novel *Quoi de neuf sur la guerre?* (Paris, 1993). The persistence (and repression) of the memory of Vichy has been analyzed in Rousso, *The Vichy Syndrome*. In this context, see also the recent works: J. F. Sweets, *Choices in Vichy France: The French Under Nazi Occupation* (New York, 1986), and W. D. Halls, *Politics, Society and Christianity in Vichy France* (Oxford, 1995). Further in O. Bartov, "The Unbearable Memory of the Next War: France, Germany, and the Trauma of 1914–18," unpublished paper (1995).

29. In this context, see esp. Mosse, *Fallen Soldiers*.

30. Helmut Kohl has made a point of double victimhood: that of the Germans under National Socialism, and that of those who had the "benefit of a late birth" like himself yet are victimized as somehow still connected to Germany's Nazi past. Ernst Nolte, Andreas Hillgruber, and Michael Stürmer have all presented Germany as a victim of either Bolshevik fears, superpower machinations, geopolitical determinants, or the burden of a negative history and the consequent loss of identity. Large sectors of the intellectual community have tended to present Germany as a victim of American cultural and nuclear imperialism; the most recent outburst of this sentiment occurred in the Gulf War. On the debate over a German history museum, see Maier, *The Unmasterable Past*, Chapter 5. See also Diner, *Der Krieg der Erinnerungen*.

31. A. Kluge, *Schlachtbeschreibung* (Frankfurt/M., 1983). See also R. G. Renner, "Hirn und Herz. Stalingrad als Gegenstand ideologischer und literarischer Diskurse," in *Stalingrad: Ereignis—Wirkung—Symbol*, ed. J. Förster (Munich, 1992), pp. 472–92.

32. One of the more recent publications is the above-cited Förster, *Stalingrad*, which notes this renewed interest. In a lecture delivered in Hamburg in February 1992 I was struck by the number of new or newly reissued books on Stalingrad exhibited at the entrance to the lecture hall. In February 1993 ZDF, in cooperation with the Russian television network Ostankino, broadcast a five-part documentary on Stalingrad developed by Guido Knopp, entitled *Decision at Stalingrad*. Joseph Vilsmaier's film *Stalingrad* (which opened also in the same month) is a grand war movie that emphasizes the sacrifice and victimhood of German soldiers. See T. W. Ryback, "Stalingrad: Letters from the Dead," TNY (February 1, 1993): 58–71.

33. On this organization, see Mosse, *Fallen Soldiers*, pp. 214–16. More generally, see J. M. Diehl, *The Thanks of the Fatherland: German Veterans after the Second World War* (Chapel Hill, 1993).

34. The Red Army is thought to have lost between four to eight times as many soldiers in Stalingrad as did the *Wehrmacht*, excluding civilians. This whole episode is reported in Ryback, *Stalingrad*.

35. Kaes, *Memory and War*.

36. Kaes, *From Hitler to Heimat*, p. 113, renders Kluge's concept of *Zusammenhang* as "seeing things in their interconnection." Santner, *Stranded Objects*, p. 154, seems to relate this concept to the knee's statement in *The Patriot*: "I am not the calf and I am not the thigh, but rather the in-between [*das Dazwischen*]." Approvingly citing

David Roberts' argument that "If in the general population there seemed to be no trace of the spirit of resistance, this spirit had disappeared into the *lacunae of history*—covered first by bombs and then by the reconstruction," Santner identifies the "non-space of the in-between" with such *lacunae* and claims that "Though this spirit has been buried, Kluge's work provides an extended argument for its continued availability to those with the proper archeological tools." These would seem to me to be the same fine tools needed for the excavation of "inner resistance" and "inner immigration" that took the place of *actual* resistance (i.e., *Widerstand* rather than *Resistenz*). In fact, I would argue that the "nonspace" was the void into which the *real* victims of Nazism disappeared both physically and in the memories of postwar Germans: Celan's "grave in the clouds." See also D. Roberts, "Alexander Kluge und die deutsche Zeitgeschichte: Der Luftangriff auf Halberstadt am 8.4.1945," in *Alexander Kluge*, ed. T. Böhm-Christl (Frankfurt/M., 1983), p. 103.

37. On the *Historikerstreit*, see Maier, *The Unmasterable Past*; Evans, *In Hitler's Shadow*; Wehler, *Entsorgung der deutschen Vergangenheit?*; Diner, *Ist der National-sozialismus Geschichte?* See also *supra*, Chapter 4.

38. A typical and commercially successful example of this trend is Wolfgang Petersen's 1982 film *The Boat*.

39. One is hard put to think of a German film or novel that makes the victims of the regime and its various agencies the focus of its narrative. Rainer Werner Fassbinder's *Lili Marleen* (1981), for instance, having implied certain atrocities occurring in the East, ends up with an evidently antisemitic portrait of foreign Jews, shown as avaricious and rich, sexually dangerous and morally perfidious. Agnieszka Holland's *Europa, Europa* (1991), a quasi-German coproduction, was not accepted as a German film by the Berlin Film Festival, and was not particularly popular in Germany, despite its rather sympathetic picture of many Germans (including Wehrmacht soldiers) and its amazing, happy end, calculated to relieve everyone's fears and guilty conscience. Though based on a true story, the film has nevertheless been rightly described as unbelievable, since it has little bearing on the fate of *most* victims. Moreover, by showing the victim as an insider with the persecutors, it evokes empathy for the perpetrator and suspicion of the victim. All this notwithstanding, this half-German film has remained a rare example in German representations of the Nazi past (see further *infra*, Chapter 8, Section III). Siegfried Lenz, Heinrich Böll, and Günter Grass, for instance, have hardly preoccupied themselves with Jews in their exhaustive literary reconstructions of the Nazi period. See further in O. Bartov, "'. . . seit die Juden weg sind': Germany, History, and Representations of Absence," in *German Studies as Cultural Studies: A User's Manual*, ed. S. Denham et al. (forthcoming).

40. An instructive discussion of this issue can be found in the section "The Idol of Origins" in Bloch's *The Historian's Craft*, pp. 29–35.

41. See, e.g., M. Fechner (ed.), *Wie Konnte es Geschehen: Auszüge aus den Tagebüchern und Bekenntnissen eines Kriegsverbrechers* (Berlin, n.d.).

42. This is most clearly reflected in Nolte, *Past That Will Not Pass*.

43. See, esp., Meinecke, *The German Catastrophe*, and Ritter, *The German Problem*.

44. This is the postmodern position taken by Kluge. There is of course by now a growing and important body of scholarship that seeks the connection between German developments and general European or Western processes, such as the crisis of modernity, the abuse of science, organic concepts of society, notions of social hygiene, etc. While this school has been somewhat vulnerable to apologetics and abuse, it has greatly enhanced our understanding of both Nazism, the Holocaust, and the potential

dangers in Western civilization. As I have argued elsewhere in this book (see, e.g., *supra*, "Introduction," and *infra*, Chapter 8), I believe that industrial killing and militarized genocide were not merely the outcome of a *crisis* of modernity, but were and remain an extreme *potential* of the modern state and society. On this see esp. Bauman, *Modernity and the Holocaust*; Lang, *Act and Idea*. And further, see Peukert, *The Weimar Republic, Inside Nazi Germany*, and *The Genesis of the "Final Solution"*. See also Koonz, *Eugenics, Gender, and Ethics*; Bock, *Racism and Sexism*; Proctor, *Racial Hygiene*; Biagioli, *Science, Modernity, and the "Final Solution"*. See also the recent useful collection, D. F. Crew, *Nazism and German Society, 1933–1945* (New York, 1994). The more traditional position relating general European trends to the rise of totalitarianism, and also of course deeply concerned with the issue of origins, was best articulated in Arendt's brilliant *The Origins of Totalitarianism*.

45. This relates, of course, also to the shift in German historiography from abstract social theories that left little room for ideology and prejudice, to detailed reconstructions of the fabric of daily life, or *Alltagsgeschichte*, which similarly sought to demonstrate the weakness of ideological penetration. On the latter see Nolan, *The Historikerstreit and Social History*. The former has been attacked (though mainly regarding its interpretation of the nineteenth century), in Blackbourn/Eley, *The Peculiarities of German History*.

46. Apart from Nolte's articles, see also contributions by Hildebrand and Fest among the revisionists, and by Jäckel, Kocka, and Habermas, among the anti-revisionists, all in *Forever in the Shadow*.

47. It is interesting to note that Nolte's first major publication insisted on the existence of an "epoch of Fascism" whose origins were to be found in the French *Action Française*. See his *Three Faces of Fascism*.

48. Here too, of course, the similarity with Reitz's *Heimat* is striking, despite the radically different approaches to the filmmaking itself, since Reitz has chosen a traditional, conservative mode that owes much to the old genre of *Heimat* literature and films popular before, during, and after the Third Reich. See Kaes, *From Hitler to Heimat*, esp. pp. 163–65. Also see H. Fehrenbach, *Cinema in Democratizing Germany: Reconstructing National Identity After Hitler* (Chapel Hill, 1995); A. Confino, "The Nation as a Local Metaphor: Heimat, National Memory and the German Empire, 1871–1918," *H&M* 5/1 (1993): 42–86.

49. *The Complete Works of Chuang Tzu* (New York, 1968), p. 49.

50. See in this context Langer, *Holocaust Testimonies*; Finkielkraut, *Remembering in Vain*; Hilberg, *Perpetrators Victims Bystanders*; Horwitz, *In the Shadow of Death*; Friedlander, *When Memory Comes*, for an indication of the kind of memories that might have been preserved and represented in German (and Austrian, and French) literary and cinematic treatments of Nazism had they not been selected out of either the minds or the texts of the makers of published and screened memory. See also *supra*, Chapter 5.

51. See W. Benjamin, "Theses on the Philosophy of History," in *Illuminations*, ed. H. Arendt (New York, 1969), pp. 254–55: "A chronicler who recites events without distinguishing between major and minor ones acts in accordance with the following truth: nothing that has ever happened should be regarded as lost for history. To be sure, only a redeemed mankind receives the fullness of its past—which is to say, only a redeemed mankind has its past become citable in all its moments. Each moment it has lived becomes a *citation à l'ordre du jour*—and that day is Judgement Day. . . . The past can be seized only as an image which flashes up at the instant when it can be recognized and is never seen again. . . . For every image of the past that is not recog-

nized by the present as one of its own concerns threatens to disappear irretrievably. . . . To articulate the past historically does not mean to recognize it 'the way it really was' (Ranke). It means to seize hold of a memory as it flashes up at a moment of danger." In this context it is ironic that recent efforts to name a street and a plaza in Berlin after Benjamin have failed. See S. Kinzer, "O Niederkirchnerstrasse, Be Some Other Name," *NYT* (Thursday, December 1, 1994): A4. Also crucial in this context is G. Perec, *W or The Memory of Childhood* (Boston, 1988 [1975]).

52. See *supra*, notes 7 and 9. It would be a sobering exercise in historical irony to compare the impact of *Holocaust* (the television series) on the Germans, with the impact of the Eichmann trial on the Israelis. On the latter, see Arendt, *Eichmann in Jerusalem*; and Segev, *The Seventh Million*, pp. 323–84. On Jewish-German and Israeli-German relations, see Stern, *The Whitewashing of the Yellow Badge*, and Zimmermann/Heilbronner, *"Normal" Relations*.

53. S. Kinzer, "Germany's Justice System Said to Favor Rightists," *NYT* (November 7, 1993): 8.

54. Müller, *Hitler's Justice*.

55. See in this context the unpublished papers by H. Peitsch, "Shaping Public Memory: A Comparison of East and West German War Novels of the 1950s," and G. Gutzmann, "Discursive Strategies on War and Violence in the Writings of Anna Seghers, Melitta Maschmann, and Christa Wolf" (1993). See also Ryan, *The Uncompleted Past*; Langer, *The Holocaust and the Literary Imagination*; H. Bosmajian, *Metaphors of Evil: Contemporary German Literature and the Shadow of Nazism* (Iowa City, 1979); P. Demetz, *Postwar German Literature: A Critical Introduction* (New York, 1970).

Chapter 8

1. This is my own translation. See Hamburger, *Paul Celan*, pp. 270–71, for the poem and an alternative translation. In writing Section I of this previously unpublished chapter I benefited from my participation in the international conference at the *Historial de la Grande Guerre* in July 1992. I would like to thank the organizers for providing me with the opportunity to tour the museum and its surroundings. Section III is a much revised version of my substantially longer chapter "Spielberg's Oskar: Hollywood Tries Evil," in Y. Loshitzky (ed.), *Spielberg's Holocaust: Critical Perspectives on Schindler's List* (forthcoming). I would like to thank Dr. Loshitzky for allowing me to publish it here. In writing Section IV I benefited from my participation in the inaugural conference of the United States Holocaust Memorial Museum in December 1993, and in the conference "Lessons and Legacies III: Memory, Memorialization, Denial," held in Dartmouth College in 1994. I would like to thank the organizers of these meetings for their kind invitations. I have used some of my comments on Nicola A. Lisus' and Richard V. Ericson's stimulating paper in the latter conference (cited below) in the very last paragraphs of this chapter. I thank Ms. Lisus for allowing me to cite this forthcoming work.

2. See also the perceptive critique by Alan Dawley, "Report on a Visit to the Historial de la Grande Guerre," *La Grande Guerre: Pays, Histoire, Mémoire. Bulletin du Centre de recherche* 7 (June 1994): 6–7.

3. See the illuminating article, Chambers, *All Quiet*.

4. Ibid.

5. J. Conrad, *Heart of Darkness*, ed. R. Kimbrough, 2d ed. (New York, 1971 [1898–99]); Herr, *Dispatches*.

6. E. Showalter, *Sexual Anarchy: Gender and Culture at the Fin de Siècle*, 2d ed. (New York, 1991), pp. 99–104.

7. Mention should be made of course of Kubrick's earlier antiwar films, *Paths of Glory* (1957) and *Dr. Strangelove or How I Learned to Stop Worrying and Love the Bomb* (1964), neither of which can be discussed here at length. While the former is a conventional, "realistic" work, based on a "true story" and therefore "authentic," the latter's black humor brings it closer to *Apocalypse Now* (as well as such films as *Catch 22* and *M.A.S.H.*). Both were influential, but it should be noted that *Paths of Glory* was about French, rather than American soldiers, whereas *Dr. Strangelove* was too strange to be taken by most viewers as anything more than a hilarious farce. Similarly, Cimino's later Vietnam films, *Born on the Fourth of July* (1984) and *Heaven and Earth* (1993) had far less impact on the public than *The Deer Hunter*. See also appropriate entries in E. Katz, *The Film Encyclopedia*, 2d ed. (New York, 1994).

8. On Renoir, see, e.g., L. Braudy, *Jean Renoir: The World of His Films*, 2d ed. (New York, 1989); C. Bertin, *Jean Renoir: A Life in Pictures* (Baltimore, 1991); Sesonske, *Jean Renoir*.

9. The Russian films by Tarkovsky and Klimov mentioned above are rarely shown in the West. Note also the Soviet/American television coproduction, based on German and Soviet newsreel material, screened in Germany in 1981 as *Der unvergessene Krieg (The Unforgotten War)*, in the USSR as *The Great Patriotic War*, and in the United States as *The Unknown War*, whose various titles were of course indicative of the different national perspectives on the war in the East.

10. See Klee, *"The Good Old Days"*; U. Borsdorf and M. Jamin (eds.), *Über Leben im Krieg: Kriegserfahrungen in einer Industrieregion 1939–1945* (Reinbek bei Hamburg, 1989), photographs on pp. 164–67. And, most recently, Heer/Naumann, *Vernichtungskrieg*, photographs immediately following cover, and on pp. 139-55, 315–21, 418–25, 480–501.

11. See also Pereboom, *La vie et rien d'autre*.

12. I refer here of course to Pascal's celebrated description of the human condition: "Imagine a number of men in chains, all under sentence of death, some of whom are each day butchered in the sight of the others; those remaining see their own condition in that of their fellows, and looking at each other with grief and despair await their turn. This is an image of the human condition." Pascal, *Pensées*, Series IV (199), p. 165. This was the origin of the title for André Malraux's novel *La Condition Humaine*, winner of the 1933 Prix Goncourt, whose central scene of execution in Shanghai is modeled on Pascal's vision: a group of chained prisoners in a dungeon, and every once in a while the door opens and one of them is led out to be executed.

13. For some reviews of the film see, e.g., J. Gross, "Hollywood and the Holocaust," *NYR* XLI/3 (February 3, 1994): 14–16; F. Bruning, "Beyond Words," *Newsday* (December 20, 1993): 50–51, 59; P. Gourevitch, "A Dissent on 'Schindler's List'," *Commentary* (February 1994): 49–52; J. Maslin, "Imagining the Holocaust to Remember It," *NYT* (December 15, 1993): C19, C23.

14. Levi, *Survival in Auschwitz* and *The Drowned and the Saved*; Hamburger, *Paul Celan*; Améry, *At the Mind's Limits*.

15. See K. Weston, "Laughing Instead of Crying: Why Oakland Teens Had Disturbing Reactions to 'Schindler's List'," *San Francisco Examiner* (January 30, 1994); S. Kleffman, "A Bid for Understanding After 'Schindler's List' Flap: Holocaust Survivors Offer to Speak to Castlemont Students," *San Francisco Chronicle/Bay Area and California/East Bay Edition* (January 20, 1994). I wish to thank Professor Anton Kaes for informing me of this incident and sending me the relevant material.

16. See also the discussion of the film *My War* in the previous section of this chapter.

17. A good example is the problematic documentary *The Eighty-First Blow*, (Israel, 1975), directed by Haim Gouri, Jacques Ehrlich, and David Bergman.

18. Interview with Claude Lanzmann by Daniel Heiman of *Le Monde*, published in a Hebrew translation in the Israeli weekly *Zeman Tel Aviv*, March 3, 1994.

19. In this context see also Ash, *The Life of Death*.

20. Rousso, *The Vichy Syndrome*.

21. For the text of the film, see Lanzmann, *Shoah*.

22. Langer, *Holocaust Testimonies*. See *supra*, Chapter 5, for a discussion of this book.

23. *Shoah* had, for instance, hardly any echo in Germany. See Kaes, *Heimat to Hitler*, p. 187.

24. See B. Lang (ed.), *Writing and the Holocaust* (New York, 1988); Young, *Writing and Rewriting the Holocaust*; Roskies, *Against the Apocalypse*; Rosenfeld, *A Double Dying*; Ezrahi, *By Words Alone*. And, of course, T. Keneally, *Schindler's List*, 2d ed. (New York, 1993 [1982]).

25. See, most recently, J. E. Young (ed.), *Holocaust Memorials: The Art of Memory in History* (New York, 1994); and idem., *The Texture of Memory*. And *infra*, Section IV.

26. N. Diamant, "The Rhetoric of Holocaust Memory: The Melodramatic Mode and the Plain Style," unpublished paper (1994); and idem., "The Boundaries of Holocaust Literature: The Emergence of a Canon" (Ph.D. dissertation: Columbia University, 1992).

27. See especially Kaes, *Hitler to Heimat*, pp. 28–35, 107–108, 132, 164, 172, 184–85. On the storm surrounding Winfried Bonengel's recent documentary *Profession: Neo-Nazi*, which covers the life of the 27–year-old Bela Ewald Althans, a Munich supporter of Nazi ideology and a denier of the Holocaust, see S. Kinzer, "Germans Ask If Film Hurts or Aids Nazis," *NYT* (Wednesday, December 15, 1993): A17.

28. G. Grass, *The Tin Drum* (Harmondsworth, 1978 [1959]).

29. On the history of Yad Vashem, see Young, *The Texture of Memory*, pp. 243–61; Segev, *The Seventh Million*, pp. 421–45.

30. On the problems and contradictions of preserving the memory of the Holocaust in Auschwitz, see the excellent article, T. W. Ryback, "Evidence of Evil," *TNY* (November 15, 1993): 68–81. Also see J. Perlez, "Decay of a 20th Century Relic: What's the Future of Auschwitz?" *NYT* (Wednesday, January 5, 1994): A6; idem., "At Warsaw Ghetto, Poles and Jews Bound by Hope," *NYT* (Tuesday, April 20, 1993): A6; J. Steinberg, "In Ceremony of Remembrance, Reminders of Human Courage," *NYT* (Monday, April 19, 1993): A1; I. Fisher, "Memories Live in Survivors of Warsaw Ghetto Battle," *NYT* (Tuesday, April 20, 1993): A1, B6; D. Margolick, "Lodz Survivors Meet and Remember," *NYT* (Friday, August 26, 1994): A6. On the German attempt to associate their victims with their own perceived victimhood in a single monument, see, e.g., S. Kinzer, "The War Memorial: To Embrace the Guilty, Too?" *NYT* (Monday, November 15, 1993): A4. On the ironies of plastic representations in post-Soviet Russia, see, e.g., S. Erlanger, "The Russians Revisit Stalin's Never-Never Land," *NYT* (Wednesday, June 1, 1994): A4.

31. For a study of the Zionist Leadership in Palestine and the Holocaust, see Porat, *The Blue and the Yellow Stars of David*.

32. For some views on the museum, see, e.g., H. Muschamp, "Shaping a Monument to Memory," in "Arts and Leisure," Section 2, *NYT* (Sunday, April 11, 1993); J. Rosen, "The Misguided Holocaust Museum," in OP-ED, *NYT* (Sunday, April 18,

1993); D. Jean Schemo, "Holocaust Museum Hailed as Sacred Debt to Dead," *NYT* (April 21, 1993): A1, A24; M. Kimmelman, "Making Art of the Holocaust: New Museum, New Works," *NYT* (Friday, April 23, 1993): A1, A24; L. Wieseltier, "After Memory," *TNR* (May 3, 1993): 16–26; L. Weissberg, "Memory Confined," *Documents* 4/5 (1994): 81–98. See also the recent essay, H. Kaplan, *Conscience and Memory: Meditations in a Museum of the Holocaust* (Chicago, 1994).

33. As an example, see D. Jean Schemo, "Anger Greets Croatian's Invitation to Holocaust Museum Dedication," *NYT* (Thursday, April 22, 1993): A1, A18; Z. Brzezinski, "'Never Again'—Except for Bosnia," in OP-ED, *NYT* (Thursday, April 22, 1993).

34. See L. Wieseltier, "The Trouble with Multiculturalism," *NYTBR* (October 23, 1994): 11; idem., "Against Identity," *TNR* (November 28, 1994): 24–32.

35. N. A. Lisus and R. V. Ericson, "Misplacing Memory: The Effects of Television Format on Holocaust Remembrance," in *Crime and the Media*, ed. R. V. Ericson (forthcoming).

36. As an example of a very different approach, see A. Kozinn, "Holocaust Memorials Can Also Be Operas," in "The Arts," *NYT* (Thursday, April 22, 1993): C17, C21.

37. Citing J. Baudrillard, *Simulations* (New York, 1983), p. 2.

Index